The
Handbook
of Style

The *SBL* Handbook of Style

*For Ancient Near Eastern,
Biblical, and Early Christian Studies*

Edited by
Patrick H. Alexander, John F. Kutsko,
James D. Ernest, Shirley A. Decker-Lucke,
and for the Society of Biblical Literature
David L. Petersen

HENDRICKSON
PUBLISHERS

© 1999 by Hendrickson Publishers, Inc.
P. O. Box 3473
Peabody, Massachusetts 01961–3473

Printed in the United States of America

ISBN 1-56563-487-X

First printing — November 1999

*This book was composed in Monotype Photina using Corel Ventura 8.
Printed and bound by Sheridan Books.*

Library of Congress Cataloging-in-Publication Data

The SBL handbook of style : for Ancient Near Eastern, Biblical, and early
Christian studies / edited by Patrick H. Alexander ... [et al.].
        p. cm.
    ISBN 1-56563-487-X (cloth)
    1. Authorship—Handbooks, manuals, etc. 2. Middle East—
Civilization—To 622—Historiography—Handbooks, manuals, etc.
3. Church history—Early church, ca. 30–600—Historiography—
Handbooks, manuals, etc. 4. Middle East—Religion—Historiography—
Handbooks, manuals, etc. 5. History, Ancient—Historiography—
Handbooks, manuals, etc. 6. Bible—Criticism, interpretation, etc.—
Handbooks, manuals, etc.   I. Title: Society of Biblical Literature
handbook of style. II. Alexander, Patrick H. III. Society of Biblical
Literature.

PN147.S26 1999
808′.027—dc21
                                                                99-046069

Table of Contents

Preface

Nearly two years in the making, not counting the fifteen years of countless prototypes, *The SBL Handbook of Style* reflects a collaborative effort between Hendrickson Publishers and the Society of Biblical Literature. This collaboration came upon the heels of a conversation about Hendrickson's style manual with Rex Matthews, editorial director at Scholars Press, who suggested that Hendrickson Publishers contact SBL associate director Gregory Glover. To Greg belongs much of the credit for working out the details and for putting Hendrickson in touch with David L. Petersen of Iliff School of Theology, in Denver. David reviewed the heart of the work, making suggestions about SBL's style preferences and offering sage editorial input. His patience, expertise, and care for certitude were most appreciated. Typesetting the project posed unique challenges; issues of extraordinary character sets, demanding designs, and constant tweaking by the obsessed editors were handled with great proficiency by Phil Frank, senior production editor, and Darren Hurlburt (who designed the book) and Doug LaBudde, production editors, of Communication Ink, Peabody, Massachusetts. The three set records in skill, endurance, and good humor. Thanks are due as well to Joe Carey for his sharp eye and helpful input. Appreciation is also due Emanuel Tov, the J. L. Magnes Professor of Bible at Hebrew University, Jerusalem. Professor Tov graciously provided the comprehensive list of the Dead Sea Scrolls in Appendix F. The generosity of Professor Tov gave the volume an added dimension of usability.

Mark Twain once remarked that he didn't give a damn for someone who could spell a word only one way; he would have hated this book. Precision—spelling that word only one way—is to editors what the Holy Grail was to Arthur's knights. This volume reflects nearly forty years of the editors' collective quests for precision, at least when it comes to everyday decisions associated with publishing in the academic fields of ancient Near Eastern, biblical, and early Christian studies. As most scholars have discovered, trying to maintain consistency in matters of style can be frustrating at best. Often it appears that there are as many ways to do something as there are scholars. Furthermore, the kinds of fine points scholars need resolved are not always addressed in the available resources, and when they are, styles may vary among books, journals, societies, and projects. *The SBL Handbook of Style* attempts to collect information as much as to dispense it; and more than dictating rules of conformity, it seeks to identify those stylistic points where the disciplines already intersect. Thus, *The SBL Handbook of Style* endeavors both to become a resource for making stylistic decisions and to be a basis for future judgments about editing and writing in these fields. Although the volume aspires to be comprehensive within its parameters, the editors realize that total comprehensiveness and consistency remain elusive. It is hoped that this volume will save writers, editors, proofreaders, and students time and energy. Should their effort be taken seriously and scholarly writing enhanced, the time required to make this happen will have been well spent.

The Editors

1   Introduction: Using This Handbook

1. Introduction: Using This Handbook

This handbook has been created to help editors, proofreaders, and professors of ancient Near Eastern studies, biblical studies, and early Christianity as well as graduate students, and perhaps even undergraduates specializing in these disciplines. Obviously a book like this cannot explicitly address every style-related question that might arise in the course of writing a book, thesis, or term paper; rather, it is meant to resolve questions arising in our particular fields that are covered inadequately, or not at all, in the standard manuals.

In preparing this *Handbook,* we have consulted various of these standard manuals, especially *The Chicago Manual of Style* (14th ed.; Chicago: University of Chicago Press, 1993; referred to hereafter as *CMS*) and the "Instructions for Contributors" in the *Journal of Biblical Literature* 117 (1998): 555–79 and also the now somewhat dated *Chicago Guide to Preparing Electronic Manuscripts* (Chicago: University of Chicago Press, 1987). Although this style manual takes precedence over these other manuals, *CMS* in particular will remain a helpful and even indispensable supplement. The next section explains the place of *CMS* and other reference works in the hierarchy of authorities.

As it is written in *CMS*, "No editor worth the title will apply identical rules to every book manuscript." At the same time, experience has taught us that minute deviations from standard style at the outset can later metastasize gruesomely, causing extra work, frustration, eye strain, and delays. To make the writing process less painful for author and publisher alike, we have decided to apply uniform standards to all books in as many details as possible.

2   Editorial Responsibilities

2. Editorial Responsibilities
    2.1 Book Style Sheet
    2.2 *The SBL Handbook of Style*
    2.3 Other Authorities
        2.3.1 Biblical Names and Terms
        2.3.2 Nonbiblical Ancient Near Eastern Names
        2.3.3 Names of Deceased Persons
        2.3.4 Place Names
        2.3.5 Other Words
        2.3.6 Unusual Words

Editors and proofreaders[1] strive to ensure that a given book both adheres to a specific style and respects the unique demands of each volume. To achieve their myriad goals, editors and proofreaders rely on "authorities." The top three authorities in this case are—in descending order:

    (1) Book style sheet (§2.1)
    (2) *The SBL Handbook of Style* (§2.2)
    (3) Other authorities (§2.3)

2.1 BOOK STYLE SHEET

Chief among the arbiters of editorial problems is the book style sheet. Inevitably, each book will present unique issues. If enough issues arise, the project editor will need to create a book style sheet. These issues, often concerning capitalization, spelling of unique terms, hyphenation, and so on, should be documented (not merely listed in alphabetical order) in the book style sheet.

2.2 *THE SBL HANDBOOK OF STYLE*

The SBL Handbook of Style is designed to address those editorial and stylistic issues that are not specific to a particular book manuscript.

---

[1]Editors and proofreaders use standardized marks when editing. These marks can be found in Appendix J.

2.3 OTHER AUTHORITIES

Questions of style that are not covered by *The SBL Handbook* or the book style sheet may be resolved by other authorities. For the orthography of proper names, we follow the authorities noted in §§2.3.1 through 2.3.5. For other questions, *CMS* may be helpful.

2.3.1   Biblical Names and Terms

For biblical names and terms, follow the version of the Bible used in your book, which should be specified in the book style sheet. If the translations are your own, indicate that. In general, we prefer the names and terms found in the NRSV or the *Anchor Bible Dictionary* (New York: Doubleday, 1992), which follows the NRSV.

2.3.2   Nonbiblical Ancient Near Eastern Names

For nonbiblical ancient Near Eastern names, use the gazetteers and indexes in the following: Michael Roaf, *Cultural Atlas of Mesopotamia* (New York: Facts on File, 1990), and John Baines and Jaromír Málek, *Atlas of Ancient Egypt* (New York: Facts on File, 1980), supplementing these sources with Jack Sasson, ed., *Civilizations of the Ancient Near East* (4 vols.; New York: Scribners, 1995).

For the titles of ancient Near Eastern texts, follow any of the resources mentioned in the previous paragraph, as well as such works as James B. Pritchard, ed., *Ancient Near Eastern Texts Relating to the Old Testament* (3d ed.; Princeton: Princeton University Press, 1969 [= *ANET*]), William W. Hallo, ed., *The Context of Scripture* (3 vols.; Leiden: E. J. Brill, 1997– [= *COS*]), or the Society of Biblical Literature Writings from the Ancient World series (= SBLWAW).

For more technical Assyriological matters, consult Riekele Borger, *Handbuch der Keilschriftliteratur* (3 vols.; Berlin, de Gruyter, 1967–1975 [= *HKL*]), which contains resources for Akkadian and Sumerian studies up to 1974. The annual "Keilschriftbibliographie" in *Orientalia* supplements *HKL*. Further issues can be resolved using Erich Ebeling et al., eds., *Reallexikon der Assyriologie* (Berlin, 1928– [*RlA*]). For more technical Egyptological questions, see Wolfgang Helck, Eberhard Otto, Wolfhart Westendorf, eds. *Lexikon der Ägyptologie* (7 vols.; Wiesbaden: Harrassowitz, 1972–1992 [= *LÄ*]). Undoubtedly, the *Encyclopedia of Egyptology*, in progress at Oxford University Press, will be an exceptional resource.

2.3.3   Names of Deceased Persons

Consult *Merriam-Webster's Biographical Dictionary* (Springfield, Mass.: Merriam-Webster, 1997).

2.3.4   PLACE NAMES

For place names, consult *Merriam-Webster's Geographical Dictionary* (3d ed.; Springfield, Mass.: Merriam-Webster, 1997).

2.3.5   OTHER WORDS

For all other words, consult *Merriam-Webster's Collegiate Dictionary* (10th ed.; Springfield, Mass.: Merriam-Webster, 1994). For compound words not in *Merriam-Webster,* see the rules and examples in *CMS.*

3   Responsibilities of an Author

Apart from the obvious task of writing the manuscript, authors have other related responsibilities before and after submitting the manuscript.

3.1 BEFORE SUBMITTING A BOOK MANUSCRIPT

3.1.1   PRELIMINARY TECHNICAL MATTERS

Before beginning to write, make sure that your electronic files will be acceptable. Production editors are able to translate files from almost any format, but if you are using obsolete hardware (like Amiga) or software (like

Chiwriter), verify ahead of time that the production department will be able to read your disk files by sending a sample file and a corresponding print-out. Include in your sample examples every type of formatting in the book, e.g., italic, boldface, superscript, footnotes.

3.1.1.1   Nonroman Fonts

If you want to use nonroman fonts but your software does not provide for them, you should mark the font changes in your file using unambiguous codes such as the following to indicate such characters.

Greek section	<gk> . . . </gk>
Hebrew section	<hb> . . . </hb>
Coptic section	<cop> . . . </cop>

If you ask, your project editor can provide a character table for you to use for each nonroman font.

3.1.1.2   Block Quotations

If your software does not provide for the marking of block quotations, use <EXT> and </EXT> to mark the beginning and the end of a text extract. Use <EXP> and </EXP> for a poetic extract.

3.1.1.3   Indenting Paragraphs

Do not use tabs to indent paragraphs. Either format paragraph indentation with your word processing program or simply indicate with a "hard return."

3.1.1.4   Notes

Use your word processor's automatic footnote feature. Remember to double-space footnotes as well as main text. Whether the book will have footnotes or endnotes, it is better to leave the notes where your word processor auto-matically stores them within the chapter files. Production editors can move this material to the appropriate place.

3.1.1.5   Hyphens and Dashes

Please distinguish between hyphens (e.g., first-century writer), en dashes (e.g., Mark 16:1–8; 1972–1983), and em dashes (e.g., "I know who you are—the Holy One of God!"). Most current word processors offer separate charac-ters for each. If yours does not, use a single hyphen to represent a hyphen or an en dash and a double hyphen for an em dash. Note that there is no space on either side of a hyphen, en dash, or em dash.

Do not use any automatic hyphenation capability that your word-processing software may have, i.e., turn off auto-hyphenation so that words will not be broken by "soft hyphens" at line endings.

3.1.1.6 Els *and Ones,* Ohs *and Zeros*

Be sure to distinguish between *els* and ones, *ohs* and zeros, and be sure to use them appropriately.

3.1.1.7 *Special Characters*

For nonroman fonts, see §3.1.1.1. If you need to use special diacritics or other characters not provided by your word-processing software, use codes enclosed in angle brackets, such as the following:

<->	macron over preceding character
<.>	dot beneath preceding character
<">	umlaut or diaeresis over preceding character
<^>	circumflex over preceding character
</>	acute accent over preceding character
<\>	grave accent over preceding character
P<gothic>	gothic uppercase p (𝔓)
<dagger>	dagger (†)

If you use other codes of your own devising, include a list when you submit the manuscript.

3.1.1.8 *Global Changes*

Be especially careful when making global changes. An improper search and replace string can introduce errors. Remember that quoted material must be cited verbatim.

3.1.1.9 *Spell-Checking*

Please spell-check all files before printing and submitting your manuscript, but take care lest your word processor beguile you into making incorrect substitutions for words not in its database.

3.1.1.10 *Spaces after Punctuation*

Only one space is needed after any punctuation that ends a sentence and also after a colon.

3.1.2 ADHERENCE TO STYLE

To avoid delays in publication, authors should conform their manuscripts to the style and format detailed in this volume. While proper style and format often concern apparently trivial details, the consequences of inconsistency can be far-reaching. Thus, for example, authors often cite primary sources inconsistently and incorrectly. Consider this: Within a work a scholar could conceivably cite Josephus's *Antiquities* as *Ant.* X,xiii.1 §258; *Antiq.* X,13,1; *Ant.* X.13.1 §258; *Antiq.* X.xiii, 1; *Ant.* X.13.1; *Antiq.* 10.13.1 §258; *Ant.* 10.258; *Ant.* X.xiii.1; *Antiq.* 10.13, 1 §258; and so on. Such a situation would create major problems for a copy editor.

3.1.3 VERIFICATION OF QUOTATIONS AND FACTS

Primary and ultimate responsibility for accuracy in fact-checking and verification of quotations (including Scripture references) must lie with the author. This includes making sure that bibliographic citations are accurate, complete, and in proper form and that quotations are accurate not only verbally but also in orthography and punctuation. No matter how many words are cited, they must be worded exactly as they appear in the original work. Errors in the original should be noted with *sic* ("so, thus, in this manner") in brackets following the error.

3.1.4 PERMISSIONS AND "FAIR USE"

It is the author's responsibility to obtain any necessary permissions for the use of text or illustrative material from other publications. Ideally the author should obtain all required permissions in writing in advance and submit copies to the publisher along with the manuscript. Authors (especially those who are inexperienced in requesting permission) may ask their editor for a standard form letter that they can fill out and print on their own letterhead. The author must pay any fees associated with obtaining permissions.

Authors are sometimes unsure about how to determine whether permission is required in a particular instance. Under the common-law practice known as "fair use," authors are permitted under many circumstances to cite other published works without securing formal permission. As a quick rule of thumb, we estimate that "fair use" permits the quotation of about five hundred words, or if the work is small, proportionately fewer; but a word count is only a crude tool in judging fair use. Authors who wish fuller guidance may seek it in *CMS* 4.51–58 and in official publications of the United States Copyright Office. Editors may at any point in the publication process require authors to obtain written permission for uses that in their own judgment exceed what is allowed by current copyright law.

3.2 SUBMITTING A MANUSCRIPT

Submit all parts of the manuscript (see §3.2.1.1) in both electronic and paper form.

3.2.1   An Electronic Manuscript

All manuscripts must be submitted in electronic form. Authors usually submit their files on 3.5-inch diskettes. The diskette's label should have the author's name, the provisional title of the book, and the name and version number of the word-processing software used.

3.2.1.1   Division into Files

Authors should provide a file for each discrete unit of text. Units of text in the front matter may include half-title page, title page, dedication or epigraph, table of contents, list of abbreviations, list of contributors, list of illustrations, list of tables, foreword, preface, acknowledgments, and introduction. (The publisher will supply the copyright page.) Units of the main text include the several chapters; but if you have any chapters that are too large for your word processor to handle as single files, you may break such chapters into two or more files. Back matter should include a bibliography and any appendix(es) or glossary. (For notes, see §3.1.1.4. Authors must normally wait for page proofs before creating indexes.)

Give files names that correspond to the chapter number or other content: CH01.DOC, CH02.DOC, BIB.DOC, INTRO.DOC, TOC.DOC, PREF.DOC, etc. (The extension should indicate the file format.)

Special text, such as lists, tables, and charts, should be produced and stored separate from the main text and files. The location of such material in the main text should be indicated clearly; for example, "insert here chart 1 (chart1.doc)."

3.2.1.2   Formatting

Use the same font and point size throughout the manuscript (except that a different font may be used for each nonroman alphabet). Do not fully justify your document; always leave text ragged right. Otherwise, do not be too concerned about document formatting. Just be sure it is complete, legible, and easily edited.

Quotations of five or more lines in any language should be formatted as a separate paragraph with all lines indented on the left, without opening and closing quotation marks. Such quotations should be double-spaced, should use the same font and point size, and should be marked with the marginal note, "extract."

3.2.2   A Paper Manuscript

All books must also be submitted in the form of a paper printout. The printout must be legible enough and durable enough to survive the diligent ministrations of copy editors, so all manuscripts should be submitted on good quality 8½" by 11" paper. Send original laser or ink-jet output, not a photocopy. All of the printout should be *double-spaced*, including block quotes and notes; margins should be ample (at least 1¼" all around). Never print on both sides of the paper. If you use continuous-feed paper, separate the sheets. The printout must match the electronic files *exactly*—do not edit the files "one more time" unless you are willing to print them "one more time" as well.

3.2.3   Backup Copies

Authors should keep both a copy of the electronic files that they submit and a copy of the printout.

3.2.4   Photos and Illustrations

The author is responsible for providing the publisher all artwork, drawings, diagrams, and photographs. The original drawings should be submitted, when possible, and photographic prints should be suitable for reproduction. See also §3.1.4.

3.3 AFTER SUBMITTING A MANUSCRIPT

3.3.1   Revisions

Before the manuscript is submitted to a copy editor, the project editor must be satisfied that it conforms to the terms of the contract; if not, it will be returned for revision. Sections 3.1 and 3.2 of this manual should be understood as describing some of the technical conditions of acceptability. In addition, the editor may find that certain structural modifications, including major deletions, additions, or revisions, are required to produce the book envisioned. It is the responsibility of the author to work with the editor to produce a manuscript that is acceptable to both. After that, a copy editor will work on the manuscript. Purely stylistic changes will not be negotiated, but where the copy editor suggests changes that could alter meaning, it is the responsibility of the author to either approve the copy editor's suggestions or provide alternatives that better suit the author's meaning. Those alternatives will be reviewed by a copy editor.

3.3.2   Proofreading

After the editing process is complete and the book has been typeset, a proofreader should inspect the results. No proofreader catches every error, however, so authors who proofread their books carefully are usually able to improve the final product. For the sake of clarity, use standard proofreading marks as described in Appendix J below.

3.3.3 INDEXING

Most scholarly books include subject and modern author indexes, and many include indexes of citations of Scripture and other ancient texts. Such indexing is the author's responsibility. In some cases, especially for multi-volume reference works and other books containing many thousands of Scripture references, it is a good idea to discuss indexing with the project editor ahead of time.

Inexperienced indexers are encouraged to read chapter 17 of *CMS* and then consult the project editor before beginning.[1] Other sections of this handbook provide specific guidelines on capitalization (§6.1), sorting (§6.2), and the treatment of compound surnames (§6.5) and names with particles (§6.4), all of which will be helpful in assembling a useful index.

---

[1] Other resources for indexing include Nancy C. Mulvany, *Indexing Books* (Chicago: University of Chicago Press, 1994), Hans H. Wellisch, *Indexing from A to Z* (2d ed.; New York: H. W. Wilson, 1996), and Larry S. Bonura, *The Art of Indexing* (New York: Wiley, 1994).

4   General Style

This section, addressed to authors, copy editors, and proofreaders, sets forth standards concerning stylistic issues that commonly cause difficulties in the main text of books. Some of these considerations apply also to notes and back matter (see especially §§7.2–3).

4.1 PUNCTUATION

4.1.1   COMMAS

Commas should enable fluent reading. That is, they should *not* be used where they make for gratuitous lurches in reading; they *should* be used where owing to syntactical ambiguity (even such as would be resolved by the end of the sentence) the reader might not otherwise construe the text correctly in one pass. The following discussions of commas indicate those uses of commas that are most problematic. Fuller discussions of the proper use of commas can be found in *CMS* 5.29–33.

4.1.2   COMMAS IN SERIES

Should a comma be used before the final conjunction in a series of three or more objects? *Yes.* Thus, in phrases like "Sarah, Rebekah, and Rachel," always put the comma after Rebekah. Note, however, that when an ampersand appears before the final term in a series no comma is used.

4.1.3   COMMAS IN RESTRICTIVE AND NONRESTRICTIVE CLAUSES

Restrictive (defining) clauses should *not* be set off with commas:

> Paul was an apostle who proclaimed Christ crucified.

> Bruce Metzger's book *The Text of the New Testament* was first published in 1964.

Nonrestrictive clauses *should* be set off with commas:

> Paul, who was one of the primary missionaries to the Gentiles, studied under Gamaliel.

> Bruce Metzger's introduction to textual criticism, *The Text of the New Testament*, was first published in 1964.

4.1.4   PARENTHETIC COMMAS

Be careful not to omit the second in a pair of parenthetic commas, as in the following examples:

> Judas returned on Nisan 21, 164 B.C.E., from his trip to . . .

> The emperor's behavior offended even Roman sensibilities when, for example, he immolated scores of innocent Christians.

Note that no parenthetic commas are used around the year when the day precedes the month or is omitted; and (following *CMS* 8.55) no commas are used with *Jr.* or *Sr.:*

Judas returned on 21 Nisan 164 B.C.E. from his trip to . . .

He published the second edition in March 1932.

Walter Wangerin Jr. spoke at the conference.

Parenthetic commas are customarily used with abbreviations for religious orders and academic degrees following proper names:

The Reverend Joseph Fitzmyer, S.J., delivered a lecture.

4.1.5   QUOTATION MARKS

The placement of quotation marks often creates problems. They belong outside periods and commas. Single quotation marks should be used to indicate quotations within double quotation marks. Note the following examples:

"Correct punctuation is vital."

I am not a "pedant."

"He says he's not a 'pedant.' "

This man, who claims he is not a "pedant," likes making rules about commas.

A question mark, however, belongs outside of the quotation marks unless it is part of the quoted or parenthetical material (*CMS* 5.28). Thus:

Why had he said, "I'm too tired to respond"?

Do you understand the word "pedant"?

He asked, "What can I do?"

Colons and semicolons also belong outside quotation marks:

S. Westerholm wrote the article " 'Letter' and 'Spirit': The Foundation of Pauline Ethics."

Quotation marks should not be used for block quotations; for a quotation within a block quotation, use double rather than single quotation marks.

4.1.6   ELLIPSIS POINTS

There should be a space before and after each dot in a set of ellipsis points. When a complete sentence is followed by ellipsis points, it should be immediately followed by the proper punctuation (whether a period, question mark, or exclamation point), with no intervening space. That punctuation mark will be followed by three—and only three—ellipsis points, as in the second and third examples below:

Right: John . . . knew who they were.
                  John knew them. . . . He had seen them before.
                  John, the youngest, . . . left home.

Wrong: John...knew who they were.
                  John ... knew who they were.

Ellipsis points are used where material has been omitted in the course of a quotation; they are generally not necessary before or after a quoted bit of text. It is acceptable to omit introductory words such as "And" and "For" from a quotation without using ellipsis points. Copy editors and proofreaders should consult *CMS* 10.39, 48–63 for directions about the proper use of ellipsis points.

4.1.7   FINAL PUNCTUATION FOR BLOCK QUOTATIONS

Quoted matter of five or more lines should generally be set off from the rest of the text in a block quotation. Scripture and other primary texts set off in this manner should conclude with punctuation, followed by the citation in parentheses:

> Thus says the Lord GOD: In the first month, on the first day of the month, you shall take a young bull without blemish, and purify the sanctuary. The priest shall take some of the blood of the sin offering and put it on the doorposts of the temple, the four corners of the ledge of the altar, and the posts of the gate of the inner court. You shall do the same on the seventh day of the month for anyone who has sinned through error or ignorance; so you shall make atonement for the temple. (Ezek 45:18–20)

4.2 NUMBERS

4.2.1   ARABIC NUMBERS

Our style requires arabic (1, 10) rather than roman (I, X) numerals. This rule is especially to hold true in bibliographic forms (volume numbers, for example). It also concerns the citing of primary sources as well (e.g., 3 John, not III John). Three exceptions to this rule are page numbers in the front matter of a book, column numbers in Qumran documents (see §8.3.5) and in many other ancient Near Eastern texts (see §5.9.2), and series numbers in Discoveries in the Judean Desert (see Appendix F). The project editor will point out in the instructions to the copy editor any other instances (such as in archaeological periods or in certain catalogs of ancient Near Eastern texts) in which roman numerals are required.

4.2.2   COMMAS IN NUMBERS

Numbers of four or more digits, except for four-digit page numbers and four-digit years, require commas. Thus:

> 3,795 pages
> 148,397 words
> page 1021
> 1296 B.C.E.
> 10,000 B.C.E.

4.2.3   INCLUSIVE NUMBERS: PAGES IN MODERN PUBLICATIONS, QUANTITIES, ETC.

SBL style follows *CMS* 8.68–73 (which allows omitting a specified number of repeated digits in the closing number in a range) *only* for the citing of page (or column) numbers in modern publications and for quantities (of commodities, money, etc.). More specifically, follow the scheme described in *CMS* 8.69. Thus:

> 10–11, 35–38, 98–99
> 100–102, 200–252
> 101–2, 204–11, 309–56
> (but 294–307)
> 1000–1004
> 1002–8
> 1002–16
> 1003–1135

But see §4.2.4 on dates and references to ancient writings.

4.2.4   INCLUSIVE NUMBERS: ANCIENT WRITINGS, DATES

All digits are used in ranges of years. All digits are used with ranges in references to premodern primary texts, whether the numbers refer to sections, chapters, verses, or pages in modern editions.

Avoid mixed use of numbers and words:

> Right: Josephus, *J.W.* 1.321–329
>   154–157 C.E.
>   502–500 B.C.E.
>   The years 1950–1951 were peaceful.
>   from 1856 to 1857
>   between 1850 and 1860
>   He was popular in the 1960s and 1970s.
>   He was popular in the '60s and '70s.
>   He was popular in the sixties and seventies.

Wrong: from 1857–68
              between 1850–60
              He was popular in the 1960s and '70s.

4.3 BIAS-FREE LANGUAGE

The generic use of masculine nouns and pronouns is increasingly unacceptable in current English usage. The assignment of gender to God is likewise best avoided. Consistent use of gender-inclusive language is primarily the author's responsibility. Editors are of course willing to help in this regard as in other stylistic matters. Especially in discussions of ancient texts and cultures, it can be difficult for copy editors to discern whether particular instances of masculine language were meant to be generic or really masculine, so authors should be especially attentive to potential problems.

Bias-free writing respects all cultures, peoples, and religions. Many readers would now regard as biased once-common usages such as *Indian* instead of the now preferred *Native American*. Uncritical use of biblical characterizations such as *the Jews* or *the Pharisees* can perpetuate religious and ethnic stereotypes. Also be aware of the connotations of alternative expressions such as the following pairs:

Hebrew Bible, Old Testament
Second Temple period, intertestamental period
deuterocanonical literature, Apocrypha

For writers and editors who need help in finding language that avoids sexual, racial, and other types of bias, we recommend *The Handbook of Nonsexist Writing*, by Casey Miller and Kate Swift (2d ed.; New York: Harper & Row, 1988), or *Guidelines for Bias-Free Writing*, by Marilyn Schwartz and the Task Force on Bias-Free Language of the Association of American University Presses (Bloomington: Indiana University Press, 1995).

4.4 EXPRESSIONS REQUIRING SPECIAL TREATMENT

Many technical terms, foreign words, proper names, etc., require definition or special treatment. The goal in these instances is always to provide the book's intended audience with the information necessary to understand the author's meaning and argument. When authors use words that may not be well known to readers at all levels of the book's intended audience, they should explain them at the first occurrence. In some books, especially textbooks, it may also be a good idea to put them in a glossary in the back matter.

17

4.4.1 SPELLING

Our hierarchy of authorities for spelling, hyphenation, and capitalization is given in §2. These norms apply even to those authors who are accustomed to using British spellings. For words other than proper nouns, *Merriam-Webster's Collegiate Dictionary* is the preferred authority; where multiple spellings are listed, use the first. Thus in general a final consonant is doubled before a verbal ending only if the final syllable is accented: *worshiping, worshiped, repelled, repelling.* For spelling examples see Appendix A below.

4.4.2 OPEN, HYPHENATED, AND CLOSED COMPOUNDS

If a compound word does not appear in the resources listed in §2.3 (and sometimes even if it does), we follow the general principles in *CMS* 6.32–42 and the rules and specific examples given in *CMS* Table 6.1. In brief: generally accepted compounds tend to be closed rather than hyphenated or open; compound adjectives tend to be left open except when ambiguity would otherwise result (which normally is the case only when the compound adjective precedes the noun it modifies, i.e., is in attributive position). Even where the resources listed in §2.3 give a hyphenated form for a compound adjective, it is preferable to leave such forms open when they are predicative rather than attributive.

Some prefixes generally form closed compounds (*ante-, anti-, co-, neo-, post-, pre-, semi-,* and quite a few others; see the list in *CMS*, pp. 229–30). As a general rule, any hyphenated compound in which the second component is a proper noun or adjective capitalizes the second term and leaves the prefix lowercase. These may be hyphenated when the base is a proper noun or adjective (*premodern,* but *pre-Nicene*), but even these hyphenated forms tend to become closed, in which case the whole word is generally capitalized if it is a noun (*Neoplatonism = neo + Platonism*) but lowercased if it is an adjective (*deuteropauline = deutero + Pauline, neoplatonic = neo + Platonic*). Not infrequently in ancient Near Eastern studies, though, style sheets permit compound forms in which both the prefix and the noun are capitalized, especially if it is a proper noun (e.g., Neo-Assyrian, Neo-Hittite). Note that *quasi-* forms hyphenated compound adjectives and open compound nouns.

Sometimes compounds that should be closed because they are formed with one of the prefixes mentioned above are left open because the closed form would be awkward (*CMS:* "misleading or puzzling"). So *CMS* lists *anti-utopian, pro-choice, pro-life,* and we agree. Sometimes having the prefix end with the same vowel that begins the base constitutes "awkward" but often it does not. Thus *CMS* accepts the curiously Dutch-looking form *neoorthodox,* but we prefer *neo-orthodox.*

So you see it can be a bit complicated. Our advice to authors: do your best, but don't obsess on it. Our advice to our copy editors: obsess and then enter your decision on the book style sheet.

18

4.4.3 CAPITALIZATION (OTHER THAN TITLES OF WORKS)

For capitalization examples see Appendix A.

For our hierarchy of authorities concerning the spelling of proper names, see §2.3; but the following special rules take precedence over those authorities. For capitalization of names with particles, see §6.4. and the examples in §6.4.3.

4.4.4 ITALICS

When discussing a specific term, it is best to set it in italics rather than quotation marks. Thus, "*Hope* occurs three times in this verse." If the term is repeated, it is not necessary to use italics thereafter. On using italics for foreign words, see §4.4.14.

4.4.5 DESIGNATIONS FOR THE BIBLE

In general, a word or phrase used as a title of the whole or a specific part of the Bible is capitalized; the name of a genre is not capitalized. Thus any ancient and modern designation for the Bible, a book of the Bible, a division of the biblical canon (e.g., Pentateuch), or a discrete section of a biblical book (e.g., Primeval History) may be a proper noun and so capitalized.

Several matters require comment. First, note that *book* and *parable* are not considered part of the title and so are lowercase, while *Letter* is considered part of the title and so *is* capitalized. Note further that *Psalms* is the title of a book, while *psalm* is usually the name of a genre (as exemplified in the many biblical *psalms*) but is sometimes part of the name of a particular psalm (such as *the Twenty-Third Psalm* or *Psalm 100*); so also *gospel* is sometimes part of a title and sometimes the name of a genre. The very same word or phrase may be used sometimes as a title and sometimes generically. For example, *the Fourth Gospel* is a commonly used alternative title for the Gospel of John, but if your central thesis is, "John was the first gospel written, although it is the fourth gospel in the canon," you are using the words generically; and *Psalms of Ascent* is the name of a discrete subsection of the book of Psalms, but *psalms of ascent* is a genre of psalms like *royal psalms*. The word *gospel* alone may be a shortened title and so capitalized. Thus in discussing the Johannine literature you might say that a certain concept "is much more prominent in the letters (or in the First Letter) than in the Gospel." Similarly, "the major themes woven by Mark into his Gospel" makes it clear that we are talking about the canonical Gospel of Mark, whereas "Mark's gospel" would mean the message that he proclaimed (which, as it happens, we know only from Mark's Gospel). The same would apply to noncanonical gospels: the days of using capitalization as a sign of reverence are past. On the other hand, there is no reason to capitalize *gospel* every time it seems to refer to one of the canonical books, still less every time it seems to refer to the canonical gospels in general. On the other hand, *the Gospels* is commonly used as the name for a specific division of the New Testament canon. On the other hand, adding a modifier, as in *the canonical gospels* or *the four gospels,* makes the noun generic, except in the phrase *the Synoptic Gospels,* which like *the Gospels* may name a subset of the canon. On the other hand, you might refer to the examples in Appendix A.

4.4.6   TITLES OF NONBIBLICAL TEXTS FROM THE ANCIENT NEAR EAST

For spelling see §2.3.2.

A title should be set in italics only when it represents a direct transliteration of the ancient language (not including personal and place names). Titles should not be set in quotation marks (except when citing the translations of a text; see §7.3.1). Thus,

> The Babylonian Epic of Creation (but, *Enuma Elish*)
> The Stela of the Vultures
> Code of Hammurabi
> The Tale of Apopis and Seqenenre

Set in lowercase the plural generic description of archives and caches (e.g., letters, ostraca, papyri, texts) and in uppercase the individual references:

> Lachish letters
> Lachish Letter 19

In those cases where texts have considerably different titles (not simply the difference, e.g., between Legend of Aqhat or Aqhat Epic), provide the reader with an explanatory comment. Thus,

> The Birth of Dawn and Dusk (also known as The Birth of the Gracious Gods, or The Birth of Shahar and Shalim).

4.4.7   NOUNS REFERRING TO GOD

Certain nouns customarily used to refer to God, to a hypostasis of the one God, or to one of the persons of the Trinity are capitalized when so used:

> Bat Qol, Comforter, Creator, Father, Immanuel, King, King of kings, Lamb, Lamb of God, Lord, Lord of lords, Maker, Messiah, Redeemer, Son, Son of God, Son of Man, Wisdom, Word.

Nontraditional designations should also be capitalized (e.g., *Parent* used as a gender-neutral substitute for *Father*). Ordinarily, noun phrases are capitalized as if they were book titles (e.g., *Son of Man*), but the second term in *King of kings* and *Lord of lords* is lowercase in accord with NRSV and NIV usage because the point in these expressions is the exaltation of the one Christ over all merely human powers. Other designations less often used outside of particular scriptural contexts are less often capitalized:

> bread of life or Bread of Life, crucified one or Crucified One, man of sorrows or Man of Sorrows, light of the world or Light of the World.

With all of these, and especially the latter category, usage varies. If the author has a preference and has been consistent, that preference should be let stand. If not, the copy editor should make consistent decisions. For biblical expressions, it can be helpful to consult the usage of a recent Bible translation such as the NRSV, the NIV, the REB, or the NJB. In any event, the copy editor should include all such items in the book's style sheet.

4.4.8 PRONOUNS REFERRING TO GOD

Avoid using gender-specific pronouns in reference to the Godhead (see §4.3). In those cases when such pronouns are unavoidable, they should not be capitalized (thus *he, him, his;* but for expressions like Third Person of the Trinity, see §4.4.7).

4.4.9 ANCIENT PERSONS

For spelling, see hierarchy of authorities in §§2.3.1–3.

The first occurrence of an ancient personal name should be accompanied by the dates of that person's life. In many cases, of course, the best that can be offered is an indication of which century the person lived in.

4.4.10 OTHER PERSONAL NAMES

For spelling, see hierarchy of authorities in §§2.3.1–3. For surnames with particles see §§6.4.1, 4. For compound surnames see §6.5.

4.4.11 ANCIENT PLACES

For spelling, see hierarchy of authorities in §§2.3.1, 2, 4.

Especially when a volume concerns ancient Near Eastern geography or archeology, locations and dates of habitation should be given at the first occurrence of ancient place names. For sites that have multiple names (ancient, biblical, premodern, modern, Arabic), give all of the names:

> Mari (Tell Hariri), Ugarit (Ras Shamra), Shechem (Tell Balatah), Jericho (Tell es-Sultân), Hazor (Tell el-Qedah), Caesarea Philippi (Banias, Panias), Bethshan (Beth-shean, Scythopolis), Samaria (Sebaste).

In some cases, it may be helpful to indicate which names are ancient, modern, etc.

> Mari (modern Tell Hariri), Laish (biblical Dan), Uruk (biblical Erech, present-day Warka), Rabbah (later Philadelphia).

Hebrew geographical names are, when needed, preceded by Tel (one *el*), arabic by Tell (two *els*). For names with the Arabic definite article *al,* follow *CMS* 9.91.

21

4.4.12   Other Geographical Terms and Names

For general reference, follow *Merriam-Webster's Geographical Dictionary* (3d ed.; Springfield, Mass.: Merriam-Webster, 1997).

The generic terms *delta, desert, gulf, island(s), lake, mount, mountain(s), nahal, nahr, river, sea, strait, tel, tell, valley, wadi* should be capitalized when used as part of a specific name (*CMS* 7.42):

> Kidron Valley, Lake Huleh, Lebanon Mountains, Ophel Ridge, Khirbet Qumran.

For spelling, see hierarchy of authorities in §§2.3.1, 2, 4; but for capitalization: *CMS* (7.43) "now recommends that when a generic term is used in the plural either before or after more than one proper name, the term should be capitalized if, in the singular form and in the same position, it would be recognized as a part of each name":

> Tigris and Euphrates Rivers

Note political divisions, such as *Central Europe*, as distinct from geographical divisions, such as *central Asia* (*CMS* 7.36, 38).

4.4.13   Events and Concepts

As a general rule, do not capitalize the names of biblical, religious, and theological (including eschatological) events and concepts:

> atonement, body and blood, body of Christ, creation, crucifixion, day of judgment, exile, exodus (from Egypt), fall, first missionary journey, kingdom of God (or heaven), man of sin, nativity (of Jesus), new covenant, passion (of Christ), resurrection, tabernacle, temple, virgin birth.

See Appendix A for more examples.

4.4.14   Words in Foreign Languages

Unusual words in modern and ancient foreign languages should be defined on first occurrence. Authors and project editors can determine if a particular book should have the Hebrew and Greek transliterated. See §5 regarding transliteration of biblical and related ancient texts. In nearly all books words in other languages using nonroman alphabets should be transliterated.

Foreign words should be italicized except for those that have passed into common English usage, which should remain in roman type. In general, consult *Merriam-Webster's Collegiate Dictionary*, 10th ed., to determine if a word falls into this latter category. Many Latin terms are familiar enough to scholars to warrant being left in roman type. *Sic* and *pace* are two notable exceptions to this rule and should always be italicized. See §8.3.14 for Latin words and abbreviations (also *CMS* 14.33).

4.4.15   DATES

Dates should be presented in the following format:

> August 15, 1979
> August 1979
> August 20 C.E. (August A.D. 20)
> August 20 B.C.E. (August 20 B.C.)

See §8.1.2 for treatment of eras.

4.4.16   LITURGICAL DAYS AND SEASONS

Names of days or seasons in the liturgical year (or in other liturgical cycles) are set roman and capitalized regardless of whether they are in English, Latin, Greek, or Hebrew:

> Ascension Day, Christmas, Christmas Eve, Christmas Day, Day of Atonement, Easter, Epiphany, Feast of the Nativity, Feast (or Festival) of Tabernacles, Lord's Day, Mother's Day, Rally Day, Super Bowl Sunday, Pascha, Passover, Pentecost, Pesach, Rosh Hashanah, Sabbath (n. and adj.), Year of Jubilee, Yom Kippur.

Note that *Day of Atonement* (a recurring event in the liturgical calendar) is capitalized; *judgment day*, referring to an eschatological event, is not (see §4.4.13).

4.4.17   LITURGICAL TEXTS

Titles of liturgical texts are capitalized:

> the Eighteen Benedictions, the Lord's Prayer, the Our Father, the Ten Commandments (which would be capitalized anyway as a canonical section).

Latin liturgical titles commonly used in English are not italicized; these are also capitalized according to English (not Latin) rules, since otherwise they would blend into the surrounding text:

> the Gloria (or Gloria in Excelsis Deo), the Gloria Patri, the Magnificat, the Nunc Dimittis, the Pater Noster, the Te Deum.

Common Hebrew liturgical terms may be transliterated informally and treated similarly:

> Amidah, Birkat Haminim, Kaddish, Shema, Shemoneh Esre.

(In nontechnical books, some of these Latin and Hebrew terms might be italicized and so capitalized according to foreign rather than English rules.)

4.4.18   ALPHABETIZED LISTS

Alphabetized lists, such as lists of abbreviations, glossaries, lists of contributors, etc., should follow the rules given in §§6.3, 6.4, 6.4.2, 6.5.

4.4.19   INDEX HEADINGS

For treatment of index headings, see §6.1.

5   Transliterating and Transcribing Ancient Texts

The project editor will decide in consultation with the author whether Hebrew, Greek, and other ancient languages will be represented in their own alphabets or transliterated into roman script. In general, there is rarely any reason to transliterate Greek in works intended for scholarly readers; for Semitic languages, transliteration may be preferable when it facilitates comparison of cognate forms. This section provides instructions to authors for cases in which transliterations are to be used. For nonroman fonts, see §3.1.1.1.

5.1 HEBREW

The author should select a Hebrew transliteration convention that reflects the level of precision necessary for the argumentation and the intended audience. An author may adopt one of two systems: (1) an academic style, which is fully reversible; that is, the system allows the reader to reproduce the Hebrew characters exactly (consonants and vowels); or (2) a general-purpose style, which is essentially phonetic.[1]

5.1.1 ACADEMIC STYLE

5.1.1.1 Consonants

CHARACTER		TRANSLITERATION	CHARACTER		TRANSLITERATION
א	ʾālep	ʾ	מ, ם	mêm	m
ב	bêt	b	נ, ן	nûn	n
ג	gîmel	g	ס	sāmek	s
ד	dālet	d	ע	ʿayin	ʿ
ה	hê	h	פ, ף	pê	p
ו	wāw	w	צ, ץ	ṣādê	ṣ
ז	zayin	z	ק	qôp	q
ח	ḥêt	ḥ	ר	rêš	r
ט	ṭêt	ṭ	שׂ	śîn	ś
י	yôd	y	שׁ	šîn	š
כ, ך	kāp	k	ת	tāw	t
ל	lāmed	l			

5.1.1.2 Vowels

CHARACTER	TRANSLITERATION		CHARACTER	TRANSLITERATION
◌ַ	pataḥ	a	◌ִי	ḥîreq yôd	î (◌ִ = îy)
◌ַ	furtive pataḥ	a	◌ָ	qāmeṣ ḥāṭûp	o
◌ָ	qāmeṣ	ā	◌ֹ	ḥōlem	ō
ה◌ָ	final qāmeṣ hê	â	◌ֹו	full ḥōlem	ô
י◌ָ	3d masc. sg. suf.	āyw	◌ֻ	short qibbûṣ	u
◌ֶ	sĕgōl	e	◌ֻ	long qibbûṣ	ū
◌ֵ	ṣērê	ē	◌ּו	šûreq	û
◌ֵי	ṣērê yôd	ê (◌ֵ = êy)	◌ֳ	ḥāṭēp qāmeṣ	ŏ
◌ֶי	sĕgōl yôd	ê (◌ֶ = êy)	◌ֲ	ḥāṭēp pataḥ	ă
◌ִ	short ḥîreq	i	◌ֱ	ḥāṭēp sĕgōl	ĕ
◌ִ	long ḥîreq	ī	◌ְ	vocal šĕwāʾ	ĕ

---

[1]See Werner Weinberg, "Transliteration and Transcription of Hebrew," *HUCA* 40–41 (1969–1970): 1–32; and idem, "On Hebrew Transliteration," *Bib* 56 (1975): 150–52.

5.1.1.3 *Stems* (Binyanim)

BASIC HEBREW STEMS

qal	*puᶜal*	*hitpaᶜel*
nipᶜal	*hipᶜil*	
piᶜel	*hopᶜal*	

BASIC ARAMAIC STEMS

peᶜal	*puᶜal*	*hitpeᶜel*
paᶜel	*hapᶜel*	*hitpaᶜal*
peᶜil	*hupᶜal*	*šapᶜel*

OTHER HEBREW AND ARAMAIC STEMS

apᶜel	*hitpalpel*	*nitpaᶜel*
etpaᶜal	*hitpoᶜlel*	*pilpel*
etpeᶜel	*ištapᶜal*	*poᶜlel*
hištapᶜal	*itpaᶜal*	*yipᶜil*
hitpaᶜlel	*itpeᶜel*	

5.1.1.4 *Notes*

(1) The consonants *hê*, *wāw*, and *yôd*, used to indicate long vowels (vowel letters, *matres lectionis*), are transliterated as a circumflex over the vowel (i.e., *â*, *ê*, *î*, *ô*, *û*); they are also taken into account when a transliteration reproduces an unpointed text (extrabiblical inscriptions, Qumran texts, Ketib, etc.) and for the purposes of alphabetization. Regarding a final *hê*, note the fem. sg. poss. ending (*malkāh*, "her king") and the feminine ending *-â* (*malkâ*, "queen"). הָ (*hê* with a *mappîq*) should be written as *-āh*.

(2) Always transliterate quiescent *ʾālep* using *ʾ*: e.g., *lōʾ*, "not"; *hûʾ*, "he"; *rōʾš*, "head"; Aram. *malkāʾ*, "the king." This rule holds even though the *ō* is placed over the right side of the *ʾ*.

(3) Transliterate short vowels written fully as *i(w)*, *o(w)*, *u(w)*: e.g., *hu(w)kkâ* for הוּכָּה.

(4) Do not indicate *begadkepat* spirantization (absence of *dāgēš lene*) unless it is important to the discussion. Exceptions may be shown by underlining the consonant: e.g., יְקֻתְאֵל = *yoqtĕʾēl* (see GKC §21).

(5) Indicate *dāgēš forte* by doubling the consonant. A euphonic *dāgēš* should not be doubled: e.g., מַה־שְּׁמוֹ = *mah-šĕmô* (see GKC §20).

(6) A silent *šĕwāʾ* is not transliterated, including when it is the second of two *šĕwāʾ*s at the end of a word: e.g., *ʾatt* for אַתְּ; *yādalt* for יָדַלְתְּ.

(7) Do not mark stress, unless it is relevant to a particular point. If stress is relevant, use an acute mark for the primary accent, and a grave mark for secondary accent.

(8) Do not capitalize transliterated proper names, although every transliteration should be capitalized at the beginning of a sentence.

(9) Use a hyphen to indicate a *maqqēp*.

5.1.2 GENERAL-PURPOSE STYLE

5.1.2.1 Consonants

א	alef	' or omit	נ, ן	nun	n	
ב	bet	b; v (spirant)	ס	samek	s	
ג	gimel	g; gh (spirant)	ע	ayin	' or omit	
ד	dalet	d; dh (spirant)	פ, ף	pe	p; f (spirant)	
ה	he	h	צ, ץ	tsade	ts	
ו	vav	v or w	ק	qof	q	
ז	zayin	z	ר	resh	r	
ח	khet	h or kh	שׂ	sin	s	
ט	tet	t	שׁ	shin	sh	
י	yod	y	ת	tav	t; th (spirant)	
כ, ך	kaf	k; kh (spirant)				
ל	lamed	l				
מ, ם	mem	m				

5.1.2.2 Vowels

ַ	patakh	a	ִי	hireq yod	i
ַ	furtive patakh	a	ָ	qamets khatuf	o
ָ	qamets	a	ֹ	holem	o
ָה	final qamets he	ah	וֹ	full holem	o
ֶ	segol	e	ֻ	short qibbuts	u
ֵ	tsere	e	ֻ	long qibbuts	u
ֵי	tsere yod	e	וּ	shureq	u
ִ	short hireq	i	ֳ	khatef qamets	o
ִ	long hireq	i	ֲ	khatef patakh	a

5.1.2.3 Stems (Binyanim)

BASIC HEBREW STEMS

Qal	Hiphil
Niphal	Hophal
Piel	Hitpael
Pual	

5.1.2.4 Notes

(1) For the spellings of common Jewish holidays and liturgical terms, see §§4.14.16–17. When spelling Hebrew terms that begin with the definite article *(ha)*, capitalize only the first letter of the word; thus, Birkat Hatorah *(not* Birkat HaTorah or Birkat haTorah).

(2) Spirant forms *(dagesh lene)* are optional, based upon convention and appearance. (In modern Hebrew, the presence or absence of the

dagesh lene generally affects the pronunciation of only *bet, kaf,* and *pe* of the *begadkepat* letters.) The main guideline is that any given decision should remain consistent throughout a manuscript.

(3) Doubled forms *(dagesh forte)* should be doubled in transliteration (e.g., *hinneh*). The two exceptions to this doubling rule are צ *(ts)* and שׁ *(sh);* these two consonants should not be doubled (e.g., מָשָׁא = *masha'*).

5.2 ARAMAIC

The systems described above for Hebrew are to be followed, even though *ṣērê* and *ḥōlem* are frequently not markers of long vowels in Aramaic.

5.3 GREEK

Whereas for Hebrew both academic and general-purpose transliteration styles are provided, for Greek only a general-purpose style is provided; for academic readers, Greek should be given in Greek characters. (In books meant for a broad audience, editors may elect to use a Greek font only in notes and parentheses, transliterating Greek words that are necessary in the main text.) Thus no provision is made for transliteration of iota subscript, diaeresis, digamma, accents, etc.: where these matter, use a Greek font. Note however that in transliteration omega and eta should be indicated with a macron. If your font has no macron, see §3.1.1.7.

α	=	*a*	ο	=	*o*
β	=	*b*	π	=	*p*
γ	=	*g*	ρ	=	*r*
γ	=	*n* (before γ, κ, ξ, χ)	ῥ	=	*rh*
δ	=	*d*	σ, ς	=	*s*
ε	=	*e*	τ	=	*t*
ζ	=	*z*	υ	=	*y* (not in diphthong)
η	=	*ē*	υ	=	*u* (in diphthongs: *au, eu, ēu,*
θ	=	*th*			*ou, ui*)
ι	=	*i*	φ	=	*ph*
κ	=	*k*	χ	=	*ch*
λ	=	*l*	ψ	=	*ps*
μ	=	*m*	ω	=	*ō*
ν	=	*n*	ʽ	=	*h* (with vowel or diphthong)
ξ	=	*x*			

5.4 COPTIC

ⲁ	=	*a*	ⲡ	=	*p*
ⲃ	=	*b*	ⲣ	=	*r*
ⲅ	=	*g*	ⲥ	=	*s*
ⲇ	=	*d*	ⲧ	=	*t*
ⲉ	=	*e*	ⲩ	=	*u*
ⲍ	=	*z*	ⲫ	=	*ph*
ⲏ	=	*ē*	ⲭ	=	*kh*
ⲑ	=	*th*	ⲯ	=	*ps*
ⲓ	=	*i*	ⲱ	=	*ō*
ⲕ	=	*k*	ϣ	=	*š*
ⲗ	=	*l*	ϥ	=	*f*
ⲙ	=	*m*	ϩ	=	*h*
ⲛ	=	*n*	ϫ	=	*j*
ⲝ	=	*ks*	ϭ	=	*č*
ⲟ	=	*o*	ϯ	=	*ti*

For the Achmimic and Boharic *ḫay*, use *ḫ*. For the supralinear stroke, use a raised italic *e* (e.g., *ᵉmpjoei*)

5.5. AKKADIAN

The transliteration of Akkadian should consistently follow either A. L. Oppenheim, et al., eds., *The Assyrian Dictionary of the Oriental Insititue of the University of Chicago* (Chicago: The Oriental Institute, 1956– [= *CAD*]) or W. von Soden, *Akkadisches Handwörterbuch* (3 vols.; Wiesbaden: Harrassowitz, 1965–1981 [= *AHw*]), with the following alphabetic representation: *a, b, d, e, g, ḫ, i, y (j in AHw), k, l, m, n, p, q, r, s, ṣ, š, t, ṭ, u, w, z*. Sumerian logograms should be set in small caps. Determinatives should be set as superscript lowercase letters. The "two" and "three" values of signs should be indicated by subscript "2" and "3" (instead of acute and grave accents). The rules for the Hebrew general-purpose style (§5.1.2) can be applied when transliterating in a nontechnical format (e.g., *misharum* instead of *mīšarum*).

5.6. EGYPTIAN

Egyptian transliteration follows either A. Gardiner (*Egyptian Grammar* [3d ed.; London: Oxford University Press, 1957], 26–27) or Rainer Hannig, *Grosses Handwörterbuch Ägyptisch-Deutsch (2800–950 v. Chr.): Die Sprache der Pharaonen* (Kulturgeschichte der antiken Welt 64; Mainz: Philipp von Zabern, 1995), xxxvii–xxxviii: *z, i (j in Hannig), y, ꜥ, w, b, f, m, n, r, h, ḥ, ḫ, ẖ, s (z, s in Hannig), š, ḳ (q in Hannig), k, g, t, ṯ, d, ḏ*. For current treatment of the Egyptian language, see Antonio Loprieno, *Ancient Egyptian: A Linguis-*

tic Introduction (Cambridge: Cambridge University Press, 1995), and Hannig's *Grosses Handwörterbuch Ägyptisch-Deutsch,* which includes an excellent discussion of various systems of Egyptian transliterations (pp. xxxvi–xlii).

5.7. UGARITIC

Ugaritic transliteration follows Cyrus H. Gordon (*Ugaritic Textbook* [AnOr 38; Rome: Pontifical Biblical Institute, 1965] = *UT*), 13–15: *a, i, u, b, g, d, ḏ, h, w, z, ḥ, ḫ, ṭ, ẓ, y, k, l, m, n, s, ṣ, ᶜ, ġ, p, ṣ, q, r, š, t, ṯ. A, i,* and *u* indicate not vowels but the variously vocalized consonantal ʾ.

5.8 OTHER ANCIENT LANGUAGES

For transliterating other Semitic languages, consult the pertinent grammars and dictionaries.

5.9 TRANSCRIBING ANCIENT TEXTS

When citing or discussing ancient texts, the following guidelines should be followed:

5.9.1 Symbols

[ ]	in both transliteration and translation, brackets indicate reconstructed text or gaps.
( )	in English translations, parentheses are used for additions to improve the sense and for transliterations immediately preceding translated words.
*	in discussions of grammatical and lexical items, asterisk indicates an unattested form.
§	section markers may be used to cite a natural division of a text (e.g., Code of Hammurabi §10) or a published division (e.g., *ARAB 2* §808).

5.9.2 Abbreviations

col(s).	column(s); usually cited as roman numerals, uppercase or lowercase, depending on edition
ep(s).	episode(s); section of an inscription or section of a common narrated event extant in more than one inscription
line(s)	always spell out
no(s).	number(s)
obv.	obverse (front) of a tablet
rec(s).	recension(s)
rev.	reverse (back) of a tablet
r	recto (often superscripted)
v	verso (often superscripted)

31

6   Indexes and Bibliographies

Most of the matters in this section concern sorting lists. The first two items apply only to indexes; the last applies only to bibliographies; the rest apply to both. For matters pertaining to bibliographies and notes, see §7.

6.1 CAPITALIZATION OF INDEX HEADINGS

Capitalize only those index headings that would be capitalized in the middle of a sentence.

6.2 SORTING PRIMARY-TEXT REFERENCES

Please pay particular attention to the following model regarding the ordering of references within indexes of primary-text references. The following general principles can be observed in the examples below: (1) When two ranges have the same starting point, the one with the earlier end point has priority. (2) A simple reference (to a chapter, a verse, or part of a verse, rather than a range) precedes a range whose starting point is the same as the simple reference. (3) We strongly discourage the use of a reference to a range with no explicitly named end point (i.e., a reference using f. or ff.); but if used such a reference would follow any simple references and precede any references to ranges whose end points are explicitly given. (4) A reference to a specified portion of a verse (or a range beginning therewith) comes after a reference to the whole verse (or a range beginning therewith).

Acts	2	2:4a
	2–3	2:4b
	2:4	2:4b–6
	2:4–7	2:4b–7

6.3 ALPHABETIZING

The two main ways of sorting are generally called letter-by-letter and word-by-word. We find these labels unhelpful, but for those who are accustomed to them: we use the word-by-word rule. A simple way of explaining this rule (and thereby demonstrating the ineptness of the "word-by-word" label) is: *proceed character-by-character and do not ignore spaces.* Letters, obviously enough, will go in alphabetical order: *a* ranks highest; *z* lowest; case and diacritics are ignored (o = ö = ø). Spaces outrank the letter *a*. Hyphens, capital letters, and quotation marks are ignored. Apostrophe ranks between space and the letter *a.* The following list gives a fuller hierarchy:

```
, [comma]
  [space]
' [apostrophe]
0
1
(etc.)
9
a, A, ä, á, å (etc.)
b
(etc.)
z
Ignored: - – . " " ' ' [hyphen, en dash, period, double and single quotation
    marks]
```

Thus, to borrow and modify the *CMS* word-by-word example:

New Deal	newel
new economics	new-fashioned
New England	newlywed
New Latin	news conference
"new math"	news release
New Testament	newsboy
New Word	newspaper
New Year's Day	newsprint
new years and old habits	newt
New, Zoe	Newton, Lady Anne
newborn	Newton, Isaac
newcomer	Newton, Rev. Philip T.

This description of the word-by-word rule does not cover all questions that may arise; it is worth noting, however, that it is probably the system your word processor's sorting function uses (some word processors will let you specify letter-by-letter or word-by-word sorting, but others just provide word-by-word without offering you an option); so in general you should probably begin alphabetizing by letting the computer do the sorting and then check for any anomalous results. For example, some word processors rank quotation marks above letters and so (in the above example) put *"new math"* at the top of the list.

6.4 NAMES WITH PARTICLES

For surnames that begin with particles (i.e., prepositions and articles) we follow two general rules: (1) Capitalize according to established usage; (2) alphabetize by the first capitalized part of the surname.

We do not conform Jewish and Arabic names in *ben* and *ibn* to the rules for particles because *ben* and *ibn* are not particles but nouns (meaning "son [of]"). *Abraham ibn Ezra* should be alphabetized as *Ibn Ezra, Abraham*. *Moses ben Maimon* would be alphabetized as *Ben Maimon, Moses* (or as *Maimonides!*). Similarly, when such a surname occurs in mid-sentence without a first name, it is capitalized ("the works of Ibn Ezra").

6.4.1 CAPITALIZATION

It is not always easy to know what constitutes established usage, since different rules apply to different particles in names of different nationalities; for example, names that have been Americanized are generally capitalized without regard to such rules. The table in §6.4.3 gives our usage for some names that occur commonly in biblical scholarship and related fields. Others may be treated by analogy with these (but be careful to follow the right model for the nationality at hand) or looked up in a standard reference work such as *Merriam-Webster's Biographical Dictionary*. If no print authority is available, you might consult the online catalog of a major university library, but these also contain many errors.

A particle in a given person's name should have the same case in running text, footnotes, bibliographies, and indexes whether or not the surname is preceded by a first name or initials. Thus:

> In his earlier works, Gerhard von Rad said . . .
> In his earlier works, von Rad said . . .
> In his earlier works, François Du Bois said . . .
> In his earlier works, Du Bois said . . .

Of course, any name with a particle at the beginning of a sentence is capitalized:

> Von Rad often said . . .

6.4.2   ALPHABETIZATION

John Van Seters should be alphabetized as *Van Seters, John*, because in this Americanized name *Van* is capitalized; *Hans von Campenhausen* should be alphabetized as *Campenhausen, Hans von*, because *von* is not capitalized. Follow this same rule even when a noncapitalized particle is separated from the main part of the surname by an apostrophe or hyphen rather than a space (as with *Jean Le Rond d'Alembert* and *Khalid Ahmad al-A'dami* in the following table).

For names beginning with *O'* or *Mc* or *Mac*, as well as names beginning with *St., Saint, Saint-, Sainte*, etc., follow the general rule given above in §6.3. These names should be "sorted as they appear" not "sorted as if spelled out"; i.e., alphabetize according to *kethiv*, not *qere* (see *CMS* 17.109). Remember that spaces are significant in sorting.

The main desideratum in an index is usefulness to the reader. Our rules are meant to be easy to follow and in accord with convention, but the sad fact is that since not all editors and publishers are careful or consistent in this matter, readers don't know what to expect and are not likely to look up a particular name in the "right" place all the time. So in indexes containing only a few names with particles, judicious use of cross-references and even double entries is encouraged.

6.4.3   EXAMPLES

The following list is a guide for capitalization as well as alphabetization. Some names without particles have been included to demonstrate correct alphabetization.

Aarde, Andries G. van
A'dami, Khalid Ahmad al-
Alembert, Jean Le Rond d'
Balthasar, Hans Urs von
Ben Maimon, Moses. *See* Maimonides
Ben-Tor, Amnon
Berardino, Angelo di
Berchem, Denis van
Bickerman, Elias J.
Böhl, Franz Marius Theodor de
   Liagre
Born, Adrianus van den
Campenhausen, Hans von
Cranenburgh, Henri van
Dake, Finis J.
D'Angelo, Mary Rose
De Boer, Willis Peter
De Lacey, D. R.

De Vries, Simon J.
Des Places, Eduard
Di Lella, Alexander A.
Díez Macho, Alejandro
Dobschütz, Ernst von
Du Buit, F. M.
Du Cange, Charles Du Fresne
Du Plessis, Paul Johannes
Dubarle, André M.
Fraine, Jean de
Geus, C. H. J. de
Grobel, Kendrick
Grønbaek, J. H.
Gröndahl, Franke
Gross, Walter
Harnack, Adolf von
or
Harnack, Adolf

Hoek, Annewies van den
Horst, P. W. van der
Houwink ten Cate, Philo H. J.
Ibn Ezra, Abraham ben Meir
Imschoot, Paul van
Jonge, H. J. de
Jonge, Marinus de
Kooij, Gerrit van der
La Mésangère, Pierre de
La Potterie, Ignace de
La Sor, William Sanford
Lacocque, André
Lagarde, Pierre de
Lagrange, Marie-Joseph
Langhe, Robert de
Laperrousaz, Ernest-Marie
Le Boulluec, Alain
Le Déaut, R.
Le Moyne, J.
Le Nain de Tillemont, Louis-
    Sebastien
Loon, Maurits Nanning van
Lubac, Henri de
Maass, F.
MacDermot, Violet
Macdonald, John
Maimonides (Moses ben Maimon)
Markus, R. A.
McKenzie, J. L.
Medico, H. E. del
Meer, Frederik van der
Moor, Johannes C. de

Oakman, Douglas E.
O'Callaghan, J.
Olmo Lete, G. del
O'Neil, Edward N.
Ortiz de Urbina, Ignacio
Osten-Sacken, Peter von der
Ploeg, J. P. M. van der
Rad, Gerhard von
Ranke, Leopold von
Rossum, J. van
Santos, Elmaro Camilo dos
Santos Otero, A. de
Saulcy, Louis Felicien Joseph
    Caignart de
Selms, Adrianus van
Smitten, Wilhelm T. in der
Soden, Hermann von
Soden, Wolfram von
Sola Pool, D. de
St. Ville, Susan M.
Strycker, Emile de
Teilhard de Chardin, Pierre
Tuya, Manuel de
Unnik, W. C. van
Van Dusen, Henry P.
Van Seters, John
Van Til, Cornelius
Vaux, Roland de
Vries, Benjamin de
Wette, W. M. L. de
Woude, A. S. van der

6.5 COMPOUND SURNAMES

Most Spanish authors and some English-speaking authors use double surnames, which should be alphabetized according to the first element. It is
often impossible to tell just from looking at such names how they should be
treated, so authors and editors are encouraged to make use of on-line
library catalogs and other resources. With English-speaking authors, the
absence of a hyphen does not necessarily mean that the two family names
do not make a double surname—although it usually does. As for names
with particles, we look to the Library of Congress for definitive guidance in
individual cases. A few examples:

Alonso Schökel, Luis
Busto Saiz, José Ramon
Díez Macho, Alejandro
García Cordero, M.
García de la Fuente, O.
Lane Fox, Robin
Payne Smith, R.
Ruiz Bueno, Daniel

but:

Santos Otero, Aurelio de
Schüssler Fiorenza, Elisabeth
Teilhard de Chardin, Pierre

Collins, Adela Yarbro
Darr, Katheryn Pfisterer
Jones, Henry Stuart

6.6 SORTING MULTIPLE BOOKS BY A SINGLE AUTHOR

In our preferred style for bibliographies, works by the same author or editor are sorted alphabetically by title. In the author-date format (see §7.4), works by a single author are sorted by date.

7   Notes and Bibliographies

Authors are responsible for supplying complete, accurate, and stylistically correct notes and bibliographies.

We prefer the traditional documentation style that uses footnotes and bibliographies (this is a production matter, so the author should not worry about the form in which it is submitted [see §3.1.1.4]). For some books using social-science methodologies, however, we use text notes and author-date citations.

For books using the author-date format, the bibliography should include all the works, and only the works, referred to in text notes. For books using the traditional format, the bibliography may cite exactly the same books referred to in notes, or it may cite a subset of these (a "select bibliography"), or it may cite the books mentioned in the notes plus others.

For books using the traditional format, complete publication data should be supplied in the first note referring to a given source. Subsequent notes referring to the same source should use a short title and the abbreviated note form exhibited in the examples in §7.2.

Standard abbreviations for titles and series should be used in the notes (see §8.4), while the entries in the bibliography should include the complete and unabbreviated references. In a similar way, "edited by" and "translated by" should be abbreviated in the notes and spelled out in the bibliography.

7.1 RULES

7.1.1 SEQUENCE OF INFORMATION

As a general rule the sequence of publishing information (that given inside parentheses in a note) is as follows: editor; translator; number of volumes; edition; series; city; publisher; date. Colons precede page numbers in journal articles, and colons separate volume and page numbers.

7.1.2 AUTHOR OR EDITOR

Whenever possible, the author's or editor's first name (not just an initial) should be provided. A space should always be left between initials. Ancient and other premodern works may be listed in bibliographies either under the name of the premodern author or under the name of the modern editor, but all premodern works should be treated the same. If works are listed by premodern author, the standard English spelling of the name should be used regardless of the spelling on the title page of the work being cited: Aristotle (not *Aristote* or *Aristoteles*), *Sophocles* (not *Sophokles*), *Jerome* (not *Hieronymus*), *Augustine* (not *Augustinus* or *Augustin*), etc. The standard English spellings may be found as headings in library catalogs. Where necessary fuller forms of names may be used: *Eusebius of Caesarea, Athanasius of Alexandria, George of the Jungle*, etc.

40

7.1.3 TITLE

7.1.3.1 Punctuation

Regardless of the punctuation or lack thereof on the title page of the book, and regardless of the language of the book, use a colon (not a period, semicolon, or comma) before every subtitle. Use a comma before a range of years at the end of a title unless the title page uses parentheses. Use semicolons between titles of separate works published in the same binding.

7.1.3.2 Format

When abbreviations such as B.C.E., C.E., etc., are used in a title, they should be set in full caps, not small caps, and italicized to agree with the rest of the title. When non-English words are used in an English title, they should be set roman when the title is italic and italic when the title is roman.

7.1.3.3 Capitalization of Titles in English

In titles in English, all words should be capitalized except articles, coordinating conjunctions, and prepositions, except when they are the first or last word in the title or subtitle. In hyphenated words, both words should be capitalized unless they are articles, coordinating conjunctions, or prepositions (unless used adverbially), or if the word is a prefix attached to anything other than a proper noun or proper adjective. In these cases the word should be lowercase. Cf. *CMS* 7.127–28.

7.1.3.4 Capitalization of Titles Not in English

For titles in languages other than English, the general rule is to capitalize only the first word of the title or subtitle and any words that would be capitalized in a normal sentence. For most languages, only proper nouns (but not proper adjectives) are capitalized. In German, nouns are capitalized, and in Dutch, proper adjectives are capitalized. For more on titles in particular languages see §§7.1.3.7–9.

7.1.3.5 Series and Multivolume Works

Series titles are set roman; titles of multivolume works are set italic. Some works could be classified either way. We treat the following as series titles:

Patrologia graeca (for Patrologiae cursus completus: Series graeca)
Patrologia latina (for Patrologiae cursus completus: Series latina)
Patrologia orientalis
Sources chrétiennes

We treat the following as multivolume works:

Ante-Nicene Fathers
Aufstieg und Niedergang der römischen Welt
Nicene and Post-Nicene Fathers, First Series
Nicene and Post-Nicene Fathers, Second Series

7.1.3.6 Primary Sources

In the body of a manuscript, cite primary sources, including biblical texts, parenthetically, inside the final punctuation.[1] Thus,

> In Luke, for example, it is the lawyer who cites the double command, whereas in Matthew and Mark it is Jesus (Matt 22:37–40; Mark 12:29–31).

> All of this occurred "In the ninth year of King Zedekiah of Judah, in the tenth month" (Jer 39:1).

If the translation is important, simply insert it following the reference.

> From Luke's point of view, "the kingdom of God is among you" (Luke 17:21 NRSV).

Likewise, if a longer passage is cited as an excerpt, the source should appear within parentheses, but this time outside the final punctuation. In excerpted material, the translator should be included unless an earlier statement has indicated the source of the translation for a given work or corpus.[2] Thus,

> Therefore according to the circumstances and temper and even age of each is the delay of baptism more profitable, yet especially in the case of little children. For where is the need of involving sponsors also in danger? They too through mortality may fail to perform their promises, or may be deceived by the growth of an evil disposition. (Tertullian, *De baptismo* 18, Gwatkin)

For citing primary sources in notes and bibliographies, see §7.3.2.

7.1.3.7 French Titles

We prefer to treat French like other modern languages, capitalizing titles according to the general rule given in §7.1.3.4 (rather than the more complicated alternative rule explained in *CMS* 9.4 n.1) and retaining the accents on upper-case vowels.

---

[1] Specific examples of how to cite ANF, NPNF, and LCL texts in notes (rather than in parentheses) and bibliographies appear in § 7.3.2.

[2] If the translation is referred to consistently, a note at the first instance indicating which edition and translation are used throughout the manuscript is appropriate.

7.1.3.8   Latin Titles

Editors in every country have a tendency to capitalize Latin titles in accord with their rules for their own language. *The SBL Handbook,* unlike *CMS,* undertakes to bring all Latin titles from all periods of history into conformity with the general rule given in §7.1.3.4: i.e., capitalize only the first word of the title (or subtitle) and any proper nouns (but not proper adjectives) included in the title.

Lest this seem too easy, we point out that one has to know a bit of Latin to differentiate between proper nouns and proper adjectives (but a brief guideline is that if the term in question has the same ending as the noun it follows, it is probably an adjectival form). We also stipulate, in accord with the practice of the Stuttgart edition of the Vulgate, that in addition to names of persons and places, proper nouns include various appellations of the one God: *Deus, Pater, Filius* (and so *Filioque*), *Trinitas,* and other terms when they are clearly used as alternative names of the deity (*Verbum, Creator,* etc.). The title of a book is also a proper noun, so that when one book title occurs within another, the included title is capitalized (i.e., its first word is capitalized) as if it were standing alone.

When an adjective is so closely associated with a proper noun that the two form in effect a compound noun, both words are capitalized:

> Sancta Trinitas, Sanctus Augustinus, Sanctus Spiritus, Beata Virgo Maria.

Analogously to our treatment of the Latin titles of liturgical texts cited in the text (§4.4.17 above), standard Latin terms for the Bible are set roman and capitalized according to English rules:

> Biblia Hebraica (when not referring to a particular published edition), Biblia Vulgata, Novum Testamentum, Vetus Testamentum.

When they occur within titles of journals and other secondary works italics are added and their capitalization is unchanged. (Any other non-italicized Latin titles of primary works could be similarly treated; but modern series titles follow the general rule. The reason for the difference is that primary texts, such as the Gloria in Excelsis Deo, would commonly be referred to in running text, where they need capitalization to make them stand out, whereas series titles usually occur only in bibliographies, notes, and abbreviation lists, where they are in no danger of being lost in surrounding prose.)

Printed editions of ancient and medieval works often have long Latin titles that are really complete sentences comprising the name of the ancient writer, the title of the work, and the name and contribution of each modern editor involved in the product. Library catalogers usually insert a colon between the main title and further descriptive information and then a slash before the part of the sentence that identifies the modern editor(s). In notes and bibliographies, the title may be truncated at the colon; but if it is not, this added punctuation (and the slash) should not be retained. See §7.1.4.3

43

regarding the translation of publication information into English. Sometimes the title of a printed edition will include the titles of several included primary works. These various titles should be separated by semicolons and each should be capitalized separately.

In a bibliography, if the works of St. Anselm are listed under the editor's name, then *Sancti Anselmi* would be retained as part of the title. If they are listed under Anselm's name, *Sancti Anselmi* should be deleted from the title. Thus this title—*Sancti Anselmi ex Beccensi abbate Cantuariensis archiepiscopi Opera: nec non Eadmeri monachi Cantuariensis Historia novorum, et alia opuscula/labore ac studio d. Gabrielis Gerberon monachi congregationis S. Mauri ad mss. fidem expurgata & aucta*—could be listed in either of the following ways:

> Gerberon, Gabriel, ed. *Sancti Anselmi ex Beccensi abbate Cantuariensis archiepiscopi Opera*. Paris, 1675.

> Anselm of Canterbury. *Opera*. Edited by Gabriel Gerberon. Paris, 1675.

Some additional examples may be helpful.

> Analecta gregoriana
> Compendia rerum iudaicarum ad Novum Testamentum
> Corpus Christianorum: Continuatio mediaevalis
> Corpus scriptorum ecclesiasticorum latinorum
> De divinis officiis
> *De glorificatione Trinitatis*
> *De Sancta Trinitate et operibus ejus*
> *De vita Cuthberti*
> *In Aristotelis Analyticorum priorum librum i commentarium*
> *Index scriptorum operumque latino-belgicorum medii aevi*
> *Monumenta Germaniae historica*
> *Patrologia orientalis*
> *Patrologiae cursus completus: Series latina*
> Sancti Ambrosii Liber de consolatione Valentiniani
> *Sancti Aurelii Augustini De doctrina christiana*
> *Sancti Bernardi Opera omnia*
> *Sic et non*
> *Summa contra gentiles*
> *Summa theologica*
> *Vigilae christianae*

7.1.3.9   Titles in Nonroman Alphabets

Titles of modern works in Hebrew and other languages using nonroman scripts should ordinarily be given in translation only. When for sufficient reason a title *is* given in such a language, capitalize only the first word and proper nouns. For Hebrew, use the informal transliteration scheme given in §5.1.2.

7.1.4 PUBLICATION INFORMATION

7.1.4.1 *Names of Presses*

The publisher's name should be abbreviated in footnotes and bibliographies by the omission of *Press, Publishing Company,* and the like except in the case of university presses and wherever else ambiguity or awkwardness would result. An ampersand should be used in a publisher's name rather than *and* (e.g., T&T Clark; Hodder & Stoughton; Farrar, Straus & Giroux). Note that the serial comma is omitted before an ampersand.

ON TITLE PAGE	IN NOTES AND BIBLIOGRAPHIES
Hendrickson Publishers	Hendrickson
Verlag Herder	Herder
Editions du Cerf	Cerf
Oxford University Press	Oxford University Press
Scholars Press	Scholars Press
JSOT Press	JSOT Press
William B. Eerdmans Publishing Company	Eerdmans
Free Press	Free Press
Neukirchener Verlag	Neukirchener Verlag

7.1.4.2 *Place of Publication*

If the title page lists more than one city, only the first city should be used in the bibliography and notes. When the city listed is not well known, reference to the state or country follows. Be careful to do this consistently; thus if you name "Grand Rapids, Mich.:" in one citation, you must name Mich. in every other citation of a publisher in Grand Rapids. State references should be abbreviated using the standard abbreviations, not postal code abbreviations (cf. §8.1.1).

7.1.4.3 *Translating Foreign-Language Publication Information*

For foreign-language publications, authors should translate everything but the title (including author's name, city of publication and the roles of contributors) into English. When an author has not done so, the copy editor should either translate such information or query the project editor. For example:

Bruxelles	Brussels
Cantabrigiae	Cambridge
Lugdunum	Lyon
Lugdunum Batavorum	Leiden
Lutetiae	Paris

München	Munich
Oxonii	Oxford
Wien	Vienna

7.1.5   PAGE NUMBERS

Avoid using *f.* and *ff.* for "following" pages; give actual page ranges.

7.2 GENERAL EXAMPLES

The following examples define SBL style for notes and bibliographies more fully than the select rules in §7.1.

7.2.1   A BOOK BY A SINGLE AUTHOR

[15] Charles H. Talbert, *Reading John: A Literary and Theological Commentary on the Fourth Gospel and the Johannine Epistles* (New York: Crossroad, 1992), 127.

[19] Talbert, *Reading John,* 22.

Talbert, Charles H. *Reading John: A Literary and Theological Commentary on the Fourth Gospel and the Johannine Epistles.* New York: Crossroad, 1992.

7.2.2   A BOOK BY TWO OR THREE AUTHORS

[4] James M. Robinson and Helmut Koester, *Trajectories through Early Christianity* (Philadelphia: Fortress, 1971), 237.

[12] Robinson and Koester, *Trajectories,* 23.

Robinson, James M., and Helmut Koester. *Trajectories through Early Christianity.* Philadelphia: Fortress, 1971.

7.2.3   A BOOK BY MORE THAN THREE AUTHORS

[7] Bernard Brandon Scott et al., *Reading New Testament Greek* (Peabody, Mass.: Hendrickson, 1993), 53.

[9] Scott et al., *Reading New Testament Greek,* 42.

Scott, Bernard Brandon, Margaret Dean, Kristen Sparks, and Frances LaZar. *Reading New Testament Greek.* Peabody, Mass.: Hendrickson, 1993.

7.2.4   A TRANSLATED VOLUME

[14] Wilhelm Egger, *How to Read the New Testament: An Introduction to Linguistic and Historical-Critical Methodology* (trans. P. Heinegg; Peabody, Mass.: Hendrickson, 1996), 28.

[18] Egger, *How to Read,* 291.

Egger, Wilhelm. *How to Read the New Testament: An Introduction to Linguistic and Historical-Critical Methodology.* Translated by P. Heinegg. Peabody, Mass.: Hendrickson, 1996.

7.2.5   THE FULL HISTORY OF A TRANSLATED VOLUME

[3] Julius Wellhausen, *Prolegomena to the History of Ancient Israel* (New York: Meridian Books, 1957), 296; repr. of *Prolegomena to the History of Israel* (trans. J. Sutherland Black and Allan Enzies, with preface by W. Robertson Smith; Edinburgh: Adam & Charles Black, 1885); trans. of *Prolegomena zur Geschichte Israels* (2d ed.; Berlin: G. Reimer, 1883).

Julius Wellhausen, *Prolegomena to the History of Ancient Israel.* New York: Meridian Books, 1957. Reprint of *Prolegomena to the History of Israel.* Translated by J. Sutherland Black and Allan Enzies, with preface by W. Robertson Smith. Edinburgh: Adam & Charles Black, 1885. Translation of *Prolegomena zur Geschichte Israels.* 2d ed. Berlin: G. Reimer, 1883.

7.2.6   A BOOK WITH ONE EDITOR

[5] Jeffrey H. Tigay, ed., *Empirical Models for Biblical Criticism* (Philadelphia: University of Pennsylvania Press, 1985), 35.

[9] Tigay, *Empirical Models,* 38.

Tigay, Jeffrey H., ed. *Empirical Models for Biblical Criticism.* Philadelphia: University of Pennsylvania Press, 1985.

7.2.7   A BOOK WITH TWO OR THREE EDITORS

[44] Robert A. Kraft and George W. E. Nickelsburg, eds., *Early Judaism and Its Modern Interpreters* (Philadelphia: Fortress, 1986), xii.

[47] Kraft and Nickelsburg, *Early Judaism,* xii.

Kraft, Robert A., and George W. E. Nickelsburg, eds. *Early Judaism and Its Modern Interpreters.* Philadelphia: Fortress, 1986.

In this instance the volume is copublished with Scholars Press; however, it is not necessary to cite both sets of publication facts.

7.2.8   A BOOK WITH MORE THAN THREE EDITORS

If a work is by three or more editors, simply list one and "et al." to indicate additional editors (without comma following the first editor's name).

[4] John F. Oates et al., eds., *Checklist of Editions of Greek and Latin Papyri, Ostraca and Tablets* (4th ed.; BASPSup 7; Atlanta: Scholars Press, 1992), 10.

Oates, John F., William H. Willis, Roger S. Bagnall, and Klaas A. Worp, eds. *Checklist of Editions of Greek and Latin Papyri, Ostraca and Tablets.* 4th ed.

Bulletin of the American Society of Papyrologists, Supplements 7. Atlanta: Scholars Press, 1992.

7.2.9 A Book with Both Author and Editor

[45]Edward Schillebeeckx, *The Schillebeeckx Reader* (ed. Robert J. Schreiter; Edinburgh: T&T Clark, 1986), 20.

Schillebeeckx, Edward. *The Schillebeeckx Reader.* Edited by Robert J. Schreiter. Edinburgh: T&T Clark, 1986.

7.2.10 A Book with Author, Editor, and Translator

[3] F. Blass and A. Debrunner. *Grammatica del greco del Nuovo Testamento* (ed. F. Rehkopf; trans. G. Pisi; Brescia: Paideia, 1982), 40.

Blass, F., and A. Debrunner. *Grammatica del greco del Nuovo Testamento.* Edited by F. Rehkopf. Translated by G. Pisi. Brescia: Paideia, 1982.

7.2.11 A Title in a Modern Work Citing a Nonroman Alphabet

See *CMS* 15.118–19.

7.2.12 An Article in an Edited Volume

[3] Harold W. Attridge, "Jewish Historiography," in *Early Judaism and Its Modern Interpreters* (ed. R. A. Kraft and G. W. E. Nickelsburg; Philadelphia: Fortress, 1986), 311–43.

[6] Attridge, "Jewish Historiography," 314–17.

If subsequent references could be confused with another article by the same author, include the information concerning the editors.

[9] Attridge, "Jewish Historiography," in Kraft and Nickelsburg, *Early Judaism,* 314–17.

Attridge, Harold A. "Jewish Historiography." Pages 311–43 in *Early Judaism and Its Modern Interpreters.* Edited by R. A. Kraft and G. W. E. Nickelsburg. Philadelphia: Fortress, 1986.

7.2.13 An Article in a Festschrift

[8] John Van Seters, "The Theology of the Yahwist: A Preliminary Sketch," in *"Wer ist wie du, Herr, unter den Göttern?": Studien zur Theologie und Religionsgeschichte Israels* (ed. I. Kottsieper et al.; Göttingen: Vandenhoeck & Ruprecht, 1995), 219–28.

[17] Van Seters, "Yahwist," 222.

Van Seters, John. "The Theology of the Yahwist: A Preliminary Sketch." Pages 219–28 in *"Wer ist wie du, Herr, unter den Göttern?": Studien zur*

Theologie und Religionsgeschichte Israels. Edited by I. Kottsieper et al. Göttingen: Vandenhoeck & Ruprecht, 1995.

7.2.14   An Introduction, Preface, or Foreword Written by Someone Other Than the Author

[2] Hendrikus Boers, introduction to *How to Read the New Testament: An Introduction to Linguistic and Historical-Critical Methodology,* by Wilhelm Egger (trans. P. Heinegg; Peabody, Mass.: Hendrickson, 1996), xi–xxi.

[6] Boers, "Introduction," xi–xx.

Boers, Hendrikus. Introduction to *How to Read the New Testament: An Introduction to Linguistic and Historical-Critical Methodology,* by Wilhelm Egger. Translated by P. Heinegg. Peabody, Mass.: Hendrickson, 1996.

7.2.15   A Revised Edition

[87] James B. Pritchard, ed., *Ancient Near Eastern Texts Relating to the Old Testament* (3d ed.; Princeton: Princeton University Press, 1969), xxi.

Pritchard, James B., ed. *Ancient Near Eastern Texts Relating to the Old Testament.* 3d ed. Princeton: Princeton University Press, 1969.

[56] Joseph Blenkinsopp, *A History of Prophecy in Israel* (rev. and enl. ed.; Louisville, Ky.: Westminster John Knox, 1996), 81.

Blenkinsopp, Joseph. *A History of Prophecy in Israel.* Rev. and enl. ed. Louisville, Ky.: Westminster John Knox, 1996.

7.2.16   A Recent Reprint Title

[5] John Van Seters, *In Search of History: Historiography in the Ancient World and the Origins of Biblical History* (New Haven: Yale University Press, 1983; repr., Winona Lake, Ind.: Eisenbrauns, 1997), 35.

Van Seters, John. *In Search of History: Historiography in the Ancient World and the Origins of Biblical History.* New Haven: Yale University Press, 1983. Repr., Winona Lake, Ind.: Eisenbrauns, 1997.

7.2.17   A Reprint Title in the Public Domain

See *CMS* 4.16–17.

[5] Gustav Adolf Deissmann, *Light from the Ancient East: The New Testament Illustrated by Recently Discovered Texts of the Graeco-Roman World* (trans. Lionel R. M. Strachan; 1927; repr., Peabody, Mass.: Hendrickson, 1995), 55.

Deissmann, Gustav Adolf. *Light from the Ancient East: The New Testament Illustrated by Recently Discovered Texts of the Graeco-Roman World.* Translated by Lionel R. M. Strachan. 1927. Repr., Peabody, Mass.: Hendrickson, 1995.

49

7.2.18   A FORTHCOMING BOOK

⁹ John E. Hartley, *Genesis* (NIBCOT 1; Peabody, Mass.: Hendrickson, forthcoming).

Hartley, John E. *Genesis.* New International Biblical Commentary on the Old Testament 1. Peabody, Mass.: Hendrickson, forthcoming.

7.2.19   A MULTIVOLUME WORK[3]

⁵ Adolf Harnack, *History of Dogma* (trans. Neil Buchanan; 7 vols.; Boston: Little, Brown & Co., 1896–1905).

⁹ Harnack, *History of Dogma,* 2:126.

Harnack, Adolf. *History of Dogma.* Translated from the 3d German ed. by Neil Buchanan. 7 vols. Boston: Little, Brown & Co., 1896–1905.

7.2.20   A TITLED VOLUME IN A MULTIVOLUME, EDITED WORK[4]

⁵ Bruce W. Winter and Andrew D. Clarke, eds., *The Book of Acts in Its Ancient Literary Setting* (vol. 1 of *The Book of Acts in Its First Century Setting;* ed. B. W. Winter; Grand Rapids: Eerdmans, 1993), 25.

¹⁶ Winter and Clarke, eds., *Acts,* 25.

Winter, Bruce W. and Andrew D. Clarke, eds. *The Book of Acts in Its Ancient Literary Setting.* Vol. 1 of *The Book of Acts in Its First Century Setting.* Edited by Bruce W. Winter. Grand Rapids: Eerdmans, 1993.

The entire multivolume series should be cited as any multivolume work, §7.2.19.

7.2.21   A CHAPTER WITHIN A TITLED VOLUME IN A MULTIVOLUME EDITED WORK

⁶⁶ Richard Bauckham, "The *Acts of Paul* As a Sequel to Acts," in *The Book of Acts in Its Ancient Literary Setting* (ed. Bruce W. Winter and Andrew D. Clarke; vol. 1 of *The Book of Acts in Its First Century Setting,* ed. Bruce W. Winter; Grand Rapids: Eerdmans, 1993), 105–52.

⁷⁸ Bauckham, "Sequel to Acts," in *Acts* (ed. Winter and Clarke), 1:107.

---

[3] When an *abbreviated* title of a multivolume work appears in a short title, it is not necessary to place a comma following the abbreviation preceding the volume and page number. This imitates the rule for journal volumes and is both more attractive and easier on the reader's eye. Multivolume lexicons, collections of primary sources, and dictionaries are candidates for this special treatment.

[4] Note §7.2.21 to see how an article in this type of volume should be cited in short title form.

Bauckham, Richard. "The *Acts of Paul* As a Sequel to Acts." Pages 105–52 in *The Book of Acts in Its Ancient Literary Setting*. Edited by Bruce W. Winter and Andrew D. Clarke. Vol. 1 of *The Book of Acts in Its First Century Setting*. Edited by Bruce W. Winter. Grand Rapids: Eerdmans, 1993.

7.2.22   A Work in a Series

Volumes that appear in series follow the standard note and bibliographic form.

[12] Otfried Hofius, *Paulusstudien* (WUNT 51; Tübingen: J. C. B. Mohr, 1989), 122.

[14] Hofius, *Paulusstudien*, 124.

Hofius, Otfried. *Paulusstudien*. Wissenschaftliche Untersuchungen zum Neuen Testament 51. Tübingen: J. C. B. Mohr, 1989.

When a series begins anew, distinguishing between the old and new series can be problematic. Virgules (e.g., SBT 2/18), or superscripts (e.g., SBT^2 18) are often used to denote the new series. The former seems more easily implemented in notes, but in either case the series' sequence should be fully spelled out in the bibliography.

[23] Joachim Jeremias, *The Prayers of Jesus* (SBT 2/6; Naperville, Ill.: Alec R. Allenson, 1967), 123–27.

[32] Jeremias, *Prayers*, 126.

Jeremias, Joachim. *The Prayers of Jesus*. Studies in Biblical Theology. Second Series 6. Naperville, Ill.: Alec R. Allenson, 1967.

7.2.23   A Journal Article

[7] Blake Leyerle, "John Chrysostom on the Gaze," *JECS* 1 (1993): 159–74.

[23] Leyerle, "Chrysostom," 161.

Leyerle, Blake. "John Chrysostom on the Gaze." *Journal of Early Christian Studies* 1 (1993): 159–74.

For articles written by more than one author, follow the examples above in §§7.2.2–3. It is not necessary to include the issue number unless the journal volume is not paginated consecutively. See §7.2.31.

7.2.24   A Journal Article with Multiple Page Locations and Volumes

[21]Hans Wildberger, "Das Abbild Gottes Gen 1:26–30," *TZ* 21 (1965): 245–59, 481–501.

Wildberger, Hans. "Das Abbild Gottes Gen 1:26–30." *Theologische Zeitschrift* 21 (1965): 245–59, 481–501.

[24]Julius Wellhausen, "Die Composition des Hexateuchs," *JDT* 21 (1876): 392–450; 22 (1877): 407–79.

Wellhausen, Julius. "Die Composition des Hexateuchs." *Jahrbuch für deutsche Theologie* 21 (1876): 392–450; 22 (1877): 407–79.

7.2.25   A JOURNAL ARTICLE REPUBLISHED IN A COLLECTED VOLUME

The citation may follow either one of the two formats.

[20] David Noel Freedman, "Pottery, Poetry, and Prophecy: An Essay on Biblical Poetry," *JBL* 96 (1977): 20; repr. in *Pottery, Poetry, and Prophecy: Studies in Early Hebrew Poetry* (Winona Lake, Ind.: Eisenbrauns, 1980).

Freedman, David Noel. "Pottery, Poetry, and Prophecy: An Essay on Biblical Poetry." *Journal of Biblical Literature* 96 (1977): 5–26. Repr. pages 1–22 in *Pottery, Poetry, and Prophecy: Studies in Early Hebrew Poetry*. Winona Lake, Ind.: Eisenbrauns, 1980.

[20] David Noel Freedman. "Pottery, Poetry, and Prophecy: An Essay on Biblical Poetry," in *Pottery, Poetry, and Prophecy: Studies in Early Hebrew Poetry* (Winona Lake, Ind.: Eisenbrauns, 1980), 14; repr. from *JBL* 96 (1977).

Freedman, David Noel. "Pottery, Poetry, and Prophecy: An Essay on Biblical Poetry." Pages 1–22 in *Pottery, Poetry, and Prophecy: Studies in Early Hebrew Poetry*. Winona Lake, Ind.: Eisenbrauns, 1980. Repr. from *Journal of Biblical Literature* 96 (1977): 5–26.

7.2.26   A BOOK REVIEW

Untitled book reviews may be cited as follows.

[8] Howard M. Teeple, review of A. Robert and A. Feuillet, *Introduction to the New Testament*, *JBR* 34 (1966): 368-70.

[21] Teeple, review of Robert and Feuillet, 369.

Teeple, Howard M. Review of A. Robert and A. Feuillet, *Introduction to the New Testament*. *Journal of Bible and Religion* 34 (1966): 368-70.

Titled book reviews should be cited as normal journal articles but with a parenthetic explanation after the title.

[9]Jaroslav Pelikan, "The Things That You're Liable to Read in the Bible" (review of David Noel Freedman, ed., *The Anchor Bible Dictionary*), *New York Times Review of Books*, December 20, 1992, 3.

Pelikan, Jaroslav. "The Things That You're Liable to Read in the Bible" (review of David Noel Freedman, ed., *The Anchor Bible Dictionary*). *New York Times Review of Books*, December 20, 1992, 3.

Review articles (reviewing multiple books) may be treated similarly, except that if too many books are reviewed to be listed in the note or bibliographic citation, then the actual title—or if none is used, a description—will be sufficient.

> 7 David Petersen, "Hebrew Bible Textbooks: A Review Article, *CRBQ* 1 (1988): 1–18.

> 14 Petersen, "Hebrew Bible Textbooks," 8.

> Petersen, David. "Hebrew Bible Textbooks: A Review Article." *Critical Review of Books in Religion* 1 (1988): 1–18.

7.2.27   AN UNPUBLISHED DISSERTATION OR THESIS

> 21 Lee E. Klosinski, "Meals in Mark" (Ph.D. diss., The Claremont Graduate School, 1988), 22–44.

> 26 Klosinski, "Meals," 23.

> Klosinski, Lee. E. "Meals in Mark." Ph.D. diss., The Claremont Graduate School, 1988.

7.2.28   AN ARTICLE IN AN ENCYCLOPEDIA OR A DICTIONARY

This form also applies to an article in a lexicon or theological dictionary if the specific entry is cited in the bibliography.

> 33 K. Stendahl, "Biblical Theology, Contemporary," *IDB* 1:418–32.

> 36 Stendahl, "Biblical Theology," 1:419.

> Stendahl, K. "Biblical Theology, Contemporary." Pages 418–32 in vol. 1 of *The Interpreter's Dictionary of the Bible*. Edited by G. A. Buttrick. 4 vols. Nashville: Abingdon, 1962.

7.2.29   AN ARTICLE IN A LEXICON OR A THEOLOGICAL DICTIONARY

For the discussion of a word or a family of words, give the entire title and page range of the article:

> 3 K. Dahn, W. Liefeld, "See, Vision, Eye," *NIDNTT* 3:511–21.

> 6 H. Beyer, "διακονέω, διακονία, κτλ," *TDNT* 2:81–93.

> 7 C. Spicq, "ἀτακτέω, ἄτακτος, ἀτάκτως," *TLNT* 1:223–24.

> 143 C. Spicq, "ἀμοιβή," *TLNT* 1:95–96.

Subsequent entries need only the dictionary reference.

> 25 Beyer, *TDNT* 2:83.

For the discussion of a specific word in an article covering a larger group of words, name just the word discussed and those pages on which it is discussed:

> 23 H. Beyer, "διακονέω," *TDNT* 2:81–87.

> 26 K. Dahn, "ὁράω," *NIDNTT* 3:511–18.

Subsequent entries need to include only the dictionary volume and page numbers.

> 32 Beyer, *TDNT* 2:87.

> 29 Dahn, *NIDNTT* 3:511.

> 147 Spicq, *TLNT* 1:95.

In the bibliography, cite only the theological dictionary.

> Brown, Colin, ed. *New International Dictionary of New Testament Theology.* 4 vols. Grand Rapids: Zondervan, 1975–1985.

> Kittel, G., and G. Friedrich, eds. *Theological Dictionary of the New Testament.* Translated by G. W. Bromiley. 10 vols. Grand Rapids: Eerdmans, 1964–1976.

> Spicq, Ceslas. *Theological Lexicon of the New Testament.* Translated and edited by James D. Ernest. 3 vols. Peabody, Mass.: Hendrickson, 1994.

7.2.30   A PAPER PRESENTED AT A PROFESSIONAL SOCIETY

> Susan Niditch, "Oral Culture and Written Documents" (paper presented at the annual meeting of the New England Region of the SBL, Worcester, Mass., 25 March 1994), 13–17.

> 25 Niditch, "Oral Culture," 14.

> Niditch, Susan. "Oral Culture and Written Documents." Paper presented at the annual meeting of the New England Region of the SBL. Worcester, Mass., March 25, 1994.

7.2.31   AN ARTICLE IN A MAGAZINE

> 8Anthony J. Saldarini, "Babatha's Story," *BAR* 24, no. 2 (March/April 1998): 28–33, 36–37, 72–74.

> Saldarini, Anthony J. "Babatha's Story." *Biblical Archaeology Review* 24, no. 2 (March/April 1998): 28–33, 36–37, 72–74.

7.3 SPECIAL EXAMPLES

7.3.1 TEXTS FROM THE ANCIENT NEAR EAST

Citing primary sources from the ancient Near East presents special problems for authors and editors. The written materials are diverse. The evidence is ever increasing. The publications of these texts are scattered throughout journals, series, and monographs. Principal editions are not always easy to find, and one may have to gather several volumes to locate the necessary transcriptions, transliterations, and translations. The diverse nature of these texts requires the translator and publisher to use a variety of formats, abbreviations, numerations, and symbols. Even at the most basic level—for example, that of the titles of texts—no consistency prevails. Thus, we offer the following paragraphs only as basic guidelines.

7.3.1.1   Citing ANET

A translated text from James B. Pritchard, ed. *Ancient Near Eastern Texts Relating to the Old Testament* (3d ed.; Princeton: Princeton University Press, 1969) conventionally is cited using the abbreviation *ANET:*

> [16] "Suppiluliumas and the Egyptian Queen," translated by Albrecht Goetze (*ANET*, 319).

> Pritchard, James B., ed. *Ancient Near Eastern Texts Relating to the Old Testament*. 3d ed. Princeton: Princeton University Press, 1969.

7.3.1.2   Citing COS

A translated text from William W. Hallo, ed. *The Context of Scripture* (3 vols.; Leiden: E. J. Brill, 1997–), is cited using the abbreviation *COS* (+ vol. no. + text no. + pages):

> [7] "The Great Hymn to the Aten," translated by Miriam Lichtheim (*COS* 1.26:44–46).

> Hallo, William W., ed. *Canonical Compositions from the Biblical World*. Vol. 1 of *The Context of Scripture*. Leiden: E. J. Brill, 1997.

7.3.1.3   Citing Other Texts

Citing a text can be as easy as citing a well-known translation:

> [5] "Erra and Ishum" (Stephanie Dalley, *Myths from Mesopotamia* [Oxford: Oxford University Press, 1991], 282–315).

> Dalley, Stephanie. *Myths from Mesopotamia*. Oxford: Oxford University Press, 1991.

> [5] "Erra and Ishum" (Benjamin Foster, *Before the Muses: An Anthology of Akkadian Literature* [Bethesda, Md.: CDL Press, 1993], 1:771–805).

Foster, Benjamin. *Before the Muses: An Anthology of Akkadian Literature.* Vol. 1. Bethesda, Md.: CDL Press, 1993.

34 "The Doomed Prince" (Miriam Lichtheim, *Ancient Egyptian Literature* [Berkeley and Los Angeles: University of California Press, 1976], 2:200–203).

34 "The Doomed Prince" (*AEL* 2:200–203).

Lichtheim, Miriam. *Ancient Egyptian Literature.* Vol. 2. Berkeley and Los Angeles: University of California Press, 1976.

Follow the convention of whatever text edition or translation you cite in your notes and bibliography (for symbols and abbreviations common to ANE texts, see §5.9):

12 "The Disappearance of the Sun God," §3 (A I 11–17) (Harry A. Hoffner Jr., *Hittite Myths* [ed. Gary M. Beckman; SBLWAW 2; Atlanta: Scholars Press, 1990], 26).

Hoffner, Harry A. Jr., *Hittite Myths.* Edited by Gary M. Beckman. SBL Writings from the Ancient World 2. Atlanta: Scholars Press, 1990.

Authors are encouraged to provide the reader with the most current edition, particularly if a transliterated text is cited:

32 Ashur Inscription, obv. lines 10–17 (Albert Kirk Grayson, *Assyrian Rulers of the Early First Millennium BC [1114–859 BC]* [The Royal Inscriptions of Mesopotamia, Assyrian Periods 2; Toronto: University of Toronto Press, 1991], 143–44).

32 Ashur Inscription, obv. lines 10–17 (RIMA 2:143–44).

Grayson, Albert Kirk. *Assyrian Rulers of the Early First Millennium BC (1114–859 BC).* The Royal Inscriptions of Mesopotamia, Assyrian Periods 2. Toronto: University of Toronto Press, 1991.

33 Esarhaddon Chronicle, lines 3–4 (Albert Kirk Grayson, *Assyrian and Babylonian Chronicles* [Texts from Cuneiform Sources; Locust Valley, N.Y.: J. J. Augustin, 1975], 125).

33 Esarhaddon Chronicle, lines 3–4 (*ABC*, 125).

Grayson, Albert Kirk. *Assyrian and Babylonian Chronicles.* Texts from Cuneiform Sources. Locust Valley, N.Y.: J. J. Augustin, 1975.

Some texts, especially letters, are conventionally cited by their number in the principal edition, without a page reference; for example, a letter from the Mari archive sent by Yasmah-Adad is cited as:

45 ARM 1.3.

Dossin, G. *Lettres.* Archives royales de Mari 1. 1946. Repr., Paris: Paul Geuthner, 1967.

If citing it from the edited version:

> ⁴⁵ARMT 1.3.

> G. Dossin, *Correspondance de Šamši-Addu et de ses fils.* Archives royales de Mari, transcrite et traduite 1. Paris: Imprimerei nationale, 1950.

7.3.2 Loeb Classical Library (Greek and Latin)

Citing a volume or work in the Loeb Classical Library, especially if the work is well known, requires only the primary reference. Ordinarily these are cited in parentheses, just as any other primary source. (See above §7.1.3.6 above on conventions for citing primary sources.)

> (Josephus, *Ant.* 2.233–235)

> ¹ Josephus, *Ant.* 2.233–235.

> ⁴ Tacitus, *Ann.* 15.18–19

As in the case of all ancient works, if the translation is being quoted, it is appropriate to cite the translator:

> (Josephus, *Ant.* 2.233–235 [Thackeray, LCL])

> ⁵ Josephus, *Ant.* 2.233–235 (Thackeray, LCL).

> ⁶ Tacitus, *Ann.* 15.18–19 (Jackson, LCL).

The bibliography provides the necessary information regarding the work.

> *Josephus.* Translated by H. St. J. Thackeray et al. 10 vols. Loeb Classical Library. Cambridge: Harvard University Press, 1926–1965.

> Tacitus. *The Histories and The Annals.* Translated by C. H. Moore and J. Jackson. 4 vols. Loeb Classical Library. Cambridge: Harvard University Press, 1937.

If a complete work within an ancient author's corpus is under consideration, the entry can reflect that.

> ¹⁴ Flavius Josephus, *The Jewish Antiquities, Books 1–19* (trans. H. St. J. Thackeray et al.; LCL; Cambridge: Harvard University Press, 1930–1965).

But the bibliography should reflect the entire collection.

> *Josephus.* Translated by H. St. J. Thackeray et al. 10 vols. LCL. Cambridge: Harvard University Press, 1926–1965.

7.3.3 Papyri, Ostraca, and Epigraphica

7.3.3.1 Papyri and Ostraca in General

When a papyrus or ostracon, or a translation thereof, is cited from the standard critical edition listed in the most recent edition of the *Checklist of Editions of Greek and Latin Papyri, Ostraca and Tablets*,[5] it is sufficient to cite by abbreviation (using the abbreviation from the *Checklist*; note that there are no spaces within the abbreviation) and inventory number.

> (P.Cair.Zen. 59003)

> [22] P.Cair.Zen. 59003.

Bibliographic information for all collections so abbreviated should be included in a list of abbreviations or short titles. If a papyrus, or a translation thereof, is quoted from a source other than the principal edition (such as, e.g., Hunt and Edgar's *Select Papyri*), the source should be identified in parentheses. In such cases, it is nevertheless preferable to use the standard abbreviation from the *Checklist* and include that abbreviation in the list of abbreviations or short titles.

> [22] P.Cair.Zen. 59003 (A. S. Hunt and C. C. Edgar, *Select Papyri* [LCL; Cambridge, Mass.: Harvard University Press, 1932] 1:96).

If *Select Papyri* or a similar collection is cited frequently, it should be abbreviated. In the case of *Select Papyri,* citation may be by selection number rather than volume and page number.

> [22] P.Cair.Zen. 59003 (Hunt and Edgar §31).

7.3.3.2 Epigraphica

Taking their cue from Oates, Willis, and Bagnall,[6] G. H. R. Horsley and John A. L. Lee offer "A Preliminary Checklist of Abbreviations of Greek Epigraphic Volumes" in *Epigraphica: Periodico Internazionale di Epigrafia* 56 (1994): 129–69. This indispensable checklist seeks "to provide a list of coherent abbreviations for Greek epigraphic volumes which are both acceptable to specialist epigraphers and comprehensible in themselves to non-specialists who have occasion to use and refer to inscriptions . . ." (p. 130). Abbreviations for a few of the more common epigraphic resources are included in §8.4 (e.g., *BGU, MAMA, SIG*), but for a more comprehensive catalogue, see Horsley and Lee's checklist.

---

[5]Edited by John F. Oates et al. The most recent print edition is the 4th (BASPSup 7; Atlanta: Scholars Press, 1992); more current is the online version at http://scriptorium.lib.duke.edu/papyrus/texts/clist.html.
[6]Ibid.

7.3.3.3   *Greek Magical Papyri*[7]

> (*PGM* III. 1–164)

> [22] *PGM* III. 1–164.

If the edition should be mentioned, cite it in parentheses following the reference, listing it in full in the bibliography.

> [22] *PGM* III. 1–164 (Betz).

> Betz, H. D. *The Greek Magical Papyri in Translation, Including the Demotic Spells.* 2d ed. Chicago: University of Chicago Press, 1996.

7.3.4   ANCIENT EPISTLES AND HOMILIES

The edition of the Cynic epistles edited by Abraham Malherbe (*The Cynic Epistles: A Study Edition* [SBLSBS 12; Atlanta: Scholars Press, 1977]) provides a convenient model for citation. Citing the Cynic Epistles or the several ancient collections of letters, homilies, etc., can be confusing on two fronts since the writings frequently bear both titles and numbers but sometimes only a number. For example, the *Epistles of Diogenes* include *Epistle 26: To Crates*, and a simple numeric designation, *Epistle 28*. Since all the epistles have numbers but not all have titles, the numbers serve as the best identifiers of the pieces and are considered sufficient citation. Line numbers should be included in specific quotations, with a comma separating the work from the line number.

> (Heraclitus, *Epistle 1*, 10)

> [34] Heraclitus, *Epistle 1*, 10.

A comma separates the epistle number (set in italic) from the line number (set in roman). If the translation itself requires notation, include it in parentheses.

> [36] Heraclitus, *Epistle 1*, 10 (Worley).

> Heraclitus. *Epistle 1*. Translated by David Worley. Page 187 in *The Cynic Epistles: A Study Edition*. Edited by A. J. Malherbe. SBLSBS 12. Atlanta: Scholars Press, 1977.

---

[7] Abbreviated, following H. D. Betz, *The Greek Magical Papyri in Translation, including the Demotic Spells* (2d ed. Chicago: University of Chicago Press, 1996). The roman numerals, even those with appended letters (e.g., *PGM* Va. 1–3), follow Preisendanz's catalogue of manuscripts. Betz retains Preisendanz's Greek text numeration (until the end of Preisendanz's list, LXXX), except he creates his own system (still dependent on *PGM*) for the demotic spells (which he identifies as *PDM*). N.B.: Spaces separate roman numerals and arabic numerals which "usually delineate the compass of individual spells within the papyrus manuscript" (ibid., xxxi).

If several authors from the collection are cited, put the full work in the bibliography:

> Malherbe, A. J., ed. *The Cynic Epistles: A Study Edition.* Society of Biblical Literature Sources for Biblical Study 12. Atlanta: Scholars Press, 1977.

7.3.5 *ANF* and *NPNF*, First and Second Series

Citing the church fathers can be confusing and frustrating since often there are a variety of levels at which one can cite. Authors may elect to cite both the primary reference and the volume and page number within a given series. If this does not become cumbersome for the reader, it is helpful to include both. In either case, it is better to use arabic numbers rather than roman numerals and to put the *ANF* or *NPNF* reference in parentheses. It is not necessary to give a full citation if a bibliography is included, and subsequent citations in the notes are identical to the first citation.

> [14] *The Clementine Homilies* 1.3 (*ANF* 8:223).

In this example the title of work appears in italics. The number 1 indicates the homily number, and 3 designates the chapter. The parenthetical information refers to the series, volume, and page number. In the bibliography, one need cite only the series information, unless the translation itself plays an integral role in the discussion. Thus:

> *The Ante-Nicene Fathers.* Edited by Alexander Roberts and James Donaldson. 1885–1887. 10 vols. Repr. Peabody, Mass.: Hendrickson, 1994.

An example in which the translation itself needs to be documented follows:

> [44] Augustine, *Letters of St. Augustin* 28.3.5 (*NPNF*[1] 1:252).

> Augustine. *The Letters of St. Augustin.* In vol. 1 of *The Nicene and Post-Nicene Fathers,* Series 1. Edited by Philip Schaff. 1886–1889. 14 vols. Repr. Peabody, Mass.: Hendrickson, 1994.

7.3.6 J.-P. Migne's *Patrologia latina* and *Patrologia graeca*

For this series, use the abbreviated form:

> [6] Gregory of Nazianzus, *Orationes theologicae* 4 (PG 36:12c).

> Patrologia latina. Edited by J.-P. Migne. 217 vols. Paris, 1844–1864.

> Patrologia graeca. Edited by J.-P. Migne. 162 vols. Paris, 1857–1886.

Regarding the roman type, see §7.3.1.5.

7.3.7   Strack-Billerbeck, *Kommentar zum Neuen Testament*

Citing Hermann Strack's and Paul Billerbeck's *Kommentar zum Neuen Testament aus Talmud und Midrasch* is simplified by using the abbreviation for the work, Str-B and the volume and page number(s). Thus a note might read:

> 3 See the discussion of ἐκρατοῦντο in Str-B 2:271.

> Strack, Hermann L., and Paul Billerbeck. *Kommentar zum Neuen Testament aus Talmud und Midrasch.* 6 vols. Munich: C. H. Beck, 1922–1961.

7.3.8   *Aufstieg und Niedergang der römischen Welt (ANRW)*

The multivolume *Aufstieg und Niedergang der römischen Welt: Geschichte und Kultur Roms im Spiegel der neueren Forschung (ANRW)* can be problematic because of the variety of levels, languages, and titles within this ongoing work. Articles appear in English, French, German, and Italian. Later volumes have the parallel English title *Rise and Decline of the Roman World*. Volumes of Part 2, *Principat*, the material most commonly cited, have separate subtitles, e.g., *Religion, Politische Geschichte, Sprache und Literatur*, etc. (with nearly 30 volumes in print). The note example below assumes that *ANRW* is listed properly in the bibliography and included in the list of abbreviations.

> 76 Graham Anderson, "The *pepaideumenos* in Action: Sophists and Their Outlook in the Early Empire," *ANRW* 33.1:80–208.

> 79 Anderson, "*Pepaideumenos*," *ANRW* 33.1:86.

> Anderson, Graham. "The *pepaideumenos* in Action: Sophists and Their Outlook in the Early Empire." *ANRW* 33.1:80–208. Part 2, *Principat*, 33.1. Edited by H. Temporini and W. Haase. New York: de Gruyter, 1989.

As a strictly bibliographical entry, *ANRW* can be entered as follows.

> Temporini, Hildegard, and Wolfgang Haase, eds. *Aufstieg und Niedergang der römischen Welt: Geschichte und Kultur Roms im Spiegel der neueren Forschung.* Part 2, *Principat*, 33.1. New York: de Gruyter, 1989.

7.3.9   Bible Commentaries

Properly citing Bible commentaries can be complex, especially when the commentaries are (1) multivolume, or (2) in a series. Commentaries are normally cited just as any other book, with the commentary series name being the only significant addition. Since editors of commentary series usually acquire rather than edit, the names of general editors need not be included in bibliographic or note references. Thus:

⁶ Morna Hooker, *The Gospel according to Saint Mark* (BNTC 2; Peabody, Mass.: Hendrickson, 1991), 223.

Hooker, Morna. *The Gospel according to Saint Mark.* Black's New Testament Commentaries 2. Peabody, Mass.: Hendrickson, 1991.

7.3.10   A SINGLE VOLUME OF A MULTIVOLUME COMMENTARY IN A SERIES

To cite a single volume of a multivolume commentary in a series keep in mind the general rule for citing a series (§7.2.22): in a note the series name is usually abbreviated and is the second element (following the number of volumes) inside the parentheses. The problem arises when volumes in a multivolume commentary do not bear the same title. Authors should decide whether to cite each volume based on a bibliographic entry of the whole work, or to cite each volume individually, both in the notes and in the bibliography. If, for example, all three volumes of Dahood's *Psalms* are used, it makes sense to cite the work as if it were any other three-volume work. Using the entire work as the basis for citation (preferred):

⁴Mitchell Dahood, *Psalms* (3 vols.; AB 16–17A; Garden City: Doubleday, 1965–1970), 3:127.

⁷Dahood, *Psalms,* 2:121.

Dahood, Mitchell. *Psalms.* 3 vols. Anchor Bible 16–17A. Garden City: Doubleday, 1965–1970.

Using individual volumes as the basis for citation:

⁷⁸Mitchell Dahood, *Psalms I, 1–50* (AB 16; Garden City: Doubleday, 1965), 44.

⁷⁹Dahood, *Psalms I, 1–50,* 78.

¹⁶Mitchell Dahood, *Psalms II, 51–100* (AB 17; Garden City: Doubleday, 1968), 347.

³⁷Dahood, *Psalms II, 51–100,* 351.

¹²⁶Mitchell Dahood, *Psalms III, 100–150* (AB 17A; Garden City: Doubleday, 1970), 478

¹³⁰Dahood, *Psalms III, 100–150,* 478.

Whichever style is chosen, the author or editor must be consistent.

7.3.11   SBL SEMINAR PAPERS

³³D. MacDonald, "Virgins, Widows, and Paul in Second Century Asia Minor," *SBL Seminar Papers, 1979* (2 vols.; SBLSP 16; Chico, Calif.: Scholars Press, 1979), 1:169–84.

MacDonald, D. "Virgins, Widows, and Paul in Second Century Asia Minor." Pages 169–84 in volume 1 of the *SBL Seminar Papers, 1979*. 2 vols. Society of Biblical Literature Seminar Papers 16. Chico, Calif.: Scholars Press, 1979.

7.3.12   A CD-ROM Reference (with a Corresponding Print Edition)

67 Duane F. Watson, "False Apostles," n.p., *ABD on CD-ROM*. Version 2.0c. 1995, 1996.

71 Watson, "False Apostles," n.p.

Watson, Duane F. "False Apostles." *The Anchor Bible Dictionary on CD-ROM*. Logos Library System Version 2.0c. 1995, 1996. Print ed.: David Noel Freedman, ed. *Anchor Bible Dictionary*. 6 vols. New York: Doubleday, 1992.

7.3.13   An Internet Publication with a Print Counterpart

URL addresses are never hyphenated at the end of a line and should be divided before the "dot" at the end of a line.

8 Charles Truehart, "Welcome to the Next Church," *Atlantic Monthly* 278 (August 1996): 37–58. Cited 5 May 1997. Online: http://www.theatlantic .com/atlantic/issues/96aug/nxtchrch/nxtchrch.htm.

12 Truehart, "Next Church," 37.

Truehart, Charles. "Welcome to the Next Church." *Atlantic Monthly* 278 (August 1996): 37–58. Cited 5 May 1997. Online: http://www.theatlantic .com/atlantic/issues/96aug/nxtchrch/nxtchrch.htm.

7.3.14   An Internet Publication without a Print Counterpart[8]

32 Matthew Thomas Farrell, "History of the Discovery of Thomas and Comments on the Text," n.p. [cited 5 May 1997]. Online: http://www.miseri .edu/davies/thomas/farrell.htm.

Farrell, Matthew Thomas. "History of the Discovery of Thomas and Comments on the Text." No pages. Cited 5 May 1997. Online: http://www .miseri.edu/davies/thomas/farrell.htm.

---

[8]For further reference, see Janice R. Walker and Todd Taylor, *The Columbia Guide to Online Style* (New York: Columbia University Press, 1998).

7.4 AUTHOR-DATE CITATIONS[9]

Authors writing in the social sciences may elect to use the author-date form of citation, although the standard bibliographic form predominates among the various disciplines. Below are select examples of author-date citations and reference list forms. Examples of citations within a text are followed by bibliographic examples (with the parenthetical form following; N.B.: capitalization rules). For additional information consult *CMS* 16.3–209.

> An elaborate treatment can be found in Talbert 1992 (51).

> The explanation for this is not clear (Leyerle 1997, 61).

> Pfuhl (1980, 65–68) notes five possible techniques.

Two citations in the same sentence:

> An agrarian society is built upon agricultural production (Lenski and Lenski 1974, 207; Lenski 1966, 192).

When an author has more than one work in the bibliography, the entries should follow this order: (1) books by author in chronological order from the oldest to the most recent; (2) books edited by that author; (3) books edited by that author and another. Thus, for books by the same author:

> Wilder, Amos. 1939. *Eschatology and Ethics in the Teaching of Jesus.* New York: Harper & Bros.

> ———. 1971. *Early Christian Rhetoric: The Language of the Gospel.* Cambridge: Harvard University Press.

When an author has two works in the same year, the designations "a" and "b" should be added to the date of publication, and the entries should follow in alphabetical order:

> (Pilch 1988a, 14)

> (Pilch 1988b, 60)

> Pilch, John J. 1988a. Interpreting Scripture: The Social Science Method. *Biblical Theology Bulletin* 18:13–19.

> ———. 1988b. Understanding Biblical Healing: Selecting the Appropriate Model. *Biblical Theology Bulletin* 18:60–66.

7.4.1 A BOOK BY A SINGLE AUTHOR

> (Talbert 1992, 22)

---

[9]The general style of *Semeia* and Semeia Studies. The bibliography itself is often called "Works Consulted."

Talbert, Charles H. 1992. *Reading John: A Literary and Theological Commentary on the Fourth Gospel and the Johannine Epistles.* New York: Crossroad.

7.4.2   A BOOK BY TWO OR THREE AUTHORS

(Robinson and Koester 1971, 23).

Robinson, James M., and Helmut Koester. 1971. *Trajectories through Early Christianity.* Philadelphia: Fortress.

7.4.3   A TRANSLATED VOLUME

(Egger 1996, 291)

Egger, Wilhelm. 1996. *How to Read the New Testament: An Introduction to Linguistic and Historical-Critical Methodology.* Translated by P. Heinegg. Peabody, Mass.: Hendrickson.

7.4.4   AN EDITED VOLUME

(Kraft and Nickelsburg 1986, 271)

Kraft, Robert A., and George W. E. Nickelsburg, eds. 1986. *Early Judaism and Its Modern Interpreters.* Philadelphia: Fortress.

7.4.5   AN ARTICLE IN A FESTSCHRIFT

(Van Seters 1995, 222)

Van Seters, John. 1995. The Theology of the Yahwist: A Preliminary Sketch. Pages 219–28 in *"Wer ist wie du, Herr, unter den Göttern?": Studien zur Theologie und Religionsgeschichte Israels.* Edited by I. Kottsieper et al. Göttingen: Vandenhoeck & Ruprecht.

7.4.6   A REPRINT TITLE

(Moore 1997, 2:228)

Moore, George Foot. 1997. *Judaism in the First Three Centuries of the Christian Era: The Age of Tannaim.* 3 vols. Cambridge: Harvard University Press, 1927–1930. Repr. 3 vols. in 2, Peabody, Mass.: Hendrickson.

7.4.7   A TITLED VOLUME IN A MULTIVOLUME WORK

(Winter 1993, 137)

Winter, Bruce W., and Andrew D. Clarke, eds. 1993. *The Book of Acts in Its Ancient Literary Setting.* Vol. 1 of *The Book of Acts in Its First Century Setting.* Edited by Bruce W. Winter. Grand Rapids: Eerdmans.

65

7.4.8   A CHAPTER WITHIN A TITLED VOLUME IN A MULTIVOLUME WORK

(Bauckham 1993, 53)

Bauckham, Richard. 1993. The *Acts of Paul* As a Sequel to Acts. Pages 105–52 in *The Book of Acts in Its Ancient Literary Setting.* Edited by Bruce W. Winter and Andrew D. Clarke. Vol. 1 of *The Book of Acts in Its First Century Setting.* Edited by Bruce W. Winter. Grand Rapids: Eerdmans.

7.4.9   A WORK IN A SERIES

(Hofius 1989, 124)

Hofius, Otfried. 1989. *Paulusstudien.* Wissenschaftliche Untersuchungen zum Neuen Testament 51. Tübingen: J. C. B. Mohr.

7.4.10   A JOURNAL ARTICLE

(Leyerle 1993, 161)

Leyerle, Blake. 1993. John Chrysostom on the Gaze. *Journal of Early Christian Studies* 1:159–74.

7.4.11   AN ARTICLE IN AN ENCYCLOPEDIA OR A DICTIONARY

(Stendahl 1962, 1:419)

Stendahl, K. 1962. Biblical Theology, Contemporary. Pages 418–32 in vol. 1 of *Interpreter's Dictionary of the Bible.* Edited by G. A. Buttrick. 4 vols. Nashville: Abingdon, 1962.

7.4.12   AN ARTICLE IN A LEXICON OR A THEOLOGICAL DICTIONARY

For the discussion of a specific word:

(Beyer 1965, 2:81–87)

Beyer, H. 1965. "διακονέω." Pages 81–87 in vol. 2 of *Theological Dictionary of the New Testament.* Edited by G. Kittel and G. Friedrich. Translated by G. Bromiley. 10 vols. Grand Rapids: Eerdmans, 1964–1976.

7.4.13   A PAPER PRESENTED AT A PROFESSIONAL SOCIETY

(Niditch 1994, 14)

Niditch, Susan. 1994. Oral Culture and Written Documents. Paper presented at the annual meeting of the New England Regional SBL. Worcester, Mass. March 25.

7.4.14 Loeb Classical Library (Greek and Latin)

Noting a volume or work in the Loeb Classical Library, especially if the work is well known, requires only the primary reference. (See Appendix H on abbreviating Greek and Latin works.) See above §7.3.2.

>   (Josephus, *Ant.* 2.233–235)

>   (Tacitus, *Ann.* 15.18–19)

Or with a translation or excerpt:

>   (Josephus, *Ant.* 2.233–235, Thackery)

When citing the full work, with an emphasis on the translator.

>   *Josephus.* 1926–1965. Translated by H. St. J. Thackeray et al. 10 vols. LCL. Cambridge: Harvard University Press.

With an emphasis on the original author (note date follows title rather than author).

>   Tacitus, Cornelius. *The Histories and The Annals.* 1937. Translated by C. H. Moore and J. Jackson. 4 vols. LCL. Cambridge: Harvard University Press.

8   Abbreviations

Authors should make the most of abbreviations. Frequently abbreviations are listed in the front matter. Thus the abbreviations for Old and New Testaments, the different versions of the Scripture, conventional journal and dictionary abbreviations, and numerous other potentially abbreviated terms should be readily used in lieu of the entire word. (See §§8.1.3–8.3 for abbreviations of periodicals, technical terms, and primary sources.) An exception to this would be if the term to be abbreviated came at the beginning of a sentence. In that case it should be spelled out.

8.1 GENERAL ABBREVIATIONS

8.1.1.   STATE ABBREVIATIONS

In bibliographies and footnotes, do not use the two-letter postal code state abbreviations; rather, use the standard, and usually longer, state abbreviations, e.g., Mass., not MA; Calif., not CA. Do not abbreviate states or other geographic names in the body of a work unless they occur in parentheses.

Ala.	Ga.	Md.	N.Mex.	S.Dak.
Alaska	Hawaii	Mass.	N.Y.	Tenn.
Ariz.	Idaho	Mich.	N.C.	Tex.
Ark.	Ill.	Minn.	N.Dak.	Utah
Calif.	Ind.	Miss.	Ohio	Vt.
Colo.	Iowa	Mo.	Okla.	Va.
Conn.	Kans.	Mont.	Oreg. *or* Ore.	Wash.
Del.	Ky.	Nebr.	Pa.	W.Va.
D.C.	La.	Nev.	R.I.	Wis. *or* Wisc.
Fla.	Maine	N.H.	S.C.	Wyo.
		N.J.		

8.1.2   ERAS

The preferred style is B.C.E. and C.E. (with periods). If you use A.D. and B.C., remember that A.D. precedes the date and B.C. follows it. (For the use of these abbreviations in titles, see §7.1.3.2.)

A.D.	anno Domini	B.C.	before Christ
A.M.	anno mundi (precedes date)	B.C.E.	before the Common Era
A.U.C.	ab urbe condita (precedes date)	C.E.	Common Era

8.1.3   TECHNICAL ABBREVIATIONS

abl.	ablative	ca.	circa
abs.	absolute, absolutely	Can.	Canaanite
acc.	accusative	cent.	century
act.	active	cf.	*confer,* compare
ad loc.	*ad locum,* at the place discussed	ch(s).	chapter(s)
adj.	adjective, adjectival	Chr	Chronicler
adv.	adverb	cj.	conjecture (regarding an uncertain reading)
Aram.	Aramaic		
art.	article	cod.	codex
Assyr.	Assyrian	col(s).	column(s)
b.	born	comm(s).	commentary, commentaries
Bibl. Aram.	Biblical Aramaic		
bibliog.	bibliography	conj.	conjunction
bis	twice	consec.	consecutive
bk.	book	const.	construct
c.	century	cont.	continued

Copt.	Coptic	impv.	imperative
D	Deuteronomist source (of the Pentateuch)	incl.	inclusive; including
		indic.	indicative
d.	died	inf.	infinitive
dat.	dative	inscr.	inscription
def.	definition	instr.	instrumental
deriv.	derivative	intrans.	intransitive
Deutero-Isa	Deutero-Isaiah or Second Isaiah	Isr.	Israelite
dim.	diminutive	J	Jahwist or Yahwist source (of the Pentateuch)
diss.	dissertation		
Dtn	Deuteronomic (history, writer)	JPS	Jewish Publication Society
Dtr	Deuteronomistic (history; writer); Deuteronomist	juss.	jussive
		K	Kethib
Dyn.	Dynasty	line(s)	[always spell out]
E	Elohist source (of the Pentateuch)	Lat.	Latin
ed(s).	editor(s), edited by	lit.	literally
e.g.	*exempli gratia,* for example	loc.	locative
Eg.	Egyptian	loc. cit.	*loco citato,* in the place cited
emph.	emphatic		
Eng.	English	LXX	Septuagint (the Greek OT)
ep(s).	episode(s); section of an inscription or section of a common narrated event extant in more than one inscription	m. or masc.	masculine
		Mand.	Mandean
		mg.	marginal
		Mid. Assyr.	Middle Assyrian
ESem.	East Semitic (language group)	Mid. Heb.	Middle Hebrew
esp.	especially	Midr.	Midrash
ET	English translation	Min. Pr.	Twelve Minor Prophets
et al.	*et alii,* and others	Moab.	Moabite
etc.	*et cetera,* and the rest	MS(S)	manuscript(s)
Eth.	Ethiopic	MT	Masoretic Text (of the OT)
ex.	example	N	Northern (source)
excl.	excluding	n(n).	note(s)
extrabibl.	extrabiblical	N.B.	*nota bene,* note carefully
f(f).	and the following one(s)	n.d.	no date
f. or fem.	feminine	n.p.	no place; no publisher; no page
fig.	figurative, figuratively		
Fr.	French	Nab.	Nabatean
frg.	fragment	neg.	negative
FS	Festschrift	neut.	neuter
fut.	future	NHC	Nag Hammadi Codex
gen.	genitive, genitival	no(s).	number(s)
Ger.	German	nom.	nominal, nominative
Gk.	Greek, referring to lexical forms, not translation	NS	new series
		NT	New Testament
HB	Hebrew Bible	obj.	object
Heb.	Hebrew	obs.	obsolete
Hitt.	Hittite	obv.	obverse (front) of a tablet
i.e.	*id est,* that is	OL	Old Latin
ibid.	*ibidem,* in the same place	op. cit.	*opere citato,* in the work cited
idem	the same		
Imp. Aram.	Imperial Aramaic	orig.	original
imper.	impersonal	OT	Old Testament
impf.	imperfect	P	Priestly source (of the Pentateuch)
impf. cons.	*imperfectum consecutivum*		

p(p).	page(s)	ser.	series
Pal.	Palestinian	sg.	singular
Palm.	Palmyrene	SSem.	South Semitic (language group)
pap.	papyrus		
par.	parallel (use to indicate textual parallels, e.g., Matt 25:14–30 par. Luke 19:11–27)	subj.	subject
		subst.	substantive, substantival
		suf.	suffix
pass.	passive	Sum.	Sumerian
passim	here and there	SUNY	State University of New York
per.	person, persons, personal		
Pers.	Persia, Persian	superl.	superlative
pf.	perfect, perfective	suppl.	supplement
Phoen.	Phoenician	s.v.	*sub verbo*, under the word
pl.	plural; plate	SWSem.	Southwest Semitic (language group)
PN	personal name		
poss.	possessive	syn.	synonym (-ous)
postbibl.	postbiblical	Syr.	Syriac
prep.	preposition, prepositional	Tg(s).	Targum(s); Targumic
pres.	present	theol.	theology; Theologie, theologisch
pron.	pronoun		
ptc.	participle	trans.	translator, translated by; transitive
Pun.	Punic		
Q	Qere	txt?	problematic or corrupted text
q.v.	*quod vide*, which see		
R	Redactor	txt em	textual emendation
re	regarding	v(v).	verse(s)
rec(s).	recension(s)	Vg.	Vulgate
reg.	register	viz.	*videlicet*, namely
repr.	reprinted	VL	Vetus Latina
resp.	respectively	voc.	vocative
rev.	revised (by)	vol(s).	volume(s)
rev.	reverse (back) of a tablet	vs.	versus
Sam.	Samaritan	WSem.	West Semitic
sec.	section	*x*	no. of times a form occurs
Sem.	Semitic		

The above list includes several abbreviations whose use we strongly discourage. The abbreviations f. and ff. (for references to ranges with no explicitly named end point) should be replaced by an exact range. Instead of using op. cit. and loc. cit. for note citations, an abbreviated citation (author's last name and a short title) is preferred.

8.2 BIBLE TEXTS, VERSIONS, ETC.

Books of the Bible cited without chapter or chapter and verse should be spelled out in the main text. Books of the Bible cited with chapter or chapter and verse should be abbreviated, unless they come at the beginning of

71

the sentence. All occurrences of biblical books in parentheses and footnotes should be abbreviated. Authors citing more than one translation of the Bible must indicate which translation is used in a particular citation. When this citation is in parentheses, a comma is not needed to separate the citation and the abbreviation of the translation, as is indicated in the fourth example below.

Right:
The passage in 1 Cor 5 is often considered crucial.
The passage, 1 Cor 5:6, is often considered crucial.
First Corinthians 5:6 is a crucial text.
"Do you not know that a little yeast leavens the whole batch of dough?" (1 Cor 5:6 NRSV).

Wrong:
1 Cor 5:6 is a crucial text.
1 Corinthians 5:6 is a crucial text.

In addition to the abbreviations for biblical books given below in §§8.3.1–3, the following abbreviations should be used:

Divisions of the canon:

HB	Hebrew Bible
NT	New Testament
OT	Old Testament

Units of text:

ch./chs.	chapter/chapters
v./vv.	verse/verses

Ancient texts, text types, and versions:

Byz.	Byzantine
Copt.	Coptic
LXX	Septuagint
MT	Masoretic Text
Syr.	Syriac
TR	Textus Receptus
Vulg.	Vulgate

Modern editions:

BF^2	British and Foreign Bible Societies, 2d edition
BHK	*Biblia Hebraica*, ed. R. Kittel
BHS	*Biblia Hebraica Stuttgartensia*
NA^{27}	*Novum Testamentum Graece*, Nestle-Aland, 27th ed.
UBS^4	*The Greek New Testament*, United Bible Societies, 4th ed.
WH	Westcott-Hort

Modern versions:

ASV	American Standard Version
CEV	Contemporary English Version
GNB	Good News Bible
GOODSPEED	*The Complete Bible: An American Translation*, E. J. Goodspeed

JB	Jerusalem Bible
KJV	King James Version
LB	Living Bible
MLB	Modern Language Bible
MOFFATT	*The New Testament: A New Translation*, James Moffatt
NAB	New American Bible
NASB	New American Standard Bible
NAV	New American Version
NEB	New English Bible
NIV	New International Version
NJB	New Jerusalem Bible
NJPS	*Tanakh: The Holy Scriptures: The New JPS Translation according to the Traditional Hebrew Text*
NKJV	New King James Version
NRSV	New Revised Standard Version
PHILLIPS	*The New Testament in Modern English*, J. B. Phillips
REB	Revised English Bible
RSV	Revised Standard Version
RV	Revised Version
TEV	Today's English Version (= Good News Bible)
WEYMOUTH	*The New Testament in Modern Speech*, R. F. Weymouth

8.3 PRIMARY SOURCES: ANCIENT TEXTS

Note that abbreviations for the Hebrew Bible/Old Testament, New Testament, Apocrypha, and Septuagint titles *do not* require a period and *are not* italicized.

8.3.1 HEBREW BIBLE/OLD TESTAMENT

Gen	Genesis	Eccl (or Qoh)	Ecclesiastes (or Qoheleth)
Exod	Exodus	Song	Song of Songs (Song of Solomon,
Lev	Leviticus	or (Cant)	or Canticles)
Num	Numbers	Isa	Isaiah
Deut	Deuteronomy	Jer	Jeremiah
Josh	Joshua	Lam	Lamentations
Judg	Judges	Ezek	Ezekiel
Ruth	Ruth	Dan	Daniel
1–2 Sam	1–2 Samuel	Hos	Hosea
1–2 Kgdms	1–2 Kingdoms (LXX)	Joel	Joel
		Amos	Amos
1–2 Kgs	1–2 Kings	Obad	Obadiah
3–4 Kgdms	3–4 Kingdoms (LXX)	Jonah	Jonah
1–2 Chr	1–2 Chronicles	Mic	Micah
Ezra	Ezra	Nah	Nahum
Neh	Nehemiah	Hab	Habakkuk
Esth	Esther	Zeph	Zephaniah
Job	Job	Hag	Haggai
Ps/Pss	Psalms	Zech	Zechariah
Prov	Proverbs	Mal	Malachi

8.3.2 NEW TESTAMENT

Matt	Matthew	1–2 Thess	1–2 Thessalonians
Mark	Mark	1–2 Tim	1–2 Timothy
Luke	Luke	Titus	Titus
John	John	Phlm	Philemon
Acts	Acts	Heb	Hebrews
Rom	Romans	Jas	James
1–2 Cor	1–2 Corinthians	1–2 Pet	1–2 Peter
Gal	Galatians	1–2–3 John	1–2–3 John
Eph	Ephesians	Jude	Jude
Phil	Philippians	Rev	Revelation
Col	Colossians		

8.3.3 APOCRYPHA AND SEPTUAGINT

Bar	Baruch	Jdt	Judith
Add Dan	Additions to Daniel	1–2 Macc	1–2 Maccabees
Pr Azar	Prayer of Azariah	3–4 Macc	3–4 Maccabees
Bel	Bel and the Dragon	Pr Man	Prayer of Manasseh
Sg Three	Song of the Three Young Men	Ps 151	Psalm 151
Sus	Susanna	Sir	Sirach/Ecclesiasticus
1–2 Esd	1–2 Esdras	Tob	Tobit
Add Esth	Additions to Esther	Wis	Wisdom of Solomon
Ep Jer	Epistle of Jeremiah		

8.3.4 OLD TESTAMENT PSEUDEPIGRAPHA

The names of authors whose works survive only in a small number of fragments should not normally be abbreviated. Abbreviations for them are included in this list (in roman type) mainly for the benefit of editors who may need to expand them.

Ahiqar	*Ahiqar*	*4 Bar.*	*4 Baruch (Paraleipomena*
Ant. bib.	Use *L.A.B.*		*Jeremiou)*
Apoc. Ab.	*Apocalypse of Abraham*	*Bib. Ant.*	Use *L.A.B.*
Apoc. Adam	*Apocalypse of Adam*	*Bk. Noah*	*Book of Noah*
Apoc. Dan.	*Apocalypse of Daniel*	*Cav. Tr.*	*Cave of Treasures*
Apoc. El. (H)	Hebrew *Apocalypse of Elijah*	*Cl. Mal.*	Cleodemus Malchus
Apoc. El. (C)	Coptic *Apocalypse of Elijah*	*Dem.*	Demetrius (the
Apoc. Ezek.	Use *Apocr. Ezek.*		Chronographer)
Apoc. Mos.	*Apocalypse of Moses*	*El. Mod.*	*Eldad and Modad*
Apoc. Sedr.	*Apocalypse of Sedrach*	*1 En.*	*1 Enoch (Ethiopic*
Apoc. Zeph.	*Apocalypse of Zephaniah*		*Apocalypse)*
Apoc. Zos.	Use *Hist. Rech.*	*2 En.*	*2 Enoch (Slavonic*
Apocr. Ezek.	*Apocryphon of Ezekiel*		*Apocalypse)*
Aris. Ex.	Aristeas the Exegete	*3 En.*	*3 Enoch (Hebrew*
Aristob.	Aristobulus		*Apocalypse)*
Artap.	Artapanus	Eup.	Eupolemus
Ascen. Isa.	*Mart. Ascen. Isa.* 6–11	*Ezek. Trag.*	Ezekiel the Tragedian
As. Mos.	*Assumption of Moses*	*4 Ezra*	*4 Ezra*
2 Bar.	*2 Baruch (Syriac Apocalypse)*	*5 Apoc. Syr. Pss.*	*Five Apocryphal Syriac*
3 Bar.	*3 Baruch (Greek Apocalypse)*		*Psalms*

Gk. Apoc. Ezra	Greek Apocalypse of Ezra	Rev. Ezra	Revelation of Ezra
Hec. Ab.	Hecataeus of Abdera	Sib. Or.	Sibylline Oracles
Hel. Syn. Pr.	Hellenistic Synagogal Prayers	Syr. Men.	Sentences of the Syriac
Hist. Jos.	History of Joseph		Menander
Hist. Rech.	History of the Rechabites	T. 12 Patr.	Testaments of the Twelve
Jan. Jam.	Jannes and Jambres		Patriarchs
Jos. Asen.	Joseph and Aseneth	T. Ash.	Testament of Asher
Jub.	Jubilees	T. Benj.	Testament of Benjamin
L.A.B.	Liber antiquitatum biblicarum	T. Dan	Testament of Dan
	(Pseudo-Philo)	T. Gad	Testament of Gad
L.A.E.	Life of Adam and Eve	T. Iss.	Testament of Issachar
Lad. Jac.	Ladder of Jacob	T. Jos.	Testament of Joseph
Let. Aris.	Letter of Aristeas	T. Jud.	Testament of Judah
Liv. Pro.	Lives of the Prophets	T. Levi	Testament of Levi
Lost Tr.	The Lost Tribes	T. Naph.	Testament of Naphtali
3 Macc.	3 Maccabees	T. Reu.	Testament of Reuben
4 Macc.	4 Maccabees	T. Sim.	Testament of Simeon
5 Macc.	5 Maccabees (Arabic)	T. Zeb.	Testament of Zebulun
Mart. Ascen. Isa.	Martyrdom and Ascension of Isaiah	T. 3 Patr.	Testaments of the Three
Mart. Isa.	Mart. Ascen. Isa. 1–5		Patriarchs
Odes Sol.	Odes of Solomon	T. Ab.	Testament of Abraham
P. J.	Use 4 Bar.	T. Isaac	Testament of Isaac
Ph. E. Poet	Philo the Epic Poet	T. Jac.	Testament of Jacob
Pr. Jac.	Prayer of Jacob	T. Adam	Testament of Adam
Pr. Jos.	Prayer of Joseph	T. Hez.	Testament of Hezekiah
Pr. Man.	Prayer of Manasseh		(Mart. Ascen. Isa.
Pr. Mos.	Prayer of Moses		3:13–4:22)
Ps.-Eup.	Pseudo-Eupolemus	T. Job	Testament of Job
Ps.-Hec.	Pseudo-Hecataeus	T. Mos.	Testament of Moses
Ps.-Orph.	Pseudo-Orpheus	T. Sol.	Testament of Solomon
Ps.-Philo	Use L.A.B.	Theod.	Theodotus, On the Jews
Ps.-Phoc.	Pseudo-Phocylides	Treat. Shem	Treatise of Shem
Pss. Sol.	Psalms of Solomon	Vis. Ezra	Vision of Ezra
Ques. Ezra	Questions of Ezra	Vis. Isa.	Use Ascen. Isa.

8.3.5 DEAD SEA SCROLLS AND RELATED TEXTS

Certain conventions are used to cite texts from Qumran and the surrounding area. The name of the site is given, abbreviated according to the list below.

Q	Qumran
Ḥev	Naḥal Ḥever
Ḥev/Se	Used for documents earlier attributed to Seiyal
Mas	Masada
Mird	Khirbet Mird
Mur	Murabbaʿat

The different caves at each site are denoted with sequential numbers, for example, 1Q, 2Q, etc. Different copies of the same composition from the same cave are indicated by the use of raised lowercase letters, e.g., 1QIsaᵃ, 1QIsaᵇ.

There is considerable diversity in nomenclature in actual use for individual documents. In most cases, it is helpful to give the number of the document to avoid confusion. In addition to the number, the descriptive name should be given in the initial citation to permit ease of identification. The number of the text should not be put in italics or bold type, e.g., 4Q520, Mur16.

The first seven scrolls removed from Cave 1, as well as the Cairo Genizah copy of the *Damascus Document*, are referred to customarily by name (not by number). The standard names and abbreviations are as follows:

1Qap Gen^{ar}	*Genesis Apocryphon*
1QH^a	*Hodayot*^a or *Thanksgiving Hymns*^a
1QpHab	*Pesher Habakkuk*
1QM	*Milḥamah* or *War Scroll*
1QS	*Serek Hayaḥad* or *Rule of the Community*
1QIsa^a	Isaiah^a
1QIsa^b	Isaiah^b
CD	Cairo Genizah copy of the *Damascus Document*

Common abbreviations for the classification of the scrolls are as follows:

apocr	Apocryphon (e.g., 1Qap Gen)
ar	Aramaic (e.g., 4QMess ar)
gr	Greek (e.g., 4QpapParaExod gr)
hebr	Hebrew (e.g., 4QTob^e hebr)
p	Pesher (e.g., 1QpHab)
paleo	Paleo-Hebrew (e.g., 11QpaleoLev)
pap	papyrus (e.g., 4QpapParaExod gr)
tg	Targum (e.g., 11QtgJob)

When a manuscript is referred to by column and line number, roman numerals are used for the column number, followed by a space, with the line number set as arabic numerals (e.g., 1QS III, 12; 1QpHab I, 2). Manuscripts of biblical texts can include the biblical citation of chapter and verse in parentheses: 4QpaleoExod^m V, 4 (9:7).

When there are several fragments and they are numbered separately within a work, the fragments should be in arabic numerals. Thus, 1Q27 1 II, 25 means text 27 from Qumran Cave 1, fragment 1, column II, line 25; 4QpIsa^c 4–7 II, 2–4 means the third copy (copy c) of a pesher on Isaiah from Qumran Cave 4, joined fragments 4 to 7, column II, lines 2 to 4. Fragments are also identified by uppercase letters (e.g., 11Q1 A [Lev 4:24–26]). (While some works use lowercase column numbers, with and without the comma [e.g., 1Q27 1 ii, 25 or 1Q27 1 ii 25], the above conventions are recommended for the sake of simplicity.)

Some of the most frequently cited texts, examples from various categories, and some of the texts whose names have been changed since first publication are given below:

NUMBER	ABBREVIATION	NAME (AND ALTERNATIVE NAMES)
1Q28a	1QSa	*Rule of the Congregation* (Appendix a to 1QS)
1Q28b	1QSb	*Rule of the Blessings* (Appendix b to 1QS)
3Q15		*Copper Scroll*
4Q17	4QExod-Lev[f]	
4Q22	4QpaleoExod[m]	
4Q82	4QXII[g]	*The Greek Minor Prophets Scroll*
4Q120	4QpapLXXLev[b]	
4Q127	4QpapParaExod gr	*ParaExodus*
4Q174	4QFlor (MidrEschat[a])	*Florilegium*, also *Midrash on Eschatology*[a]
4Q175	4QTest	*Testimonia*
4Q177	4QCatena[a] (MidrEschat[b])	*Catena*[a], also *Midrash on Eschatology*[b]
4Q180	4QAgesCreat	*Ages of Creation*
4Q182	4QCatena[b] (MidrEschat[c])	*Catena*[b], also *Midrash on Eschatology*[c]
4Q242	4QPrNab ar	*Prayer of Nabonidus*
4Q246	4QapocrDan ar	*Apocryphon of Daniel*
4Q252	4QCommGen A	*Commentary on Genesis A*, formerly *Patriarchal Blessings* or *Pesher Genesis*
4Q265	4QSD	*Serek Damascus*
4Q266	4QD[a]	*Damascus Document*[a]
4Q274	4QTohorot A	*Tohorot A*
4Q285		*Sefer Hamilhamah*
4Q299	4QMyst[a]	*Mysteries*[a]
4Q320	4QCalDoc A	*Calendrical Document A*, formerly *Mishmarot A*
4Q365	4QRP[c]	*Reworked Pentateuch*[c]
4Q378	4QapocrJosh[a]	*Apocryphon of Joshua*[a], formerly *Psalms of Joshua*[a]
4Q394	4QMMT[a]	*Miqsat Ma'aśê ha-Torah*[a]
4Q400	4QShirShabb[a]	*Songs of the Sabbath Sacrifice*[a]
4Q414	4QRitPur A	*Ritual Purity A*, formerly *Baptismal Liturgy*
4Q418	4QInstruction[a]	*Instruction*[a], formerly *Sapiental Work A*[a]
4Q434	4QBarki Nafshi[a]	*BarkhiNafshi*[a]
4Q502	4QpapRitMar	*Ritual of Marriage*
4Q503	4QpapPrQuot	*Prières quotidiennes* or *Daily Prayers*
4Q504	4QDibHam[a]	*Dibre Hame'orot*[a] or *Words of the Luminaries*[a]
4Q507	4QPrFêtes[a]	*Prières pour les fêtes*[a] or *Festival Prayers*[a]
4Q510	4QShir[a]	*Shirot*[a] or *Songs of the Sage*[a]
4Q512	4QpapRitPur B	*Ritual Purity B*
4Q521	4QMessAp	*Messianic Apocalypse*
4Q525	4QBeat	*Beatitudes*
11Q5	11QPs[a]	*Psalms Scroll*[a]
11Q10	11QtgJob	*Targum of Job*
11Q11	11QApPs[a]	*Apocryphal Psalms*[a]
11Q13	11QMelch	*Melchizedek*
11Q18	11QNJ ar	*New Jerusalem*
11Q19	11QT[a]	*Temple Scroll*[a]

Appendix F contains an exhaustive list of Dead Sea Scroll texts, numbers, and principle publications.

8.3.6 PHILO

Abr.		*Leg.* 1, 2, 3	*Legum allegoriae* I, II, III
Abr.	*De Abrahamo*	*Alleg. Interp.* 1, 2, 3	*Allegorical Interpretation* 1, 2, 3
Abraham	*On the Life of Abraham*		
		Legat.	*Legatio ad Gaium*
Aet.	*De aeternitate mundi*	Embassy	*On the Embassy to Gaius*
Eternity	*On the Eternity of the World*		
		Migr.	*De migratione Abrahami*
		Migration	*On the Migration of Abraham*
Agr.	*De agricultura*		
Agriculture	*On Agriculture*		
		Mos. 1, 2	*De vita Mosis* I, II
Anim.	*De animalibus*	Moses 1, 2	*On the Life of Moses* 1, 2
Animals	*Whether Animals Have Reason* (= Alexander)		
		Mut.	*De mutatione nominum*
		Names	*On the Change of Names*
Cher.	*De cherubim*		
Cherubim	*On the Cherubim*	*Opif.*	*De opificio mundi*
		Creation	*On the Creation of the World*
Conf.	*De confusione linguarum*		
Confusion	*On the Confusion of Tongues*	*Plant.*	*De plantatione*
		Planting	*On Planting*
Contempl.	*De vita contemplativa*		
Contempl. Life	*On the Contemplative Life*	*Post.*	*De posteritate Caini*
		Posterity	*On the Posterity of Cain*
Congr.	*De congressu eruditionis gratia*		
		Praem.	*De praemiis et poenis*
Prelim. Studies	*On the Preliminary Studies*	Rewards	*On Rewards and Punishments*
Decal.	*De decalogo*		
Decalogue	*On the Decalogue*	*Prob.*	*Quod omnis probus liber sit*
		Good Person	*That Every Good Person Is Free*
Deo	*De Deo*		
God	*On God*	*Prov.* 1, 2	*De providentia* I, II
		Providence 1, 2	*On Providence* 1, 2
Det.	*Quod deterius potiori insidari soleat*	QE 1, 2	*Quaestiones et solutiones in Exodum* I, II
Worse	*That the Worse Attacks the Better*	QE 1, 2	*Questions and Answers on Exodus* 1, 2
Deus	*Quod Deus sit immutabilis*		
Unchangeable	*That God Is Unchangeable*	QG 1, 2, 3, 4	*Quaestiones et solutiones in Genesin* I, II, III, IV
Ebr.	*De ebrietate*	QG 1, 2, 3, 4	*Questions and Answers on Genesis* 1, 2, 3, 4
Drunkenness	*On Drunkenness*		
		Sacr.	*De sacrificiis Abelis et Caini*
Exsecr.	*De exsecrationibus*	Sacrifices	*On the Sacrifices of Cain and Abel*
Curses	*On Curses* (= Rewards 127–72)		
		Sobr.	*De sobrietate*
Flacc.	*In Flaccum*	Sobriety	*On Sobriety*
Flaccus	*Against Flaccus*		
		Somn. 1, 2	*De somniis* I, II
Fug.	*De fuga et inventione*	Dreams 1, 2	*On Dreams* 1, 2
Flight	*On Flight and Finding*		
		Spec. 1, 2, 3, 4	*De specialibus legibus* I, II, III, IV
Gig.	*De gigantibus*		
Giants	*On Giants*	*Spec. Laws* 1, 2, 3, 4	*On the Special Laws*
Her.	*Quis rerum divinarum heres sit*	*Virt.*	*De virtutibus*
Heir	*Who Is the Heir?*	Virtues	*On the Virtues*
Hypoth.	*Hypothetica*		
Hypothetica	*Hypothetica*		
Ios.	*De Iosepho*		
Joseph	*On the Life of Joseph*		

8.3.7 JOSEPHUS

Vita	*Vita*	*A.J.*	*Antiquitates judaicae*
Life	*The Life*	*Ant.*	*Jewish Antiquities*
C. Ap.	*Contra Apionem*	*B.J.*	*Bellum judaicum*
Ag. Ap.	*Against Apion*	*J.W.*	*Jewish War*

8.3.8 MISHNAH, TALMUD, AND RELATED LITERATURE

Abbreviations distinguish the versions of the Talmudic tractates: *y.* for Jerusalem and *b.* for Babylonian. A prefixed *t.* denotes the tractates of the Tosefta and an *m.* those of the Mishnah. A prefixed *bar.* denotes a baraita (an authoritative Tannaitic rule external to the Mishnah). When citing the Mishnah, a colon separates the chapter from the paragraph (i.e., *mishnah*); thus, *m. Ber.* 1:1. The standard way to cite the Talmud is by folio and side (a or b); thus, *b. Ber. 2a.* The third column contains nontechnical transliterations following the general-purpose Hebrew transliteration style (§5.1.2).

ᶜAbod. Zar.	*ᶜAbodah Zarah*	*Avodah Zarah*
ʾAbot	*ʾAbot*	*Avot*
ᶜArak.	*ᶜArakin*	*Arakhin*
B. Bat.	*Baba Batra*	*Bava Batra*
B. Meṣiᶜa	*Baba Meṣiᶜa*	*Bava Metzi'a*
B. Qam.	*Baba Qamma*	*Bava Qamma*
Bek.	*Bekorot*	*Bekhorot*
Ber.	*Berakot*	*Berakhot*
Beṣah	*Beṣah (=Yom Ṭob)*	*Betzah (= Yom Tov)*
Bik.	*Bikkurim*	*Bikkurim*
Demai	*Demai*	*Demai*
ᶜErub.	*ᶜErubin*	*Eruvin*
ᶜEd.	*ᶜEduyyot*	*Eduyyot*
Giṭ.	*Giṭṭin*	*Gittin*
Ḥag.	*Ḥagigah*	*Hagigah*
Ḥal.	*Ḥallah*	*Hallah*
Hor.	*Horayot*	*Horayot*
Ḥul.	*Ḥullin*	*Hullin*
Kelim	*Kelim*	*Kelim*
Ker.	*Kerithot*	*Keritot*
Ketub.	*Ketubbot*	*Ketubbot*
Kil.	*Kilʾayim*	*Kil'ayim*
Maᶜaś. Š.	*Maᶜaśer Šeni*	*Ma'aser Sheni*
Maᶜaś.	*Maᶜaśerot*	*Ma'aserot*
Mak.	*Makkot*	*Makkot*
Makš.	*Makširin*	*Makhshirin*
Meg.	*Megillah*	*Megillah*
Meᶜil.	*Meᶜilah*	*Me'ilah*
Menaḥ.	*Menaḥot*	*Menahot*
Mid.	*Middot*	*Middot*
Miqw.	*Miqwaʾot*	*Mikwa'ot*
Moʾed	*Moʾed*	*Mo'ed*

79

Moʾed Qaṭ.	*Moʾed Qaṭan*	*Mo'ed Qatan*
Naš.	*Našim*	*Nashim*
Naz.	*Nazir*	*Nazir*
Ned.	*Nedarim*	*Nedarim*
Neg.	*Negaʿim*	*Nega'im*
Nez.	*Neziqin*	*Neziqin*
Nid.	*Niddah*	*Niddah*
ʾOhal.	*ʾOhalot*	*Ohalot*
ʿOr.	*ʿOrlah*	*Orlah*
Parah	*Parah*	*Parah*
Peʾah	*Peʾah*	*Pe'ah*
Pesaḥ.	*Pesaḥim*	*Pesahim*
Qinnim	*Qinnim*	*Qinnim*
Qidd.	*Qiddušin*	*Qiddushin*
Qod.	*Qodašim*	*Qodashim*
Roš Haš.	*Roš Haššanah*	*Rosh HaShanah*
Sanh.	*Sanhedrin*	*Sanhedrin*
Šabb.	*Šabbat*	*Shabbat*
Šeb.	*Šebiʿit*	*Shevi'it*
Šebu.	*Šebuʿot*	*Shevu'ot*
Seder	*Seder*	*Seder*
Šeqal.	*Šeqalim*	*Sheqalim*
Soṭah	*Soṭah*	*Sotah*
Sukkah	*Sukkah*	*Sukkah*
Taʿan.	*Taʿanit*	*Ta'anit*
Tamid	*Tamid*	*Tamid*
Tem.	*Temurah*	*Temurah*
Ter.	*Terumot*	*Terumot*
Ṭehar.	*Ṭeharot*	*Teharot*
Ṭ. Yom	*Ṭebul Yom*	*Tevul Yom*
ʿUq.	*ʿUqṣin*	*Uqtzin*
Yad.	*Yadayim*	*Yadayim*
Yebam.	*Yebamot*	*Yevamot*
Yoma	*Yoma (= Kippurim)*	*Yoma*
Zabim	*Zabim*	*Zavim*
Zebaḥ.	*Zebaḥim*	*Zevahim*
Zera.	*Zeraʿim*	*Zera'im*

8.3.9 TARGUMIC TEXTS

Tg. Onq.	*Targum Onqelos*
Tg. Neb.	*Targum of the Prophets*
Tg. Ket.	*Targum of the Writings*
Frg. Tg.	*Fragmentary Targum*
Sam. Tg.	*Samaritan Targum*
Tg. Isa.	*Targum Isaiah*
Tg. Neof.	*Targum Neofiti*
Tg. Ps.-J.	*Targum Pseudo-Jonathan*
Tg. Yer. I	*Targum Yerušalmi*
Tg. Yer. II	*Targum Yerušalmi I*
Yem. Tg.	*Yemenite Targum*
Tg. Esth. I, II	*First or Second Targum of Esther*

8.3.10 OTHER RABBINIC WORKS

The third column lists the titles according to the general-purpose style (§5.1.2).

ᶜAbad.	*ᶜAbadim*	*Avadim*
ʾAbot R. Nat.	*ʾAbot de Rabbi Nathan*	*Avot of Rabbi Nathan*
ʾAg. Ber.	*ʾAggadat Berešit*	*Aggadat Bereshit*
Bab.	*Babylonian I(used alone)*	*Babylonian*
Der. Er. Rab.	*Derek Ereṣ Rabbah*	*Derekh Eretz Rabbah*
Der. Er. Zuṭ.	*Derek Ereṣ Zuṭa*	*Derekh Eretz Zuta*
Gem.	*Gemara*	*Gemara*
Gerim	*Gerim*	*Gerim*
Kallah	*Kallah*	*Kallah*
Kallah Rab.	*Kallah Rabbati*	*Kallah Rabbati*
Kutim	*Kutim*	*Kutim*
Mas. Qet.	*Massektot Qeṭannot*	*Massekhtot Qetannot*
Mek.	*Mekilta*	*Mekilta*
Mez.	*Mezuzah*	*Mezuzah*
Midr.	*Midrash I(+ biblical book)*	*Midrash*
Pal.	*Palestinian I(used alone)*	*Palestinian*
Pesiq. Rab.	*Pesiqta Rabbati*	*Pesiqta Rabbati*
Pesiq. Rab Kah.	*Pesiqta de Rab Kahana*	*Pesiqta of Rab Kahana*
Pirqe R. El.	*Pirqe Rabbi Eliezer*	*Pirqe Rabbi Eliezer*
Rab. (e.g., Gen. Rab.= Genesis Rabbah)	*Rabbah (+ biblical book)*	*Rabbah*
S. Eli. Rab.	*Seder Eliyahu Rabbah*	*Seder Eliyahu Rabbah*
S. Eli. Zut.	*Seder Eliyahu Zuta*	*Seder Eliyahu Zuta*
Sem.	*Semaḥot*	*Semahot*
Sep. Torah	*Seper Torah*	*Sefer Torah*
Sipra	*Sipra*	*Sifra*
Sipre	*Sipre*	*Sifre*
Ṣiṣit	*Ṣiṣit*	*Tzitzit*
Sop.	*Soperim*	*Soferim*
S. ᶜOlam Rab.	*Seder ᶜOlam Rabbah*	*Seder Olam Rabbah*
Tanḥ.	*Tanḥuma*	*Tanhuma*
Tep.	*Tepillin*	*Tefillin*
Yal.	*Yalquṭ*	*Yalqut*

8.3.11 APOSTOLIC FATHERS

Barn.	*Barnabas*
1–2 Clem.	*1–2 Clement*
Did.	*Didache*
Diogn.	*Diognetus*
Herm. Mand.	Shepherd of Hermas, *Mandate*
Herm. Sim.	Shepherd of Hermas, *Similitude*
Herm. Vis.	Shepherd Hermas, *Vision*
Ign. Eph.	Ignatius, *To the Ephesians*
Ign. Magn.	Ignatius, *To the Magnesians*
Ign. Smyrn.	Ignatius, *To the Smyrnaeans*
Ign. Phld.	Ignatius, *To the Philadelphians*
Ign. Rom.	Ignatius, *To the Romans*
Ign. Pol.	Ignatius, *To Polycarp*

Ign. *Trall.*	Ignatius, *To the Trallians*
Mart. Pol.	*Martyrdom of Polycarp*
Pol. *Phil*	Polycarp, *To the Philippians*

8.3.12 Nag Hammadi Codices

Nag Hammadi Codices (=NHC) are identified by the codex number (I) followed by treatise number (1).

Pr. Paul	I,1 *Prayer of the Apostle Paul*
Ap. Jas.	I,2 *Apocryphon of James*
Gos. Truth	I,3 *Gospel of Truth*
Treat. Res.	I,4 *Treatise on the Resurrection*
Tri. Trac.	I,5 *Tripartite Tractate*
Ap. John	II,1 *Apocryphon of John*
Gos. Thom.	II,2 *Gospel of Thomas*
Gos. Phil.	II,3 *Gospel of Philip*
Hyp. Arch.	II,4 *Hypostasis of the Archons*
Orig. World	II,5 *On the Origin of the World*
Exeg. Soul	II,6 *Exegesis of the Soul*
Thom. Cont.	II,7 *Book of Thomas the Contender*
Ap. John	III,1 *Apocryphon of John*
Gos. Eg.	III,2 *Gospel of the Egyptians*
Eugnostos	III,3 *Eugnostos the Blessed*
Soph. Jes. Chr.	III,4 *Sophia of Jesus Christ*
Dial. Sav.	III,5 *Dialogue of the Savior*
Ap. John	IV,1 *Apocryphon of John*
Gos. Eg.	IV,2 *Gospel of the Egyptians*
Eugnostos	V,1 *Eugnostos the Blessed*
Apoc. Paul	V,2 *Apocalypse of Paul*
1 Apoc. Jas.	V,3 *(First) Apocalypse of James*
2 Apoc. Jas.	V,4 *(Second) Apocalypse of James*
Apoc. Adam	V,5 *Apocalypse of Adam*
Acts Pet. 12 Apos.	VI,1 *Acts of Peter and the Twelve Apostles*
Thund.	VI,2 *Thunder: Perfect Mind*
Auth. Teach.	VI,3 *Authoritative Teaching*
Great Pow.	VI,4 *Concept of our Great Power*
Plato Rep.	VI,5 *Plato, Republic 588b–589b*
Disc. 8–9	VI,6 *Discourse on the Eighth and Ninth*
Pr. Thanks.	VI,7 *Prayer of Thanksgiving*
Asclepius	VI,8 *Asclepius 21–29*
Paraph. Shem	VII,1 *Paraphrase of Shem*
Treat. Seth	VII,2 *Second Treatise of the Great Seth*
Apoc. Pet.	VII,3 *Apocalypse of Peter*
Teach. Silv.	VII,4 *Teachings of Silvanus*
Steles Seth	VII,5 *Three Steles of Seth*
Zost.	VIII,1 *Zostrianos*
Ep. Pet. Phil.	VIII,2 *Letter of Peter to Philip*
Melch.	IX,1 *Melchizedek*
Norea	IX,2 *Thought of Norea*
Testim. Truth	IX,3 *Testimony of Truth*
Marsanes	X *Marsanes*
Interp. Know.	XI,1 *Interpretation of Knowledge*
Val. Exp.	XI,2 *A Valentinian Exposition*

On Anointing	*XI,2a On the Anointing*
On Bap. A	*XI,2b On Baptism A*
On Bap. B	*XI,2c On Baptism B*
On Euch. A	*XI,2d On the Eucharist A*
On Euch. B	*XI,2e On the Eucharist B*
Allogenes	*XI,3 Allogenes*
Hypsiph.	*XI,4 Hypsiphrone*
Sent. Sextus	*XII,1 Sentences of Sextus*
Gos. Truth	*XII,2 Gospel of Truth*
Frm.	*XII,3 Fragments*
Trim. Prot.	*XIII,1 Trimorphic Protennoia*
Orig. World.	*XIII,2 On the Origin of the World*
Gos. Mary	*BG,1 Gospel of Mary*
Ap. John	*BG,2 Apocryphon of John*
Soph. Jes. Chr.	*BG,3 Sophia of Jesus Christ*
Act Pet.	*BG,4 Act of Peter*

8.3.13 NEW TESTAMENT APOCRYPHA AND PSEUDEPIGRAPHA

Acts Andr.	*Acts of Andrew*
Acts Andr. Mth.	*Acts of Andrew and Matthias*
Acts Andr. Paul	*Acts of Andrew and Paul*
Acts Barn.	*Acts of Barnabas*
Acts Jas.	*Acts of James the Great*
Acts John	*Acts of John*
Acts John Pro.	*Acts of John (by Prochorus)*
Acts Paul	*Acts of Paul*
Acts Pet.	*Acts of Peter*
Acts Pet. (Slav.)	*Acts of Peter (Slavonic)*
Acts Pet. Andr.	*Acts of Peter and Andrew*
Acts Pet. Paul	*Acts of Peter and Paul*
Acts Phil.	*Acts of Philip*
Acts Phil. (Syr.)	*Acts of Philip (Syriac)*
Acts Pil.	*Acts of Pilate*
Acts Thad.	*Acts of Thaddaeus*
Acts Thom.	*Acts of Thomas*
Apoc. Pet.	*Apocalypse of Peter*
Ap. John	*Apocryphon of John*
Apoc. Dosith.	*Apocalypse of Dositheus*
Apoc. Messos	*Apocalypse of Messos*
Apoc. Thom.	*Apocalypse of Thomas*
Apoc. Vir.	*Apocalypse of the Virgin*
(Apocr.) Ep. Tit.	*Apocryphal Epistle of Titus*
(Apocr.) Gos. John	*Apocryphal Gospel of John*
Apos. Con.	*Apostolic Constitutions and Canons*
Ps.-Abd.	*Apostolic History of Pseudo-Abdias*
(Arab.) Gos. Inf.	*Arabic Gospel of the Infancy*
(Arm.) Gos. Inf.	*Armenian Gospel of the Infancy*
Asc. Jas.	*Ascents of James*
Assum. Vir.	*Assumption of the Virgin*
Bk. Barn.	*Book of the Resurrection of Christ by Barnabas the Apostle*
Bk. Elch.	*Book Elchasai*
Cerinthus	*Cerinthus*
3 Cor.	*3 Corinthians*

Ep. Alex.	*Epistle to the Alexandrians*
Ep. Apos.	*Epistle to the Apostles*
Ep. Chr. Abg.	*Epistle of Christ and Abgar*
Ep. Chr. Heav.	*Epistle of Christ from Heaven*
Ep. Lao.	*Epistle to the Laodiceans*
Ep. Lent.	*Epistle of Lentulus*
Ep. Paul Sen.	*Epistles of Paul and Seneca*
Gos. Barn.	*Gospel of Barnabas*
Gos. Bart.	*Gospel of Bartholomew*
Gos. Bas.	*Gospel of Basilides*
Gos. Bir. Mary	*Gospel of the Birth of Mary*
Gos. Eb.	*Gospel of the Ebionites*
Gos. Eg.	*Gospel of the Egyptians*
Gos. Eve	*Gospel of Eve*
Gos. Gam.	*Gospel of Gamaliel*
Gos. Heb.	*Gospel of the Hebrews*
Gos. Marcion	*Gospel of Marcion*
Gos. Mary	*Gospel of Mary*
Gos. Naass.	*Gospel of the Naassenes*
Gos. Naz.	*Gospel of the Nazarenes*
Gos. Nic.	*Gospel of Nicodemus*
Gos. Pet.	*Gospel of Peter*
Ps.-Mt.	*Gospel of Pseudo-Matthew*
Gos. Thom.	*Gospel of Thomas*
Gos. Trad. Mth.	*Gospel and Traditions of Matthias*
Hist. Jos. Carp.	*History of Joseph the Carpenter*
Hymn Dance	*Hymn of the Dance*
Hymn Pearl	*Hymn of the Pearl*
Inf. Gos. Thom.	*Infancy Gospel of Thomas*
Inf. Gos.	*Infancy Gospels*
Mart. Bart.	*Martyrdom of Bartholomew*
Mart. Mt.	*Martyrdom of Matthew*
Mart. Paul	*Martyrdom of Paul*
Mart. Pet.	*Martyrdom of Peter*
Mart. Pet. Paul	*Martyrdom of Peter and Paul*
Mart. Phil.	*Martyrdom of Philip*
Melkon	*Melkon*
Mem. Apos.	*Memoria of Apostles*
Pre. Pet.	*Preaching of Peter*
Prot. Jas.	*Protevangelium of James*
Ps.-Clem.	*Pseudo-Clementines*
Rev. Steph.	*Revelation of Stephen*
Sec. Gos. Mk.	*Secret Gospel of Mark*
Vis. Paul	*Vision of Paul*

8.3.14   Classical and Ancient Christian Writings

When citing a particular work only once, spell it out rather than abbreviating it, especially if many readers might not be familiar with the work in question. If the same work is cited many times, however, or if many different works are cited, use abbreviations within notes or parentheses to avoid cluttering the book with spelled-out titles.

We have consulted a number of standard references: the various Oxford Greek and Latin lexicons and dictionaries, the *Dictionnaire latin-français des auteurs chrétiens* (Turnhout: Brepols, 1967), the *TLG Canon* (New York: Oxford University Press, 1990), and others. We do not, however, follow any of these without exception for several reasons: none of them covers the whole field of ancient and late antique, Greek and Latin, Christian and non-Christian writers; most of them are inconsistent internally and with other complementary works; and most of them abbreviate at least some works too concisely for readers not specializing in classical studies or patristics.

We therefore provide not only the table in Appendix H but also a set of rules. If the work you need to abbreviate is not in the table, similar titles may be; and if not, you can use the rules to devise an acceptable abbreviation of your own.

Rules for abbreviating Latin titles:

(1) Abbreviate titles of works but not names of authors (except as in rule 12 below).

(2) Latin and Greek titles are capitalized according to the rules for Latin (see §7.1.3.8).

(3) The first letter of an abbreviation is always uppercase; otherwise, case in the abbreviation follows case in the spelled-out title.

(4) With regard to Latin orthography: we prefer *v* and *j* for consonantal *u* and *i*.

(5) Do not use acronymns. (In a monograph on Eusebius, the author may elect to use *HE* rather than *Hist. eccl.*, but otherwise *Hist. eccl.* is more helpful to readers.) Do not use acronym-abbreviation hybrids such as *DMort.* or *JTr.* Do not abbreviate by omitting vowels, as in *Phdr.* for *Phaedrus*. (An exception would be a standard biblical abbreviation, such as *Phlm* for *Philemon* [cf. §§8.3.2 and 8.3.15].)

(6) Rather, abbreviate words by truncating them and placing a period at the point of truncation. Don't truncate between consonants; truncate after a consonant rather than after a vowel where possible. The abbreviation should normally contain at least a whole syllable. Thus: use *Phaedr.* rather than *Phaed.* for *Phaedrus*, *Socr.* rather than *Soc.* for *Socrates*, *coll.* rather than *col.* for *collatio*, *parad.* rather than *para.* for *paradoxa*, and *Thras.* rather than *Thr.* for *Thrasonidis*.

(7) Do not double a final consonant in an abbreviation to indicate a plural; e.g., use *Can. ap.* not *Cann. app.* for a reference in *Canones apostolicae*.

(8) For Latin titles that begin with prepositions *(De, In, Contra, Adversus, Pro, Ad)*, the abbreviation includes the preposition (or its abbreviation) only if one of the following holds: (1) The work is a commentary, homily, etc., whose title consists of *In* plus the name of the primary text. (2) The preposition is followed by a noun too short to be abbreviated, so that omitting the preposition would result in an abbreviation

beginning with a noun in a case other than the nominative. (3) With-out the preposition, this work could be confused with another whose name is similarly abbreviated, as with Demosthenes' orations for and against Phormio. Similarly, prepositions within a title are omitted in the absence of like complications: *Enarrationes in Psalmos* is abbrevi-ated *Enarrat. Ps.*, not *Enarrat. in Ps.* Note that in the table, an initial preposition is ignored in alphabetizing the abbreviations.

(9)   Like prepositions, *et* is omitted from abbreviations.

(10)   When a single author has several numbered works by the same name, we prefer in the abbreviation to place the numeral (always arabic in the abbreviations though roman in the spelled-out Latin title) before the name and italicize it. This keeps the treatise number from being confused with a section, chapter, or paragraph number and is consistent with the usage for numbered biblical books. On the other hand, sometimes such works are commonly treated as books of a unified opus; in which case the number follows the name, is set roman, and is followed immediately by a period and a section number.

(11)   Where different authors have works with the same title, use the same abbreviation for each author; and where the same word occurs in different titles, try to use the same abbreviation for the same word. Here is a list of words that occur commonly in titles and their abbreviations:

adv.	adversus	hist.	historia
an.	anima; analytica; animal, animalia	hom.	homilia
		hymn.	hymnus
anth.	anthologia	int.	interpretatio
ap.	apostolicus	metam.	metamorphoses
apol.	apologia	metaph.	metaphysica
Apoll.	Apollo, Apollonius, etc.	mete.	meteorologica
Arian.	Arianus	od.	odae
bell.	bellum	or.	orator, oratoria, oratio
catech.	catechesis	orac.	oraculum
c.	contra	orig.	origo, originalis
comm.	commentarius, commentarium, commentariolum	Orig.	Origen
		pr.	prior
cor.	corona	pol.	politicus. politeia
d.	deus	post.	posterior
eccl.	ecclesiasticus	quaest.	quaestiones
enarrat.	enarratio	res.	resurrectio
ep.	epistula	rhet.	rhetor, rhetorica
epigr.	epigrammata	sat.	satirae, saturae
eth.	ethica	schol.	scholia
ev.	evangelium, evangelicus	sel.	selecta
Ev.	Evangelium	spir.	spiritus
exc.	excerpta	tract.	tractatus
exp.	expositio	virg.	virgo, virgines
expl.	explanatio	virginit.	virginitas
fr.	fragmentum, fragmenta	vit.	vita

(12) Similarly, where the title of one work (e.g., a biblical book or a treatise of Aristotle) occurs in the title of another (such as a commentary or a translation), the abbreviation for the primary work should be incorporated (and capitalized) in the abbreviation of the secondary work. The abbreviation for the secondary work is not simply identical to the abbreviation for the primary work. Rather, if it is a translation, it should begin with an abbreviation for the name of the original author (for examples, see under Rufinus and Jerome for their translations of Origen; this is the only circumstance in which we abbreviate authors' names); if the secondary work is a commentary of some kind, its abbreviation should begin with *Comm., Enarrat., Hom., Tract.,* or the like, or at least with *In.*

8.3.15   LATIN NAMES OF BIBLICAL BOOKS

The following table provides abbreviations for the Latin names of biblical books. For the benefit of those not familiar with the Latin Bible, the English name of each book is also given. These abbreviations for the Latin names of the books of the Bible follow the *Dictionnaire latin-français des auteurs chrétiens* (Turnhout: Brepols, 1967) except as modified according to the following hierarchy of rules: (1) unabbreviated forms are used only for short, uninflected forms; (2) where possible, these Latin abbreviations conform to the abbreviations given below for the English book names, except that the Latin abbreviations are italicized and followed by a period; (3) otherwise, these Latin abbreviations conform to the rules given above. For numbered books, the abbreviation should use arabic numbers set italic; e.g., a patristic commentary on 1 Chronicles, if such had been written, might be titled *Commentarii in primum Paralipomenorum librum* and abbreviated *Comm. 1 Par.*[1]

	LATIN TITLE	ENGLISH TITLE
	Vetus Testamentum	Old Testament
Abd.	*Abdias*	Obadiah
Agg.	*Aggaeus*	Haggai
Am.	*Amos*	Amos
Bar.	*Baruch*	Baruch
Cant.	*Canticum canticorum*	Song of Songs
Dan.	*Daniel*	Daniel
Deut.	*Deuteronomium*	Deuteronomy
Eccl.	*Ecclesiastes*	Ecclesiastes
Ecclesiastic.	*Ecclesiasticus*	Sirach
Esdr.	*Esdras*	Esdras and Ezra
Esth.	*Esther*	Esther
Exod.	*Exodus*	Exodus

[1] Some writers use inflected forms of Hebrew names that other writers leave uninflected. When inflected names are used, abbreviated forms must have a period. For example, Commentarius in Joel would be abbreviated *Comm. Joel* (no period after Joel); but *Commentarius in Joelem* is abbreviated *Comm. Joel.*, since in this case an accusative ending is being dropped.

Ezech.	*Ezechiel*	Ezekiel
Gen.	*Genesis*	Genesis
Hab.	*Habacuc*	Habakkuk
Isa.	*Isaias*	Isaiah
Jer.	*Jeremias*	Jeremiah
Jes. Nav.	*Jesus Nave (= Josue)*	Joshua
Job	*Job*	Job
Joel	*Joel*	Joel
Jon.	*Jonas*	Jonah
Jos.	*Josue*	Joshua
Judic.	*Judices*	Judges
Judith	*Judith*	Judith
Lam.	*Lamentationes*	Lamentations
Lev.	*Leviticus*	Leviticus
Macc.	*Macchabaei*	Maccabees
Mal.	*Malachias*	Malachi
Mich.	*Michaeas*	Micah
Nah.	*Nahum*	Nahum
Num.	*Numeri*	Numbers
Or. Man.	*Oratio Manasse*	Prayer of Manasseh
Os.	*Osee*	Hosea
Par.	*Paralipomena*	Chronicles
Prov.	*Proverbia Salomonis*	Proverbs
Ps.	*Psalmi*	Psalms
Reg.	*Reges*	Kings
Ruth	*Ruth*	Ruth
Sap.	*Sapientia*	Wisdom
Soph.	*Sophonias*	Zephaniah
Tob.	*Tobias*	Tobit
Zach.	*Zacharias*	Zechariah
	Novum Testamentum	New Testament
Act.	*Actus apostolorum*	Acts
Apoc.	*Apocalypsis*	Revelation
Col.	*Pauli epistula ad Colossenses*	Colossians
Cor.	*Pauli epistulae ad Corinthios*	Corinthians
Eph.	*Pauli epistula ad Ephesios*	Ephesians
Gal.	*Pauli epistula ad Galatas*	Galatians
Heb.	*Pauli epistula ad Hebraeos*	Hebrews
Jac.	*Epistula Jacobi*	James
Jo.	*Euangelium Joannis*	John
Jo. ep.	*Johannis epistulae*	John
Jud.	*Epistula Judae*	Jude
Laod.	*Epistula ad Laodicenses*	Laodiceans
Luc.	*Evangelium Lucae*	Luke
Marc.	*Evangelium Marci*	Mark
Matt.	*Evangelium Matthaei*	Matthew
Pet.	*Epistulae Petri*	Peter
Phil.	*Pauli epistula ad Philippenses*	Philippians
Phlm.	*Pauli epistula ad Philemonem*	Philemon
Rom.	*Pauli epistula ad Romanos*	Romans
Thess.	*Pauli epistulae ad Thessalonicenses*	Thessalonians
Tim.	*Pauli epistulae ad Timotheum*	Timothy
Tit.	*Pauli epistula ad Titum*	Titus

8.3.16   PAPYRI, OSTRACA, EPIGRAPHICAL CITATIONS, ETC.

The standard resource for abbreviating Greek papyri, ostraca, and tablets is the *Checklist of Editions of Greek and Latin Papyri, Ostraca and Tablets* (ed. J. F. Oates, et al.; 4th ed.; BASPSup 7; Atlanta: Scholars Press, 1992). When collections or selections of papyri are given, include the source of the citation. Thus,

> 4 P.Ryl. 77.32–47 (LCL; *Select Papyri* 2.154–159).

> *Select Papyri.* Translated by A. S. Hunt and C. C. Edgar. 5 vols. LCL. Cambridge: Harvard University Press.

See above §7.3.3

8.3.17   ANCIENT NEAR EASTERN TEXTS

No standard list of abbreviations exists for the diverse and ever-growing body of primary material that falls under the general classification of the ancient Near East. Indeed, in many cases, several titles exist for a particular text (e.g., The Babylonian Epic of Creation or *Enuma Elish*). Often, the abbreviations associated with texts from these regions are based not on a particular title, but on the text editions wherein these writings are principally found (e.g., EA 15 for Amarna letter no. 15 in the edition of J. A. Knudtzon, *Die el-Amarna Tafeln* [Leipzig: J. C. Hinrichs, 1915]. Further guidelines for citing these texts can be found in §§2.3.2, 4.4.6, and 7.3.1.

8.4 SECONDARY SOURCES: JOURNALS, PERIODICALS, MAJOR REFERENCE WORKS, AND SERIES

Abbreviations for works not listed below should follow Siegfried M. Schwertner, *Internationales Abkürzungsverzeichnis für Theologie und Grenzgebiete* (2d ed.; Berlin: de Gruyter, 1992 [=IATG²]). Abbreviations use superscripted numbers to indicate multiple editions. Superscripted numbers should not be used in bibliographic or note citations. See, e.g., §7.2.15.

8.4.1   ALPHABETIZED BY SOURCE

ABAW	Abhandlungen der Bayrischen Akademie der Wissenschaften
ADOG	Abhandlungen der deutschen Orientgesellschaft
AHAW	Abhandlungen der Heidelberger Akademie der Wissenschaften
ALASP	Abhandlungen zur Literatur Alt-Syren-Palästinas und Mesopotamiens
ASAW	Abhandlungen der Sächsischen Akademie der Wissenschaften

ATANT	Abhandlungen zur Theologie des Alten und Neuen Testaments
ANTC	Abingdon New Testament Commentaries
AbrN	*Abr-Nahrain*
AbrNSup	Abr-Nahrain: Supplement Series
AAS	*Acta apostolicae sedis*
ACO	*Acta conciliorum oecumenicorum.* Edited by E. Schwartz. Berlin, 1914–
AMS	*Acta martyrum et sanctorum Syriace.* Edited by P. Bedjan. 7 vols. Paris, 1890–1897
AcOr	*Acta orientalia*
ASS	*Acta sanctae sedis*
AASS	*Acta sanctorum quotquot toto orbe coluntur.* Antwerp, 1643–
ASNU	Acta seminarii neotestamentici upsaliensis
AcT	*Acta theologica*
ATDan	Acta theologica danica
BGU	*Aegyptische Urkunden aus den Königlichen Staatlichen Museen zu Berlin, Griechische Urkunden.* 15 vols. Berlin, 1895–1983.
Aeg	*Aegyptus*
Aev	*Aevum: Rassegna de scienze, storiche, linguistiche, e filologiche*
AJBS	*African Journal of Biblical Studies*
ÄgAbh	Ägyptologische Abhandlungen
ÄF	Ägyptologische Forschungen
AHw	*Akkadisches Handwörterbuch.* W. von Soden. 3 vols. Wiesbaden, 1965–1981
Altaner	Altaner, B. *Patrologie.* 8th ed. Freiburg, 1978
AbB	*Altbabylonische Briefe in Umschrift und Übersetzung.* Edited by F. R. Kraus. Leiden, 1964–
AO	*Der Alte Orient*
ATD	Das Alte Testament Deutsch
AOAT	Alter Orient und Altes Testament
AOBib	Altorientalische Bibliothek
ABAT2	*Altorientalische Bilder zum Alten Testament.* Edited by H. Gressmann. 2d ed. Berlin, 1927
AoF	Altorientalische Forschungen
AOTAT	*Altorientalische Texte zum Alten Testament.* Edited by H. Gressmann. 2d ed. Berlin, 1926
ATA	Alttestamentliche Abhandlungen
AARDS	American Academy of Religion Dissertation Series
ABQ	*American Baptist Quarterly*
AER	*American Ecclesiastical Review*
AHR	*American Historical Review*
AJAS	*American Journal of Arabic Studies*
AJA	*American Journal of Archaeology*
AJP	*American Journal of Philology*
AJSL	*American Journal of Semitic Languages and Literature*
AJT	*American Journal of Theology*
AOS	American Oriental Series
AOSTS	American Oriental Society Translation Series

APSP	*American Philosophical Society Proceedings*
ASOR	American Schools of Oriental Research
ASP	*American Studies in Papyrology*
ATLA	American Theological Library Association
ACEBT	*Amsterdamse Cahiers voor Exegese en bijbelse Theologie*
AAeg	*Analecta aegyptiaca*
AnBib	Analecta biblica
AnBoll	Analecta Bollandiana
ALBO	Analecta lovaniensia biblica et orientalia
AnOr	Analecta orientalia
Anám	*Anámnesis*
AnSt	*Anatolian Studies*
AB	Anchor Bible
ABD	*Anchor Bible Dictionary.* Edited by D. N. Freedman. 6 vols. New York, 1992
ABRL	Anchor Bible Reference Library
ACCS	Ancient Christian Commentary on Scripture
ACW	Ancient Christian Writers. 1946–
AEL	*Ancient Egyptian Literature.* M. Lichtheim. 3 vols. Berkeley, 1971–1980
AEO	*Ancient Egyptian Onomastica.* A. H. Gardiner. 3 vols. London, 1947
ANEP	*The Ancient Near East in Pictures Relating to the Old Testament.* Edited by J. B. Pritchard. Princeton, 1954
ANESTP	*The Ancient Near East: Supplementary Texts and Pictures Relating to the Old Testament.* Edited by J. B. Pritchard. Princeton, 1969.
ANET	*Ancient Near Eastern Texts Relating to the Old Testament.* Edited by J. B. Pritchard. 3d ed. Princeton, 1969
ARAB	*Ancient Records of Assyria and Babylonia.* Daniel David Luckenbill. 2 vols. Chicago, 1926–1927
ARE	*Ancient Records of Egypt.* Edited by J. H. Breasted. 5 vols. Chicago, 1905–1907. Reprint, New York, 1962
ANQ	*Andover Newton Quarterly*
AUSS	*Andrews University Seminary Studies*
Ang	*Angelicum*
AThR	*Anglican Theological Review*
AASF	Annales Academiae scientiarum fennicae
ASAE	*Annales du Service des antiquités de l'Egypte*
AT	*Annales theologici*
AION	*Annali dell'Istituto Orientale di Napoli*
AAA	Annals of Archaeology and Anthropology
AE	*Année épigraphique*
AnPhil	*L'année philologique*
AIPHOS	*Annuaire de l'Institut de philologie et d'histoire orientales et slaves*
AEB	*Annual Egyptological Bibliography*
AASOR	Annual of the American Schools of Oriental Research
Bar-Ilan	*Annual of Bar-Ilan University*
ADAJ	*Annual of the Department of Antiquities of Jordan*

AJBI	*Annual of the Japanese Biblical Institute*
ALUOS	*Annual of Leeds University Oriental Society*
ASTI	*Annual of the Swedish Theological Institute*
ANF	*Ante-Nicene Fathers*
AnthLyrGraec	*Anthologia lyrica graeca*. Edited by E. Diehl. Leipzig, 1954–
AnL	*Anthropological Linguistics*
Anton	*Antonianum*
Anuari	*Anuari de filología*
AÖAW	Anzeiger der Österreichischen Akademie der Wissenschaften
AAHG	*Anzeiger für die Altertumswissenschaft*
AMWNE	*Apocalypticism in the Mediterranean World and the Near East.* Proceedings of the International Colloquium on Apocalypticism. Edited by D. Hellholm. Uppsala, 1979
APOT	*The Apocrypha and Pseudepigrapha of the Old Testament.* Edited by R. H. Charles. 2 vols. Oxford, 1913
AOT	*The Apocryphal Old Testament.* Edited by H. F. D. Sparks. Oxford, 1984
APAT	*Die Apokryphen und Pseudepigraphen des Alten Testaments.* Translated and edited by E. Kautzsch. 2 vols. Tübingen, 1900
ArSt	Arabian Studies
ArBib	The Aramaic Bible
AJSUFS	Arbeiten aus dem Juristischen Seminar der Universität Freiburg, Schweiz
ANTJ	Arbeiten zum Neuen Testament und Judentum
AGJU	Arbeiten zur Geschichte des antiken Judentums und des Urchristentums
AGSU	Arbeiten zur Geschichte des Spätjudentums und Urchristentums
ALGHJ	Arbeiten zur Literatur und Geschichte des hellenistischen Judentums
ANTF	Arbeiten zur neutestamentlichen Textforschung
AzTh	Arbeiten zur Theologie
Arch	*Archaeology*
ABW	*Archaeology in the Biblical World*
AA	*Archäologischer Anzeiger*
AfK	*Archiv für Keilschriftforschung*
AfOB	Archiv für Orientforschung: Beiheft
AfO	*Archiv für Orientforschung*
APF	*Archiv für Papyrusforschung*
ARG	*Archiv für Reformationsgeschichte*
AR	*Archiv für Religionswissenschaft*
ArOr	*Archiv Orientální*
ASSR	*Archives de sciences sociales des religions*
ARM	Archives royales de Mari
ARMT	Archives royales de Mari, transcrite et traduite
ATG	*Archivo teológico granadino*
AsTJ	*Asbury Theological Journal*
ATJ	*Ashland Theological Journal*
AJT	*Asia Journal of Theology*

Asp	*Asprenas: Rivista di scienze teologiche*
AsSeign	*Assemblées du Seigneur*
AJSR	*Association for Jewish Studies Review*
ABC	*Assyrian and Babylonian Chronicles.* A. K. Grayson. TCS 5. Locust Valley, New York, 1975
ABL	*Assyrian and Babylonian Letters Belonging to the Kouyunjik Collections of the British Museum.* Edited by R. F. Harper. 14 vols. Chicago, 1892–1914
ADD	*Assyrian Deeds and Documents.* C. H. W. Johns. 4 vols. Cambridge, 1898–1923
CAD	*The Assyrian Dictionary of the Oriental Institute of the University of Chicago.* Chicago, 1956–
ARI	*Assyrian Royal Inscriptions.* A. K. Grayson. 2 vols. RANE. Wiesbaden, 1972–1976
AS	Assyriological Studies
AB	*Assyriologische Bibliothek*
ABZ	*Assyrisch-babylonische Zeichenliste.* Rykle Borger. 3d ed. AOAT 33/33A. Neukirchen-Vluyn, 1986
Atiqot	ᶜ*Atiqot*
AVTRW	Aufsätze und Vorträge zur Theologie und Religionswissenschaft
ANRW	*Aufstieg und Niedergang der römischen Welt: Geschichte und Kultur Roms im Spiegel der neueren Forschung.* Edited by H. Temporini and W. Haase. Berlin, 1972–
ACNT	Augsburg Commentaries on the New Testament
AugStud	*Augustinian Studies*
Aug	*Augustinianum*
AuOr	*Aula orientalis*
AGLB	*Aus der Geschichte der lateinischen Bibel (= Vetus Latina: Die Reste der altlateinischen Bibel: Aus der Geschichte der lateinischen Bibel).* Freiburg: Herder, 1957–
ACR	*Australasian Catholic Record*
ATR	*Australasian Theological Review*
ABR	*Australian Biblical Review*
ANZSTR	Australian and New Zealand Studies in Theology and Religion
AJBA	*Australian Journal of Biblical Archaeology*
Bab	*Babyloniaca*
BOR	*Babylonian and Oriental Record*
BIN	*Babylonian Inscriptions in the Collection of James B. Nies*
BWL	*Babylonian Wisdom Literature.* W. G. Lambert. Oxford, 1960
BaghM	*Baghdader Mitteilungen*
BBMS	Baker Biblical Monograph Series
BEB	*Baker Encyclopedia of the Bible.* Edited by W. A. Elwell. 2 vols. Grand Rapids, 1988
BAG	Bauer, W., W. F. Arndt, and F. W. Gingrich. *Greek-English Lexicon of the New Testament and Other Early Christian Literature.* Chicago, 1957

BAGD	Bauer, W., W. F. Arndt, F. W. Gingrich, and F. W. Danker. *Greek-English Lexicon of the New Testament and Other Early Christian Literature.* 2d ed. Chicago, 1979
BDAG	Bauer, W., F. W. Danker, W. F. Arndt, and F. W. Gingrich. *Greek-English Lexicon of the New Testament and Other Early Christian Literature.* 3d ed. Chicago, 1999
BZAW	Beihefte zur Zeitschrift für die alttestamentliche Wissenschaft
BZNW	Beihefte zur Zeitschrift für die neutestamentliche Wissenschaft
BZRGG	Beihefte zur Zeitschrift für Religions- und Geistesgeschichte
BAP	*Beiträge zum altbabylonischen Privatrecht.* Bruno Meissner. Leipzig, 1893
BzA	Beiträge zur Assyriologie
BBET	Beiträge zur biblischen Exegese und Theologie
BEATAJ	Beiträge zur Erforschung des Alten Testaments und des antiken Judentum
BEvT	Beiträge zur evangelischen Theologie
BFCT	Beiträge zur Förderung christlicher Theologie
BGBE	Beiträge zur Geschichte der biblischen Exegese
BHT	Beiträge zur historischen Theologie
BWA(N)T	Beiträge zur Wissenschaft vom Alten (und Neuen) Testament
BSGW	Berichte der Sächsischen Gesellschaft der Wissenschaften
BerMatÖAI	Berichte und Materialien des Österreichischen archäologischen Instituts
BJVF	*Berliner Jahrbuch für Vor- und Frühgeschichte*
BTZ	*Berliner Theologische Zeitschrift*
Ber	*Berytus*
BeO	*Bibbia e oriente*
BK	*Bibel und Kirche*
BibLeb	*Bibel und Leben*
BL	*Bibel und Liturgie*
BiBh	*Bible Bhashyam*
BTS	*Bible et terre sainte*
BVC	*Bible et vie chrétienne*
BRev	*Bible Review*
BSC	Bible Student's Commentary
TBT	*The Bible Today*
BT	*The Bible Translator*
BHK	*Biblia Hebraica.* Edited by R. Kittel. Stuttgart, 1905–1906, 1925^2, 1937^3, 1951^4, 1973^{16}
BHS	*Biblia Hebraica Stuttgartensia.* Edited by K. Elliger and W. Rudolph. Stuttgart, 1983
ByF	*Biblia y fe*
BiPa	Biblia Patristica: Index des citations et allusions bibliques dans la littérature. Paris, 1975–
Bib	*Biblica*
BibOr	Biblica et orientalia
BA	*Biblical Archaeologist*
BARead	*Biblical Archaeologist Reader*

BAR	*Biblical Archaeology Review*
BFT	Biblical Foundations in Theology
BI	*Biblical Illustrator*
BibInt	*Biblical Interpretation*
BR	*Biblical Research*
BTB	*Biblical Theology Bulletin*
BV	*Biblical Viewpoint*
BW	*The Biblical World: A Dictionary of Biblical Archaeology.* Edited by C. F. Pfeiffer. Grand Rapids, 1966
BAC	Biblioteca de autores cristianos
BCR	Biblioteca di cultura religiosa
HumTeo	Biblioteca humanística e teológica
BETL	Bibliotheca ephemeridum theologicarum lovaniensium
BHG	*Bibliotheca hagiographica Graece.* Brussels, 1977
BHL	*Bibliotheca hagiographica latina antiquae et mediae aetatis.* 2 vols. Brussels, 1898–1901
BHO	*Bibliotheca hagiographica orientalis.* Brussels, 1910
BMes	Bibliotheca mesopotamica
BO	*Bibliotheca orientalis*
BSac	*Bibliotheca sacra*
Teubner	Bibliotheca scriptorum graecorum et romanorum teubneriana
BibB	Biblische Beiträge
BN	*Biblische Notizen*
BibS(F)	Biblische Studien (Freiburg, 1895–)
BibS(N)	Biblische Studien (Neukirchen, 1951–)
BZ	*Biblische Zeitschrift*
BKAT	Biblischer Kommentar, Altes Testament. Edited by M. Noth and H. W. Wolff
BRL2	*Biblisches Reallexikon.* 2d ed. Edited by K. Galling. HAT 1/1. Tübingen, 1977
BHH	*Biblisch-historisches Handwörterbuch: Landeskunde, Geschichte, Religion, Kultur.* Edited by B. Reicke and L. Rost. 4 vols. Göttingen, 1962–1966
BLit	*Bibliothèque liturgique*
Bijdr	*Bijdragen: Tijdschrift voor filosofie en theologie*
BNTC	Black's New Testament Commentaries
BDF	Blass, F., A. Debrunner, and R. W. Funk. *A Greek Grammar of the New Testament and Other Early Christian Literature.* Chicago, 1961
Böhl	Böhl, F. M. Th. de Liagre. *Opera minora: Studies en bijdragen op Assyriologisch en Oudtestamentisch terrein.* Groningen, 1953
BBB	Bonner biblische Beiträge
BJ	*Bonner Jahrbücher*
B&R	*Books and Religion*
BAT	Die Botschaft des Alten Testaments
Bousset-Gressmann	Bousset, W., and H. Gressmann, *Die Religion des Judentums im späthellenistischen Zeitalter.* 3d ed. Tübingen, 1926
BJS	Brown Judaic Studies

BDB	Brown, F., S. R. Driver, and C. A. Briggs. *A Hebrew and English Lexicon of the Old Testament*. Oxford, 1907
BBB	*Bulletin de bibliographie biblique*
BCH	*Bulletin de correspondance hellénique*
BHEAT	*Bulletin d'histoire et d'exégèse de l'Ancien Testament*
BAGB	*Bulletin de l'Association G. Budé*
BIFAO	*Bulletin de l'Institut français d'archéologie orientale*
BSAA	*Bulletin de la Société archéologique d'Alexandrie*
BSAC	*Bulletin de la Société d'archéologie copte*
BLE	*Bulletin de littérature ecclésiastique*
BThAM	*Bulletin de théologie ancienne et médiévale*
BCPE	*Bulletin du Centre protestant d'études*
BBR	*Bulletin for Biblical Research*
BBS	*Bulletin of Biblical Studies*
BASOR	*Bulletin of the American Schools of Oriental Research*
BASORSup	Bulletin of the American Schools of Oriental Research: Supplement Series
BASP	*Bulletin of the American Society of Papyrologists*
BASPSup	Bulletin of the American Society of Papyrologists: Supplement
BAIAS	*Bulletin of the Anglo-Israel Archeological Society*
BCSR	*Bulletin of the Council on the Study of Religion*
BIOSCS	*Bulletin of the International Organization for Septuagint and Cognate Studies*
BIES	*Bulletin of the Israel Exploration Society (= Yediot)*
BJPES	*Bulletin of the Jewish Palestine Exploration Society*
BJRL	*Bulletin of the John Rylands University Library of Manchester*
BSOAS	*Bulletin of the School of Oriental and African Studies*
Burg	*Burgense*
BurH	*Buried History*
ByzF	*Byzantinische Forschungen*
ByzZ	*Byzantinische Zeitschrift*
Byzantion	*Byzantion*
CahRB	Cahiers de la Revue biblique
CRTL	Cahiers de la Revue théologique de Louvain
CaE	*Cahiers évangile*
CahT	Cahiers Théologiques
CBTJ	*Calvary Baptist Theological Journal*
CTJ	*Calvin Theological Journal*
CAH	Cambridge Ancient History
CBC	Cambridge Bible Commentary
CGTC	Cambridge Greek Testament Commentary
CGTSC	Cambridge Greek Testament for Schools and Colleges
CHJ	*Cambridge History of Judaism*. Ed. W. D. Davies and Louis Finkelstein. Cambridge, 1984–
CML	*Canaanite Myths and Legends*. Edited by G. R. Driver. Edinburgh, 1956. Edited by J. C. L. Gibson, 1978[2]
CTAED	*Canaanite Toponyms in Ancient Egyptian Documents*. S. Ahituv. Jerusalem, 1984

CJT	*Canadian Journal of Theology*
Car	*Carthagiensia*
CBQMS	Catholic Biblical Quarterly Monograph Series
CBQ	*Catholic Biblical Quarterly*
CHR	*Catholic Historical Review*
CBM	Chester Beatty Monographs
CSJH	Chicago Studies in the History of Judaism
ChrCent	*Christian Century*
ChrLit	*Christianity and Literature*
ChrEg	*Chronique d'Egypte*
CH	*Church History*
CQ	*Church Quarterly*
CQR	*Church Quarterly Review*
Chm	*Churchman*
CClCr	*Civiltà classica e cristiana*
CANE	*Civilizations of the Ancient Near East.* Edited by J. Sasson. 4 vols. New York, 1995
CF	*Classical Folia*
CJ	*Classical Journal*
CP	*Classical Philology*
CQ	*Classical Quarterly*
CW	*Classical World*
CWS	Classics of Western Spirituality. New York, 1978–
CPG	*Clavis patrum graecorum.* Edited by M. Geerard. 5 vols. Turnhout, 1974–1987
CPL	*Clavis patrum latinorum.* Edited by E. Dekkers. 2d ed. Steenbrugis, 1961
Coll	*Collationes*
ColT	*Collectanea theologica*
CAGN	*Collected Ancient Greek Novels.* Edited by B. P. Reardon. Berkeley, 1989
Budé	Collection des universités de France, publiée sous le patronage de l'Association Guillaume Budé
Colloq	*Colloquium*
COut	Commentaar op het Oude Testament
CAT	Commentaire de l'Ancien Testament
CNT	Commentaire du Nouveau Testament
CV	*Communio viatorum*
Cmio	*Communio: Commentarii internationales de ecclesia et theología*
Comm	*Communio*
CRINT	Compendia rerum iudaicarum ad Novum Testamentum
Comp	*Compostellanum*
CRAI	Comptes rendus de l'Académie des inscriptions et belles-lettres
CDME	*A Concise Dictionary of Middle Egyptian.* Edited by R. O. Faulkner. Oxford, 1962
CUL	*A Concordance of the Ugaritic Literature.* R. E. Whitaker. Cambridge, Mass., 1972
CTM	*Concordia Theological Monthly*

97

CTQ	*Concordia Theological Quarterly*
ConBOT	Coniectanea biblica: Old Testament Series
ConBNT	Coniectanea neotestamentica or Coniectanea biblica: New Testament Series
COS	*The Context of Scripture.* Edited by W. W. Hallo. 3 vols. Leiden, 1997–
CC	Continental Commentaries
Cont	*Continuum*
CBET	Contributions to Biblical Exegesis and Theology
CA	*Convivium assisiense*
CCath	Corpus Catholicorum
CCCM	Corpus Christianorum: Continuatio mediaevalis. Turnhout, 1969–
CCSG	Corpus Christianorum: Series graeca. Turnhout, 1977–
CCSL	Corpus Christianorum: Series latina. Turnhout, 1953–
CTA	*Corpus des tablettes en cunéiformes alphabétiques découvertes à Ras Shamra-Ugarit de 1929 à 1939.* Edited by A. Herdner. Mission de Ras Shamra 10. Paris, 1963
CIC	*Corpus inscriptionum chaldicarum*
CIG	*Corpus inscriptionum graecarum.* Edited by A. Boeckh. 4 vols. Berlin, 1828–1877
CII	*Corpus inscriptionum iudaicarum.* Edited by J. B. Frey. 2 vols. Rome, 1936–1952
CIJ	*Corpus inscriptionum judaicarum*
CIL	*Corpus inscriptionum latinarum*
CIS	*Corpus inscriptionum semiticarum*
CPJ	*Corpus papyrorum judaicorum.* Edited by V. Tcherikover. 3 vols. Cambridge, 1957–1964.
CSCO	Corpus scriptorum christianorum orientalium. Edited by I. B. Chabot et al. Paris, 1903–
CSEL	Corpus scriptorum ecclesiasticorum latinorum
CSHB	Corpus scriptorum historiae byzantinae
CSRB	*Council on the Study of Religion: Bulletin*
CAP	Cowley, A. E. *Aramaic Papyri of the Fifth Century B.C.* Oxford, 1923
CNS	*Cristianesimo nella storia*
CTR	*Criswell Theological Review*
CRBR	*Critical Review of Books in Religion*
Crux	*Crux*
CB	*Cultura bíblica*
CTU	*The Cuneiform Alphabetic Texts from Ugarit, Ras Ibn Hani, and Other Places.* Edited by M. Dietrich, O. Loretz, and J. Sanmartín. Münster, 1995.
RawlCu	*The Cuneiform Inscriptions of Western Asia.* Edited by H. C. Rawlinson. London, 1891
CT	*Cuneiform Texts from Babylonian Tablets in the British Museum*
CCT	*Cuneiform Texts from Cappadocian Tablets in the British Museum*
CurBS	*Currents in Research: Biblical Studies*
CurTM	*Currents in Theology and Mission*

DTT	*Dansk teologisk tidsskrift*
DSD	*Dead Sea Discoveries*
Di	*Dialog*
DHA	*Dialogues d'histoire ancienne*
DBT	*Dictionary of Biblical Theology.* Edited by X. Léon-Dufour. 2d ed. 1972
DCG	*Dictionary of Christ and the Gospels.* Edited by J. Hastings. 2 vols. Edinburgh, 1908
DCB	*Dictionary of Christian Biography.* Edited by W. Smith and H. Wace. 4 vols. London, 1877–1887
DCH	*Dictionary of Classical Hebrew.* Edited by D. J. A. Clines. Sheffield, 1993–
DDD	*Dictionary of Deities and Demons in the Bible.* Edited by K. van der Toorn, B. Becking, and P. W. van der Horst. Leiden, 1995
DJG	*Dictionary of Jesus and the Gospels.* Edited by J. B. Green and S. McKnight. Downers Grove, 1992
DLE	*Dictionary of Late Egyptian.* Edited by L. H. Lesko and B. S. Lesko. 4 vols. Berkeley, 1982–1989
DLNT	*Dictionary of the Later New Testament and Its Developments.* Edited by R. P. Martin and P. H. Davids. Downers Grove, 1997
DNWSI	*Dictionary of the North-West Semitic Inscriptions.* J. Hoftijzer and K. Jongeling. 2 vols. Leiden, 1995
DPL	*Dictionary of Paul and His Letters.* Edited by G. F. Hawthorne and R. P. Martin. Downers Grove, 1993
DACL	*Dictionnaire d'archéologie chrétienne et de liturgie.* Edited by F. Cabrol. 15 vols. Paris, 1907–1953
DB	*Dictionnaire de la Bible.* Edited by F. Vigouroux. 5 vols. 1895–1912
DBSup	*Dictionnaire de la Bible: Supplément.* Edited by L. Pirot and A. Robert. Paris, 1928–
DTC	*Dictionnaire de théologie catholique.* Edited by A. Vacant et al. 15 vols. Paris, 1903–1950
DISO	*Dictionnaire des inscriptions sémitiques de l'ouest.* Edited by Ch. F. Jean and J. Hoftijzer. Leiden, 1965
Did	*Didaskalia*
DBAT	*Dielheimer Blätter zum Alten Testament und seiner Rezeption in der Alten Kirche*
DJD	Discoveries in the Judaean Desert
DissAb	Dissertation Abstracts
DivThom	*Divus Thomas*
DPAC	*Dizionario patristico e di antichità cristiane.* Edited by A. di Berardino. 3 vols. Casale Monferrato, 1983–1988
DOTT	*Documents from Old Testament Times.* Edited by D. W. Thomas, London, 1958
DRev	*Downside Review*
DrewG	*Drew Gateway*
Duchesne	Duchesne, L., ed. *Le Liber pontificalis.* 2 vols. Paris, 1886, 1892. Reprinted with 3d vol. by C. Vogel. Paris, 1955–1957
DOP	*Dumbarton Oaks Papers*

99

DunRev	*Dunwoodie Review*
ECR	*Eastern Churches Review*
EMC	*Echos du monde classique/Classical Views*
EB	Echter Bibel
EfMex	*Efemerides mexicana*
EgT	*Eglise et théologie*
ECT	*Egyptian Coffin Texts.* Edited by A. de Buck and A. H. Gardiner. Chicago, 1935–1947
EA	El-Amarna tablets. According to the edition of J. A. Knudtzon. *Die el-Amarna-Tafeln.* Leipzig, 1908–1915. Reprint, Aalen, 1964. Continued in A. F. Rainey, *El-Amarna Tablets, 359–379.* 2d revised ed. Kevelaer, 1978
Elenchus	*Elenchus bibliographicus biblicus* of *Biblica,* Rome, 1985–
EnchBib	*Enchiridion biblicum*
Enc	*Encounter*
EncJud	*Encyclopaedia Judaica.* 16 vols. Jerusalem, 1972
EAEHL	*Encyclopedia of Archaeological Excavations in the Holy Land.* Edited by M. Avi-Yonah. 4 vols. Jerusalem, 1975
EEC	*Encyclopedia of Early Christianity.* Edited by E. Ferguson. 2d ed. New York, 1990
ER	*The Encyclopedia of Religion.* Edited by M. Eliade. 16 vols. New York, 1987
ERE	*Encyclopedia of Religion and Ethics.* Edited by J. Hastings. 13 vols. New York, 1908–1927. Reprint, 7 vols., 1951
EECh	*Encyclopedia of the Early Church.* Edited by A. di Berardino. Translated by A. Walford. New York, 1992
ETL	*Ephemerides theologicae lovanienses*
EEA	*L'epigrafia ebraica antica.* S. Moscati. Rome, 1951
Epiph	*Epiphany*
ERAS	*Epithètes royales akkadiennes et sumériennes.* M.-J. Seux. Paris, 1967
ErJb	*Eranos-Jahrbuch*
ErIsr	*Eretz-Israel*
ETS	Erfurter theologische Studien
EdF	Erträge der Forschung
EstAg	*Estudio Agustiniano*
EstBib	*Estudios bíblicos*
EstEcl	*Estudios eclesiásticos*
EFN	Estudios de filología neotestamentaria. Cordova, Spain, 1988–
EstMin	*Estudios mindonienses*
EstTeo	*Estudios teológicos*
EBib	*Etudes bibliques*
EPap	*Etudes de papyrologie*
EPRO	Etudes préliminaires aux religions orientales dans l'empire romain
ETR	*Etudes théologiques et religieuses*
EuroJTh	*European Journal of Theology*
EvJ	*Evangelical Journal*
EvQ	*Evangelical Quarterly*

100

EvK	Evangelische Kommentare
EvT	*Evangelische Theologie*
EKL	*Evangelisches Kirchenlexikon.* Edited by Erwin Fahlbusch et al. 4 vols. 3d ed. Göttingen, 1985–1996
EKKNT	Evangelisch-katholischer Kommentar zum Neuen Testament
ELKZ	*Evangelisch-Lutherische Kirchenzeitung*
Even-Shoshan	Even-Shoshan, A., ed. *A New Concordance of the Bible.* Jerusalem, 1977, 1983[4]
ExAud	*Ex auditu*
Exeg	*Exegetica* [Japanese]
EDNT	*Exegetical Dictionary of the New Testament.* Edited by H. Balz, G. Schneider. ET. Grand Rapids, 1990–1993
EHAT	Exegetisches Handbuch zum Alten Testament
ExpTim	*Expository Times*
FBBS	Facet Books, Biblical Series
FC	Fathers of the Church. Washington, D.C., 1947–
FCB	Feminist Companion to the Bible
FoiVie	*Foi et vie*
FO	*Folia orientalia*
FT	*Folia theologica*
FOTL	Forms of the Old Testament Literature
FB	Forschung zur Bibel
FiE	*Forschungen in Ephesos*
FF	*Forschungen und Fortschritte*
FAT	Forschungen zum Alten Testament
FRLANT	Forschungen zur Religion und Literatur des Alten und Neuen Testaments
ForFasc	*Forum Fascicles*
FBE	Forum for Bibelsk Eksegese
Foster, *Muses*	Foster, Benjamin R. *Before the Muses: An Anthology of Akkadian Literature.* 2 vols. Bethesda, 1993
FF	Foundations and Facets
FGH	*Die Fragmente der griechischen Historiker.* Edited by F. Jacoby. Leiden, 1954–1964
FHG	Fragmenta historicorum graecorum. Paris, 1841–1870
Fran	*Franciscanum*
FZPhTh	*Freiburger Zeitschrift für Philosophie und Theologie*
FMSt	Frühmittelalterliche Studien
Fund	*Fundamentum*
GTTOT	*The Geographical and Topographical Texts of the Old Testament.* Edited by J. J. Simons. Studia Francisci Scholten memoriae dicata 2. Leiden, 1959
GP	*Géographie de la Palestine.* F. M. Abel. 2 vols. Paris, 1933
GTT	*Gereformeerd theologisch tijdschrift*
GS	*Gesammelte Studien*
Gesenius, *Thesaurus*	Gesenius, W. *Thesaurus philologicus criticus linguae hebraeae et chaldaeae Veteris Testamenti.* Vols. 1–3. Leipzig, 1829–1842
GKC	*Gesenius' Hebrew Grammar.* Edited by E. Kautzsch. Translated by A. E. Cowley. 2d. ed. Oxford, 1910

101

Gn	*Gnomon*
GTA	Göttinger theologischer Arbeiten
GNS	*Good News Studies*
GCDS	*Graphic Concordance to the Dead Sea Scrolls.* Edited by J. H. Charlesworth et al. Tübingen, 1991
GR	*Greece and Rome*
GOTR	*Greek Orthodox Theological Review*
GRBS	*Greek, Roman, and Byzantine Studies*
L&N	*Greek-English Lexicon of the New Testament: Based on Semantic Domains.* Edited by J. P. Louw and E. A. Nida. 2d ed. New York, 1989
Greg	*Gregorianum*
GCS	Die griechische christliche Schriftsteller der ersten [drei] Jahrhunderte
GAG	*Grundriss der akkadischen Grammatik.* W. von Soden. 2d ed. Rome, 1969
GVG	*Grundriss der vergleichenden Grammatik der semitischen Sprachen.* C. Brockelmann, 2 vols. Berlin, 1908–1913. Reprint, Hildesheim, 1961
GAT	Grundrisse zum Alten Testament
GNT	Grundrisse zum Neuen Testament
GBS	Guides to Biblical Scholarship
HKL	*Handbuch der Keilschriftliteratur.* R. Borger. 3 vols. Berlin, 1967–1975
NE	*Handbuch der nordsemitischen Epigraphik.* Edited by M. Lidzbarski. Weimar, 1898. Reprint, Hildesheim, 1962
HO	Handbuch der Orientalistik
HAT	Handbuch zum Alten Testament
HNT	Handbuch zum Neuen Testament
HKAT	Handkommentar zum Alten Testament
HKNT	Handkommentar zum Neuen Testament
HBC	*Harper's Bible Commentary.* Edited by J. L. Mays et al. San Francisco, 1988.
HNTC	Harper's New Testament Commentaries
HBD	*HarperCollins Bible Dictionary.* Edited by P. J. Achtemeier et al. 2d ed. San Francisco, 1996
Harris	Harris, Z. S. *A Grammar of the Phoenician Language.* AOS 8. New Haven, 1936. Reprint, 1990
HDR	Harvard Dissertations in Religion
HSM	Harvard Semitic Monographs
HSS	Harvard Semitic Studies
HSCP	*Harvard Studies in Classical Philology*
HTR	*Harvard Theological Review*
HTS	Harvard Theological Studies
HRCS	Hatch, E. and H. A. Redpath. *Concordance to the Septuagint and Other Greek Versions of the Old Testament.* 2 vols. Oxford, 1897. Suppl., 1906. Reprint, 3 vols. in 2, Grand Rapids, 1983
HAR	*Hebrew Annual Review*
HS	*Hebrew Studies*

HUCA	*Hebrew Union College Annual*
HSAT	*Die Heilige Schrift des Alten Testaments.* Edited by E. Kautzsch and A. Bertholet. 4th ed. Tübingen, 1922–1923
Hell	*Hellenica: Recueil d'épigraphie, de numismatique et d'antiquités grecques*
Hen	*Henoch*
HTKNT	Herders theologischer Kommentar zum Neuen Testament
Herm	*Hermanthena*
HUT	Hermeneutische Untersuchungen zur Theologie
HvTSt	*Hervormde teologiese studies*
Hesperia	*Hesperia: Journal of the American School of Classical Studies at Athens*
HeyJ	*Heythrop Journal*
HibJ	*Hibbert Journal*
HTB	Histoire du texte biblique. Lausanne, 1996–
HR	*History of Religions*
HT	*History Today*
HTh	*Ho Theológos*
Hok	*Hokhma*
HolBD	*Holman Bible Dictionary.* Edited by T. C. Butler. Nashville, 1991
HSem	Horae semiticae. 9 vols. London, 1908–1912
HBT	*Horizons in Biblical Theology*
Hor	*Horizons*
Imm	*Immanuel*
IDS	*In die Skriflig*
IJT	*Indian Journal of Theology*
ICUR	*Inscriptiones christianae urbis Romae.* Edited by J. B. de Rossi. Rome, 1857–1888
IG	*Inscriptiones graecae.* Editio minor. Berlin, 1924–
ILCV	*Inscriptiones latinae christianae veteres.* Edited by E. Diehl. 2d ed. Berlin, 1961
ITP	Hayim Tadmor, *The Inscriptions of Tiglath-Pileser III, King of Assyria.* Jerusalem, 1994
ICC	International Critical Commentary
IESS	*International Encyclopedia of the Social Sciences.* Edited by D. L. Sills. New York, 1968–
ISBE	*International Standard Bible Encyclopedia.* Edited by G. W. Bromiley. 4 vols. Grand Rapids, 1979–1988
ITC	International Theological Commentary
IKaZ	*Internationale katholische Zeitschrift*
IKZ	*Internationale kirchliche Zeitschrift*
IZBG	*Internationale Zeitschriftenschau für Bibelwissenschaft und Grenzgebiete*
IATG²	Schwertner, Siegfried M. *Internationales Abkürzungsverzeichnis für Theologie und Grenzgebeite.* 2d ed. Berlin, 1992
Int	*Interpretation*
IBC	Interpretation: A Bible Commentary for Teaching and Preaching.

IB	*Interpreter's Bible.* Edited by G. A. Buttrick et al. 12 vols. New York, 1951–1957
IDB	*The Interpreter's Dictionary of the Bible.* Edited by G. A. Buttrick. 4 vols. Nashville, 1962
IDBSup	*Interpreter's Dictionary of the Bible: Supplementary Volume.* Edited by K. Crim. Nashville, 1976
IBHS	*An Introduction to Biblical Hebrew Syntax.* B. K. Waltke and M. O'Connor. Winona Lake, Indiana, 1990
Iran	*Iran*
Iraq	*Iraq*
IAR	Iraq Archaeological Reports
Irén	*Irénikon*
IBS	*Irish Biblical Studies*
ITQ	*Irish Theological Quarterly*
Isd	*Isidorianum*
IEJ	*Israel Exploration Journal*
IOS	*Israel Oriental Society*
IPN	*Die israelitischen Personennamen.* M. Noth. BWANT 3/10. Stuttgart, 1928. Reprint, Hildesheim, 1980
IRT	Issues in Religion and Theology
IstMitt	*Istanbuler Mitteilungen*
Istina	*Istina*
Itala	*Itala: Das Neue Testament in altlateinischer Überlieferung.* 4 vols. Berlin, 1938–1963
Iter	*Iter*
Itin (Portugal)	*Itinerarium* (Portugal)
Itin (Italy)	*Itinerarium* (Italy)
JEOL	*Jaarbericht van het Vooraziatisch-Egyptisch Gezelschap (Genootschap) Ex oriente lux*
Jahnow	Jahnow, J. *Das hebräische Leichenlied im Rahmen der Völkerdichtung.* Giessen, 1923
JdI	*Jahrbuch des deutschen archäologischen Instituts*
JAC	Jahrbuch für Antike und Christentum
JDT	*Jahrbuch für deutsche Theologie*
JET	*Jahrbuch für Evangelische Theologie*
JÖAI	*Jahreshefte des Österreichischen archäologischen Instituts*
Jastrow	Jastrow, M. *A Dictionary of the Targumim, the Talmud Babli and Yerushalmi, and the Midrashic Literature.* 2d ed. New York, 1903
Jeev	*Jeevadhara*
JBC	*Jerome Biblical Commentary.* Edited by R. E. Brown et al. Englewood Cliffs, 1968
JB	Jerusalem Bible
JAL	Jewish Apocryphal Literature Series
JBQ	*Jewish Bible Quarterly*
JDS	Jewish Desert Studies
JE	*The Jewish Encyclopedia.* Edited by I. Singer. 12 vols. New York, 1925
JLA	*Jewish Law Annual*

JQR	*Jewish Quarterly Review*
JQRMS	Jewish Quarterly Review Monograph Series
JSQ	*Jewish Studies Quarterly*
JWSTP	*Jewish Writings of the Second Temple Period: Apocrypha, Pseudepigrapha, Qumran Sectarian Writings, Philo, Josephus.* Edited by M. E. Stone. CRINT 2.2. Assen/Philadelphia, 1984
Jian Dao	*Jian Dao*
JHNES	Johns Hopkins Near Eastern Studies
JLCRS	Jordan Lectures in Comparative Religion Series
JJT	*Josephinum Journal of Theology*
Joüon	Joüon, P. *A Grammar of Biblical Hebrew.* Translated and revised by T. Muraoka. 2 vols. Subsidia biblica 14/1–2. Rome, 1991
JA	*Journal asiatique*
JSSR	*Journal for the Scientific Study of Religion*
JSJ	*Journal for the Study of Judaism in the Persian, Hellenistic, and Roman Periods*
JSNT	*Journal for the Study of the New Testament*
JSNTSup	Journal for the Study of the New Testament: Supplement Series
JSOT	*Journal for the Study of the Old Testament*
JSOTSup	Journal for the Study of the Old Testament: Supplement Series
JSP	*Journal for the Study of the Pseudepigrapha*
JSPSup	Journal for the Study of the Pseudepigrapha: Supplement Series
JTC	*Journal for Theology and the Church*
JAAL	*Journal of Afroasiatic Languages*
ZAC	*Journal of Ancient Christianity*
JACiv	*Journal of Ancient Civilizations*
JAS	*Journal of Asian Studies*
JBR	*Journal of Bible and Religion*
JBL	*Journal of Biblical Literature*
JCS	*Journal of Cuneiform Studies*
JECS	*Journal of Early Christian Studies*
JEH	*Journal of Ecclesiastical History*
JES	*Journal of Ecumenical Studies*
JEA	*Journal of Egyptian Archaeology*
JFSR	*Journal of Feminist Studies in Religion*
JHS	*Journal of Hellenic Studies*
JJA	*Journal of Jewish Art*
JJS	*Journal of Jewish Studies*
JJP	*Journal of Juristic Papyrology*
JMedHist	*Journal of Medieval History*
JMES	*Journal of Middle Eastern Studies*
JMS	*Journal of Mithraic Studies*
JNES	*Journal of Near Eastern Studies*
JNSL	*Journal of Northwest Semitic Languages*
JPJ	*Journal of Progressive Judaism*
JR	*Journal of Religion*

105

JRE	*Journal of Religious Ethics*
JRH	*Journal of Religious History*
JRelS	*Journal of Religious Studies*
JRT	*Journal of Religious Thought*
JRitSt	*Journal of Ritual Studies*
JRS	*Journal of Roman Studies*
JSS	*Journal of Semitic Studies*
JSem	*Journal of Semitics*
JAAR	*Journal of the American Academy of Religion*
JAOS	*Journal of the American Oriental Society*
JANESCU	*Journal of the Ancient Near Eastern Society of Columbia University*
JESHO	*Journal of the Economic and Social History of the Orient*
JETS	*Journal of the Evangelical Theological Society*
JHI	*Journal of the History of Ideas*
JPOS	*Journal of the Palestine Oriental Society*
JRAS	*Journal of the Royal Asiatic Society*
JSSEA	*Journal of the Society for the Study of Egyptian Antiquities*
JSOR	*Journal of the Society of Oriental Research*
JTS	*Journal of Theological Studies*
JTSA	*Journal of Theology for Southern Africa*
JOTT	*Journal of Translation and Textlinguistics*
Jud	*Judaica*
Judaica	*Judaica: Beiträge zum Verständnis des jüdischen Schicksals in Vergangenheit und Gegenwart*
Judaism	*Judaism*
JDS	Judean Desert Studies
JSHRZ	*Jüdische Schriften aus hellenistisch-römischer Zeit*
Kairós	*Kairós*
KI	*Kanaanäische Inschriften (Moabitisch, Althebraisch, Phonizisch, Punisch).* Edited by M. Lidzbarski. Giessen, 1907
KAI	*Kanaanäische und aramäische Inschriften.* H. Donner and W. Röllig. 2d ed. Wiesbaden, 1966–1969
KK	*Katorikku Kenkyu*
K&D	Keil, C. F., and F. Delitzsch, *Biblical Commentary on the Old Testament.* Translated by J. Martin et al. 25 vols. Edinburgh, 1857–1878. Reprint, 10 vols., Peabody, Mass., 1996
KTU	*Die keilalphabetischen Texte aus Ugarit.* Edited by M. Dietrich, O. Loretz, and J. Sanmartín. AOAT 24/1. Neukirchen-Vluyn, 1976. 2d enlarged ed. of *KTU: The Cuneiform Alphabetic Texts from Ugarit, Ras Ibn Hani, and Other Places.* Edited by M. Dietrich, O. Loretz, and J. Sanmartín. Münster, 1995 (= *CTU*)
KB	*Keilinschriftliche Bibliothek.* Edited by E. Schrader. 6 vols. Berlin, 1889–1915
KAH 1	*Keilschrifttexte aus Assur historischen Inhalts.* L. Messerschmidt. Vol. 1. WVDOG 16. Leipzig, 1911
KAH 2	*Keilschrifttexte aus Assur historischen Inhalts.* O. Schroeder. Vol. 2. WVDOG 37. Leipzig, 1922

106

KAR	*Keilschrifttexte aus Assur religiösen Inhalts.* Edited by E. Ebeling. Leipzig, 1919–1923
KBo	*Keilschrifttexte aus Boghazköi.* WVDOG 30, 36, 68–70, 72–73, 77–80, 82–86, 89–90. Leipzig, 1916–
KUB	*Keilschrifturkunden aus Boghazköi*
Kerux	*Kerux*
KD	*Kerygma und Dogma*
KS	*Kirjath-Sepher*
KlPauly	*Der kleine Pauly*
KlT	Kleine Texte
KBL	Koehler, L., and W. Baumgartner, *Lexicon in Veteris Testamenti libros.* 2d ed. Leiden, 1958
HALOT	Koehler, L., W. Baumgartner, and J. J. Stamm, *The Hebrew and Aramaic Lexicon of the Old Testament.* Translated and edited under the supervision of M. E. J. Richardson. 4 vols. Leiden, 1994–1999
HAL	Koehler, L., W. Baumgartner, and J. J. Stamm. *Hebräisches und aramäisches Lexikon zum Alten Testament.* Fascicles 1–5, 1967–1995 (KBL3). ET: *HALOT*
KVRG	Kölner Veroffentlichungen zur Religionsgeschichte
KAT	Kommentar zum Alten Testament
KBANT	Kommentare und Beiträge zum Alten und Neuen Testament
KEK	Kritisch-exegetischer Kommentar über das Neue Testament (Meyer-Kommentar)
Kuhn	Kuhn, K. G. *Konkordanz zu den Qumrantexten.* Göttingen, 1960
KHC	Kurzer Hand-Commentar zum Alten Testament
Lane	Lane, E. W. *An Arabic-English Lexicon.* 8 vols. London. Reprint, 1968
Laur	*Laurentianum*
LTP	*Laval théologique et philosophique*
LD	Lectio divina
LSS	*Leipziger semitische Studien*
Leš	*Lešonénu*
Levant	*Levant*
LTK	*Lexicon für Theologie und Kirche*
LIMC	*Lexicon iconographicum mythologiae classicae.* Edited by H. C. Ackerman and J.-R. Gisler. 8 vols. Zurich, 1981–1997
LexSyr	*Lexicon syriacum.* C. Brockelmann. 2d ed. Halle, 1928
LÄ	*Lexikon der Ägyptologie.* Edited by W. Helck, E. Otto, and W. Westendorf. Wiesbaden, 1972
LTQ	*Lexington Theological Quarterly*
LASBF	*Liber annuus Studii biblici franciscani*
LCC	Library of Christian Classics. Philadelphia, 1953–
LEC	Library of Early Christianity
LSJ	Liddell, H. G., R. Scott, H. S. Jones, *A Greek-English Lexicon.* 9th ed. with revised supplement. Oxford, 1996
LB	*Linguistica Biblica*
List	*Listening: Journal of Religion and Culture*
LAE	*Literature of Ancient Egypt.* W. K. Simpson. New Haven, 1972

LJPSTT	Literature of the Jewish People in the Period of the Second Temple and the Talmud
LAPO	Littératures anciennes du Proche-Orient
LW	*Living Word*
LCL	Loeb Classical Library
LS	*Louvain Studies*
Lum	*Lumen*
LumVie	*Lumière et vie*
LUÅ	Lunds universitets årsskrift
LQ	*Lutheran Quarterly*
LR	*Lutherische Rundschau*
Maarav	*Maarav*
MCuS	*Manchester Cuneiform Studies*
Mandl	Mandelkern, S. *Veteris Testamenti concordantiae hebraicae atque chaldaicae, etc.* Reprint, 1925. 2d ed. Jerusalem, 1967
MARI	*Mari: Annales de recherches interdisciplinaires*
MSJ	*The Master's Seminary Journal*
MSL	*Materialien zum sumerischen Lexikon.* Benno Landsberger, ed.
McCQ	*McCormick Quarterly*
Med	*Medellin*
MS	*Mediaeval Studies*
MEFR	*Mélanges d'archéologie et d'histoire de l'école français de Rome*
MUSJ	*Mélanges de l'Université Saint-Joseph*
MScRel	*Mélanges de science religieuse*
MelT	*Melita theologica*
MPAIBL	Mémoires présentés à l'Academie des inscriptions et belles-lettres
MAAR	Memoirs of the American Academy in Rome
MDB	*Mercer Dictionary of the Bible.* Edited by W. E. Mills. Macon, 1990
MBS	Message of Biblical Spirituality
MTSR	*Method and Theory in the Study of Religion*
Mid-Stream	*Mid-Stream*
Mils	*Milltown Studies*
MCom	*Miscelánea Comillas*
MEAH	*Miscelánea de estudios arabes y hebraicos*
MAOG	Mitteilungen der Altorientalischen Gesellschaft
MDOG	Mitteilungen der Deutschen Orient-Gesellschaft
MVAG	Mitteilungen der Vorderasiatisch-ägyptischen Gesellschaft. Vols. 1–44. 1896–1939
MDAI	*Mitteilungen des Deutschen archäologischen Instituts*
MIOF	*Mitteilungen des Instituts für Orientforschung*
MSU	Mitteilungen des Septuaginta-Unternehmens
MNTC	Moffatt New Testament Commentary
MGWJ	*Monatschrift für Geschichte und Wissenschaft des Judentums*
MdB	*Le Monde de la Bible*
HUCM	Monographs of the Hebrew Union College
MAMA	*Monumenta Asiae Minoris Antiqua.* Manchester and London, 1928–1993

108

MM	Moulton, J. H., and G. Milligan. *The Vocabulary of the Greek Testament*. London, 1930. Reprint, Peabody, Mass., 1997
MBPF	Münchener Beiträge zur Papyrusforschung und antiken Rechtsgeschichte
MTZ	*Münchener theologische Zeitschrift*
Mursurillo	Mursurillo, H., ed. and trans. *The Acts of the Christian Martyrs*. Oxford, 1972
Mus	*Muséon: Revue d'études orientales*
MH	*Museum helveticum*
NAWG	*Nachrichten (von) der Akademie der Wissenschaften in Göttingen*
NHC	Nag Hammadi Codices
NHL	*Nag Hammadi Library in English*. Edited by J. M. Robinson. 4th rev. ed. Leiden, 1996
NHS	Nag Hammadi Studies
NETR	*Near East School of Theology Theological Review*
NGTT	*Nederduitse gereformeerde teologiese tydskrif*
NedTT	*Nederlands theologisch tijdschrift*
Nem	*Nemalah*
Neot	*Neotestamentica*
NEchtB	Neue Echter Bibel
NJahrb	*Neue Jahrbücher für das klassiche Altertum (1898–1925); Neue Jahrbücher für Wissenschaft und Jugendbildung (1925–1936)*
NKZ	*Neue kirchliche Zeitschrift*
NTD	Das Neue Testament Deutsch
DNP	*Der neue Pauly: Enzyklopädie der Antike*. Edited by H. Cancik and H. Schneider. Stuttgart, 1996–
NTAbh	Neutestamentliche Abhandlungen
NTF	Neutestamentliche Forschungen
NAC	New American Commentary
NBD[2]	*New Bible Dictionary*. Edited by J. D. Douglas and N. Hillyer. 2d ed. Downers Grove, 1982
NBf	*New Blackfrairs*
NCE	*New Catholic Encyclopedia*. Edited by W. J. McDonald et al. 15 vols. New York, 1967
NCB	New Century Bible
NewDocs	*New Documents Illustrating Early Christianity*. Edited by G. H. R. Horsley and S. Llewelyn. North Ryde, N.S.W., 1981–
NEAEHL	*The New Encyclopedia of Archaeological Excavations in the Holy Land*. Edited by E. Stern. 4 vols. Jerusalem, 1993
NFT	New Frontiers in Theology
NIBCNT	New International Biblical Commentary on the New Testament
NIBCOT	New International Biblical Commentary on the Old Testament
NICNT	New International Commentary on the New Testament
NICOT	New International Commentary on the Old Testament
NIDBA	*New International Dictionary of Biblical Archaeology*. Edited by E. M. Blaiklock and R. K. Harrison. Grand Rapids, 1983
NIDNTT	*New International Dictionary of New Testament Theology*. Edited by C. Brown. 4 vols. Grand Rapids, 1975–1985

109

NIDOTTE	*New International Dictionary of Old Testament Theology and Exegesis.* Edited by W. A. VanGemeren. 5 vols. Grand Rapids, 1997
NIDB	*New International Dictionary of the Bible.* Edited by J. D. Douglas and M. C. Tenney. Grand Rapids, 1987
NIGTC	New International Greek Testament Commentary
NIB	*The New Interpreter's Bible*
NJBC	*The New Jerome Biblical Commentary.* Edited by R. E. Brown et al. Englewood Cliffs, 1990
NTA	*New Testament Abstracts*
NTG	New Testament Guides
NTGF	New Testament in the Greek Fathers
NTL	New Testament Library
NTS	*New Testament Studies*
NTTS	New Testament Tools and Studies
NPNF[1]	*Nicene and Post-Nicene Fathers,* Series 1
NPNF[2]	*Nicene and Post-Nicene Fathers,* Series 2
NTT	*Norsk Teologisk Tidsskrift*
Notes	*Notes on Translation*
NRTh	*La nouvelle revue théologique*
NABU	*Nouvelles assyriologiques breves et utilitaires*
NV	*Nova et vetera*
NovT	*Novum Testamentum*
NTOA	Novum Testamentum et Orbis Antiquus
NovTSup	Novum Testamentum Supplements
NuMu	*Nuevo mundo*
Numen	*Numen: International Review for the History of Religions*
NumC	*Numismatic Chronicle*
ÖTK	Ökumenischer Taschenbuch-Kommentar
OTA	*Old Testament Abstracts*
OTE	*Old Testament Essays*
OTG	Old Testament Guides
OTL	Old Testament Library
OTP	*Old Testament Pseudepigrapha.* Edited by J. H. Charlesworth. 2 vols. New York, 1983
OTS	Old Testament Studies
OiC	*One in Christ*
OBO	Orbis biblicus et orientalis
OrAnt	*Oriens antiquus*
OrChr	*Oriens christianus*
OrSyr	*L'orient syrien*
OIC	*Oriental Institute Communications*
OIP	Oriental Institute Publications
OrChrAn	Orientalia christiana analecta
OCP	*Orientalia christiana periodica*
OLA	Orientalia lovaniensia analecta
OLP	Orientalia lovaniensia periodica
Or	*Orientalia* (NS)
OLZ	*Orientalistische Literaturzeitung*

110

OGIS	*Orientis graeci inscriptiones selectae.* Edited by W. Dittenberger. 2 vols. Leipzig, 1903–1905
Orita	*Orita*
ÖBS	Österreichische biblische Studien
OtSt	*Oudtestamentische Studiën*
OBT	Overtures to Biblical Theology
OCD	*Oxford Classical Dictionary.* Edited by S. Hornblower and A. Spawforth. 3d ed. Oxford, 1996
OCT	Oxford Classical Texts/Scriptorum classicorum bibliotheca oxoniensis
ODCC	*The Oxford Dictionary of the Christian Church.* Edited by F. L. Cross and E. A. Livingstone. 2d ed. Oxford, 1983
OECT	Oxford Early Christian Texts. Edited by H. Chadwick. Oxford, 1970–
OCuT	Oxford Editions of Cuneiform Texts
OEANE	*The Oxford Encyclopedia of Archaeology in the Near East.* Edited by E. M. Meyers. New York, 1997
Pacifica	*Pacifica*
PRU	*Le palais royal d'Ugarit*
PJ	*Palästina-Jahrbuch*
PEFQS	Palestine Exploration Fund Quarterly Statement
PEQ	*Palestine Exploration Quarterly*
PDM	*Papyri demoticae magicae.* Demotic texts in *PGM* corpus as collated in H. D. Betz, ed. *The Greek Magical Papyri in Translation, including the Demotic Spells.* Chicago, 1996
PGM	*Papyri graecae magicae: Die griechischen Zauberpapyri.* Edited by K. Preisendanz. Berlin, 1928
PapyCast	Papyrologica Castroctaviana, Studia et textus. Barcelona, 1967–
Parab	*Parabola*
ParOr	*Parole de l'orient*
PaVi	*Parole di vita*
PGL	*Patristic Greek Lexicon.* Edited by G. W. H. Lampe. Oxford, 1968
PTS	Patristische Texte und Studien
PG	Patrologia graeca [= Patrologiae cursus completus: Series graeca]. Edited by J.-P. Migne. 162 vols. Paris, 1857–1886
PL	Patrologia latina [= Patrologiae cursus completus: Series latina]. Edited by J.-P. Migne. 217 vols. Paris, 1844–1864
PO	Patrologia orientalis
PS	Patrologia syriaca. Rev. ed. I. Ortiz de Urbina. Rome, 1965
PW	Pauly, A. F. *Paulys Realencyclopädie der classischen Altertumswissenschaft.* New edition G. Wissowa. 49 vols. Munich, 1980
PNTC	Pelican New Testament Commentaries
PSTJ	*Perkins (School of Theology) Journal*
PerTeol	*Perspectiva teológica*
PRSt	*Perspectives in Religious Studies*
Per	*Perspectives*

Phil	*Philologus*
Phon	*Phonetica*
PTMS	Pittsburgh Theological Monograph Series
Pneuma	*Pneuma: Journal for the Society of Pentecostal Studies*
POut	De Prediking van het Oude Testament
Presb	*Presbyterion*
PSB	*Princeton Seminary Bulletin*
ProEccl	*Pro ecclesia*
PAAJR	*Proceedings of the American Academy of Jewish Research*
PIBA	Proceedings of the Irish Biblical Association
PIASH	Proceedings of the Israel Academy of Sciences and Humanities
Proof	*Prooftexts: A Journal of Jewish Literary History*
Protest	*Protestantesimo*
PzB	*Protokolle zur Bibel*
Proy	*Proyección*
PVTG	Pseudepigrapha Veteris Testamenti Graece
Qad	*Qadmoniot*
QD	Quaestiones disputatae
QDAP	*Quarterly of the Department of Antiquities in Palestine*
QR	*Quarterly Review*
Quasten	Quasten, J. *Patrology.* 4 vols. Westminster, 1953–1986
QC	*Qumran Chronicle*
RS	Ras Shamra
RSP	*Ras Shamra Parallels*
RdT	*Rassegna di teologia*
RE	*Realencyklopädie für protestantische Theologie und Kirche*
RlA	*Reallexikon der Assyriologie.* Edited by Erich Ebeling et al. Berlin, 1928–
RÄR	*Reallexikon der ägyptischen Religionsgeschichte.* H. Bonnet. Berlin, 1952
RLV	*Reallexikon der Vorgeschichte.* Edited by M. Ebert. Berlin, 1924–1932
RAC	*Reallexikon für Antike und Christentum.* Edited by T. Kluser et al. Stuttgart, 1950–
RechBib	Recherches bibliques
RechPap	*Recherches de papyrologie*
RSR	*Recherches de science religieuse*
RTAM	*Recherches de théologie ancienne et médiévale*
RANE	Records of the Ancient Near East
RefLitM	*Reformed Liturgy and Music*
RefR	*Reformed Review*
RTR	*Reformed Theological Review*
RNT	Regensburger Neues Testament
RST	Regensburger Studien zur Theologie
RelSoc	*Religion and Society*
RelArts	Religion and the Arts
R&T	*Religion and Theology*

112

RGG	*Religion in Geschichte und Gegenwart.* Edited by K. Galling. 7 vols. 3d ed. Tübingen, 1957–1965
RelEd	*Religious Education*
RelS	*Religious Studies*
RelStTh	*Religious Studies and Theology*
RelSRev	*Religious Studies Review*
RES	*Répertoire d'épigraphie sémitique*
ResQ	*Restoration Quarterly*
RevExp	*Review and Expositor*
RR	*Review of Religion*
RRelRes	*Review of Religious Research*
RBB	*Revista biblica brasileira*
RevistB	*Revista bíblica*
RCT	*Revista catalana de teología*
RCB	*Revista de cultura bíblica*
RIBLA	*Revista de interpretación bíblica latino-americana*
RSO	*Revista degli studi orientali*
REB	*Revista eclesiástica brasileira*
RET	*Revista española de teología*
RAr	*Revue archéologique*
RBPH	*Revue belge de philologie et d'histoire*
RBén	*Revue bénédictine*
RB	*Revue biblique*
RA	*Revue d'assyriologie et d'archéologie orientale*
REg	*Revue d'égyptologie*
RHE	*Revue d'histoire ecclésiastique*
RHPR	*Revue d'histoire et de philosophie religieuses*
RHR	*Revue de l'histoire des religions*
RUO	*Revue de l'université d'Ottawa*
RevPhil	*Revue de philologie*
RevQ	*Revue de Qumran*
RSém	*Revue de sémitique*
RTP	*Revue de théologie et de philosophie*
REA	*Revue des études anciennes*
REAug	*Revue des études augustiniennes*
REG	*Revue des études grecques*
REJ	*Revue des études juives*
RES	*Revue des études sémitiques*
RSPT	*Revue des sciences philosophiques et théologiques*
RevScRel	*Revue des sciences religieuses*
RHA	*Revue hittite et asianique*
RIDA	*Revue internationale des droits de l'antiquité*
RRef	*La revue réformée*
RTL	*Revue théologique de Louvain*
RThom	*Revue thomiste*
RStB	*Ricerche storico bibliche*
RivB	*Rivista biblica italiana*
RSO	*Rivista degli studi orientali*

RivSR	*Rivista di scienze religiose*
RSC	*Rivista di studi classici*
RSF	*Rivista di studi fenici*
RocT	*Roczniki teologiczne*
RomBarb	*Romanobarbarica*
RQ	*Römische Quartalschrift für christliche Altertumskunde und Kirchengeschichte*
RoMo	Rowohlts Monographien
RIMA	The Royal Inscriptions of Mesopotamia, Assyrian Periods
RIMB	The Royal Inscriptions of Mesopotamia, Babylonian Periods
RIME	The Royal Inscriptions of Mesopotamia, Early Periods
RIM	The Royal Inscriptions of Mesopotamia Project. Toronto
RIMS	The Royal Inscriptions of Mesopotamia, Supplements
RISA	*Royal Inscriptions of Sumer and Akkad.* Edited by G. A. Barton. New Haven, 1929
RBL	*Ruch biblijny i liturgiczny*
SP	Sacra pagina
SacEr	*Sacris erudiri: Jaarboek voor Godsdienstwetenschappen*
Salm	*Salmanticensis*
SB	*Sammelbuch griechischer Urkunden aus Aegypten.* Edited by F. Preisigke et al. Vols. 1– , 1915–
SAQ	Sammlung ausgewählter Kirchen- und dogmengeschichtlicher Quellenschriften
Sap	*Sapienza*
SJOT	*Scandinavian Journal of the Old Testament*
Schol	*Scholastik*
SQAW	Schriften und Quellen der alten Welt
SThU	*Schweizerische theologische Umschau*
SThZ	*Schweizerische theologische Zeitschrift*
ScEs	*Science et esprit*
ScEccl	*Sciences ecclésiastiques*
SJT	*Scottish Journal of Theology*
SFulg	*Scripta fulgentina*
ScrHier	Scripta hierosolymitana
ScrTh	*Scripta theologica*
ScrVict	*Scriptorium victoriense*
Scr	*Scripture*
ScrB	*Scripture Bulletin*
ScrC	*Scripture in Church*
ScC	*La scuola cattolica*
SecCent	Second Century
Sef	*Sefarad*
Semeia	*Semeia*
SemeiaSt	Semeia Studies
SSS	Semitic Study Series
Sem	*Semitica*
SMBen	Série monographique de Benedictina: Section paulinienne
STRev	*Sewanee Theological Review*
Shofar	*Shofar*

114

SIDIC	*SIDIC* (Journal of the Service internationale de documentation judeo-chrétienne)
SDAW	Sitzungen der deutschen Akademie der Wissenschaften zu Berlin
SHAW	Sitzungen der heidelberger Akademie der Wissenschaften
SÖAW	Sitzungen der österreichischen Akademie der Wissenschaften in Wien
SBAW	Sitzungsberichte der bayerischen Akademie der Wissenschaften
SPAW	Sitzungsberichte der preussischen Akademie der Wissenschaften
SK	*Skrif en kerk*
Sobornost	*Sobornost*
SWBA	Social World of Biblical Antiquity
SOTSMS	Society for Old Testament Studies Monograph Series
SNTSMS	Society for New Testament Studies Monograph Series
SBL	Society of Biblical Literature
SBLABS	Society of Biblical Literature Archaeology and Biblical Studies
SBLBAC	Society of Biblical Literature The Bible and American Culture
SBLBMI	Society of Biblical Literature The Bible and Its Modern Interpreters
SBLBSNA	Society of Biblical Literature Biblical Scholarship in North America
SBLCP	Society of Biblical Literature Centennial Publications
SBLDS	Society of Biblical Literature Dissertation Series
SBLEJL	Society of Biblical Literature Early Judaism and Its Literature
SBLMasS	Society of Biblical Literature Masoretic Studies
SBLMS	Society of Biblical Literature Monograph Series
SBLNTGF	Society of Biblical Literature The New Testament in the Greek Fathers
SBLRBS	Society of Biblical Literature Resources for Biblical Study
SBLSP	*Society of Biblical Literature Seminar Papers*
SBLSCS	Society of Biblical Literature Septuagint and Cognate Studies
SBLSBS	Society of Biblical Literature Sources for Biblical Study
SBLTT	Society of Biblical Literature Texts and Translations
SBLSymS	Society of Biblical Literature Symposium Series
SBLWAW	Society of Biblical Literature Writings from the Ancient World
Sound	*Soundings*
SB	Sources bibliques
SC	Sources chrétiennes. Paris: Cerf, 1943–
SwJT	*Southwestern Journal of Theology*
Spec	*Speculum*
SLJT	*St. Luke's Journal of Theology*
SVTQ	*St. Vladimir's Theological Quarterly*
SAA	State Archives of Assyria
SAAB	*State Archives of Assyria Bulletin*
SAAS	State Archives of Assyria Studies
StZ	Stimmen der Zeit

115

SVF	*Stoicorum veterum fragmenta.* H. von Arnim. 4 vols. Leipzig, 1903–1924
Str-B	Strack, H. L., and P. Billerbeck. *Kommentar zum Neuen Testament aus Talmud und Midrasch.* 6 vols. Munich, 1922–1961
Str	*Stromata*
SMSR	*Studi e materiali di storia delle religioni*
SEL	*Studi epigrafici e linguistici*
SCHNT	Studia ad corpus hellenisticum Novi Testamenti
SA	Studia anselmiana
StudBib	Studia Biblica
StC	Studia catholica
SEAug	Studia ephemeridis Augustinianum
SE	*Studia evangelica I, II, III* (= TU 73 [1959], 87 [1964], 88 [1964]. etc.)
SVTP	Studia in Veteris Testamenti pseudepigraphica
SJ	Studia judaica
StudMon	Studia monastica
StudNeot	Studia neotestamentica
StudOr	Studia orientalia
SPap	*Studia papyrologica*
StPat	*Studia patavina*
StPatr	Studia patristica
SPhilo	*Studia philonica*
StPB	Studia post-biblica
SSN	Studia semitica neerlandica
StSin	Studia Sinaitica
Su	*Studia theologica varsaviensia*
ST	*Studia theologica*
SANT	Studien zum Alten und Neuen Testaments
SNT	Studien zum Neuen Testament
SNTSU	Studien zum Neuen Testament und seiner Umwelt
SUNT	Studien zur Umwelt des Neuen Testaments
SD	Studies and Documents
StABH	Studies in American Biblical Hermeneutics
SAOC	Studies in Ancient Oriental Civilizations
SAC	Studies in Antiquity and Christianity
SBA	Studies in Biblical Archaeology
SBT	Studies in Biblical Theology
SCH	Studies in Church History
SCR	*Studies in Comparative Religion*
SHT	Studies in Historical Theology
SSEJC	*Studies in Early Judaism and Christianity*
SJLA	Studies in Judaism in Late Antiquity
StOR	Studies in Oriental Religions
SR	*Studies in Religion*
SHR	Studies in the History of Religions (supplement to *Numen*)
SHANE	Studies in the History of the Ancient Near East
STDJ	*Studies on the Texts of the Desert of Judah*

SBFLA	*Studii biblici Franciscani liber annus*
SMT	*Studii Montis Regii*
SNTA	Studiorum Novi Testamenti Auxilia
St	*Studium*
STJ	*Stulos Theological Journal*
SBS	Stuttgarter Bibelstudien
SBAB	Stuttgarter biblische Aufsatzbände
SBB	Stuttgarter biblische Beiträge
SBM	Stuttgarter biblische Monographien
SKKNT	Stuttgarter kleiner Kommentar, Neues Testament
SubBi	*Subsidia biblica*
Sumer	*Sumer: A Journal of Archaeology and History in Iraq*
SL	*Sumerisches Lexikon.* Edited by A. Deimel. 8 vols. Rome, 1928–1950
PWSup	Supplement to PW
NovTSup	Supplements to Novum Testamentum
VTSup	Supplements to Vetus Testamentum
SEG	Supplementum epigraphicum graecum
SEÅ	*Svensk exegetisk årsbok*
STK	*Svensk teologisk kvartalskrift*
SIG	*Sylloge inscriptionum graecarum.* Edited by W. Dittenberger. 4 vols. 3d ed. Leipzig, 1915–1924
SymBU	Symbolae biblicae upsalienses
SO	Symbolae osloenses
Tarbiz	*Tarbiz*
TA	*Tel Aviv*
TI	*Teologia iusi*
Teol	*Teología*
TV	*Teología y vida*
TRSR	Testi e ricerche di scienze religiose
TGI	*Textbuch zur Geschichte Israels.* Edited by K. Galling. 2d ed. Tübingen, 1968
TUAT	*Texte aus der Umwelt des Alten Testaments.* Edited by Otto Kaiser. Gütersloh, 1984–
T&K	*Texte & Kontexte*
TSAJ	Texte und Studien zum antiken Judentum
TU	Texte und Untersuchungen
TUGAL	Texte und Untersuchungen zur Geschichte der altchristlichen Literatur
TCL	Textes cunéiformes. Musée du Louvre
TS	Texts and Studies
TCS	Texts from Cuneiform Sources
Text	*Textus*
Them	*Themelios*
ThViat	*Theologia viatorum*
Theol	*Theologica*
TDNT	*Theological Dictionary of the New Testament.* Edited by G. Kittel and G. Friedrich. Translated by G. W. Bromiley. 10 vols. Grand Rapids, 1964–1976

TDOT	*Theological Dictionary of the Old Testament.* Edited by G. J. Botterweck and H. Ringgren. Translated by J. T. Willis, G. W. Bromiley, and D. E. Green. 8 vols. Grand Rapids, 1974–
TTE	*The Theological Educator*
TLNT	*Theological Lexicon of the New Testament.* C. Spicq. Translated and edited by J. D. Ernest. 3 vols. Peabody, Mass., 1994
TLOT	*Theological Lexicon of the Old Testament.* Edited by E. Jenni, with assistance from C. Westermann. Translated by M. E. Biddle. 3 vols. Peabody, Mass., 1997
TS	*Theological Studies*
TWOT	*Theological Wordbook of the Old Testament.* Edited by R. L. Harris, G. L. Archer Jr. 2 vols. Chicago, 1980
ThH	Théologie historique
TGl	*Theologie und Glaube*
TP	*Theologie und Philosophie*
Theo	*Theologika*
TPQ	*Theologisch-praktische Quartalschrift*
ThT	*Theologisch tijdschrift*
TBei	*Theologische Beiträge*
TBl	*Theologische Blätter*
TB	Theologische Bücherei: Neudrucke und Berichte aus dem 20. Jahrhundert
TF	*Theologische Forschung*
TLZ	*Theologische Literaturzeitung*
TQ	*Theologische Quartalschrift*
TRE	*Theologische Realenzyklopädie.* Edited by G. Krause and G. Müller. Berlin, 1977–
TRev	*Theologische Revue*
TRu	*Theologische Rundschau*
ThSt	Theologische Studiën
TSK	*Theologische Studien und Kritiken*
TVM	Theologische Verlagsgemeinschaft: Monographien
TWNT	*Theologische Wörterbuch zum Neuen Testament.* Edited by G. Kittel and G. Friedrich. Stuttgart, 1932–1979
TZ	*Theologische Zeitschrift*
THKNT	Theologischer Handkommentar zum Neuen Testament
THAT	*Theologisches Handwörterbuch zum Alten Testament.* Edited by E. Jenni, with assistance from C. Westermann. 2 vols., Stuttgart, 1971–1976
ThWAT	*Theologisches Wörterbuch zum Alten Testament.* Edited by G. J. Botterweck and H. Ringgren. Stuttgart, 1970–
ThPQ	*Theologisch-praktische Quartalschrift*
TD	*Theology Digest*
ThTo	*Theology Today*
TLG	*Thesaurus linguae graecae: Canon of Greek Authors and Works.* Edited by L. Berkowitz and K. A. Squitier. 3d ed. Oxford, 1990
TLL	*Thesaurus linguae latinae*
Payne Smith	*Thesaurus syriacus.* Edited by R. Payne Smith. Oxford, 1879–1901

TTKi	*Tidsskrift for Teologi og Kirke*
TvT	*Tijdschrift voor theologie*
TimesLitSupp	*Times Literary Supplement*
TBC	Torch Bible Commentaries
TJT	*Toronto Journal of Theology*
TPINTC	TPI New Testament Commentaries
TAPA	*Transactions of the American Philological Association*
TGUOS	Transactions of the Glasgow University Oriental Society
Transeu	*Transeuphratène*
TThSt	Trierer theologische Studien
TTZ	*Trierer theologische Zeitschrift*
TJ	*Trinity Journal*
TTJ	*Trinity Theological Journal*
TUMSR	Trinity University Monograph Series in Religion
Trumah	*Trumah*
TCW	*Tydskrif vir Christelike Wetenskap*
TynBul	*Tyndale Bulletin*
TNTC	Tyndale New Testament Commentaries
TOTC	Tyndale Old Testament Commentaries
UF	*Ugarit-Forschungen*
UNP	*Ugaritic Narrative Poetry.* Edited by Simon B. Parker. SBLWAW 9. Atlanta, 1997
UT	*Ugaritic Textbook.* C. H. Gordon. AnOr 38. Rome, 1965
UHP	*Ugaritic-Hebrew Philology.* M. Dahood. 2d ed. Rome, 1989
UBL	Ugaritisch-biblische Literatur
USQR	*Union Seminary Quarterly Review*
UJEnc	*The Universal Jewish Encyclopedia.* Edited by I. Landman. 10 vols. New York, 1939–1943
UNT	Untersuchungen zum Neuen Testament
UUA	Uppsala Universitetsårsskrift
UrE	Ur Excavations
UrET	Ur Excavations: Texts
VCaro	*Verbum caro*
VD	*Verbum domini*
VS	*Verbum Salutie*
VF	*Verkündigung und Forschung*
VL	*Vetus Latina: Die Reste der altlateinischen Bibel.* Edited by E. Beuron, 1949–
VT	*Vetus Testamentum*
VTSup	Vetus Testamentum Supplements
Vid	*Vidyajyoti*
VSpir	*Vie spirituelle*
VC	*Vigiliae christianae*
VH	*Vivens homo*
VAT	Vorderasiatische Abteilung Tontafel. Vorderasiatisches Museum, Berlin
VAB	Vorderasiatische Bibliothek
VE	*Vox evangelica*
VR	*Vox reformata*

119

VS	*Vox scripturae*
Wehr	Wehr, H. *A Dictionary of Modern Written Arabic.* Edited by J. M. Cowan. Ithaca, 1961, 1976[3]
WO	*Die Welt des Orients*
WC	Westminster Commentaries
WDB	*Westminster Dictionary of the Bible*
WHAB	*Westminster Historical Atlas of the Bible*
WTJ	*Westminster Theological Journal*
WZKM	*Wiener Zeitschrift für die Kunde des Morgenlandes*
WZKSO	*Wiener Zeitschrift für die Kunde Süd- und Ostasiens*
WMANT	Wissenschaftliche Monographien zum Alten und Neuen Testament
WUANT	Wissenschaftliche Untersuchungen zum Alten und Neuen Testament
WUNT	Wissenschaftliche Untersuchungen zum Neuen Testament
WVDOG	Wissenschaftliche Veröffentlichungen der deutschen Orientgesellschaft
WZ	*Wissenschaftliche Zeitschrift*
WW	*Word and World*
WBC	Word Biblical Commentary
WHJP	World History of the Jewish People
WD	*Wort und Dienst*
WÄS	*Wörterbuch der ägyptischen Sprache.* A. Erman and H. Grapow. 5 vols. Berlin, 1926–1931. Reprint, 1963
WKAS	*Das Wörterbuch der klassischen arabischen Sprache.* Edited by M. Ullmann. 1957– .
WUS	*Das Wörterbuch der ugaritischen Sprache.* J. Aistleitner. Edited by O. Eissfeldt. 3d ed. Berlin, 1967
WTM	*Das Wörterbuch über die Talmudim und Midraschim.* J. Levy. 2d ed. 1924
YCS	Yale Classical Studies
YOSR	Yale Oriental Series, Researches
YOS	Yale Oriental Series, Texts
ZDMG	*Zeitschrift der deutschen morgenländischen Gesellschaft*
ZDMGSup	Zeitschrift der deutschen morgenländischen Gesellschaft: Supplementbände
ZDPV	*Zeitschrift des deutschen Palästina-Vereins*
ZÄS	*Zeitschrift für ägyptische Sprache und Altertumskunde*
ZAH	*Zeitschrift für Althebräistik*
ZABR	*Zeitschrift für altorientalische und biblische Rechtgeschichte*
ZAC	*Zeitschrift für Antikes Christentum*
ZABeih	Zeitschrift für Assyriologie: Beihefte
ZA	*Zeitschrift für Assyriologie*
ZAW	*Zeitschrift für die alttestamentliche Wissenschaft*
ZNW	*Zeitschrift für die neutestamentliche Wissenschaft und die Kunde der älteren Kirche*
ZEE	*Zeitschrift für evangelische Ethik*
ZHT	*Zeitschrift für historische Theologie*
ZKT	*Zeitschrift für katholische Theologie*

ZKG	*Zeitschrift für Kirchengeschichte*
ZKunstG	*Zeitschrift für Kunstgeschichte*
ZPE	*Zeitschrift für Papyrologie und Epigraphik*
ZRGG	*Zeitschrift für Religions- und Geistesgeschichte*
ZS	*Zeitschrift für Semitistik und verwandte Gebiete*
ZST	*Zeitschrift für systematische Theologie*
ZTK	*Zeitschrift für Theologie und Kirche*
ZWKL	*Zeitschrift für Wissenschaft und kirchliches Leben*
ZWT	*Zeitschrift für wissenschaftliche Theologie*
Zion	*Zion*
ZPEB	*Zondervan Pictorial Encyclopedia of the Bible.* Edited by M. C. Tenney. 5 vols. Grand Rapids, 1975
Zorell	Zorell, F. *Lexicon hebraicum et aramaicum Veteris Testamenti.* Rome, 1968
ZB	Zürcher Bibel
ZBK	Zürcher Bibelkommentare

8.4.2 ALPHABETIZED BY ABBREVIATION

AA	*Archäologischer Anzeiger*
AAA	Annals of Archaeology and Anthropology
AAeg	*Analecta aegyptiaca*
AAHG	*Anzeiger für die Altertumswissenschaft*
AARDS	American Academy of Religion Dissertation Series
AAS	*Acta apostolicae sedis*
AASF	Annales Academiae scientiarum fennicae
AASOR	Annual of the American Schools of Oriental Research
AASS	*Acta sanctorum quotquot toto orbe coluntur.* Antwerp, 1643–
AB	Anchor Bible
AB	*Assyriologische Bibliothek*
ABAT2	*Altorientalische Bilder zum Alten Testament.* Edited by H. Gressmann. 2d ed. Berlin, 1927
ABAW	Abhandlungen der Bayrischen Akademie der Wissenschaften
AbB	*Altbabylonische Briefe in Umschrift und Übersetzung.* Edited by F. R. Kraus. Leiden, 1964–
ABC	*Assyrian and Babylonian Chronicles.* A. K. Grayson. TCS 5. Locust Valley, New York, 1975
ABD	*Anchor Bible Dictionary.* Edited by D. N. Freedman. 6 vols. New York, 1992
ABL	*Assyrian and Babylonian Letters Belonging to the Kouyunjik Collections of the British Museum.* Edited by R. F. Harper. 14 vols. Chicago, 1892–1914
ABQ	*American Baptist Quarterly*
ABR	*Australian Biblical Review*
ABRL	Anchor Bible Reference Library
AbrN	*Abr-Nahrain*
AbrNSup	Abr-Nahrain: Supplement Series
ABW	*Archaeology in the Biblical World*

ABZ	*Assyrisch-babylonische Zeichenliste.* Rykle Borger. 3d ed. AOAT 33/33A. Neukirchen-Vluyn, 1986
ACCS	Ancient Christian Commentary on Scripture
ACEBT	*Amsterdamse Cahiers voor Exegese en bijbelse Theologie*
ACNT	Augsburg Commentaries on the New Testament
ACO	*Acta conciliorum oecumenicorum.* Edited by E. Schwartz. Berlin, 1914–
AcOr	*Acta orientalia*
ACR	*Australasian Catholic Record*
AcT	*Acta theologica*
ACW	Ancient Christian Writers. 1946–
ADAJ	*Annual of the Department of Antiquities of Jordan*
ADD	*Assyrian Deeds and Documents.* C. H. W. Johns. 4 vols. Cambridge, 1898–1923
ADOG	Abhandlungen der deutschen Orientgesellschaft
AE	*Année épigraphique*
AEB	*Annual Egyptological Bibliography*
Aeg	*Aegyptus*
AEL	*Ancient Egyptian Literature.* M. Lichtheim. 3 vols. Berkeley, 1971–1980
AEO	*Ancient Egyptian Onomastica.* A. H. Gardiner. 3 vols. London, 1947
AER	*American Ecclesiastical Review*
Aev	*Aevum: Rassegna de scienze, storiche, linguistiche, e filologiche*
AfK	*Archiv für Keilschriftforschung*
AfO	*Archiv für Orientforschung*
AfOB	Archiv für Orientforschung: Beiheft
ÄF	Ägyptologische Forschungen
ÄgAbh	Ägyptologische Abhandlungen
AGBL	*Aus der Geschichte der lateinischen Bibel (= Vetus Latina: Die Reste der altlateinischen Bibel: Aus der Geschichte der lateinischen Bibel).* Freiburg: Herder, 1957–
AGJU	Arbeiten zur Geschichte des antiken Judentums und des Urchristentums
AGSU	Arbeiten zur Geschichte des Spätjudentums und Urchristentums
AHAW	Abhandlungen der Heidelberger Akademie der Wissenschaften
AHR	*American Historical Review*
AHw	*Akkadisches Handwörterbuch.* W. von Soden. 3 vols. Wiesbaden, 1965–1981
AION	*Annali dell'Istituto Orientale di Napoli*
AIPHOS	*Annuaire de l'Institut de philologie et d'histoire orientales et slaves*
AJA	*American Journal of Archaeology*
AJAS	*American Journal of Arabic Studies*
AJBA	*Australian Journal of Biblical Archaeology*
AJBI	*Annual of the Japanese Biblical Institute*
AJBS	*African Journal of Biblical Studies*

AJP	*American Journal of Philology*
AJSL	*American Journal of Semitic Languages and Literature*
AJSR	*Association for Jewish Studies Review*
AJSUFS	Arbeiten aus dem Juristischen Seminar der Universität Freiburg, Schweiz
AJT	*American Journal of Theology*
AJT	*Asia Journal of Theology*
ALASP	Abhandlungen zur Literatur Alt-Syren-Palästinas und Mesopotamiens
ALBO	Analecta lovaniensia biblica et orientalia
ALGHJ	Arbeiten zur Literatur und Geschichte des hellenistischen Judentums
Altaner	Altaner, B. *Patrologie.* 8th ed. Freiburg, 1978
ALUOS	*Annual of Leeds University Oriental Society*
AMS	*Acta martyrum et sanctorum Syriace.* Edited by P. Bedjan. 7 vols. Paris, 1890–1897
AMWNE	*Apocalypticism in the Mediterranean World and the Near East.* Proceedings of the International Colloquium on Apocalypticism. Edited by D. Hellholm. Uppsala, 1979
Anám	*Anámnesis*
AnBib	Analecta biblica
AnBoll	Analecta Bollandiana
ANEP	*The Ancient Near East in Pictures Relating to the Old Testament.* Edited by J. B. Pritchard. Princeton, 1954
ANESTP	*The Ancient Near East: Supplementary Texts and Pictures Relating to the Old Testament.* Edited by J. B. Pritchard. Princeton, 1969.
ANET	*Ancient Near Eastern Texts Relating to the Old Testament.* Edited by J. B. Pritchard. 3d ed. Princeton, 1969
ANF	*Ante-Nicene Fathers*
Ang	*Angelicum*
AnL	*Anthropological Linguistics*
AnOr	Analecta orientalia
AnPhil	*L'année philologique*
ANQ	*Andover Newton Quarterly*
ANRW	*Aufstieg und Niedergang der römischen Welt: Geschichte und Kultur Roms im Spiegel der neueren Forschung.* Edited by H. Temporini and W. Haase. Berlin, 1972–
AnSt	*Anatolian Studies*
ANTC	Abingdon New Testament Commentaries
ANTF	Arbeiten zur neutestamentlichen Textforschung
AnthLyrGraec	*Anthologia lyrica graeca.* Edited by E. Diehl. Leipzig, 1954–
ANTJ	Arbeiten zum Neuen Testament und Judentum
Anton	*Antonianum*
Anuari	*Anuari de filología*
ANZSTR	Australian and New Zealand Studies in Theology and Religion
AO	*Der Alte Orient*
AOAT	Alter Orient und Altes Testament

AÖAW	Anzeiger der Österreichischen Akademie der Wissenschaften
AOBib	Altorientalische Bibliothek
AoF	Altorientalische Forschungen
AOS	American Oriental Series
AOSTS	American Oriental Society Translation Series
AOT	*The Apocryphal Old Testament.* Edited by H. F. D. Sparks. Oxford, 1984
AOTAT	*Altorientalische Texte zum Alten Testament.* Edited by H. Gressmann. 2d ed. Berlin, 1926
APAT	*Die Apokryphen und Pseudepigraphen des Alten Testaments.* Translated and edited by E. Kautzsch. 2 vols. Tübingen, 1900
APF	*Archiv für Papyrusforschung*
APOT	*The Apocrypha and Pseudepigrapha of the Old Testament.* Edited by R. H. Charles. 2 vols. Oxford, 1913
APSP	*American Philosophical Society Proceedings*
AR	*Archiv für Religionswissenschaft*
ARAB	*Ancient Records of Assyria and Babylonia.* Daniel David Luckenbill. 2 vols. Chicago, 1926–1927
ArBib	The Aramaic Bible
Arch	*Archaeology*
ARE	*Ancient Records of Egypt.* Edited by J. H. Breasted. 5 vols. Chicago, 1905–1907. Reprint, New York, 1962
ARG	*Archiv für Reformationsgeschichte*
ARI	*Assyrian Royal Inscriptions.* A. K. Grayson. 2 vols. RANE. Wiesbaden, 1972–1976
ARM	Archives royales de Mari
ARMT	Archives royales de Mari, transcrite et traduite
ArOr	*Archiv Orientální*
ArSt	Arabian Studies
AS	Assyriological Studies
ASAE	*Annales du service des antiquités de l'Egypte*
ASAW	Abhandlungen der Sächsischen Akademie der Wissenschaften
ASNU	Acta seminarii neotestamentici upsaliensis
ASOR	American Schools of Oriental Research
ASP	*American Studies in Papyrology*
Asp	*Asprenas: Rivista di scienze teologiche*
ASS	*Acta sanctae sedis*
AsSeign	*Assemblées du Seigneur*
ASSR	*Archives de sciences sociales des religions*
ASTI	*Annual of the Swedish Theological Institute*
AsTJ	*Asbury Theological Journal*
AT	*Annales theologici*
ATA	Alttestamentliche Abhandlungen
ATANT	Abhandlungen zur Theologie des Alten und Neuen Testaments
ATD	Das Alte Testament Deutsch
ATDan	Acta theologica danica
ATG	*Archivo teológico granadino*

Atiqot	*ʿAtiqot*
ATJ	*Ashland Theological Journal*
ATLA	American Theological Library Association
AThR	*Anglican Theological Review*
ATR	*Australasian Theological Review*
Aug	*Augustinianum*
AugStud	*Augustinian Studies*
AuOr	*Aula orientalis*
AUSS	*Andrews University Seminary Studies*
AVTRW	Aufsätze und Vorträge zur Theologie und Religionswissenschaft
AzTh	Arbeiten zur Theologie
B&R	*Books and Religion*
BA	*Biblical Archaeologist*
Bab	*Babyloniaca*
BAC	Biblioteca de autores cristianos
BAG	Bauer, W., W. F. Arndt, and F. W. Gingrich. *Greek-English Lexicon of the New Testament and Other Early Christian Literature.* Chicago, 1957
BAGB	*Bulletin de l'Association G. Budé*
BAGD	Bauer, W., W. F. Arndt, F. W. Gingrich, and F. W. Danker. *Greek-English Lexicon of the New Testament and Other Early Christian Literature.* 2d ed. Chicago, 1979
BaghM	*Baghdader Mitteilungen*
BAIAS	*Bulletin of the Anglo-Israel Archeological Society*
BAP	*Beiträge zum altbabylonischen Privatrecht.* Bruno Meissner. Leipzig, 1893
BAR	*Biblical Archaeology Review*
BARead	*Biblical Archaeologist Reader*
Bar-Ilan	*Annual of Bar-Ilan University*
BASOR	*Bulletin of the American Schools of Oriental Research*
BASORSup	Bulletin of the American Schools of Oriental Research: Supplement Series
BASP	*Bulletin of the American Society of Papyrologists*
BASPSup	Bulletin of the American Society of Papyrologists: Supplement
BAT	Die Botschaft des Alten Testaments
BBB	Bonner biblische Beiträge
BBB	*Bulletin de bibliographie biblique*
BBET	Beiträge zur biblischen Exegese und Theologie
BBMS	Baker Biblical Monograph Series
BBR	*Bulletin for Biblical Research*
BBS	*Bulletin of Biblical Studies*
BCH	*Bulletin de correspondance hellénique*
BCPE	*Bulletin du Centre protestant d'études*
BCR	Biblioteca di cultura religiosa
BCSR	*Bulletin of the Council on the Study of Religion*

BDAG   Bauer, W., F. W. Danker, W. F. Arndt, and F. W. Gingrich. *Greek-English Lexicon of the New Testament and Other Early Christian Literature.* 3d ed. Chicago, 1999

BDB   Brown, F., S. R. Driver, and C. A. Briggs. *A Hebrew and English Lexicon of the Old Testament.* Oxford, 1907

BDF   Blass, F., A. Debrunner, and R. W. Funk. *A Greek Grammar of the New Testament and Other Early Christian Literature.* Chicago, 1961

BEATAJ   Beiträge zur Erforschung des Alten Testaments und des antiken Judentum

BEB   *Baker Encyclopedia of the Bible.* Edited by W. A. Elwell. 2 vols. Grand Rapids, 1988

BeO   *Bibbia e oriente*

Ber   *Berytus*

BerMatÖAI   Berichte und Materialien des Österreichischen archäologischen Instituts

BETL   Bibliotheca ephemeridum theologicarum lovaniensium

BEvT   Beiträge zur evangelischen Theologie

BFCT   Beiträge zur Förderung christlicher Theologie

BFT   Biblical Foundations in Theology

BGBE   Beiträge zur Geschichte der biblischen Exegese

BGU   *Aegyptische Urkunden aus den Königlichen Staatlichen Museen zu Berlin, Griechische Urkunden.* 15 vols. Berlin, 1895–1983.

BHEAT   *Bulletin d'histoire et d'exégèse de l'Ancien Testament*

BHG   *Bibliotheca hagiographica Graece.* Brussels, 1977

BHH   *Biblisch-historisches Handwörterbuch: Landeskunde, Geschichte, Religion, Kultur.* Edited by B. Reicke and L. Rost. 4 vols. Göttingen, 1962–1966

BHK   *Biblia Hebraica.* Edited by R. Kittel. Stuttgart, 1905–1906, 1925^2, 1937^3, 1951^4, 1973^{16}

BHL   *Bibliotheca hagiographica latina antiquae et mediae aetatis.* 2 vols. Brussels, 1898–1901

BHO   *Bibliotheca hagiographica orientalis.* Brussels, 1910

BHS   *Biblia Hebraica Stuttgartensia.* Edited by K. Elliger and W. Rudolph. Stuttgart, 1983

BHT   Beiträge zur historischen Theologie

BI   *Biblical Illustrator*

Bib   *Biblica*

BibB   Biblische Beiträge

BiBh   *Bible Bhashyam*

BibInt   *Biblical Interpretation*

BibLeb   *Bibel und Leben*

BibOr   Biblica et orientalia

BibS(F)   Biblische Studien (Freiburg, 1895–)

BibS(N)   Biblische Studien (Neukirchen, 1951–)

BIES   *Bulletin of the Israel Exploration Society (= Yediot)*

BIFAO   *Bulletin de l'Institut français d'archéologie orientale*

Bijdr   *Bijdragen: Tijdschrift voor filosofie en theologie*

BIN   *Babylonian Inscriptions in the Collection of James B. Nies*

BIOSCS	*Bulletin of the International Organization for Septuagint and Cognate Studies*
BiPa	Biblia Patristica: Index des citations et allusions bibliques dans la littérature. Paris, 1975–
BJ	*Bonner Jahrbücher*
BJPES	*Bulletin of the Jewish Palestine Exploration Society*
BJRL	*Bulletin of the John Rylands University Library of Manchester*
BJS	Brown Judaic Studies
BJVF	*Berliner Jahrbuch für Vor- und Frühgeschichte*
BK	*Bibel und Kirche*
BKAT	Biblischer Kommentar, Altes Testament. Edited by M. Noth and H. W. Wolff
BL	*Bibel und Liturgie*
BLE	*Bulletin de littérature ecclésiastique*
BLit	*Bibliothèque liturgique*
BMes	Bibliotheca mesopotamica
BN	*Biblische Notizen*
BNTC	Black's New Testament Commentaries
BO	*Bibliotheca orientalis*
Böhl	Böhl, F. M. Th. de Liagre. *Opera minora: Studies en bijdragen op Assyriologisch en Oudtestamentisch terrein.* Groningen, 1953
BOR	*Babylonian and Oriental Record*
Bousset-Gressmann	Bousset, W., and H. Gressmann, *Die Religion des Judentums im späthellenistischen Zeitalter.* 3d ed. Tübingen, 1926
BR	*Biblical Research*
BRev	*Bible Review*
BRL2	*Biblisches Reallexikon.* 2d ed. Edited by K. Galling. HAT 1/1. Tübingen, 1977
BSAA	*Bulletin de la Société archéologique d'Alexandrie*
BSac	*Bibliotheca sacra*
BSAC	*Bulletin de la Société d'archéologie copte*
BSC	Bible Student's Commentary
BSGW	Berichte der Sächsischen Gesellschaft der Wissenschaften
BSOAS	*Bulletin of the School of Oriental and African Studies*
BT	*The Bible Translator*
BTB	*Biblical Theology Bulletin*
BThAM	*Bulletin de théologie ancienne et médiévale*
BTS	*Bible et terre sainte*
BTZ	*Berliner Theologische Zeitschrift*
Budé	Collection des universités de France, publiée sous le patronage de l'Association Guillaume Budé
Burg	*Burgense*
BurH	*Buried History*
BV	*Biblical Viewpoint*
BVC	*Bible et vie chrétienne*
BW	*The Biblical World: A Dictionary of Biblical Archaeology.* Edited by C. F. Pfeiffer. Grand Rapids, 1966
BWA(N)T	Beiträge zur Wissenschaft vom Alten (und Neuen) Testament
BWL	*Babylonian Wisdom Literature.* W. G. Lambert. Oxford, 1960

127

ByF	*Biblia y fe*
Byzantion	*Byzantion*
ByzF	*Byzantinische Forschungen*
ByzZ	*Byzantinische Zeitschrift*
BZ	*Biblische Zeitschrift*
BzA	Beiträge zur Assyriologie
BZAW	Beihefte zur Zeitschrift für die alttestamentliche Wissenschaft
BZNW	Beihefte zur Zeitschrift für die neutestamentliche Wissenschaft
BZRGG	Beihefte zur Zeitschrift für Religions- und Geistesgeschichte
CA	*Convivium assisiense*
CAD	*The Assyrian Dictionary of the Oriental Institute of the University of Chicago.* Chicago, 1956–
CaE	*Cahiers évangile*
CAGN	*Collected Ancient Greek Novels.* Edited by B. P. Reardon. Berkeley, 1989
CAH	Cambridge Ancient History
CahRB	Cahiers de la Revue biblique
CahT	Cahiers Théologiques
CANE	*Civilizations of the Ancient Near East.* Edited by J. Sasson. 4 vols. New York, 1995
CAP	Cowley, A. E. *Aramaic Papyri of the Fifth Century B.C.* Oxford, 1923
Car	*Carthagiensia*
CAT	Commentaire de l'Ancien Testament
CB	*Cultura bíblica*
CBC	Cambridge Bible Commentary
CBET	Contributions to Biblical Exegesis and Theology
CBM	Chester Beatty Monographs
CBQ	*Catholic Biblical Quarterly*
CBQMS	Catholic Biblical Quarterly Monograph Series
CBTJ	*Calvary Baptist Theological Journal*
CC	Continental Commentaries
CCath	Corpus Catholicorum
CCCM	Corpus Christianorum: Continuatio mediaevalis. Turnhout, 1969–
CClCr	*Civiltà classica e cristiana*
CCSG	Corpus Christianorum: Series graeca. Turnhout, 1977–
CCSL	Corpus Christianorum: Series latina. Turnhout, 1953–
CCT	*Cuneiform Texts from Cappadocian Tablets in the British Museum*
CDME	*A Concise Dictionary of Middle Egyptian.* Edited by R. O. Faulkner. Oxford, 1962
CF	*Classical Folia*
CGTC	Cambridge Greek Testament Commentary
CGTSC	Cambridge Greek Testament for Schools and Colleges
CH	*Church History*
CHJ	*Cambridge History of Judaism.* Ed. W. D. Davies and Louis Finkelstein. Cambridge, 1984–

Chm	*Churchman*
CHR	*Catholic Historical Review*
ChrCent	*Christian Century*
ChrEg	*Chronique d'Egypte*
ChrLit	*Christianity and Literature*
CIC	*Corpus inscriptionum chaldicarum*
CIG	*Corpus inscriptionum graecarum.* Edited by A. Boeckh. 4 vols. Berlin, 1828–1877
CII	*Corpus inscriptionum iudaicarum.* Edited by J. B. Frey. 2 vols. Rome, 1936–1952
CIJ	*Corpus inscriptionum judaicarum*
CIL	*Corpus inscriptionum latinarum*
CIS	*Corpus inscriptionum semiticarum*
CJ	*Classical Journal*
CJT	*Canadian Journal of Theology*
Cmio	*Communio: Commentarii internationales de ecclesia et theología*
CML	*Canaanite Myths and Legends.* Edited by G. R. Driver. Edinburgh, 1956. Edited by J. C. L. Gibson, 1978[2]
CNS	*Cristianesimo nella storia*
CNT	Commentaire du Nouveau Testament
Coll	*Collationes*
Colloq	*Colloquium*
ColT	*Collectanea theologica*
Comm	*Communio*
Comp	*Compostellanum*
ConBNT	Coniectanea neotestamentica or Coniectanea biblica: New Testament Series
ConBOT	Coniectanea biblica: Old Testament Series
Cont	*Continuum*
COS	*The Context of Scripture.* Edited by W. W. Hallo. 3 vols. Leiden, 1997–
COut	Commentaar op het Oude Testament
CP	*Classical Philology*
CPG	*Clavis patrum graecorum.* Edited by M. Geerard. 5 vols. Turnhout, 1974–1987
CPJ	*Corpus papyrorum judaicorum.* Edited by V. Tcherikover. 3 vols. Cambridge, 1957–1964.
CPL	*Clavis patrum latinorum.* Edited by E. Dekkers. 2d ed. Steenbrugis, 1961
CQ	*Church Quarterly*
CQ	*Classical Quarterly*
CQR	*Church Quarterly Review*
CRAI	Comptes rendus de l'Académie des inscriptions et belles-lettres
CRBR	*Critical Review of Books in Religion*
CRINT	Compendia rerum iudaicarum ad Novum Testamentum
CRTL	Cahiers de la Revue théologique de Louvain
Crux	*Crux*

CSCO	Corpus scriptorum christianorum orientalium. Edited by I. B. Chabot et al. Paris, 1903–
CSEL	Corpus scriptorum ecclesiasticorum latinorum
CSHB	Corpus scriptorum historiae byzantinae
CSJH	Chicago Studies in the History of Judaism
CSRB	*Council on the Study of Religion: Bulletin*
CT	*Cuneiform Texts from Babylonian Tablets in the British Museum*
CTA	*Corpus des tablettes en cunéiformes alphabétiques découvertes à Ras Shamra-Ugarit de 1929 à 1939.* Edited by A. Herdner. Mission de Ras Shamra 10. Paris, 1963
CTAED	*Canaanite Toponyms in Ancient Egyptian Documents.* S. Ahituv. Jerusalem, 1984
CTJ	*Calvin Theological Journal*
CTM	*Concordia Theological Monthly*
CTQ	*Concordia Theological Quarterly*
CTR	*Criswell Theological Review*
CTU	*The Cuneiform Alphabetic Texts from Ugarit, Ras Ibn Hani, and Other Places.* Edited by M. Dietrich, O. Loretz, and J. Sanmartín. Münster, 1995.
CUL	*A Concordance of the Ugaritic Literature.* R. E. Whitaker. Cambridge, Mass., 1972
CurBS	*Currents in Research: Biblical Studies*
CurTM	*Currents in Theology and Mission*
CV	*Communio viatorum*
CW	*Classical World*
CWS	Classics of Western Spirituality. New York, 1978–
DACL	*Dictionnaire d'archéologie chrétienne et de liturgie.* Edited by F. Cabrol. 15 vols. Paris, 1907–1953
DB	*Dictionnaire de la Bible.* Edited by F. Vigouroux. 5 vols. 1895–1912
DBAT	*Dielheimer Blätter zum Alten Testament und seiner Rezeption in der Alten Kirche*
DBSup	*Dictionnaire de la Bible: Supplément.* Edited by L. Pirot and A. Robert. Paris, 1928–
DBT	*Dictionary of Biblical Theology.* Edited by X. Léon-Dufour. 2d ed. 1972
DCB	*Dictionary of Christian Biography.* Edited by W. Smith and H. Wace. 4 vols. London, 1877–1887
DCG	*Dictionary of Christ and the Gospels.* Edited by J. Hastings. 2 vols. Edinburgh, 1908
DCH	*Dictionary of Classical Hebrew.* Edited by D. J. A. Clines. Sheffield, 1993–
DDD	*Dictionary of Deities and Demons in the Bible.* Edited by K. van der Toorn, B. Becking, and P. W. van der Horst. Leiden, 1995
DHA	*Dialogues d'histoire ancienne*
Di	*Dialog*
Did	*Didaskalia*
DISO	*Dictionnaire des inscriptions sémitiques de l'ouest.* Edited by Ch. F. Jean and J. Hoftijzer. Leiden, 1965

DissAb	Dissertation Abstracts
DivThom	*Divus Thomas*
DJD	Discoveries in the Judaean Desert
DJG	*Dictionary of Jesus and the Gospels.* Edited by J. B. Green and S. McKnight. Downers Grove, 1992
DLE	*Dictionary of Late Egyptian.* Edited by L. H. Lesko and B. S. Lesko. 4 vols. Berkeley, 1982–1989
DLNT	*Dictionary of the Later New Testament and Its Developments.* Edited by R. P. Martin and P. H. Davids. Downers Grove, 1997
DNP	*Der neue Pauly: Enzyklopädie der Antike.* Edited by H. Cancik and H. Schneider. Stuttgart, 1996–
DNWSI	*Dictionary of the North-West Semitic Inscriptions.* J. Hoftijzer and K. Jongeling. 2 vols. Leiden, 1995
DOP	*Dumbarton Oaks Papers*
DOTT	*Documents from Old Testament Times.* Edited by D. W. Thomas, London, 1958
DPAC	*Dizionario patristico e di antichità cristiane.* Edited by A. di Berardino. 3 vols. Casale Monferrato, 1983–1988
DPL	*Dictionary of Paul and His Letters.* Edited by G. F. Hawthorne and R. P. Martin. Downers Grove, 1993
DRev	*Downside Review*
DrewG	*Drew Gateway*
DSD	*Dead Sea Discoveries*
DTC	*Dictionnaire de théologie catholique.* Edited by A. Vacant et al. 15 vols. Paris, 1903–1950
DTT	*Dansk teologisk tidsskrift*
Duchesne	Duchesne, L., ed. *Le Liber pontificalis.* 2 vols. Paris, 1886, 1892. Reprinted with 3d vol. by C. Vogel. Paris, 1955–1957
DunRev	*Dunwoodie Review*
EA	El-Amarna tablets. According to the edition of J. A. Knudtzon. *Die el-Amarna-Tafeln.* Leipzig, 1908–1915. Reprint, Aalen, 1964. Continued in A. F. Rainey, *El-Amarna Tablets, 359–379.* 2d revised ed. Kevelaer, 1978
EAEHL	*Encyclopedia of Archaeological Excavations in the Holy Land.* Edited by M. Avi-Yonah. 4 vols. Jerusalem, 1975
EB	Echter Bibel
EBib	*Etudes bibliques*
ECR	*Eastern Churches Review*
ECT	*Egyptian Coffin Texts.* Edited by A. de Buck and A. H. Gardiner. Chicago, 1935–1947
EdF	Erträge der Forschung
EDNT	*Exegetical Dictionary of the New Testament.* Edited by H. Balz, G. Schneider. ET. Grand Rapids, 1990–1993
EEA	*L'epigrafia ebraica antica.* S. Moscati. Rome, 1951
EEC	*Encyclopedia of Early Christianity.* Edited by E. Ferguson. 2d ed. New York, 1990
EECh	*Encyclopedia of the Early Church.* Edited by A. di Berardino. Translated by A. Walford. New York, 1992
EfMex	*Efemerides mexicana*

EFN	Estudios de filología neotestamentaria. Cordova, Spain, 1988–
EgT	*Eglise et théologie*
EHAT	Exegetisches Handbuch zum Alten Testament
EKKNT	Evangelisch-katholischer Kommentar zum Neuen Testament
EKL	*Evangelisches Kirchenlexikon.* Edited by Erwin Fahlbusch et al. 4 vols. 3d ed. Göttingen, 1985–1996
Elenchus	*Elenchus bibliographicus biblicus* of *Biblica,* Rome, 1985–
ELKZ	*Evangelisch-Lutherische Kirchenzeitung*
EMC	*Echos du monde classique/Classical Views*
Enc	*Encounter*
EnchBib	*Enchiridion biblicum*
EncJud	*Encyclopaedia Judaica.* 16 vols. Jerusalem, 1972
EPap	*Etudes de papyrologie*
Epiph	*Epiphany*
EPRO	Etudes préliminaires aux religions orientales dans l'empire romain
ER	*The Encyclopedia of Religion.* Edited by M. Eliade. 16 vols. New York, 1987
ERAS	*Epithètes royales akkadiennes et sumériennes.* M.-J. Seux. Paris, 1967
ERE	*Encyclopedia of Religion and Ethics.* Edited by J. Hastings. 13 vols. New York, 1908–1927. Reprint, 7 vols., 1951
ErIsr	*Eretz-Israel*
ErJb	*Eranos-Jahrbuch*
EstAg	*Estudio Agustiniano*
EstBib	*Estudios bíblicos*
EstEcl	*Estudios eclesiásticos*
EstMin	*Estudios mindonienses*
EstTeo	*Estudios teológicos*
ETL	*Ephemerides theologicae lovanienses*
ETR	*Etudes théologiques et religieuses*
ETS	Erfurter theologische Studien
EuroJTh	*European Journal of Theology*
Even-Shoshan	Even-Shoshan, A., ed. *A New Concordance of the Bible.* Jerusalem, 1977, 1983[4]
EvJ	*Evangelical Journal*
EvK	Evangelische Kommentare
EvQ	*Evangelical Quarterly*
EvT	*Evangelische Theologie*
ExAud	*Ex auditu*
Exeg	*Exegetica* [Japanese]
ExpTim	*Expository Times*
FAT	Forschungen zum Alten Testament
FB	Forschung zur Bibel
FBBS	Facet Books, Biblical Series
FBE	Forum for Bibelsk Eksegese
FC	Fathers of the Church. Washington, D.C., 1947–
FCB	Feminist Companion to the Bible
FF	*Forschungen und Fortschritte*

FF	Foundations and Facets
FGH	*Die Fragmente der griechischen Historiker.* Edited by F. Jacoby. Leiden, 1954–1964
FHG	Fragmenta historicorum graecorum. Paris, 1841–1870
FiE	*Forschungen in Ephesos*
FMSt	Frühmittelalterliche Studien
FO	*Folia orientalia*
FoiVie	*Foi et vie*
ForFasc	*Forum Fascicles*
Foster, *Muses*	Foster, Benjamin R. *Before the Muses: An Anthology of Akkadian Literature.* 2 vols. Bethesda, 1993
FOTL	Forms of the Old Testament Literature
Fran	*Franciscanum*
FRLANT	Forschungen zur Religion und Literatur des Alten und Neuen Testaments
FT	*Folia theologica*
Fund	*Fundamentum*
FZPhTh	*Freiburger Zeitschrift für Philosophie und Theologie*
GAG	*Grundriss der akkadischen Grammatik.* W. von Soden. 2d ed. Rome, 1969
GAT	Grundrisse zum Alten Testament
GBS	Guides to Biblical Scholarship
GCDS	*Graphic Concordance to the Dead Sea Scrolls.* Edited by J. H. Charlesworth et al. Tübingen, 1991
GCS	Die griechische christliche Schriftsteller der ersten [drei] Jahrhunderte
Gesenius, *Thesaurus*	Gesenius, W. *Thesaurus philologicus criticus linguae hebraeae et chaldaeae Veteris Testamenti.* Vols. 1–3. Leipzig, 1829–1842
GKC	*Gesenius' Hebrew Grammar.* Edited by E. Kautzsch. Translated by A. E. Cowley. 2d. ed. Oxford, 1910
Gn	*Gnomon*
GNS	*Good News Studies*
GNT	Grundrisse zum Neuen Testament
GOTR	*Greek Orthodox Theological Review*
GP	*Géographie de la Palestine.* F. M. Abel. 2 vols. Paris, 1933
GR	*Greece and Rome*
GRBS	*Greek, Roman, and Byzantine Studies*
Greg	*Gregorianum*
GS	*Gesammelte Studien*
GTA	Göttinger theologischer Arbeiten
GTT	*Gereformeerd theologisch tijdschrift*
GTTOT	*The Geographical and Topographical Texts of the Old Testament.* Edited by J. J. Simons. Studia Francisci Scholten memoriae dicata 2. Leiden, 1959
GVG	*Grundriss der vergleichenden Grammatik der semitischen Sprachen.* C. Brockelmann, 2 vols. Berlin, 1908–1913. Reprint, Hildesheim, 1961

133

HAL	Koehler, L., W. Baumgartner, and J. J. Stamm. *Hebräisches und aramäisches Lexikon zum Alten Testament.* Fascicles 1–5, 1967–1995 (KBL3). ET: *HALOT*
HALOT	Koehler, L., W. Baumgartner, and J. J. Stamm, *The Hebrew and Aramaic Lexicon of the Old Testament.* Translated and edited under the supervision of M. E. J. Richardson. 4 vols. Leiden, 1994–1999
HAR	*Hebrew Annual Review*
Harris	Harris, Z. S. *A Grammar of the Phoenician Language.* AOS 8. New Haven, 1936. Reprint, 1990
HAT	Handbuch zum Alten Testament
HBC	*Harper's Bible Commentary.* Edited by J. L. Mays et al. San Francisco, 1988.
HBD	*HarperCollins Bible Dictionary.* Edited by P. J. Achtemeier et al. 2d ed. San Francisco, 1996
HBT	*Horizons in Biblical Theology*
HDR	Harvard Dissertations in Religion
Hell	*Hellenica: Recueil d'épigraphie, de numismatique et d'antiquités grecques*
Hen	*Henoch*
Herm	*Hermanthena*
Hesperia	*Hesperia: Journal of the American School of Classical Studies at Athens*
HeyJ	*Heythrop Journal*
HibJ	*Hibbert Journal*
HKAT	Handkommentar zum Alten Testament
HKL	*Handbuch der Keilschriftliteratur.* R. Borger. 3 vols. Berlin, 1967–1975
HKNT	Handkommentar zum Neuen Testament
HNT	Handbuch zum Neuen Testament
HNTC	Harper's New Testament Commentaries
HO	Handbuch der Orientalistik
Hok	*Hokhma*
HolBD	*Holman Bible Dictionary.* Edited by T. C. Butler. Nashville, 1991
Hor	*Horizons*
HR	*History of Religions*
HRCS	Hatch, E. and H. A. Redpath. *Concordance to the Septuagint and Other Greek Versions of the Old Testament.* 2 vols. Oxford, 1897. Suppl., 1906. Reprint, 3 vols. in 2, Grand Rapids, 1983
HS	*Hebrew Studies*
HSAT	*Die Heilige Schrift des Alten Testaments.* Edited by E. Kautzsch and A. Bertholet. 4th ed. Tübingen, 1922–1923
HSCP	*Harvard Studies in Classical Philology*
HSem	Horae semiticae. 9 vols. London, 1908–1912
HSM	Harvard Semitic Monographs
HSS	Harvard Semitic Studies
HT	*History Today*
HTB	Histoire du texte biblique. Lausanne, 1996–

134

HTh	*Ho Theológos*
HTKNT	Herders theologischer Kommentar zum Neuen Testament
HTR	*Harvard Theological Review*
HTS	Harvard Theological Studies
HUCA	*Hebrew Union College Annual*
HUCM	Monographs of the Hebrew Union College
HumTeo	Biblioteca humanística e teológica
HUT	Hermeneutische Untersuchungen zur Theologie
HvTSt	*Hervormde teologiese studies*
IAR	Iraq Archaeological Reports
IATG²	Schwertner, Siegfried M. *Internationales Abkürzungsverzeichnis für Theologie und Grenzgebeite.* 2d ed. Berlin, 1992
IB	*Interpreter's Bible.* Edited by G. A. Buttrick et al. 12 vols. New York, 1951–1957
IBC	Interpretation: A Bible Commentary for Teaching and Preaching.
IBHS	*An Introduction to Biblical Hebrew Syntax.* B. K. Waltke and M. O'Connor. Winona Lake, Indiana, 1990
IBS	*Irish Biblical Studies*
ICC	International Critical Commentary
ICUR	*Inscriptiones christianae urbis Romae.* Edited by J. B. de Rossi. Rome, 1857–1888
IDB	*The Interpreter's Dictionary of the Bible.* Edited by G. A. Buttrick. 4 vols. Nashville, 1962
IDBSup	*Interpreter's Dictionary of the Bible: Supplementary Volume.* Edited by K. Crim. Nashville, 1976
IDS	*In die Skriflig*
IEJ	*Israel Exploration Journal*
IESS	*International Encyclopedia of the Social Sciences.* Edited by D. L. Sills. New York, 1968–
IG	*Inscriptiones graecae.* Editio minor. Berlin, 1924–
IJT	*Indian Journal of Theology*
IKaZ	*Internationale katholische Zeitschrift*
IKZ	*Internationale kirchliche Zeitschrift*
ILCV	*Inscriptiones latinae christianae veteres.* Edited by E. Diehl. 2d ed. Berlin, 1961
Imm	*Immanuel*
Int	*Interpretation*
IOS	*Israel Oriental Society*
IPN	*Die israelitischen Personennamen.* M. Noth. BWANT 3/10. Stuttgart, 1928. Reprint, Hildesheim, 1980
Iran	*Iran*
Iraq	*Iraq*
Irén	*Irénikon*
IRT	Issues in Religion and Theology
ISBE	*International Standard Bible Encyclopedia.* Edited by G. W. Bromiley. 4 vols. Grand Rapids, 1979–1988
Isd	*Isidorianum*
Istina	*Istina*

IstMitt	*Istanbuler Mitteilungen*
Itala	*Itala: Das Neue Testament in altlateinischer Überlieferung.* 4 vols. Berlin, 1938–1963
ITC	International Theological Commentary
Iter	*Iter*
Itin (Italy)	*Itinerarium* (Italy)
Itin (Portugal)	*Itinerarium* (Portugal)
ITP	Hayim Tadmor, *The Inscriptions of Tiglath-Pileser III, King of Assyria.* Jerusalem, 1994
ITQ	*Irish Theological Quarterly*
IZBG	*Internationale Zeitschriftenschau für Bibelwissenschaft und Grenzgebiete*
JA	*Journal asiatique*
JAAL	*Journal of Afroasiatic Languages*
JAAR	*Journal of the American Academy of Religion*
JAC	Jahrbuch für Antike und Christentum
JACiv	*Journal of Ancient Civilizations*
Jahnow	Jahnow, I. *Das hebräische Leichenlied im Rahmen der Völkerdichtung.* Giessen, 1923
JAL	Jewish Apocryphal Literature Series
JANESCU	*Journal of the Ancient Near Eastern Society of Columbia University*
JAOS	*Journal of the American Oriental Society*
JAS	*Journal of Asian Studies*
Jastrow	Jastrow, M. *A Dictionary of the Targumim, the Talmud Babli and Yerushalmi, and the Midrashic Literature.* 2d ed. New York, 1903
JB	Jerusalem Bible
JBC	*Jerome Biblical Commentary.* Edited by R. E. Brown et al. Englewood Cliffs, 1968
JBL	*Journal of Biblical Literature*
JBQ	*Jewish Bible Quarterly*
JBR	*Journal of Bible and Religion*
JCS	*Journal of Cuneiform Studies*
JdI	*Jahrbuch des deutschen archäologischen Instituts*
JDS	Jewish Desert Studies
JDS	Judean Desert Studies
JDT	*Jahrbuch für deutsche Theologie*
JE	*The Jewish Encyclopedia.* Edited by I. Singer. 12 vols. New York, 1925
JEA	*Journal of Egyptian Archaeology*
JECS	*Journal of Early Christian Studies*
Jeev	*Jeevadhara*
JEH	*Journal of Ecclesiastical History*
JEOL	*Jaarbericht van het Vooraziatisch-Egyptisch Gezelschap (Genootschap) Ex oriente lux*
JES	*Journal of Ecumenical Studies*
JESHO	*Journal of the Economic and Social History of the Orient*
JET	*Jahrbuch für Evangelische Theologie*

JETS	*Journal of the Evangelical Theological Society*
JFSR	*Journal of Feminist Studies in Religion*
JHI	*Journal of the History of Ideas*
JHNES	Johns Hopkins Near Eastern Studies
JHS	*Journal of Hellenic Studies*
Jian Dao	*Jian Dao*
JJA	*Journal of Jewish Art*
JJP	*Journal of Juristic Papyrology*
JJS	*Journal of Jewish Studies*
JJT	*Josephinum Journal of Theology*
JLA	*Jewish Law Annual*
JLCRS	Jordan Lectures in Comparative Religion Series
JMedHist	*Journal of Medieval History*
JMES	*Journal of Middle Eastern Studies*
JMS	*Journal of Mithraic Studies*
JNES	*Journal of Near Eastern Studies*
JNSL	*Journal of Northwest Semitic Languages*
JÖAI	*Jahreshefte des Österreichischen archäologischen Instituts*
JOTT	*Journal of Translation and Textlinguistics*
Joüon	Joüon, P. *A Grammar of Biblical Hebrew*. Translated and revised by T. Muraoka. 2 vols. Subsidia biblica 14/1–2. Rome, 1991
JPJ	*Journal of Progressive Judaism*
JPOS	*Journal of the Palestine Oriental Society*
JQR	*Jewish Quarterly Review*
JQRMS	Jewish Quarterly Review Monograph Series
JR	*Journal of Religion*
JRAS	*Journal of the Royal Asiatic Society*
JRE	*Journal of Religious Ethics*
JRelS	*Journal of Religious Studies*
JRH	*Journal of Religious History*
JRitSt	*Journal of Ritual Studies*
JRS	*Journal of Roman Studies*
JRT	*Journal of Religious Thought*
JSem	*Journal of Semitics*
JSHRZ	*Jüdische Schriften aus hellenistisch-römischer Zeit*
JSJ	*Journal for the Study of Judaism in the Persian, Hellenistic, and Roman Periods*
JSNT	*Journal for the Study of the New Testament*
JSNTSup	Journal for the Study of the New Testament: Supplement Series
JSOR	*Journal of the Society of Oriental Research*
JSOT	*Journal for the Study of the Old Testament*
JSOTSup	Journal for the Study of the Old Testament: Supplement Series
JSP	*Journal for the Study of the Pseudepigrapha*
JSPSup	Journal for the Study of the Pseudepigrapha: Supplement Series
JSQ	*Jewish Studies Quarterly*

137

JSS	*Journal of Semitic Studies*
JSSEA	*Journal of the Society for the Study of Egyptian Antiquities*
JSSR	*Journal for the Scientific Study of Religion*
JTC	*Journal for Theology and the Church*
JTS	*Journal of Theological Studies*
JTSA	*Journal of Theology for Southern Africa*
Jud	*Judaica*
Judaica	*Judaica: Beiträge zum Verständnis des jüdischen Schicksals in Vergangenheit und Gegenwart*
Judaism	*Judaism*
JWSTP	*Jewish Writings of the Second Temple Period: Apocrypha, Pseudepigrapha, Qumran Sectarian Writings, Philo, Josephus.* Edited by M. E. Stone. CRINT 2.2. Assen/Philadelphia, 1984
K&D	Keil, C. F., and F. Delitzsch, *Biblical Commentary on the Old Testament.* Translated by J. Martin et al. 25 vols. Edinburgh, 1857–1878. Reprint, 10 vols., Peabody, Mass., 1996
KAH 1	*Keilschrifttexte aus Assur historischen Inhalts.* L. Messerschmidt. Vol. 1. WVDOG 16. Leipzig, 1911
KAH 2	*Keilschrifttexte aus Assur historischen Inhalts.* O. Schroeder. Vol. 2. WVDOG 37. Leipzig, 1922
KAI	*Kanaanäische und aramäische Inschriften.* H. Donner and W. Röllig. 2d ed. Wiesbaden, 1966–1969
Kairós	*Kairós*
KAR	*Keilschrifttexte aus Assur religiösen Inhalts.* Edited by E. Ebeling. Leipzig, 1919–1923
KAT	Kommentar zum Alten Testament
KB	*Keilinschriftliche Bibliothek.* Edited by E. Schrader. 6 vols. Berlin, 1889–1915
KBANT	Kommentare und Beiträge zum Alten und Neuen Testament
KBL	Koehler, L., and W. Baumgartner, *Lexicon in Veteris Testamenti libros.* 2d ed. Leiden, 1958
KBo	*Keilschrifttexte aus Boghazköi.* WVDOG 30, 36, 68–70, 72–73, 77–80, 82–86, 89–90. Leipzig, 1916–
KD	*Kerygma und Dogma*
KEK	Kritisch-exegetischer Kommentar über das Neue Testament (Meyer-Kommentar)
Kerux	*Kerux*
KHC	Kurzer Hand-Commentar zum Alten Testament
KI	*Kanaanäische Inschriften (Moabitisch, Althebraisch, Phonizisch, Punisch).* Edited by M. Lidzbarski. Giessen, 1907
KK	*Katorikku Kenkyu*
KlPauly	*Der kleine Pauly*
KlT	Kleine Texte
KS	*Kirjath-Sepher*
KTU	*Die keilalphabetischen Texte aus Ugarit.* Edited by M. Dietrich, O. Loretz, and J. Sanmartín. AOAT 24/1. Neukirchen-Vluyn, 1976. 2d enlarged ed. of *KTU: The Cuneiform Alphabetic Texts from Ugarit, Ras Ibn Hani, and Other Places.* Edited by M. Dietrich, O. Loretz, and J. Sanmartín. Münster, 1995 (= *CTU*)

138

KUB	*Keilschrifturkunden aus Boghazköi*
Kuhn	Kuhn, K. G. *Konkordanz zu den Qumrantexten.* Göttingen, 1960
KVRG	Kölner Veroffentlichungen zur Religionsgeschichte
L&N	*Greek-English Lexicon of the New Testament: Based on Semantic Domains.* Edited by J. P. Louw and E. A. Nida. 2d ed. New York, 1989
LAE	*Literature of Ancient Egypt.* W. K. Simpson. New Haven, 1972
Lane	Lane, E. W. *An Arabic-English Lexicon.* 8 vols. London. Reprint, 1968
LAPO	Littératures anciennes du Proche-Orient
LASBF	*Liber annuus Studii biblici franciscani*
Laur	*Laurentianum*
LÄ	*Lexikon der Ägyptologie.* Edited by W. Helck, E. Otto, and W. Westendorf. Wiesbaden, 1972
LB	*Linguistica Biblica*
LCC	Library of Christian Classics. Philadelphia, 1953–
LCL	Loeb Classical Library
LD	Lectio divina
LEC	Library of Early Christianity
Leš	*Lešonénu*
Levant	*Levant*
LexSyr	*Lexicon syriacum.* C. Brockelmann. 2d ed. Halle, 1928
LIMC	*Lexicon iconographicum mythologiae classicae.* Edited by H. C. Ackerman and J.-R. Gisler. 8 vols. Zurich, 1981–1997
List	*Listening: Journal of Religion and Culture*
LJPSTT	Literature of the Jewish People in the Period of the Second Temple and the Talmud
LQ	*Lutheran Quarterly*
LR	*Lutherische Rundschau*
LS	*Louvain Studies*
LSJ	Liddell, H. G., R. Scott, H. S. Jones, *A Greek-English Lexicon.* 9th ed. with revised supplement. Oxford, 1996
LSS	*Leipziger semitische Studien*
LTK	*Lexicon für Theologie und Kirche*
LTP	*Laval théologique et philosophique*
LTQ	*Lexington Theological Quarterly*
LUÅ	Lunds universitets årsskrift
Lum	*Lumen*
LumVie	*Lumière et vie*
LW	*Living Word*
MAAR	Memoirs of the American Academy in Rome
Maarav	*Maarav*
MAMA	*Monumenta Asiae Minoris Antiqua.* Manchester and London, 1928–1993
Mandl	Mandelkern, S. *Veteris Testamenti concordantiae hebraicae atque chaldaicae, etc.* Reprint, 1925. 2d ed. Jerusalem, 1967
MAOG	Mitteilungen der Altorientalischen Gesellschaft
MARI	*Mari: Annales de recherches interdisciplinaires*

139

MBPF	Münchener Beiträge zur Papyrusforschung und antiken Rechtsgeschichte
MBS	Message of Biblical Spirituality
McCQ	*McCormick Quarterly*
MCom	*Miscelánea Comillas*
MCuS	*Manchester Cuneiform Studies*
MDAI	*Mitteilungen des Deutschen archäologischen Instituts*
MDB	*Mercer Dictionary of the Bible.* Edited by W. E. Mills. Macon, 1990
MdB	*Le Monde de la Bible*
MDOG	Mitteilungen der Deutschen Orient-Gesellschaft
MEAH	*Miscelánea de estudios arabes y hebraicos*
Med	*Medellin*
MEFR	*Mélanges d'archéologie et d'histoire de l'école français de Rome*
MelT	*Melita theologica*
MGWJ	*Monatschrift für Geschichte und Wissenschaft des Judentums*
MH	*Museum helveticum*
Mid-Stream	*Mid-Stream*
Mils	*Milltown Studies*
MIOF	*Mitteilungen des Instituts für Orientforschung*
MM	Moulton, J. H., and G. Milligan. *The Vocabulary of the Greek Testament.* London, 1930. Reprint, Peabody, Mass., 1997
MNTC	Moffatt New Testament Commentary
MPAIBL	Mémoires présentés à l'Academie des inscriptions et belles-lettres
MS	*Mediaeval Studies*
MScRel	*Mélanges de science religieuse*
MSJ	*The Master's Seminary Journal*
MSL	*Materialien zum sumerischen Lexikon.* Benno Landsberger, ed.
MSU	Mitteilungen des Septuaginta-Unternehmens
MTSR	*Method and Theory in the Study of Religion*
MTZ	*Münchener theologische Zeitschrift*
Mursurillo	Mursurillo, H., ed. and trans. *The Acts of the Christian Martyrs.* Oxford, 1972
Mus	*Muséon: Revue d'études orientales*
MUSJ	*Mélanges de l'Université Saint-Joseph*
MVAG	Mitteilungen der Vorderasiatisch-ägyptischen Gesellschaft. Vols. 1–44. 1896–1939
NABU	*Nouvelles assyriologiques breves et utilitaires*
NAC	New American Commentary
NAWG	*Nachrichten (von) der Akademie der Wissenschaften in Göttingen*
NBD²	*New Bible Dictionary.* Edited by J. D. Douglas and N. Hillyer. 2d ed. Downers Grove, 1982
NBf	*New Blackfrairs*
NCB	New Century Bible
NCE	*New Catholic Encyclopedia.* Edited by W. J. McDonald et al. 15 vols. New York, 1967
NE	*Handbuch der nordsemitischen Epigraphik.* Edited by M. Lidzbarski. Weimar, 1898. Reprint, Hildesheim, 1962

140

NEAEHL	*The New Encyclopedia of Archaeological Excavations in the Holy Land.* Edited by E. Stern. 4 vols. Jerusalem, 1993
NEchtB	Neue Echter Bibel
NedTT	*Nederlands theologisch tijdschrift*
Nem	*Nemalah*
Neot	*Neotestamentica*
NETR	*Near East School of Theology Theological Review*
NewDocs	*New Documents Illustrating Early Christianity.* Edited by G. H. R. Horsley and S. Llewelyn. North Ryde, N.S.W., 1981–
NFT	New Frontiers in Theology
NGTT	*Nederduitse gereformeerde teologiese tydskrif*
NHC	Nag Hammadi Codices
NHL	*Nag Hammadi Library in English.* Edited by J. M. Robinson. 4th rev. ed. Leiden, 1996
NHS	Nag Hammadi Studies
NIB	*The New Interpreter's Bible*
NIBCNT	New International Biblical Commentary on the New Testament
NIBCOT	New International Biblical Commentary on the Old Testament
NICNT	New International Commentary on the New Testament
NICOT	New International Commentary on the Old Testament
NIDB	*New International Dictionary of the Bible.* Edited by J. D. Douglas and M. C. Tenney. Grand Rapids, 1987
NIDBA	*New International Dictionary of Biblical Archaeology.* Edited by E. M. Blaiklock and R. K. Harrison. Grand Rapids, 1983
NIDNTT	*New International Dictionary of New Testament Theology.* Edited by C. Brown. 4 vols. Grand Rapids, 1975–1985
NIDOTTE	*New International Dictionary of Old Testament Theology and Exegesis.* Edited by W. A. VanGemeren. 5 vols. Grand Rapids, 1997
NIGTC	New International Greek Testament Commentary
NJahrb	*Neue Jahrbücher für das klassiche Altertum (1898–1925); Neue Jahrbücher für Wissenschaft und Jugendbildung (1925–1936)*
NJBC	*The New Jerome Biblical Commentary.* Edited by R. E. Brown et al. Englewood Cliffs, 1990
NKZ	*Neue kirchliche Zeitschrift*
Notes	*Notes on Translation*
NovT	*Novum Testamentum*
NovTSup	Novum Testamentum Supplements
NovTSup	Supplements to Novum Testamentum
NPNF[1]	*Nicene and Post-Nicene Fathers, Series 1*
NPNF[2]	*Nicene and Post-Nicene Fathers, Series 2*
NRTh	*La nouvelle revue théologique*
NTA	*New Testament Abstracts*
NTAbh	Neutestamentliche Abhandlungen
NTD	Das Neue Testament Deutsch
NTF	Neutestamentliche Forschungen
NTG	New Testament Guides

NTGF	New Testament in the Greek Fathers
NTL	New Testament Library
NTOA	Novum Testamentum et Orbis Antiquus
NTS	*New Testament Studies*
NTT	*Norsk Teologisk Tidsskrift*
NTTS	New Testament Tools and Studies
NumC	*Numismatic Chronicle*
Numen	*Numen: International Review for the History of Religions*
NuMu	*Nuevo mundo*
NV	*Nova et vetera*
OBO	Orbis biblicus et orientalis
ÖBS	Österreichische biblische Studien
OBT	Overtures to Biblical Theology
OCD	*Oxford Classical Dictionary.* Edited by S. Hornblower and A. Spawforth. 3d ed. Oxford, 1996
OCP	*Orientalia christiana periodica*
OCT	Oxford Classical Texts/Scriptorum classicorum bibliotheca oxoniensis
OCuT	Oxford Editions of Cuneiform Texts
ODCC	*The Oxford Dictionary of the Christian Church.* Edited by F. L. Cross and E. A. Livingstone. 2d ed. Oxford, 1983
OEANE	*The Oxford Encyclopedia of Archaeology in the Near East.* Edited by E. M. Meyers. New York, 1997
OECT	Oxford Early Christian Texts. Edited by H. Chadwick. Oxford, 1970–
OGIS	*Orientis graeci inscriptiones selectae.* Edited by W. Dittenberger. 2 vols. Leipzig, 1903–1905
OiC	*One in Christ*
OIC	*Oriental Institute Communications*
OIP	Oriental Institute Publications
OLA	Orientalia lovaniensia analecta
OLP	Orientalia lovaniensia periodica
OLZ	*Orientalistische Literaturzeitung*
Or	*Orientalia* (NS)
OrAnt	*Oriens antiquus*
OrChr	*Oriens christianus*
OrChrAn	Orientalia christiana analecta
Orita	*Orita*
OrSyr	*L'orient syrien*
OTA	*Old Testament Abstracts*
OTE	*Old Testament Essays*
OTG	Old Testament Guides
ÖTK	Ökumenischer Taschenbuch-Kommentar
OTL	Old Testament Library
OTP	*Old Testament Pseudepigrapha.* Edited by J. H. Charlesworth. 2 vols. New York, 1983
OTS	Old Testament Studies
OtSt	*Oudtestamentische Studiën*
PAAJR	*Proceedings of the American Academy of Jewish Research*

142

Pacifica	*Pacifica*
Parab	*Parabola*
PapyCast	Papyrologica Castroctaviana, Studia et textus. Barcelona, 1967–
ParOr	*Parole de l'orient*
PaVi	*Parole di vita*
Payne Smith	*Thesaurus syriacus.* Edited by R. Payne Smith. Oxford, 1879–1901
PDM	*Papyri demoticae magicae.* Demotic texts in *PGM* corpus as collated in H. D. Betz, ed. *The Greek Magical Papyri in Translation, including the Demotic Spells.* Chicago, 1996
PEFQS	Palestine Exploration Fund Quarterly Statement
PEQ	*Palestine Exploration Quarterly*
Per	*Perspectives*
PerTeol	*Perspectiva teológica*
PG	Patrologia graeca [= Patrologiae cursus completus: Series graeca]. Edited by J.-P. Migne. 162 vols. Paris, 1857–1886
PGL	*Patristic Greek Lexicon.* Edited by G. W. H. Lampe. Oxford, 1968
PGM	*Papyri graecae magicae: Die griechischen Zauberpapyri.* Edited by K. Preisendanz. Berlin, 1928
Phil	*Philologus*
Phon	*Phonetica*
PIASH	Proceedings of the Israel Academy of Sciences and Humanities
PIBA	Proceedings of the Irish Biblical Association
PJ	*Palästina-Jahrbuch*
PL	Patrologia latina [= Patrologiae cursus completus: Series latina]. Edited by J.-P. Migne. 217 vols. Paris, 1844–1864
Pneuma	*Pneuma: Journal for the Society of Pentecostal Studies*
PNTC	Pelican New Testament Commentaries
PO	Patrologia orientalis
POut	De Prediking van het Oude Testament
Presb	*Presbyterion*
ProEccl	*Pro ecclesia*
Proof	*Prooftexts: A Journal of Jewish Literary History*
Protest	*Protestantesimo*
Proy	*Proyección*
PRSt	*Perspectives in Religious Studies*
PRU	*Le palais royal d'Ugarit*
PS	Patrologia syriaca. Rev. ed. I. Ortiz de Urbina. Rome, 1965
PSB	*Princeton Seminary Bulletin*
PSTJ	*Perkins (School of Theology) Journal*
PTMS	Pittsburgh Theological Monograph Series
PTS	Patristische Texte und Studien
PVTG	Pseudepigrapha Veteris Testamenti Graece
PW	Pauly, A. F. *Paulys Realencyclopädie der classischen Altertumswissenschaft.* New edition G. Wissowa. 49 vols. Munich, 1980

143

PWSup	Supplement to PW
PzB	*Protokolle zur Bibel*
Qad	*Qadmoniot*
QC	*Qumran Chronicle*
QD	Quaestiones disputatae
QDAP	*Quarterly of the Department of Antiquities in Palestine*
QR	*Quarterly Review*
Quasten	Quasten, J. Patrology. 4 vols. Westminster, 1953–1986
R&T	*Religion and Theology*
RA	*Revue d'assyriologie et d'archéologie orientale*
RAC	*Reallexikon für Antike und Christentum.* Edited by T. Kluser et al. Stuttgart, 1950–
RANE	Records of the Ancient Near East
RAr	*Revue archéologique*
RÄR	*Reallexikon der ägyptischen Religionsgeschichte.* H. Bonnet. Berlin, 1952
RawlCu	*The Cuneiform Inscriptions of Western Asia.* Edited by H. C. Rawlinson. London, 1891
RB	*Revue biblique*
RBB	*Revista biblica brasileira*
RBén	*Revue bénédictine*
RBL	*Ruch biblijny i liturgiczny*
RBPH	*Revue belge de philologie et d'histoire*
RCB	*Revista de cultura bíblica*
RCT	*Revista catalana de teología*
RdT	*Rassegna di teologia*
RE	*Realencyklopädie für protestantische Theologie und Kirche*
REA	*Revue des études anciennes*
REAug	*Revue des études augustiniennes*
REB	*Revista eclesiástica brasileira*
RechBib	Recherches bibliques
RechPap	*Recherches de papyrologie*
RefLitM	*Reformed Liturgy and Music*
RefR	*Reformed Review*
REg	*Revue d'égyptologie*
REG	*Revue des études grecques*
REJ	*Revue des études juives*
RelArts	Religion and the Arts
RelEd	*Religious Education*
RelS	*Religious Studies*
RelSoc	*Religion and Society*
RelSRev	*Religious Studies Review*
RelStTh	*Religious Studies and Theology*
RES	*Répertoire d'épigraphie sémitique*
RES	*Revue des études sémitiques*
ResQ	*Restoration Quarterly*
RET	*Revista española de teología*
RevExp	*Review and Expositor*
RevistB	*Revista bíblica*

144

RevPhil	*Revue de philologie*
RevQ	*Revue de Qumran*
RevScRel	*Revue des sciences religieuses*
RGG	*Religion in Geschichte und Gegenwart.* Edited by K. Galling. 7 vols. 3d ed. Tübingen, 1957–1965
RHA	*Revue hittite et asianique*
RHE	*Revue d'histoire ecclésiastique*
RHPR	*Revue d'histoire et de philosophie religieuses*
RHR	*Revue de l'histoire des religions*
RIBLA	*Revista de interpretación bíblica latino-americana*
RIDA	*Revue internationale des droits de l'antiquité*
RIM	The Royal Inscriptions of Mesopotamia Project. Toronto
RIMA	The Royal Inscriptions of Mesopotamia, Assyrian Periods
RIMB	The Royal Inscriptions of Mesopotamia, Babylonian Periods
RIME	The Royal Inscriptions of Mesopotamia, Early Periods
RIMS	The Royal Inscriptions of Mesopotamia, Supplements
RISA	*Royal Inscriptions of Sumer and Akkad.* Edited by G. A. Barton. New Haven, 1929
RivB	*Rivista biblica italiana*
RivSR	*Rivista di scienze religiose*
RlA	*Reallexikon der Assyriologie.* Edited by Erich Ebeling et al. Berlin, 1928–
RLV	*Reallexikon der Vorgeschichte.* Edited by M. Ebert. Berlin, 1924–1932
RNT	Regensburger Neues Testament
RocT	*Roczniki teologiczne*
RomBarb	*Romanobarbarica*
RoMo	Rowohlts Monographien
RQ	*Römische Quartalschrift für christliche Altertumskunde und Kirchengeschichte*
RR	*Review of Religion*
RRef	*La revue réformée*
RRelRes	*Review of Religious Research*
RS	Ras Shamra
RSC	*Rivista di studi classici*
RSém	*Revue de sémitique*
RSF	*Rivista di studi fenici*
RSO	*Revista degli studi orientali*
RSO	*Rivista degli studi orientali*
RSP	*Ras Shamra Parallels*
RSPT	*Revue des sciences philosophiques et théologiques*
RSR	*Recherches de science religieuse*
RST	Regensburger Studien zur Theologie
RStB	*Ricerche storico bibliche*
RTAM	*Recherches de théologie ancienne et médiévale*
RThom	*Revue thomiste*
RTL	*Revue théologique de Louvain*
RTP	*Revue de théologie et de philosophie*

RTR	*Reformed Theological Review*
RUO	*Revue de l'université d'Ottawa*
SA	Studia anselmiana
SAA	State Archives of Assyria
SAAB	*State Archives of Assyria Bulletin*
SAAS	State Archives of Assyria Studies
SAC	Studies in Antiquity and Christianity
SacEr	*Sacris erudiri: Jaarboek voor Godsdienstwetenschappen*
Salm	*Salmanticensis*
SANT	Studien zum Alten und Neuen Testaments
SAOC	Studies in Ancient Oriental Civilizations
Sap	*Sapienza*
SAQ	Sammlung ausgewählter Kirchen- und dogmen- geschichtlicher Quellenschriften
SB	*Sammelbuch griechischer Urkunden aus Aegypten.* Edited by F. Preisigke et al. Vols. 1– , 1915–
SB	Sources bibliques
SBA	Studies in Biblical Archaeology
SBAB	Stuttgarter biblische Aufsatzbände
SBAW	Sitzungsberichte der bayerischen Akademie der Wissenschaften
SBB	Stuttgarter biblische Beiträge
SBFLA	*Studii biblici Franciscani liber annus*
SBL	Society of Biblical Literature
SBLABS	Society of Biblical Literature Archaeology and Biblical Studies
SBLBAC	Society of Biblical Literature The Bible and American Culture
SBLBMI	Society of Biblical Literature The Bible and Its Modern Interpreters
SBLBSNA	Society of Biblical Literature Biblical Scholarship in North America
SBLCP	Society of Biblical Literature Centennial Publications
SBLDS	Society of Biblical Literature Dissertation Series
SBLEJL	Society of Biblical Literature Early Judaism and Its Literature
SBLMasS	Society of Biblical Literature Masoretic Studies
SBLMS	Society of Biblical Literature Monograph Series
SBLNTGF	Society of Biblical Literature The New Testament in the Greek Fathers
SBLRBS	Society of Biblical Literature Resources for Biblical Study
SBLSBS	Society of Biblical Literature Sources for Biblical Study
SBLSCS	Society of Biblical Literature Septuagint and Cognate Studies
SBLSP	*Society of Biblical Literature Seminar Papers*
SBLSymS	Society of Biblical Literature Symposium Series
SBLTT	Society of Biblical Literature Texts and Translations
SBLWAW	Society of Biblical Literature Writings from the Ancient World
SBM	Stuttgarter biblische Monographien
SBS	Stuttgarter Bibelstudien
SBT	Studies in Biblical Theology
SC	Sources chrétiennes. Paris: Cerf, 1943–
ScC	*La scuola cattolica*

146

ScEccl	*Sciences ecclésiastiques*
ScEs	*Science et esprit*
SCH	Studies in Church History
SCHNT	Studia ad corpus hellenisticum Novi Testamenti
Schol	*Scholastik*
Scr	*Scripture*
SCR	*Studies in Comparative Religion*
ScrB	*Scripture Bulletin*
ScrC	*Scripture in Church*
ScrHier	Scripta hierosolymitana
ScrTh	*Scripta theologica*
ScrVict	*Scriptorium victoriense*
SD	Studies and Documents
SDAW	Sitzungen der deutschen Akademie der Wissenschaften zu Berlin
SE	*Studia evangelica I, II, III* (= TU 73 [1959], 87 [1964], 88 [1964]. etc.)
SEAug	Studia ephemeridis Augustinianum
SEÅ	*Svensk exegetisk årsbok*
SecCent	*Second Century*
Sef	*Sefarad*
SEG	Supplementum epigraphicum graecum
SEL	*Studi epigrafici e linguistici*
Sem	*Semitica*
Semeia	*Semeia*
SemeiaSt	Semeia Studies
SFulg	*Scripta fulgentina*
SHANE	Studies in the History of the Ancient Near East
SHAW	Sitzungen der heidelberger Akademie der Wissenschaften
Shofar	*Shofar*
SHR	Studies in the History of Religions (supplement to *Numen*)
SHT	Studies in Historical Theology
SIDIC	*SIDIC* (Journal of the Service internationale de documentation judeo-chrétienne)
SIG	*Sylloge inscriptionum graecarum.* Edited by W. Dittenberger. 4 vols. 3d ed. Leipzig, 1915–1924
SJ	Studia judaica
SJLA	Studies in Judaism in Late Antiquity
SJOT	*Scandinavian Journal of the Old Testament*
SJT	*Scottish Journal of Theology*
SK	*Skrif en kerk*
SKKNT	Stuttgarter kleiner Kommentar, Neues Testament
SL	*Sumerisches Lexikon.* Edited by A. Deimel. 8 vols. Rome, 1928–1950
SLJT	*St. Luke's Journal of Theology*
SMBen	Série monographique de Benedictina: Section paulinienne
SMSR	*Studi e materiali di storia delle religioni*
SMT	*Studii Montis Regii*
SNT	Studien zum Neuen Testament

SNTA	Studiorum Novi Testamenti Auxilia
SNTSMS	Society for New Testament Studies Monograph Series
SNTSU	Studien zum Neuen Testament und seiner Umwelt
SO	Symbolae osloenses
SÖAW	Sitzungen der österreichischen Akademie der Wissenschaften in Wien
Sobornost	*Sobornost*
SOTSMS	Society for Old Testament Studies Monograph Series
Sound	*Soundings*
SP	Sacra pagina
SPap	*Studia papyrologica*
SPAW	Sitzungsberichte der preussischen Akademie der Wissenschaften
Spec	*Speculum*
SPhilo	*Studia philonica*
SQAW	Schriften und Quellen der alten Welt
SR	*Studies in Religion*
SSEJC	*Studies in Early Judaism and Christianity*
SSN	Studia semitica neerlandica
SSS	Semitic Study Series
ST	*Studia theologica*
St	*Studium*
StABH	Studies in American Biblical Hermeneutics
StC	Studia catholica
STDJ	*Studies on the Texts of the Desert of Judah*
SThU	*Schweizerische theologische Umschau*
SThZ	*Schweizerische theologische Zeitschrift*
STJ	*Stulos Theological Journal*
STK	*Svensk teologisk kvartalskrift*
StOR	Studies in Oriental Religions
StPat	*Studia patavina*
StPatr	Studia patristica
StPB	Studia post-biblica
Str	*Stromata*
Str-B	Strack, H. L., and P. Billerbeck. *Kommentar zum Neuen Testament aus Talmud und Midrasch.* 6 vols. Munich, 1922–1961
STRev	*Sewanee Theological Review*
StSin	Studia Sinaitica
StudBib	Studia Biblica
StudMon	Studia monastica
StudNeot	Studia neotestamentica
StudOr	Studia orientalia
StZ	Stimmen der Zeit
Su	*Studia theologica varsaviensia*
SubBi	*Subsidia biblica*
Sumer	*Sumer: A Journal of Archaeology and History in Iraq*
SUNT	Studien zur Umwelt des Neuen Testaments
SVF	*Stoicorum veterum fragmenta.* H. von Arnim. 4 vols. Leipzig, 1903–1924

SVTP	Studia in Veteris Testamenti pseudepigraphica
SVTQ	*St. Vladimir's Theological Quarterly*
SWBA	Social World of Biblical Antiquity
SwJT	*Southwestern Journal of Theology*
SymBU	Symbolae biblicae upsalienses
T&K	*Texte & Kontexte*
TA	*Tel Aviv*
TAPA	*Transactions of the American Philological Association*
Tarbiz	*Tarbiz*
TB	Theologische Bücherei: Neudrucke und Berichte aus dem 20. Jahrhundert
TBC	Torch Bible Commentaries
TBei	*Theologische Beiträge*
TBl	*Theologische Blätter*
TBT	*The Bible Today*
TCL	Textes cunéiformes. Musée du Louvre
TCS	Texts from Cuneiform Sources
TCW	*Tydskrif vir Christelike Wetenskap*
TD	*Theology Digest*
TDNT	*Theological Dictionary of the New Testament.* Edited by G. Kittel and G. Friedrich. Translated by G. W. Bromiley. 10 vols. Grand Rapids, 1964–1976
TDOT	*Theological Dictionary of the Old Testament.* Edited by G. J. Botterweck and H. Ringgren. Translated by J. T. Willis, G. W. Bromiley, and D. E. Green. 8 vols. Grand Rapids, 1974–
Teol	*Teología*
Teubner	Bibliotheca scriptorum graecorum et romanorum teubneriana
Text	*Textus*
TF	*Theologische Forschung*
TGI	*Textbuch zur Geschichte Israels.* Edited by K. Galling. 2d ed. Tübingen, 1968
TGl	*Theologie und Glaube*
TGUOS	Transactions of the Glasgow University Oriental Society
THAT	*Theologisches Handwörterbuch zum Alten Testament.* Edited by E. Jenni, with assistance from C. Westermann. 2 vols., Stuttgart, 1971–1976
Them	*Themelios*
Theo	*Theologika*
Theol	*Theologica*
ThH	Théologie historique
THKNT	Theologischer Handkommentar zum Neuen Testament
ThPQ	*Theologisch-praktische Quartalschrift*
ThSt	Theologische Studiën
ThT	*Theologisch tijdschrift*
ThTo	*Theology Today*
ThViat	*Theologia viatorum*
ThWAT	*Theologisches Wörterbuch zum Alten Testament.* Edited by G. J. Botterweck and H. Ringgren. Stuttgart, 1970–
TI	*Teologia iusi*

149

TimesLitSupp	*Times Literary Supplement*
TJ	*Trinity Journal*
TJT	*Toronto Journal of Theology*
TLG	*Thesaurus linguae graecae: Canon of Greek Authors and Works.* Edited by L. Berkowitz and K. A. Squitier. 3d ed. Oxford, 1990
TLL	*Thesaurus linguae latinae*
TLNT	*Theological Lexicon of the New Testament.* C. Spicq. Translated and edited by J. D. Ernest. 3 vols. Peabody, Mass., 1994
TLOT	*Theological Lexicon of the Old Testament.* Edited by E. Jenni, with assistance from C. Westermann. Translated by M. E. Biddle. 3 vols. Peabody, Mass., 1997
TLZ	*Theologische Literaturzeitung*
TNTC	Tyndale New Testament Commentaries
TOTC	Tyndale Old Testament Commentaries
TP	*Theologie und Philosophie*
TPINTC	TPI New Testament Commentaries
TPQ	*Theologisch-praktische Quartalschrift*
TQ	*Theologische Quartalschrift*
Transeu	*Transeuphratène*
TRE	*Theologische Realenzyklopädie.* Edited by G. Krause and G. Müller. Berlin, 1977–
TRev	*Theologische Revue*
TRSR	Testi e ricerche di scienze religiose
TRu	*Theologische Rundschau*
Trumah	*Trumah*
TS	Texts and Studies
TS	*Theological Studies*
TSAJ	Texte und Studien zum antiken Judentum
TSK	*Theologische Studien und Kritiken*
TTE	*The Theological Educator*
TThSt	Trierer theologische Studien
TTJ	*Trinity Theological Journal*
TTKi	*Tidsskrift for Teologi og Kirke*
TTZ	*Trierer theologische Zeitschrift*
TU	Texte und Untersuchungen
TUAT	*Texte aus der Umwelt des Alten Testaments.* Edited by Otto Kaiser. Gütersloh, 1984–
TUGAL	Texte und Untersuchungen zur Geschichte der altchristlichen Literatur
TUMSR	Trinity University Monograph Series in Religion
TV	*Teología y vida*
TVM	Theologische Verlagsgemeinschaft: Monographien
TvT	*Tijdschrift voor theologie*
TWNT	*Theologische Wörterbuch zum Neuen Testament.* Edited by G. Kittel and G. Friedrich. Stuttgart, 1932–1979
TWOT	*Theological Wordbook of the Old Testament.* Edited by R. L. Harris, G. L. Archer Jr. 2 vols. Chicago, 1980
TynBul	*Tyndale Bulletin*
TZ	*Theologische Zeitschrift*

150

UBL	Ugaritisch-biblische Literatur
UF	*Ugarit-Forschungen*
UHP	*Ugaritic-Hebrew Philology.* M. Dahood. 2d ed. Rome, 1989
UJEnc	*The Universal Jewish Encylopedia.* Edited by I. Landman. 10 vols. New York, 1939–1943
UNP	*Ugaritic Narrative Poetry.* Edited by Simon B. Parker. SBLWAW 9. Atlanta, 1997
UNT	Untersuchungen zum Neuen Testament
UrE	Ur Excavations
UrET	Ur Excavations: Texts
USQR	*Union Seminary Quarterly Review*
UT	*Ugaritic Textbook.* C. H. Gordon. AnOr 38. Rome, 1965
UUA	Uppsala Universitetsårskrift
VAB	Vorderasiatische Bibliothek
VAT	Vorderasiatische Abteilung Tontafel. Vorderasiatisches Museum, Berlin
VC	*Vigiliae christianae*
VCaro	*Verbum caro*
VD	*Verbum domini*
VE	*Vox evangelica*
VF	*Verkündigung und Forschung*
VH	*Vivens homo*
Vid	*Vidyajyoti*
VL	*Vetus Latina: Die Reste der altlateinischen Bibel.* Edited by E. Beuron, 1949–
VR	*Vox reformata*
VS	*Verbum Salutie*
VS	*Vox scripturae*
VSpir	*Vie spirituelle*
VT	*Vetus Testamentum*
VTSup	Supplements to Vetus Testamentum
VTSup	Vetus Testamentum Supplements
WÄS	*Wörterbuch der ägyptischen Sprache.* A. Erman and H. Grapow. 5 vols. Berlin, 1926–1931. Reprint, 1963
WBC	Word Biblical Commentary
WC	Westminster Commentaries
WD	*Wort und Dienst*
WDB	*Westminster Dictionary of the Bible*
Wehr	Wehr, H. *A Dictionary of Modern Written Arabic.* Edited by J. M. Cowan. Ithaca, 1961, 1976[3]
WHAB	*Westminster Historical Atlas of the Bible*
WHJP	World History of the Jewish People
WKAS	*Das Wörterbuch der klassischen arabischen Sprache.* Edited by M. Ullmann. 1957– .
WMANT	Wissenschaftliche Monographien zum Alten und Neuen Testament
WO	*Die Welt des Orients*
WTJ	*Westminster Theological Journal*

WTM	*Das Wörterbuch über die Talmudim und Midraschim.* J. Levy. 2d ed. 1924
WUANT	Wissenschaftliche Untersuchungen zum Alten und Neuen Testament
WUNT	Wissenschaftliche Untersuchungen zum Neuen Testament
WUS	*Das Wörterbuch der ugaritischen Sprache.* J. Aistleitner. Edited by O. Eissfeldt. 3d ed. Berlin, 1967
WVDOG	Wissenschaftliche Veröffentlichungen der deutschen Orientgesellschaft
WW	*Word and World*
WZ	*Wissenschaftliche Zeitschrift*
WZKM	*Wiener Zeitschrift für die Kunde des Morgenlandes*
WZKSO	*Wiener Zeitschrift für die Kunde Süd- und Ostasiens*
YCS	Yale Classical Studies
YOS	Yale Oriental Series, Texts
YOSR	Yale Oriental Series, Researches
ZA	*Zeitschrift für Assyriologie*
ZABeih	Zeitschrift für Assyriologie: Beihefte
ZABR	*Zeitschrift für altorientalische und biblische Rechtgeschichte*
ZAC	*Zeitschrift für Antikes Christentum/Journal of Ancient Christianity*
ZAH	*Zeitschrift für Althebräistik*
ZÄS	*Zeitschrift für ägyptische Sprache und Altertumskunde*
ZAW	*Zeitschrift für die alttestamentliche Wissenschaft*
ZB	Zürcher Bibel
ZBK	Zürcher Bibelkommentare
ZDMG	*Zeitschrift der deutschen morgenländischen Gesellschaft*
ZDMGSup	Zeitschrift der deutschen morgenländischen Gesellschaft: Supplementbände
ZDPV	*Zeitschrift des deutschen Palästina-Vereins*
ZEE	*Zeitschrift für evangelische Ethik*
ZHT	*Zeitschrift für historische Theologie*
Zion	*Zion*
ZKG	*Zeitschrift für Kirchengeschichte*
ZKT	*Zeitschrift für katholische Theologie*
ZKunstG	*Zeitschrift für Kunstgeschichte*
ZNW	*Zeitschrift für die neutestamentliche Wissenschaft und die Kunde der älteren Kirche*
Zorell	Zorell, F. *Lexicon hebraicum et aramaicum Veteris Testamenti.* Rome, 1968
ZPE	*Zeitschrift für Papyrologie und Epigraphik*
ZPEB	*Zondervan Pictorial Encyclopedia of the Bible.* Edited by M. C. Tenney. 5 vols. Grand Rapids, 1975
ZRGG	*Zeitschrift für Religions- und Geistesgeschichte*
ZS	*Zeitschrift für Semitistik und verwandte Gebiete*
ZST	*Zeitschrift für systematische Theologie*
ZTK	*Zeitschrift für Theologie und Kirche*
ZWKL	*Zeitschrift für Wissenschaft und kirchliches Leben*
ZWT	*Zeitschrift für wissenschaftliche Theologie*

Appendix A:
Capitalization and Spelling Examples

See above §4.4.3 for general rules of capitalization and §2.3 for other authorities.

A

Aaronic (referring to duties and office of priests)

Aaronide (referring to genealogy and descent of Aaron)

ʿabiru/ʿapiru (note ʿayins) (see ḫabiru/ḫapiru): Apiru

ablative

Abba

abomination of desolation (with or without quotes)

Abrahamic covenant

Achaemenid

ad hoc

Adapa

affix (any prefix, suffix, or infix)

Adonai

agape (roman); as Greek word, *agapē*

age of grace

Age (for archaeological periods, such as Bronze Age and Iron Age)

agraphon, pl. agrapha

Ahiram Inscription

Ahmose

Ahura Mazda

Akedah

Akhetaten (Tell el-Amarna)

Akiba (not Akiva or Aqiba)

Akkadian

Aktionsart

Aleppo Codex

Alpha and Omega (as titles of Christ)

Amarna age, letters, tablets

Am Ha'arets

amillennial(ism)

amphictyony

Anat

ancient Near East (noun)

ancient Near Eastern (adj.)

angel of the Lord

Angel of the Lord, the

ante-Christian

antediluvian

ante-Nicene fathers

antichrist, the

anti-Christian

antimonarchic

anti-Semitic

anti-Semitism

Apiru

Apocalypse, the (the book of Revelation)

apocalyptic

Apocrypha, the

apocryphal

Apology of Hattusilis

apothegm

Apostle Paul (but Paul the apostle, etc.)

apostle(s), the (the twelve apostles)

Apostles' Creed

apostolic

apostolic age

apostolic council/fathers

Apostolic Fathers (corpus of writings)

a priori

Aramaean

archaeology

archbishop of Canterbury (but Archbishop Smith)

Area x (archaeological reports; area followed by number)

ark (Noah's)

ark of the covenant

Ascension Day (as liturgical day)

ascension, the

Asclepius (not Asklepios)

Asherah

153

ashlar masonry
Ashur (city and god)
Ashurbanipal
Ashurnasirpal
Assyrian Empire
Assyrian King List
Astarte
atheist
Athirat
atonement, the
Atonement, the Day of
Atrahasis Epic
Augsburg Confession

B

Baal (Not Baʿal, unless in Semitic
    transcription)
Baal and Anath
Baal-shamayn
baalism
Babylonian captivity
Babylonian Chronicle
Babylonian Empire
Babylonian King List
baptism
baptism in/with/of the Holy Spirit
baptism, the (of Christ)
Bar Kokhba (person)
Bar Kokhba revolt
baraita (rabbinic gloss)
baraita (pl. *baraitoth*; for
    pronouncements as such)
Baraita (the specific rabbinic work)
Baraita (for collections; e.g., *Baraita de
    Sifrei, Baraita de Niddah, Baraita of
    Rabbi Adda*)
Bat Qol (or *bat qol*)
battle of Armageddon
battle of Carchemish, etc.
beast, the
Beatitudes, the
bedouin (singular and plural)
Behistun
Ben Sira
Ben-hadad
Benedictus (Song of Zechariah)
betrayal, the
Bible

biblical
bilingual
bishop of Rome (but Bishop Smith)
Black Obelisk
Blessing of Moses
blood of Christ
Bodmer papyri
body of Christ
book of the covenant
book of Genesis (etc.)
book of the law
Book of Life
boustrophedon
Bread of Life or bread of life
bridegroom, the (Christ)
bulla (pl. bullae)
burnt offering

C

caesura
Cairo Genizah
call of Amos, etc.
canon, the
captivity, the
cartouche
catalogue
Catholic (faith)
catholic (universal)
Catholic Church
Catholic Epistles (or Letters)
casuistic
CD-ROM
central hill country
century (the first century; first-century
    [adj.])
cereal offering
Chaldean
charismatic (noun and adj.)
charismatic movement
Chebar River
Chester Beatty papyri
chief priest
chosen people
Christian (noun and adj.)
Christian era
christianize
Christlike
christocentric

christological
Christology
christophany
Chronicler, the
church (body of Christ)
church (institution)
church age
church father(s) (but the Fathers of the church)
city of David
city of God
city-state
Classical Arabic
coastal plain
Code of Hammurabi
Codex Alexandrinus, Codex Vaticanus, etc.
colon (pl. cola; also bicola, tricola)
Comforter, the
commandment (first, second, etc.; but Ten Commandments)
Community Rule (1QS) (see also *Manual of Discipline*)
conquest period
coregency
coregent
cosmogony
council
Council of Trent
covenant (old covenant, new covenant)
Covenant Code (Exod 21–23)
creation, the
Creation Epic or Epic of Creation (= *Enuma Elish*)
Creator
crown prince
cross (upon which the crucifixion took place)
cross, the (synecdoche for the entire salvation event)
Crucified One or crucified one, the
crucifixion of Christ
crucifixion, the
Crusades
cupbearer
curse, the
Cyrus Cylinder

D

daghesh forte
daghesh lene
D stem
Damascus Covenant (see preferred *Damascus Document*)
Damascus Document (CD)
Danel (legendary king in Ugaritic text)
David's champions
Davidic (adj.; see Davidide)
Davidic monarchy/kingdom/covenant
Davidide (member of the royal house)
Day of Atonement
day of judgment
day of Pentecost
Day of the Lord
Dead Sea Scrolls (but a Dead Sea scroll)
Decalogue (Ten Commandments)
deity of Christ
Deity, the
demiurge
demotic
Deutero-Isaiah
Deutero-Zechariah
deuterocanonical
Deuteronomic
Deuteronomic source
Deuteronomist
Deuteronomistic History/Historian
deuteropauline
devil, the
diacritical mark
Diaspora (the event or the dispersed community)
Diatessaron
diglot
diphthong
disciples
Dispersion
distich
divided kingdom
divided monarchy
divine
Divine Warrior
Documentary Hypothesis
dunam

Dynasty (as in Eighteenth or 18th
    Dynasty; note Twelfth-Thirteenth
    Dynasties)

E

E account
Ea
early church
early church fathers
Early Church Fathers (title of work)
Easter
Eastern Orthodox Church
Eden
Edict of Ammisaduqa
editio princeps
Eighteen Benedictions
elect, God's elect
Elephantine papyri
Elohist source
e-mail
Emperor Constantine
emperor, an
Empire, Neo-Babylonian/Roman etc.
empire, the
end time, the
end-time (adj.)
Enheduanna
Enlil
Enuma Elish (see Creation Epic)
ephod
Epic of Creation (see Creation Epic)
Epic of Gilgamesh
epilogue
Epistle to the Romans (etc.)
Epistles, Paul's (etc.)
Epistles, the
eponym
Eridu Genesis
Erra
Erra Epic
eschatology
Esdraelon Plain
Etemenanki
etiological (not aetiological)
etiology (not aetiology)
eternal life
eternity
etymology/etymological

Eucharist
eucharistic
evangelist (John the; the fourth, etc.)
evangelist (popular)
evangelize
Execration texts
exile (the condition)
exile, the (the Babylonian captivity)
exilic
ex nihilo
exodus, the
extispicy (the oracular reading of viscera)
extrabiblical

F

faith
fall of humanity
fall of Jerusalem
fall, the
Farewell Discourses (in John)
Father, the (referring to God)
Fathers, the (but church fathers; *Early
    Church Fathers* [38–vol. collection]
    but early church fathers)
favissa (pl. favissae) (pits for burying
    cult objects)
feast day
Feast of Firstfruits
Feast of Pentecost (etc.)
Feast of Tabernacles
Fertile Crescent
fertility god(dess)
Festival of Weeks/Booths/Passover
Festschrift(en)
First Evangelist
First Jewish Revolt
first missionary journey
First Temple period
firstborn
firstfruits
Fish Gate
flood, the
footwashing
form criticism
Former Prophets
fosse (ditch, moat)
Four Document Hypothesis
Fourth Evangelist

Fourth Gospel
Fourth Philosophy
funerary offerings

G

G stem
gaon
gaonic
garden of Eden
gehenna
gematria
General Epistles (or General Letters)
genizah, a
Gentile(s) (noun and adj.)
geographical name
ger (pl. *gerim*)
Gezer Calendar
Gilgamesh
glaçis (pl. glaçis)
gnosis
gnostic (noun and adj.)
Gnosticism
God Almighty
God Most High
Godhead
godless
godlike
godly
golden calf, the
good news
gospel (a book of the gospel genre); gospel (= the good news, the kerygma)
gospels (generically); Gospels, the (a division of the canon)
goy (pl. goyim)
Great Commission, the
Great Rift Valley (= Jordan Valley)
Greco-Roman
Greek (noun and adj.)
Greek Testament
Grundlage(n)
guilt offering

H

ḥabiru/ḫapiru (see ʿabiru/ʿapiru): Habiru
hades
haggadah (not aggadah)

haggadic (not aggadic)
hagiographa
halakah (not halaka)
halakic (not halakhic)
half-brother
half-tribe
hallelujah
hanging gardens
Hanukkah
hapax legomenon (pl. *hapax legomena*)
haplography
Hasidic
Hasidim
Hasmonean
Hatti
Hattusas (Boghazköy)
Haustafel(n)
he-locale
heaven
Hebraism
Hebrew Bible
hectare
Heilsgeschichte
hell
Hellenism
Hellenistic
hellenize
hendiadys
henotheism
Heptateuch
Herodian
hesed
Hexaemeron
Hexapla (Hexaplaric)
hieroglyph
high priest
hill country
Hillel the Elder
Historical Books (of the Bible)
history of religions school
Hittite Law Code
Holiness Code (Lev 17–26)
Holy City
Holy Land
holy of holies
holy war
Horus
house of David
humanity

Hurrian
Hymns of Thanksgiving (1QH)

I

idolaters
imago Dei
Immanuel
Imperial Aramaic
Inanna's Descent to the Netherworld
incarnation
Indo-European
infancy gospels
infix
Instruction of Amenemhet
intertestamental
intertestamental period
ipsissima verba
ipsissima vox
Ishme-Dagan
Ishtar
Israelite settlement
ʿIzbet Ṣarṭah

J

Jacobian
Jamnia
Jannaeus
JEDP
Jehovah
Jerusalem Council
Jew
Jewish
Jewish War
Johanan (not Yohanan)
Johannine
Journey of Wen-Amon
Jubilee, Jubilee Year
Judah
Judah the Patriarch
Judaic
Judaism
Judaizer(s)
Judea
Judean
judgment day

K

Kabbalah
Kanesh (Kultepe)
Karatepe inscription
Kassite
Keret Epic (or Kirta)
kerygma
Kethib
Ketubim or Ketuvim (a division of the
    canon)
Khirbet
Khirbet el-Qôm
Khirbet Qumran
Kimchi
King (referring to God)
King Herod
king list (but Sumerian King List, etc.)
king of Israel
King of kings
kingdom of God/heaven
kingdom, the
King's Highway
Koine Greek
Koran: use Qur'an instead
Kuntillet ʿAjrûd

L

Lachish letters
Lachish Ostracon *x*
Lamb of God, the
Lamentation over the Destruction of
    Sumer and Ur
Lamentation over the Destruction of Ur
land of Israel
lapidary
last day, the
last days
Last Judgment, the
Last Supper, the
Latter Prophets
law (versus grace)
law book
law code
law of Moses, Jewish law, law of Israel
Law, the (Pentateuch; a division of the
    canon)
Laws of Ur-Nammu

lectio brevior/difficilior/facilior
Legend of King Keret/Kirta
Legend of Sargon, The
lemma
Leningrad Codex (or Leningradensis)
Letter of Aristeas
Letter to the Galatians (etc.)
Letters, the
Levant, the
Levantine
Level 4 (archaeological reports, level
    followed by number)
Leviathan
levirate
Levite
Levitical
lex talionis
Light of the World or light of the world
limmu lists
lingua franca (roman)
Literature, Second Temple (etc.)
lithic
loanword
locus classicus
Locus *x* (archaeological reports,
    followed by number)
logion (pl. logia)
Logogram
Lord, the (referring to one of the
    persons of the Trinity)
Lord's Day
Lord's Prayer
Lord's Supper
Lord of Hosts
Lord of lords
lordship
lordship of Christ
Lower Egypt (political division)
lower Galilee (geographical division)
Lukan
Luke–Acts

M

Ma'at
Maccabean
Madeba Map
magi
Magnificat (Song of Mary)

Major Prophets, the (a division of the
    canon)
Maker, the (referring to God)
man of sin
Man of Sorrows or man of sorrows
Manichaen
Manual of Discipline (1QS) (see also
    Community Rule)
Mari letters, tablets
Mark Antony
Markan
Masorah
Masoretes
masoretic (but Masoretic Text)
mater lectionis (pl. *matres lectionis*)
Matthean
medieval
Megillah (pl. Megilloth)
Memphite Theology
menorah
mercy seat
merkabah (not merkevah or merkaba)
Merneptah
Merneptah Stela
Merodach-baladan
messiah (in general)
Messiah, the
messiahship
messianic
messianic age
metheg
Mican
microliths
Middle Ages
Middle Assyrian Laws
Middle Assyrian period
Middle Babylonian period
middle Euphrates
middot
midrash (pl. midrashim)
midrashic
mighty men
mina
minor judges
Minor Prophets, the (a division of the
    canon)
minuscule
Mishnah
Mishnaic Hebrew

159

Mitanni
Moabite Stone
monarchic period
moon-god
Mosaic covenant
Mosaic law
Mot (Death personified)
Mount of Olives
Mount of Transfiguration
Mount Sinai
mud brick (noun)
mud-brick (adj.)
Muhammad (not Mohammed)
Muraba'at
Murashu archive
Muratorian Canon/Fragment
Muslim (not Moslem)
Mycenaean
Myth and Ritual school
mythopoeic

N

N stem
Nabatean
Nag Hammadi codices
nahal
Nahal Ḥever
name of God
Naram-sin
Narmer
nation-state
nativity, the
nawamis (beehive burials)
Nazirite
Near East
Nebiim or Nevi'im (a division of the
  canon)
Nebuchadnezzar (unless Nebuchadrezzar
  is important to the point)
Neco
Negev (not Negeb)
Neo-Assyrian period (but Neo-Assyrian
  Empire)
Neo-Babylonian period (but Neo-
  Babylonian Empire)
neo-Evangelicalism
Neofiti
Neo-Hittite

neo-orthodoxy
neo-Pentecostalism
neoplatonic
neoplatonism
Nergal and Ereshkigal
Nevi'im
new age
new covenant
new heaven and new earth
new Jerusalem
New Moon (festival)
new moon, the
New Testament (noun and adj.)
New World (as opposed to Old World)
New Year festival
Nicene Creed
Nile Delta
Nineveh
nomina sacra
noncanonical
non-Christian (but unchristian)
nonidolatrous
non-Pauline
north Arabia
northern Israel
northern kingdom
Northwest Semitic
notariqon
Nuzi texts (not Nuzu)

O

Official Aramaic
Old Assyrian period
Old Babylonian period
old covenant
Old Latin
Old South Arabic
Old Syriac
Old Testament (noun and adj.)
Old World
Omride dynasty
Omrides
only begotten of the Father
only begotten Son
Onqelos
oral law
Oral Torah
oral tradition

Orient
oriental
orientalist
original sin
Orthodox (Judaism; Eastern Orthodox)
orthodoxy
Orthostat(s)
Osiris
ostracon (pl. ostraca)
Oxyrhynchus papyri (but cf. POxy 250)

P

pagan
palace complex
Paleo-Canaanite
paleography
palimpsest
papponymy
papyrus (pl. papyri)
parable of the Good Samaritan
parable of the Wicked Tenants (etc.)
paradise
Paraleipomenon
parallelismus membrorum
Parousia, the
paschal
passim (roman)
Passion Narrative
passion, the
Passover (noun and adj.)
Passover Seder
Pastoral Epistles
patriarchal narratives
patriarchal period/age
patriarchs, the
patristic(s)
Pauline Epistles (or Letters)
Pentateuch
pentateuchal
Pentecost
pentecostal (adj.)
Pentecostal (noun)
penult/penultima
people of Israel
percent (spelled out in text; % in
    parentheses)
pericope (pl. pericopae)
period of the judges

period, as in Roman period,
    Chalcolithic period (cf. Age/Empire),
    First Intermediate period
Persian Empire
person of Christ
personal name
persons of the Trinity (but Third Person
    of the Trinity)
pesher
Peshitta
Petrine
Phaestos Disk
Pharaoh (when used as a proper name)
Pharisaic
Pharisees
pilgrim festivals
Piye (Piankhy)
place name
plain (as in Esdraelon plain)
Pleistocene
plene writing
Poetic(al) Books (of the Bible)
Pope John XXIII
pope, the
post-Nicene
postbiblical
postdiluvian
postexilic
potsherd (not potshard)
pre-Christian
prediluvian
preexilic
premillennial(ism)
premonarchic
priesthood of Christ
priesthood, the
Priestly Code/Document
Priestly source
priestly writings
Prison Epistles
promised land
Prophecy of Neferti
Prophet Jeremiah
Prophetic(al) Books (of the Bible)
prophets
Prophets, the (a division of the canon)
Protestant(ism)
Proto-Sinaitic
Proto-Semitic

Proto-urban period
Proverbs/Words of Ahiqar
Psalm 23, the Twenty-third Psalm
psalm, a
Psalms of Ascent (section of the book of
    Psalms); psalms of ascent (genre of
    psalms)
psalms, royal
psalmist, the
Psalter, the (book of Psalms)
pseudepigrapha (in general)
Pseudepigrapha, the
pseudepigraphic (adj.)

Q

Qadesh
Qere
qinah
Qoheleth
Queen of Heaven
Queen of Sheba
queen of the South
quiescent letter
Qumran
Qumranic
Qur'an (not Koran)

R

rabbi(s)
rabbinic
Rameses (place)
Ramesses (person)
Ramesside
Re (not Ra)
Received Text
Redeemer, the (referring to Jesus)
Reformation, the
Reformers
resurrection, the
return, the
risen Lord
Roman Empire
Roman Senate
root form
Rosh Hashanah
royal psalms

Rule of the Community (see preferred
    Community Rule or *Manual of
    Discipline*)

S

Sabbath, the (noun and adj.)
Sabbatical cycle
Sabbatical Year
Sadducees
salvation history
Samaritan Chronicle(s)/Pentateuch
Sanhedrin, the
Satan
satanic
satrap
Satrapy
Savior, the (referring to Jesus)
scarab
scribal
scribe
scriptio continua
scriptural
Scripture
Scriptures
Sea Peoples
Sea-Land
Second Cataract (Nile)
Second Council of Nicea
second coming
Second Evangelist
Second Isaiah
second missionary journey
Second Temple period/literature
Sed festival
Sefire Stela
segholate
Seleucids
Semitic
Semitism(s)
seminomadic
sensus plenior
Septuagint
Sermon on the Mount (in Matthew)
Sermon on the Plain (in Luke)
Servant of the Lord (Second Isaiah)
servant passages
Servant Songs
settlement period

Shalmaneser
shalom
Shamash
sheikh
Shema, the
Sheol
shofar(s)
Siddur
Siloam Inscription
Siloam Pool (but pool of Siloam)
sin offering
Sitz im Leben
Son, the (referring to Jesus)
Son of God
Son of Man
Song of Deborah
Song of Moses
Song of the Sea
Song of Ullikummis
sopherim
source criticism
southern kingdom
spirit of God
Spirit, the
Spirit Baptism
spring (as in Gihon spring)
stela (pl. stelae)
stich
Stoic(ism)
store cities
storm-god
Story/Tale of Sinuhe
Story/Tale of Two Brothers
Stratum *x* (archaeological reports;
    stratum followed by number)
Succession Narrative
Suffering Servant
Sumerian Law Code
sun-god
syllabary
synagogue
synoptic (adj.)
Synoptic Gospels, the
Synoptic Problem, the
Synoptics, the
Syria-Palestine
Syro-Palestinian

T

Ta'anach
tabernacle
Table of Nations
Tale of Aqhat
Tale of Sinuhe
Tale of Two Brothers
Talmud
talmudic
Tanak (*Tanakh* for the JPS edition)
Tannaim
Tannaitic
Targum (pl. Targumim)
Targum of Jonathan (etc.)
targumic
tell/tel
Tell Deir 'Allā
Tell Fekheriye
Telepinu Myth
televangelist
Temple Mount
temple, the; Solomon's temple
Ten Commandments
Tendenz
terra-cotta (noun and adj.)
Testaments, both
testimonia
Tetragram/Tetragrammaton
Tetrateuch
Textus Receptus
theophoric
Third Dynasty of Ur (or Ur III period)
Third Evangelist
third missionary journey
third world (noun)
third-world (adj.)
threshing floor
throne name
Thutmose
Tiglath-pileser
titulary
torah (instruction)
Torah, the (a division of the canon)
Tosefta
toward
Trans-Euphrates
transfiguration, the
Transjordan(ian)

treaty form
Trinity (cap. when referring to God);
    Holy Trinity; Trinitarian (as in
    Trinitarian controversies)
Tukulti-Ninurta Epic
Tutankhamun
twelve apostles
twelve tribes
Twelve, the
twelve-tribe league
Twenty-first Psalm (etc.)

U

Ugarit (Ras Shamra)
Ugaritic
Upper Egypt
unchristian
Uncial
underworld (adj.)
Underworld, the
united kingdom
united monarchy
Upper Egypt
upper Galilee
upper Mesopotamia
Ur III period (or Third Dynasty of Ur)
Urim and Thummim
Ur-text
utopia

V

vassal treaties
vaticinium ex eventu
verb form
versions, the (Greek versions, Coptic
    versions, etc.)
vice-regent
virgin birth, the
Virgin, the (Mary)
vis-à-vis
Vorlage(n)
Vulgate

W

wadi(s)
Wadi ed-Daliyeh/Qelt (etc.)

Wailing Wall
War Scroll (1QM)
Way of the Sea
Way, the
West Bank
West Semitic
Western church
Western text
Western Wall
whole burnt offering
whole offering
wilderness (but Wilderness of Zin)
wilderness wanderings
wisdom (movement, quality)
Wisdom (personified)
Wisdom literature
wisdom tradition
wise men
word of God
Word, the (= Jesus)
wordplay
worldview
worship/worshiper/worshiping
Writings, the (a division of the
    canon)
Written Torah

Y

Yahweh (not Jahweh)
Yahwist (not Jahwist) source
Yam (Sea personified)
Yamhad
Yarim-Lim
Yavneh (not Jamnia)
Year of Jubilee
Yom Kippur (Day of Atonement)

Z

Zadokite Fragments (see preferred
    Damascus Document)
Zealots
ziggurat
Zimri-Lim
Ziusudra Myth
Zoroastrian(ism)

Appendix B:
Ancient Near Eastern Dates and Periods

For dates of ancient Near Eastern periods and rulers, consult the appropriate chapter in *Civilizations of the Ancient Near East* (ed. Jack M. Sasson; 4 vols.; New York: Scribners, 1995), volume 2, part 5 ("History and Culture"). Unless dates for rulers and dynasties are themselves the subject of discussion, it is convenient to use the Middle Chronology for citing dates for Egypt, Mesopotamia, and Anatolia, especially those before the first millennium B.C.E. All dates should be given in full: thus, 587–539 B.C.E. For Egypt, capitalize Dynasty but lowercase period: thus, Eighteenth Dynasty, Early Dynastic period, Middle Kingdom period, First Intermediate period, classical period, Hellenistic period; for Mesopotamia, use Old Babylonian period, Ur III Dynasty, etc. The third-millennium empire of Sargon and his descendants can be cited either as the Akkade or Agage period.

ANE DYNASTIES AND RULERS

Region	Pages in *CANE*, vol. 2
ANE Dynasties	660–61
Egypt	712–14
Mesopotamia	808, 814–15, 818–19
Persia	1005, 1009, 1014
Anatolia	1092, 1098–1099
Syria-Palestine	1202 (Syria), 1210–1211 (Phoenicia), 1212 (Israel), 1222 (Ebla), 1260 (Ugarit)

ANE Archaeological Periods

Paleolithic	25,000–10,000 B.C.E.
Mesolithic	10,000–8000 B.C.E.
Neolithic	8000–3800 B.C.E
Prepottery Neolithic	
Pottery Neolithic	
Chalcolithic	4000–3400 B.C.E.
Early Chalcolithic	
Late Chalcolithic	
Early Bronze Age (I–IV)	3400–2000 B.C.E.
Middle Bronze Age (I–III)	2000–1550/1500 B.C.E.
Late Bronze Age (I–II)	1550/1500–1200 B.C.E.
Iron Age (I–III)	1200–539/500 B.C.E.
Persian period	539/500–323 B.C.E.
Hellenistic period	323–37 B.C.E.
Roman period	37 B.C.E.–324 C.E.
Byzantine period	324–640 C.E.

Appendix C:
Ezra Traditions

Text	Book of Ezra	Book of Nehemiah	Paraphrase of 2 Chr 35–36; all of Ezra; Neh 7:38–8:12; and a story about Darius's bodyguards	A Latin Apocalypse (a pseudepigraph)
Hebrew Bible	Ezra	Nehemiah		
Greek (LXX)	2 Esdras (Esdras β)		1 Esdras (α)	
Vulgate	1 Esdras	2 Esdras	3 Esdras	4 Esdras
later Latin MSS	1 Esdras		3 Esdras	2 Esdras= 1–2 4 Esdras= 3–14 5 Esdras= 15–16
NRSV	Ezra	Nehemiah	1 Esdras	2 Esdras
NAB	Ezra	Nehemiah		

Modern scholarly Title	Vulgate	NRSV
5 Ezra	4 Esdras 1–2	2 Esdras 1–2
4 Ezra	4 Esdras 3–14	2 Esdras 3–14
6 Ezra	4 Esdras 15–16	2 Esdras 15–16

Appendix D:
Hebrew Bible/Old Testament Canons

D.1 The Jewish Canon
D.2 The Roman Catholic Canon
D.3 The Eastern Orthodox Canon
D.4 The Protestant Canon

D.1 The Jewish Canon[1]

THE HEBREW BIBLE *(Tanakh)*

Torah *(Torah)*
Genesis *(Bereshit)*
Exodus *(Shemot)*
Leviticus *(Wayyiqra')*
Numbers *(Bemidbar)*
Deuteronomy *(Devarim)*

Prophets *(Nevi'im)*
Former Prophets *(Nevi'im Rishonim):*
   Joshua *(Yehoshu'a)*
   Judges *(Shofetim)*
   1–2 Samuel *(Shemu'el 'aleph* and *bet)*
   1–2 Kings *(Melakim 'aleph* and *bet)*
Latter Prophets *(Nevi'im 'Aharonim):*
   Isaiah *(Yesha'yahu)*
   Jeremiah *(Yirmeyahu)*
   Ezekiel *(Yehezqe'l)*
   The Twelve *(Tere 'Asar):*
      Hosea *(Hoshe'a)*
      Joel *(Yo'el)*
      Amos *('Amos)*
      Obadiah *('Ovadyah)*
      Jonah *(Yonah)*
      Micah *(Mikah)*
      Nahum *(Nahum)*
      Habakkuk *(Havaqquq)*
      Zephaniah *(Tsefanyah)*
      Haggai *(Haggay)*
      Zechariah *(Zekaryah)*
      Malachi *(Mal'aki)*

Writings *(Ketuvim)*
Psalms *(Tehillim)*
Proverbs *(Mishle)*
Job *('Iyyov)*
Song of Songs *(Shir Hashirim)*
Ruth *(Ruth)*
Lamentations *('Ekah)*
Ecclesiastes *(Qoheleth)*
Esther *('Esther)*
Daniel *(Daniyye'l)*
Ezra *('Ezra')*
Nehemiah *(Nehemyah)*
1–2 Chronicles *(Divre Hayyamim 'aleph* and
   bet)

---

[1] The traditional number of books in the Jewish canon is twenty-four (the twelve minor prophets are considered one, as are Ezra and Nehemiah). The italic titles in parentheses are transliterations of the Hebrew titles.

D.2 The Roman Catholic Canon[2]

OLD TESTAMENT *(Vetus Testamentum)*

Penateuch

Genesis *(Genesis)*
Exodus *(Exodus)*
Leviticus *(Leviticus)*
Numbers *(Numeri)*
Deuteronomy *(Deuteronomium)*

Historical Books

Joshua *(Josue)*
Judges *(Judices)*
Ruth *(Ruth)*
1 Samuel *(1 Samuel [1 Reges])*
2 Samuel *(2 Samuel [2 Reges])*
1 Kings *([3] 1 Reges)*
2 Kings *([4] 2 Reges)*
1 Chronicles *(1 Paralipomena)*
2 Chronicles *(2 Paralipomena)*
Ezra *(1 Esdras)*
Nehemiah *(2 Esdras)*
Tobit (Tobias)
Judith (Judith)
Esther *[with 6 additions] (Esther)*
1 Maccabees (1 Macchabaei)
2 Maccabees (2 Macchabaei)

Wisdom Books

Job *(Job)*
Psalms *(Psalmi)*
Proverbs *(Proverbia Salomonis)*
Ecclesiastes *(Ecclesiastes)*
Song of Songs *(Canticum canticorum)*
Wisdom of Solomon (Sapientia)
Ecclesiasticus (Ecclesiasticus)

Prophetic Books

Isaiah *(Isaias)*
Jeremiah *(Jeremias)*
Lamentations *(Lamentationes)*
Baruch [chapter 6 = the Epistle of Jeremiah]
    (Baruch)
Ezekiel *(Ezechiel)*
Daniel *[with 3 additions: the Prayer of Aza-*
    riah and the Song of the Three Young
    Men, Susanna, and Bel and the Dragon]
    (Daniel)
Hosea *(Osee)*
Joel *(Joel)*
Amos *(Amos)*
Obadiah *(Abdias)*
Jonah *(Jonas)*
Micah *(Michaeas)*
Nahum *(Nahum)*
Habakkuk *(Habacuc)*
Zephaniah *(Sophonias)*
Haggai *(Aggaeus)*
Zechariah *(Zacharias)*
Malachi *(Malachias)*

---

[2]The traditional number of books in the Roman Catholic canon is forty-nine. English titles in italic appear in the Roman Catholic canon, but not in the Protestant canon. The order of books in Roman Catholic Bibles varies. The above order reflects current editions, such as the Jerusalem Bible and the New American Bible. The italic titles in parentheses are those found in the Latin Vulgate. The appendix of the Latin Vulgate contains 3 Esdras, 4 Esdras, and the Prayer of Manasseh.

D.3 The Orthodox Canon[3]

THE OLD TESTAMENT

Historical Books

Genesis *(Genesis)*
Exodus *(Exodos)*
Leviticus *(Leuitikon)*
Numbers *(Arithmoi)*
Deuteronomy *(Deuteronomion)*
Joshua *(Iēsous)*
Judges *(Kritai)*
Ruth *(Routh)*
1 Kingdoms *(Basileiōn A')*[4]
2 Kingdoms *(Basileiōn B')*
3 Kingdoms *(Basileiōn G')*
4 Kingdoms *(Basileiōn D')*
1 Chronicles *(Paraleipomenōn A')*
2 Chronicles *(Paraleipomenōn B')*
1 Esdras *(Esdras A')*[5]
2 Esdras *(Esdras B')*
Nehemiah *(Neemias)*
Tobit *(Tōbit)*
Judith *(Ioudith)*
Esther *[with 6 additions] (Esthēr)*
1 Maccabees *(Makkabaiōn A')*
2 Maccabees *(Makkabaiōn B')*
3 Maccabees *(Makkabaiōn G')*

Poetic and Didactic Books

Psalms *[with Psalm 151] (Psalmoi)*
Job *(Iōb)*
Proverbs *(Paroimiai Solomōntos)*
Ecclesiastes *(Ekklēsiastēs)*
Song of Songs *(Asma)*
Wisdom of Solomon *(Sophia Solomōntos)*
Wisdom of Sirach *(Sophia Seirach)*

Prophetic Books

Hosea *(Ōsēe)*
Amos *(Amōs)*
Micah *(Michaias)*
Joel *(Iōēl)*
Obadiah *(Abdiou)*
Jonah *(Iōnas)*
Nahum *(Naoum)*
Habakkuk *(Abakoum)*
Zephaniah *(Sophonias)*
Haggai *(Aggaios)*
Zechariah *(Zacharias)*
Malachi *(Malachias)*
Isaiah *(Ēsaias)*
Jeremiah *(Ieremias)*
Baruch *(Barouch)*
Lamentations of Jeremiah *(Thrēnoi)*
Epistle of Jeremiah *(Epistolē Ieremiou)*
Ezekiel *(Iezekiēl)*
Daniel *[with the Prayer of Azariah, the Song of the Three Youths, Susanna, and Bel and the Dragon] (Daniēl)*

---

[3] *Orthodox* here refers to the Greek and Russian Orthodox churches, the Slavonic Bible being the traditional text of the latter. In Orthodox Bibles, 4 Maccabees and the Prayer of Manasseh—and in Slavonic, 3 Esdras—are in an appendix. The editors thank Father Theodore Stylianopoulos for his assistance with this page.

[4] 1 and 2 Kingdoms are the books of Samuel; 3 and 4 Kingdoms are the books of Kings.

[5] This 1 Esdras (= 1 Esdras in the Apocrypha of the NRSV) is called 2 Esdras in Slavonic Bibles. The 2 Esdras in this canon is equivalent to the book of Ezra in the NRSV; in some Bibles it also includes Nehemiah.

D.4 The Protestant Canon

THE OLD TESTAMENT

Penateuch
Genesis
Exodus
Leviticus
Numbers
Deuteronomy

Historical Books
Joshua
Judges
Ruth
1 Samuel
2 Samuel
1 Kings
2 Kings
1 Chronicles
2 Chronicles
Ezra
Nehemiah
Esther

Poetic Books
Job
Psalms
Proverbs
Ecclesiastes
Song of Songs

Prophetic Books
Isaiah
Jeremiah
Lamentations
Ezekiel
Daniel
Hosea
Joel
Amos
Obadiah
Jonah
Micah
Nahum
Habakkuk
Zephaniah
Haggai
Zechariah
Malachi

Appendix E:
English/Hebrew/Greek Versification Compared

ENGLISH	HEBREW	GREEK
Genesis		
	31:48a, 47, 51, 52a, 48b, 49, 50a, 52b	31:46b–52
31:55	32:1	
32:1–32	32:2–33	
	35:16 & 21, 17–20, 22a	35:16–21
Exodus		
8:1–4	7:26–29	
8:5–32	8:1–28	
	20: 14, 15, 13	20:13–15
22:1	21:37	
22:2–31	22:1–30	
	35:9–12, 17, 13–14, 16, 19, 15	35:8–11, 12, 15–16, 17, 18, 19b
	36:8–9	37:1–2
	36:20–34	37:18–20
	36:35–38	37:8–6
	37:1–24	38:1–17
	37:29	38:25
	38:1–7	38:21–24
	38:8	38:26
	38:9–23	37:7–21
	38:24–31	39:1–10
	39:1–31	36:8b–40
	39:32	39:11
	39:33–43	39:13–23
	40:8–10, 12–27, 29, 33, 38	40:6b–8, 10–25, 26, 27–32
	40:30–32	38:27
Leviticus		
6:1–7	5:20–26	
6:8–30	6:1–23	
Numbers		
	1:26–37, 24–25	1:24–37
	6:22, 23, 27, 24, 25, 26	6:22–26
16:36–50	17:1–15	
17:1–13	17:16–28	
26:1 (first clause)	25:19	
	26:19–27, 15–18, 44–47, 28–43	26:15–47
29:40	30:1	
30:1–16	30:2–17	

ENGLISH	HEBREW	GREEK
Deuteronomy		
12:32	13:1	
13:1–18	13:2–19	
22:30	23:1	
23:1–25	23:2–26	
29:1	28:69	
29:2–29	29:1–28	
Joshua		
	8:30–33; 9:3–27	9:3–33
	19:48, 47	19:47–48
1 Samuel		
20:42 (last clause)	21:1	
21:1–15	21:2–16	
23:29	24:1	
24:1–22	24:2–23	
2 Samuel		
18:33	19:1	
19:1–43	19:2–44	
1 Kings (3 Kingdoms)		
	4:7–8, 2–4, 9–14	4:20–21, 22–24, 25–30
	4:18, 19, 17	4:17, 18, 19
	5:1a	10:30
4:21–34	5:1–14	
	5:15–30, 32b	5:1–16, 17
5:1–18	5:15–32	
	5:31–32a	6:2–3
	6:37–38, 2–3, 14, 4–10, 15–36	6:4–5, 6–7, 8, 9–15, 16–34
	7:13–18, 21, 19–20, 23–24, 26, 25	7:1–6, 7, 8–9, 10–11, 12–13
	7:27–51, 1–12	7:14–37, 38–50
	9:15, 17–19, 20–22	10:23–24a, 24b, 25
	10:23–26	10:26–29
	10:27–29	10:31–33
	11:4, 3, 7, 5, 8, 6	11:3–8
18:33 (last half)	18:34 (first half)	
20:2 (last half)	20:3 (first half)	
	21:20	20:21
22:22 (first clause)	22:21 (last clause)	
22:43 (last half)	22:44	
22:44–53	22:45–54	

ENGLISH	HEBREW	GREEK
2 Kings		
11:21	12:1	
12:1–21	12:2–22	
1 Chronicles		
6:1–15	5:27–41	
6:16–81	6:1–66	
12:4	12:4–5	
12:5–40	12:6–41	
2 Chronicles		
2:1	1:18	
2:2–18	2:1–17	
14:1	13:23	
14:2–15	14:1–14	
Nehemiah		
4:1–6	3:33–38	
4:7–23	4:1–17	
9:38	10:1	
10:1–39	10:2–40	
Job		
41:1–8	40:25–32	
41:9–34	41:1–26	
Psalms[1]		
3:title	3:1	
3:1–8	3:2–9	
4:title	4:1	
4:1–8	4:2–9	
5:title	5:1	
5:1–12	5:2–13	
6:title	6:1	
6:1–10	6:2–11	
7:title	7:1	
7:1–17	7:2–18	
8:title	8:1	
8:1–9	8:2–10	
9:title	9:1	
9:1–20	9:2–21	
	10:1–18	9:22–39
11–113		**10–112**
11:title	11:1 (first clause)	
12:title	12:1	
12:1–8	12:2–9	
13:title	13:1	
13:1–5	13:2–6	
13:6	13:6 (last half)	
14:title	14:1 (first clause)	
15:title	15:1 (first clause)	
16:title	16:1 (first clause)	
17:title	17:1 (first clause)	

ENGLISH	HEBREW	GREEK
Psalms		
18:title	18:1–2 (first clause)	
18:1–50	18:2–51	
19:title	19:1	
19:1–14	19:2–15	
20:title	20:1	
20:1–9	20:2–10	
21:title	21:1	
21:1–13	21:2–14	
22:title	22:1	
22:1–31	22:2–32	
23:title	23:1 (first clause)	
24–28:title	24–28:1 (first clause)	
29:title	29:1 (first clause)	
30:title	30:1	
30:1–12	30:2–13	
31:title	31:1	
31:1–24	31:2–25	
32:title	32:1 (first clause)	
34:title	34:1	
34:1–22	34:2–23	
35:title	35:1 (first word)	
36:title	36:1	
36:1–12	36:2–13	
37:title	37:1 (first word)	
38:title	38:1	
38:1–22	38:2–23	
39:title	39:1	
39:1–13	39:2–14	
40:title	40:1	
40:1–17	40:2–18	
41:title	41:1	
41:1–13	41:2–14	
42:title	42:1	
42:1–11	42:2–12	
44:title	44:1	
44:1–26	44:2–27	
45:title	45:1	
45:1–17	45:2–18	
46:title	46:1	
46:1–11	46:2–12	
47:title	47:1	
47:1–9	47:2–10	
48:title	48:1	
48:1–14	48:2–15	
49:title	49:1	
49:1–20	49:2–21	
50:title	50:1 (first clause)	
51:title	51:1–2	
51:1–19	51:2–21	
52:title	52:1–2 (first clause)	
52:1–9	52:2–11	
53:title	53:1	
53:1–6	53:2–7	

[1]Bold numbers refer to whole chapters and chapter ranges.

ENGLISH	HEBREW	GREEK
Psalms		
54:title	54:1–2	
54:1–7	54:2–9	
55:title	55:1	
55:1–23	55:2–24	
56:title	56:1	
56:1–23	56:2–24	
57:title	57:1	
57:1–11	57:2–12	
58:title	58:1	
58:1–11	58:2–12	
59:title	59:1	
59:1–17	59:2–18	
60:title	60:1–2	
60:1–12	60:3–14	
61:title	61:1	
61:1–8	61:2–9	
62:title	62:1	
62:1–12	62:2–13	
63:title	63:1	
63:1–11	63:2–12	
64:title	64:1	
64:1–10	64:2–11	
65:title	65:1	
65:1–13	65:2–14	
66:title	66:1 (first clause)	
67:title	67:1	
67:1–7	67:2–8	
68:title	68:1	
68:1–35	68:2–36	
69:title	69:1	
69:1–36	69:2–37	
70:title	70:1	
70:1–5	70:2–6	
72:title	72:1 (first word)	
73:title	73:1 (first clause)	
74:title	74:1 (first clause)	
74:1–10	74:2–11	
76:title	76:1	
76:1–12	76:2–13	
77:title	77:1	
77:1–20	77:2–21	
78:title	78:1 (first clause)	
79:title	79:1 (first clause)	
80:title	80:1	
80:1–19	80:2–20	
81:title	81:1	
81:1–16	81:2–17	
82:title	82:1 (first clause)	
83:title	83:1	
83:1–18	83:2–19	
84:title	84:1	
84:1–12	84:2–13	
85:title	85:1	
85:1–13	85:2–14	
86:title	86:1 (first clause)	

ENGLISH	HEBREW	GREEK
Psalms		
87:title	87:1 (first clause)	
88:title	88:1	
88:1–18	88:2–19	
89:title	89:1	
89:1–52	89:2–53	
90:title	90:1 (first clause)	
92:title	92:1	
92:1–15	92:2–16	
98:title	98:1 (first word)	
100:title	100:1 (first clause)	
101:title	101:1 (first clause)	
102:title	102:1	
102:1–28	102:2–29	
103:title	103:1 (first word)	
108:title	108:1	
108:1–13	108:2–14	
109, 110, 120–134, 138, 139:title	109, 110, 120–134, 138, 139:1 (first clause)	
	114:1–8	113:1–8
	115:1–4	113:9–12
	116:1–9	114
	116:10–19	115
117–147:11		**116–146**
140:title	140:1	
140:1–13	140:2–14	
141:title	141:1 (first clause)	
142:title	142:1	
142:1–6	142:2–7	
143:title	143:1 (first clause)	
144:title	144:1 (first word)	
145:title	145:1 (first clause)	
	147:12–20	147:1–9

ENGLISH	HEBREW	GREEK
Proverbs		
	16:6; 15:28; 16:7; 15:29; 16:8–9; 15:30–33a; 16:5, 4a	15:27b–16:4, 6, 9
	20:20–22, 10–13, 23–30	20:10a–12, 13b–16, 17–24
	30:1–14; 24:23–34; 30:15–33; 31:1–9, 10–31	24:24–37, 38–49, 50–68, 69–77; 29:28–49

ENGLISH	HEBREW	GREEK
Ecclesiastes		
5:1	4:17	
5:2–20	5:1–19	

174

ENGLISH	HEBREW	GREEK
Song of Songs		
6:13	7:1	
7:1–13	7:2–14	
Isaiah		
9:1	8:23	
9:2–21	9:1–20	
63:19	63:19a	
64:1	63:19b	
64:2–12	64:1–11	
Jeremiah		
9:1	8:23	
9:2–26	9:1–25	
	25:15–38	32:1–24
	26	33
	27:2–22	34:1–18
	28	35
	29	36
	30	37
	31:1–34, 37, 35, 36, 38–40	38:1–34, 35–37, 38–40
	32	39
	33	40
	34	41
	35	42
	36	43
	37	44
	38	45
	39	46
	40	47
	41	48
	42	49
	43	50
	44:1–30; 45:1–5	51:1–30, 31–35
	46:2–28	26:2–28
	47:1–7	29:1–7
	48	31
	49:1–5, 28–33, 23–27	30:1–5, 6–11, 12–27
	49:7–22	29:8–23
	49:34a–39	25:14–19
	49:36b	26:1
	50	27
	51	28
Ezekiel		
	7:6–9, 3–5	7:3–9
20:45–49	21:1–5	
21:1–32	21:6–37	
Daniel		
4:1–3	3:31–33	
4:4–37	4:1–34	
5:31	6:1	
6:1–28	6:2–29	

ENGLISH	HEBREW	GREEK
Hosea		
1:10–11	2:1–2	
2:1–23	2:3–25	
11:12	12:1	
12:1–14	12:2–15	
13:16	14:1	
14:1–9	14:2–10	
Joel		
2:28–32	3:1–5	
3:1–21	4:1–21	
Jonah		
1:17	2:1	
2:1–10	2:2–11	
Micah		
5:1	4:14	
5:2–15	5:1–14	
Nahum		
1:15	2:1	
2:1–13	2:2–14	
Zechariah		
1:18–21	2:1–4	
2:1–13	2:5–17	
Malachi		
4:1–6	3:19–24	

Appendix F:[1]
Texts from the Judean Desert

by Emanuel Tov

Introduction

This list revises three earlier versions:[2]

> E. Tov with the collaboration of S. J. Pfann, *Companion Volume to The Dead Sea Scrolls on Microfiche—A Comprehensive Facsimile Edition of the Texts from the Judean Desert* (Leiden: E. J. Brill and IDC, 1993).

> E. Tov with the collaboration of S. J. Pfann, *Companion Volume to The Dead Sea Scrolls Microfiche Edition* (2d rev. ed.; Leiden: E. J. Brill and IDC, 1995).

> E. Tov, "A List of the Texts from the Judaean Desert," in *The Dead Sea Scrolls after Fifty Years—A Comprehensive Assessment* (ed. P. W. Flint and J. C. VanderKam; 2 vols.; Leiden: E. J. Brill, 1999), 2: 669–717.

The list contains the following data for all the texts from the Judean Desert:

Column 1. The sequential number in the list of the texts from the individual sites in the Judean Desert.

Column 2. The name of the composition as published in DJD or the most central publication outside that series (e.g., the large texts from Cave 1, as well as some texts from Cave 11, which were not scheduled to be included in DJD). In the nomenclature of DJD, a distinction is made between raised lowercase letters designating different copies of the same composition, such as 4QGen[b] and 4QGen[c], and uppercase letters designating independent compositions within a certain literary genre, such as 4QTohorot A and 4QTohorot B. The names also contain references to the material (pap = papyrus), language (ar = Aramaic; gr = Greek; lat = Latin; nab = Nabataean; sem = Semitic), and script (paleo = paleo-Hebrew; cr = cryptic [A or B]). All other documents are in Hebrew, written on leather.

Column 3. For Qumran texts (section 1): the siglum used in R. E. Brown, J. A. Fitzmyer, W. G. Oxtoby, and J. Teixidor, *A Preliminary*

---

[1] Emanuel Tov has kindly provided the Appendix of Texts from the Judean Desert. As of this printing, the table is not in its final form. The data in this table are constantly being updated, especially regarding Cave 4 and some of the sites outside Qumran. Future printings will include these updates. The Society is grateful to Professor Tov for allowing its publication now, since it represents the most complete and up-to-date list of Dead Sea Scroll texts and will be invaluable to students and scholars.

[2] In the compilation and editing of this list over the years, I have been ably assisted by Claire Pfann (during the first half of this decade) and Janice Karnis (during the second half of this decade). J. Karnis also prepared the present manuscript.

176

Concordance to the Hebrew and Aramaic Fragments from Qumran Caves II–X, Including Especially, the Unpublished Material from Cave IV (Göttingen: privately printed, 1988). For texts from sites other than Qumran (sections 2–13): the plate numbers in the early publication.

Column 4. The inventory number of the fragments in the Rockefeller Museum building (a number without details), the Shrine of the Book, Israel Museum (SHR), as well as other locations: Bibliothèque nationale de Paris (BNP), Department of Antiquities of Jordan (DAJ), and others. An asterisked number (e.g., 216*) refers to a parallel series of numbers assigned to the documents from Naḥal Ḥever and Masada which were transferred from the Shrine of the Book to the Rockefeller Museum building in 1996.

Column 5. Former sigla, such as C53 (C = Cross; M = Milik; Sl = Strugnell; Sn = Skehan; Sy = Starcky; Ul = Ulrich).

Column 6. Short bibliographical references mentioning the names of the editors and publication details (usually DJD) together with the plate number(s). The abbreviations are provided in the Bibliographical Abbreviations below.

The items in the List of Texts from the Judean Desert are grouped according to the sites at which they were found—first Qumran, and thereafter all other sites arranged from north to south:

No.	Site
1	Qumran
2	Wadi Daliyeh
3	Ketef Jericho
4	Khirbet Mird
5	Wadi Nar
6	Wadi Ghweir
7	Wadi Murabbaʿat
8	Wadi Sdeir
9	Naḥal Ḥever
10	Naḥal Ḥever/Seiyal
11	Naḥal Mishmar
12	Naḥal Ṣeʾelim
13	Masada

Bibliographical Abbreviations

APHM	Grohmann, A. *Arabic Papyri from Hirbet el-Mird*. Bibliothèque du Muséon 52. Louvain: Publications Universitaires, 1963.
BE	Milik, J. T. *The Books of Enoch*. Oxford: Clarendon, 1976.
Ben Sira Scroll	Yadin, Y. *The Ben Sira Scroll from Masada*. Jerusalem: Israel Exploration Society and the Shrine of the Book, 1965.
DIWD	Cross, F. M. "The Papyri and Their Historical Implications." Pages 17–29, 57–60, pls. 59–63, 80, 81 in *Discoveries in the Wadi ed-Daliyeh*. Edited by P. W. Lapp and N. L. Lapp. Annual of the American Schools of Oriental Research 41. Cambridge, Mass.: American Schools of Oriental Research, 1974.
DJD	Discoveries in the Judaean Desert (of Jordan)

A partial list of the volumes in this series follows:

Barthélemy, D., and J. T. Milik. *Qumran Cave 1*. DJD I. Oxford: Clarendon Press, 1955.

Benoit, P., J. T. Milik, and R. de Vaux. *Les grottes de Murabba'at*. DJD II. Oxford: Clarendon Press, 1961.

Baillet, M., J. T. Milik, and R. de Vaux. *Les "petites grottes" de Qumrân*. DJDJ III. Oxford: Clarendon Press, 1962.

Sanders, J. A. *The Psalms Scroll of Qumran Cave 11 (11QPs^a)*. DJDJ IV. Oxford: Clarendon Press, 1965.

Allegro, J. M. *Qumran Cave 4.I (4Q158–4Q186)*. DJDJ V. Oxford: Clarendon Press, 1968.

de Vaux, R. and J. T. Milik. *Qumrân grotte 4.II*. DJD VI. Oxford: Clarendon Press, 1977.

Baillet, M. *Qumrân grotte 4.III (4Q482–4Q520)*. DJD VII. Oxford: Clarendon Press, 1982.

Tov, E. *The Greek Minor Prophets Scroll from Nahal Hever (8HevXIIgr)*. DJD VIII. Oxford: Clarendon Press, 1990.

Skehan, P. W., E. Ulrich, and J. E. Sanderson. *Qumran Cave 4.IV: Palaeo-Hebrew and Greek Biblical Manuscripts*. DJD IX. Oxford: Clarendon Press, 1992.

Qimron, E., and J. Strugnell. *Qumran Cave 4.V: Miqsat Ma'ase ha-Torah*. DJD X. Oxford: Clarendon Press, 1994.

Eshel, E., H. Eshel, C. Newsom, B. Nitzan, E. Schuller, and A. Yardeni, in consultation with J. C. VanderKam and M. Brady. *Qumran Cave 4.VI: Poetical and Liturgical Texts, Part 1*. DJD XI. Oxford: Clarendon Press, 1997.

Ulrich, E., and F. M. Cross. *Qumran Cave 4.VII: Genesis to Numbers*. DJD XII. Oxford: Clarendon Press, 1994.

Attridge, H. W., T. Elgvin, J. Milik, S. Olyan, J. Strugnell, E. Tov, J. VanderKam, and S. White, in consultation with J. C. VanderKam. *Qumran Cave 4.VIII: Parabiblical Texts, Part 1*. DJD XIII. Oxford: Clarendon Press, 1994.

Ulrich, E., F. M. Cross, S. W. Crawford, J. A. Duncan, P. W. Skehan, E. Tov, and J. T. Barrera. *Qumran Cave 4.IX: Deuteronomy to Kings*. DJD XIV. Oxford: Clarendon Press, 1995.

Ulrich, E., F. M. Cross, R. E. Fuller, J. E. Sanderson, P. W. Skehan, and E. Tov. *Qumran Cave 4.X: The Prophets*. DJD XV. Oxford: Clarendon Press, 1997.

Baumgarten, J. M. *Qumran Cave 4.XIII: The Damascus Document (4Q266–273)*. DJD XVIII. Oxford: Clarendon Press, 1996.

Broshi, M., E. Eshel, J. Fitzmyer, E. Larson, C. Newsom, L. Schiffman, M. Smith, M. Stone, J. Strugnell, and A. Yardeni, in consultation with J. C. VanderKam. *Qumran Cave 4.XIV: Parabiblical Texts, Part 2*. DJD XIX. Oxford: Clarendon Press, 1995.

Elgvin, T., et al., in consultation with J. A. Fitzmyer. *Qumran Cave 4.XV: Sapiential Texts, Part 1*. DJD XX. Oxford: Clarendon Press, 1997.

Brooke, G. J., J.Collins, P. Flint, J. Greenfield, E. Larson, C. Newsom, É. Puech, L. H. Schiffman, M. Stone, and J. Trebolle Barrera, in consultation with J. Vanderkam, partially based on earlier transcriptions by J. T. Milik and J. Strugnell. *Qumran Cave 4.XVII: Parabiblical Texts, Part 3*. DJD XXII. Oxford: Clarendon Press, 1996.

García Martínez, F., E. J. C. Tigchelaar, and A. S. van der Woude. *Manuscripts from Qumran Cave 11 (11Q2–18, 11Q20–30)*. DJD XXIII. Oxford: Clarendon Press, 1997.

Leith, M. J. W. *Wadi Daliyeh Seal Impressions*. DJD XXIV. Oxford: Clarendon Press, 1997.

Puech, É. *Textes Hebreux (4Q521–4Q528, 4Q576–4Q579): Qumran Cave 4.XVIII*. DJD XXV. Oxford: Clarendon Press, 1997.

Alexander, P., and G. Vermes. *Qumran Cave 4.XIX: 4QSerekh Ha-Yaḥad*. DJD XXVI. Oxford: Clarendon Press, 1998.

Cotton, H. M., and A. Yardeni. *Aramaic, Hebrew, and Greek Documentary Texts from Nahal Hever and Other Sites, with an Appendix Containing Alleged Qumran Texts*. DJD XXVII. Oxford: Clarendon Press, 1997.

Strugnell, J., D. J. Harrington, and T. Elgvin, in consultation with J. A. Fitzmyer. *Sapiential Texts, Part 2: Cave 4.XXIV*. DJD XXXIV. Oxford: Clarendon Press, 1999.

DSSHU   Sukenik, E. L. *The Dead Sea Scrolls of the Hebrew University*. Jerusalem: Magnes, 1955.

DSSSMM   Burrows, M., ed. *The Dead Sea Scrolls of St. Mark's Monastery*. 2 vols. New Haven: American Schools of Oriental Research, 1951.

EAEHL   Bar Adon, P. "Judean Desert Caves—The Nahal Mishmar Caves," Pages 683–90 in vol. 3 of *Encyclopedia of Archaeological Excavations in the Holy Land*. Edited by M. Avi-Yonah and E. Stern. Jerusalem: Israel Exploration Society and Massada, 1977.

ErIsr   *Eretz-Israel*.

Genesis Apocryphon   Avigad, N., and Y. Yadin. *A Genesis Apocryphon: A Scroll from the Wilderness of Judaea*. Jerusalem: Magnes and Heikhal Ha-Sefer, 1956.

IEJ   *Israel Exploration Journal*.

JDS   Judean Desert Studies.

A partial list of the volumes in this series follows:

Lewis, N., ed. *The Documents from the Bar Kokhba Period in the Cave of the Letters:The Greek Papyri*. JDS 2. Jerusalem: Israel Exploration Society, the Hebrew University of Jerusalem, and the Shrine of the Book, 1989.

Yadin, Y., and J. C. Greenfield, *The Documents from the Bar Kokhba Period in the Cave of the Letters: Aramaic and Nabatean Signatures and Subscriptions*. JDS 2. Jerusalem: Israel Exploration Society, the Hebrew University of Jerusalem, and the Shrine of the Book, 1989.

Cotton, H. JDS 3. In press.

Yadin, Y., J. C. Greenfield, A. Yardeni, and B. Levine. JDS. In press.

Masada I   Yadin, Y., and J. Naveh. *Masada I: The Yigael Yadin Excavations 1963-1965, Final Reports: The Aramaic and Hebrew Ostraca and Jar Inscriptions*. Jerusalem: Israel Exploration Society and the Hebrew University of Jerusalem, 1989.

Masada II   Cotton, H., and J. Geiger. *Masada II, The Yigal Yadin Excavations 1963–1965, Final Reports: The Latin and Greek Documents*. Jerusalem: Israel Exploration Society, 1989.

179

Masada VI	Talmon, S. "Hebrew Fragments from Masada." Pages 1–149 in *Masada VI, The Yigal Yadin Excavations 1963–1965, Final Reports*. Edited by S. Talmon and Y. Yadin. Jerusalem: Israel Exploration Society, 1999.
PHLS	Freedman, D. N., and K. A. Mathews. *The Paleo-Hebrew Leviticus Scroll*. Winona Lake, Ind.: American Schools of Oriental Research and Eisenbrauns, 1985.
RB	*Revue biblique*.
RevQ	*Revue de Qumran*.
SQC	Trever, J. C. *Scrolls from Qumran Cave I* (= *Three Scrolls from Qumran*). Jerusalem: Albright Institute of Archaeology and the Shrine of the Book, 1972.
Tefillin from Qumran	Yadin, Y. *Tefillin from Qumran*. Jerusalem: Israel Exploration Society and the Shrine of the Book, 1969.
Temple Scroll	Yadin, Y. *The Temple Scroll*. 3 vols. Jerusalem: Israel Exploration Society, 1983.

Abbreviations of Texts from the Judean Desert[3]

apGen	Genesis Apocryphon
apocr	apocryphon
D	Damascus Document
DibHam	*Dibre Hame'orot* (Words of the Luminaries)
DM	*Dibre Moshe* (Words of Moses)
En	Enoch
Enastr	Enoch, astronomical books
EnGiants	Enoch, Giants
EpJer	Epistle of Jeremiah
Flor	Florilegium
H(od)	*Hodayot* (Thanksgiving Scroll)
Hym/Pr	Hymns or Prayers
Hym/Sap	Sapiential or Hymnic fragments
JN	Jerusalem nouvelle (New Jerusalem)
Lit	Liturgy
M	*Milḥamah* (War Scroll)
Mez	Mezuza
MMT	*Miqṣat Maʿaśê ha-Torah* (Some of the Torah Observations)
MSM	*Midrash Sefer Moshe*
Myst	Mysteries
NJ	New Jerusalem
Ord	Ordinances
p	*pesher*
par	paraphrase

---

[3] In the following abbreviations, italics indicate only transliterated titles. When citing any Dead Sea Scroll text, however, italicize the title (e.g., *Genesis Apocryphon*, *Dibre Moshe* or *Words of Moses*, and *Temple Scroll*). Also, the following titles contain spellings as they appear in the printed volumes, though these may differ in transliteration styles (e.g., *ha-Torah* and *Hame'orot*).

Phyl	Phylactery
ps	pseudo-
Pr	Prayer(s)
PrFêtes	Prières pour les fêtes
PrQuot	Prières quotidiennes
RitMar	Rituel de mariage
RitPur	Rituel de purification
RP	Reworked Pentateuch (*olim* PP, Pentateuchal Paraphrase)
S	*Serekh ha-Yaḥad* (Manual of Discipline)
sap	sapiential
ShirShabb	*Shirot ʿOlat Hashabbat* (Songs of the Sabbath Sacrifice)
T	Temple Scroll
Tanḥ	Tanḥumim
Test	Testimonia
tg	targum
TLevi	Testament of Levi
TNaph	Testament of Naphtali
Unid.	unidentified

General Abbreviations

A	Allegro
A	in list of negatives of 11QTªᵃ: early reconstructions
ABMC	Ancient Biblical Manuscript Center, Claremont, Calif.
ap	apocryphon
ar	Aramaic
arab	Arabic
ASOR	American School of Oriental Research (now known as the Albright Institute)
bdl	bundle
BA	Babatha archive
BK	Bar Kochba
BNP	Bibliothèque nationale de Paris
BT	Baillet
C	Cross
CNRS	Centre National de la Recherche Scientifique
col.	column
cpa	Christian Palestinian Aramaic
cr(ypt)	cryptic
D	in list of negatives of 11QTᵃ: fragments with the "domino wad"
DAJ	Department of Antiquities of Jordan
E(B)	École Biblique
EG	Ein Gedi
frag.	fragment
G	Department of Antiquities of Jordan (purchased by the government)
gr	Greek
H	Hunzinger
Ḥev	Naḥal Ḥever
IAA	Israel Antiquities Authority

181

IDAM	Israel Department of Antiquities and Museums (now the IAA)
inv.	museum inventory number
ir	infrared
J	Palestine Archaeological Museum, Jerusalem
JWS	Jerusalem West Semitic Project
Kh.	Khirbet
lat	Latin
LB	Late Bronze Age
loc.	locus, loci
M	Milik
M	in list of negatives of 11QT^a: mirror image
Mas	Masada
MB	Middle Bronze Age
ms	manuscript
Mur	Murabbaʿat
nab	Nabatean
ostr	ostracon
paleo	paleo-Hebrew
PAM	Palestine Archaeological Museum
pap	papyrus
Q	Qumran
R	in list of negatives of 11QT^a: infrared
r	recto
SBL	Society of Biblical Literature
Se	Seiyal
SHR	Shrine of the Book, Israel Museum, Jerusalem
SL	Strugnell
SN	Skehan
SY	Starcky
T	McCormick Theological Seminary
uv	ultraviolet
V	Vatican library
v	verso

1. Qumran

Item No.	Composition	Concordance	Inv	Former Sigla	Publication
1Q1	Gen		BNP		Barthélemy, DJD I (1955), pl. VIII
1Q2	Exod		BNP		Barthélemy, DJD I (1955), pl. VIII
1Q3	paleoLev (and paleoNum?)		BNP		Barthélemy, DJD I (1955), pls. VIII–IX
1Q4	Deut^a		BNP		Barthélemy, DJD I (1955), pl. IX
1Q5	Deut^b		673		Barthélemy, DJD I (1955), pl. X
1Q6	Judg		BNP		Barthélemy, DJD I (1955), pl. XI
1Q7	Sam		BNP		Barthélemy, DJD I (1955), pl. XI
1QIsa^a	Isa^a		SHR		Burrows, DSSSMM I (1950)
	col. I (Isa 1:1–26)				Burrows, DSSSMM I (1950), pl. I
	col. II (Isa 1:26–2:21)				Burrows, DSSSMM I (1950), pl. II
	col. III (Isa 2:21–3:24)				Burrows, DSSSMM I (1950), pl. III
	col. IV (Isa 3:24–5:14)				Burrows, DSSSMM I (1950), pl. IV
	col. V (Isa 5:14–6:7)				Burrows, DSSSMM I (1950), pl. V
	col. VI (Isa 6:7–7:15)				Burrows, DSSSMM I (1950), pl. VI
	col. VII (Isa 7:15–8:8)				Burrows, DSSSMM I (1950), pl. VII
	col. VIII (Isa 8:8–9:11)				Burrows, DSSSMM I (1950), pl. VIII
	col. IX (Isa 9:11–10:14)				Burrows, DSSSMM I (1950), pl. IX
	col. X (Isa 10:14–11:12)				Burrows, DSSSMM I (1950), pl. X
	col. XI (Isa 11:12–14:1)				Burrows, DSSSMM I (1950), pl. XI
	col. XII (Isa 14:1–29)				Burrows, DSSSMM I (1950), pl. XII
	col. XIII (Isa 14:29–16:14)				Burrows, DSSSMM I (1950), pl. XIII
	col. XIV (Isa 16:14–18:7)				Burrows, DSSSMM I (1950), pl. XIV
	col. XV (Isa 18:7–19:23)				Burrows, DSSSMM I (1950), pl. XV
	col. XVI (Isa 19:23–21:15)				Burrows, DSSSMM I (1950), pl. XVI
	col. XVII (Isa 21:15–22:24)				Burrows, DSSSMM I (1950), pl. XVII
	col. XVIII (Isa 22:24–24:4)				Burrows, DSSSMM I (1950), pl. XVIII
	col. XIX (Isa 24:4–25:5)				Burrows, DSSSMM I (1950), pl. XIX
	col. XX (Isa 25:6–26:18)				Burrows, DSSSMM I (1950), pl. XX
	col. XXI (Isa 26:19–28:2)				Burrows, DSSSMM I (1950), pl. XXI
	col. XXII (Isa 28:2–24)				Burrows, DSSSMM I (1950), pl. XXII
	col. XXIII (Isa 28:24–29:21)				Burrows, DSSSMM I (1950), pl. XXIII
	col. XXIV (Isa 29:21–30:20)				Burrows, DSSSMM I (1950), pl. XXIV
	col. XXV (Isa 30:20–31:4)				Burrows, DSSSMM I (1950), pl. XXV
	col. XXVI (Isa 31:5–33:1)				Burrows, DSSSMM I (1950), pl. XXVI
	col. XXVII (Isa 33:1–24)				Burrows, DSSSMM I (1950), pl. XXVII
	col. XXVIII (Isa 34:1–36:2)				Burrows, DSSSMM I (1950), pl. XXVIII
	col. XXIX (Isa 36:3–20)				Burrows, DSSSMM I (1950), pl. XXIX
	col. XXX (Isa 36:20–37:24)				Burrows, DSSSMM I (1950), pl. XXX
	col. XXXI (Isa 37:24–38:8)				Burrows, DSSSMM I (1950), pl. XXXI
	col. XXXII (Isa 38:8–40:2)				Burrows, DSSSMM I (1950), pl. XXXII
	col. XXXIII (Isa 40:2–28)				Burrows, DSSSMM I (1950), pl. XXXIII
	col. XXXIV (Isa 40:28–41:23)				Burrows, DSSSMM I (1950), pl. XXXIV
	col. XXXV (Isa 41:23–42:17)				Burrows, DSSSMM I (1950), pl. XXXV
	col. XXXVI (Isa 42:18–43:20)				Burrows, DSSSMM I (1950), pl. XXXVI
	col. XXXVII (Isa 43:20–44:23)				Burrows, DSSSMM I (1950), pl. XXXVII
	col. XXXVIII (Isa 44:23–45:21)				Burrows, DSSSMM I (1950), pl. XXXVIII
	col. XXXIX (Isa 45:21–47:11)				Burrows, DSSSMM I (1950), pl. XXXIX
	col. XL (Isa 47:11–49:4)				Burrows, DSSSMM I (1950), pl. XL
	col. XLI (Isa 49:4–50:1)				Burrows, DSSSMM I (1950), pl. XLI
	col. XLII (Isa 50:1–51:13)				Burrows, DSSSMM I (1950), pl. XLII
	col. XLIII (Isa 51:13–52:12)				Burrows, DSSSMM I (1950), pl. XLIII
	col. XLIV (Isa 52:13–54:4)				Burrows, DSSSMM I (1950), pl. XLIV
	col. XLV (Isa 54:4–55:8)				Burrows, DSSSMM I (1950), pl. XLV
	col. XLVI (Isa 55:8–57:2)				Burrows, DSSSMM I (1950), pl. XLVI
	col. XLVII (Isa 57:2–58:6)				Burrows, DSSSMM I (1950), pl. XLVII
	col. XLVIII (Isa 58:6–59:17)				Burrows, DSSSMM I (1950), pl. XLVIII

	col. XLIX (Isa 59:17–61:4)		Burrows, *DSSSMM* I (1950), pl. XLIX
	col. L (Isa 61:4–63:4)		Burrows, *DSSSMM* I (1950), pl. L
	col. LI (Isa 63:4–65:4)		Burrows, *DSSSMM* I (1950), pl. LI
	col. LII (Isa 65:4–18)		Burrows, *DSSSMM* I (1950), pl. LII
	col. LIII (Isa 65:19–66:14)		Burrows, *DSSSMM* I (1950), pl. LIII
	col. LIV (Isa 66:14–24)		Burrows, *DSSSMM* I (1950), pl. LIV
1Q8	Isa[b] (unopened scroll)		Sukenik, *DSSHU* (1950), pls. 1–15; figs. 10, 18–21
	frag. 1 (Isa 7:22–8:1)	677	Barthélemy, DJD I (1955), pl. XII
	frag. 1 (Isa 10:17–19)	SHR	Sukenik, *DSSHU* (1955), pl. I
	frag. 2 (Isa 12:3–13:8)	677	Barthélemy, DJD I (1955), pl. XII
	frag. 2 (Isa 13:16–19)	SHR	Sukenik, *DSSHU* (1955), pl. I
	frag. 3 (Isa 15:3–16:2)	677	Barthélemy, DJD I (1955), pl. XII
	frag. 3 (Isa 16:7–11)	SHR	Sukenik, *DSSHU* (1955), pl. I
	frag. 4 (Isa 19:7–17)	677	Barthélemy, DJD I (1955), pl. XII
	frag. 4 (Isa 19:20–20:1)	SHR	Sukenik, *DSSHU* (1955), pl. I
	frag. 5 (Isa 22:11–18)	677	Barthélemy, DJD I (1955), pl. XII
	frag. 5 (Isa 22:24–23:4)	SHR	Sukenik, *DSSHU* (1955), pl. I
	frag. 6 (Isa 24:18–25:8)	677	Barthélemy, DJD I (1955), pl. XII
	frag. 6 (Isa 26:1–5)	SHR	Sukenik, *DSSHU* (1955), pl. II
	frag. 6 bis (Isa 28:15–20)	SHR	Sukenik, *DSSHU* (1955), pl. II
	frag. 7 (Isa 29:1–8)	SHR	Sukenik, *DSSHU* (1955), pl. II
	frag. 8 (Isa 30:10–14)	SHR	Sukenik, *DSSHU* (1955), pl. II
	frag. 9 (Isa 30:21–26)	SHR	Sukenik, *DSSHU* (1955), pl. II
	frag. 10 (Isa 35:4–5)	SHR	Sukenik, *DSSHU* (1955), pl. II
	frag. 11 (Isa 37:8–12)	SHR	Sukenik, *DSSHU* (1955), pl. II
	col. I + frag. 12 (Isa 38:12–40:3)	SHR	Sukenik, *DSSHU* (1955), pl. III
	col. II (Isa 41:3–23)	SHR	Sukenik, *DSSHU* (1955), pl. IV
	col. III + frag. 13 (Isa 43:1–27)	SHR	Sukenik, *DSSHU* (1955), pl. V
	col. IV (Isa 44:21–45:13)	SHR	Sukenik, *DSSHU* (1955), pl. VI
	col. V (Isa 46:3–47:14)	SHR	Sukenik, *DSSHU* (1955), pl. VII
	col. VI (Isa 47:17–49:15)	SHR	Sukenik, *DSSHU* (1955), pl. VIII
	col. VII (Isa 50:7–51:10)	SHR	Sukenik, *DSSHU* (1955), pl. IX
	col. VIII (Isa 52:7–54:6)	SHR	Sukenik, *DSSHU* (1955), pl. X
	col. IX (Isa 55:2–57:4)	SHR	Sukenik, *DSSHU* (1955), pl. XI
	col. X (Isa 57:17–59:8)	SHR	Sukenik, *DSSHU* (1955), pl. XII
	col. XI (Isa 59:20–61:2)	SHR	Sukenik, *DSSHU* (1955), pl. XIII
	col. XII (Isa 62:2–64:8)	SHR	Sukenik, *DSSHU* (1955), pl. XIV
	col. XIII (Isa 65:17–66:24)	SHR	Sukenik, *DSSHU* (1955), pl. XV
	frag. 6	677	Barthélemy, DJD I (1955), pl. XII
1Q9	Ezek	677	Barthélemy, DJD I (1955), pl. XII
1Q10	Ps[a]		Barthélemy, DJD I (1955), pl. XIII
1Q11	Ps[b]		Barthélemy, DJD I (1955), pl. XIII
1Q12	Ps[c]		Barthélemy, DJD I (1955), pl. XIII
1Q13	Phyl	DAJ	Barthélemy, DJD I (1955), pl. XIV
1Q14	pMic	BNP	Milik, DJD I (1955), pl. XV
1QpHab	pHab	SHR	Burrows, *DSSSMM* (1950), vol. I
	col. I		Trever, *SQC* (1972), 150–151
	col. II		Trever, *SQC* (1972), 150–151
	col. III		Trever, *SQC* (1972), 152–153
	col. IV		Trever, *SQC* (1972), 152–153
	col. V		Trever, *SQC* (1972), 154–155
	col. VI		Trever, *SQC* (1972), 154–155
	col. VII		Trever, *SQC* (1972), 156–157
	col. VIII		Trever, *SQC* (1972), 156–157
	col. IX		Trever, *SQC* (1972), 158–159
	col. X		Trever, *SQC* (1972), 158–159
	col. XI		Trever, *SQC* (1972), 160–161
	col. XII		Trever, *SQC* (1972), 160–161
	col. XIII		Trever, *SQC* (1972), 162–163

1Q15	pZeph	BNP	Milik, DJD I (1955), pl. XV
1Q16	pPs	BNP	Milik, DJD I (1955), pl. XVI
1Q17	Jub[a]	DAJ	Milik, DJD I (1955), pl. XVI
1Q18	Jub[b]	DAJ	Milik, DJD I (1955), pl. XVI
1Q19	Noah	647, DAJ	Milik, DJD I (1955), pl. XVI
1Q19bis	Noah	A. Samuel	Trever, *RevQ* 5 (1964–66): 323–44
1Q20	apGen ar (unopened scroll)	SHR	Avigad, Yadin, *Genesis Apocryphon* (1956)
1QapGen	Excavated frags. from cave	DAJ	Milik, DJD I (1955), pl. XVII
	col. I (frag. pulled from side of scroll)	A. Samuel, SHR	Morgenstern, Qimron, Sivan, *AbrN* 33 (1995): 30–54
	col. II		Avigad, Yadin, *Genesis Apocryphon* (1956)
	col. III		Morgenstern, Qimron, Sivan, *AbrN* 33 (1995): 30–54
	col. IV		Morgenstern, Qimron, Sivan, *AbrN* 33 (1995): 30–54
	col. V		Morgenstern, Qimron, Sivan, *AbrN* 33 (1995): 30–54
	col. VI		Morgenstern, Qimron, Sivan, *AbrN* 33 (1995): 30–54
	col. VII		Morgenstern, Qimron, Sivan, *AbrN* 33 (1995): 30–54
	col. VIII		Morgenstern, Qimron, Sivan, *AbrN* 33 (1995): 30–54
	col. IX		Avigad, Yadin, *Genesis Apocryphon* (1956)
	col. X		Morgenstern, Qimron, Sivan, *AbrN* 33 (1995): 30–54
	col. XI		Morgenstern, Qimron, Sivan, *AbrN* 33 (1995): 30–54
	col. XII		Greenfield, Qimron, AbrNSup 3 (1992), 70–77
	col. XIII		Morgenstern, Qimron, Sivan, *AbrN* 33 (1995): 30–54
	col. XIV		Morgenstern, Qimron, Sivan, *AbrN* 33 (1995): 30–54
	col. XV		Morgenstern, Qimron, Sivan, *AbrN* 33 (1995): 30–54
	col. XVI		Morgenstern, Qimron, Sivan, *AbrN* 33 (1995): 30–54
	col. XVII		Morgenstern, Qimron, Sivan, *AbrN* 33 (1995): 30–54
	col. XVIII		Avigad, Yadin, *Genesis Apocryphon* (1956)
	col. XIX		Avigad, Yadin, *Genesis Apocryphon* (1956)
	col. XX		Avigad, Yadin, *Genesis Apocryphon* (1956)
	col. XXI		Avigad, Yadin, *Genesis Apocryphon* (1956)
	col. XXII		Avigad, Yadin, *Genesis Apocryphon* (1956)
1Q21	TLevi ar	647	Milik, DJD I (1955), pl. XVII
1Q22	DM (apocrMoses[a]?)	DAJ	Milik, DJD I (1955), pls. XVIII–XIX
1Q23	EnGiants[a] ar	DAJ	Milik, DJD I (1955), pls. XIX–XX; re-edition: Stuckenbruck, DJD XXXVI (2000)
1Q24	EnGiants[b]? ar	BNP	Milik, DJD I (1955), pl. XX; Stuckenbruck, DJD XXXVI (2000)
1Q25	Apocryphal Prophecy	BNP	Milik, DJD I (1955), pl. XX
1Q26	Instruction (*olim* Wisdom Apocryphon)	BNP	Milik, DJD I (1955), pl. XX; re-edition: Strugnell, Harrington, DJD XXXIV (1999)
1Q27	Myst	DAJ	Milik, DJD I (1955), pls. XXI–XXII
1Q28	S title	663	Milik, DJD I (1955), pl. XXII
1QS	S	SHR	Burrows, *DSSSMM* (1951), vol. II
	col. I		Trever, *SQC* (1972), 126–127
	col. II		Trever, *SQC* (1972), 128–129
	col. III		Trever, *SQC* (1972), 130–131
	col. IV		Trever, *SQC* (1972), 132–133
	col. V		Trever, *SQC* (1972), 134–135
	col. VI		Trever, *SQC* (1972), 136–137

	col. VII		Trever, *SQC* (1972), 138–139
	col. VIII		Trever, *SQC* (1972), 140–141
	col. IX		Trever, *SQC* (1972), 142–143
	col. X		Trever, *SQC* (1972), 144–145
	col. XI		Trever, *SQC* (1972), 146–147
1Q28a	Sa	DAJ	Barthélemy, DJD I (1955), pls. XXII–XXIV
1Q28b	Sb	662–664, 1000	Milik, DJD I (1955), pls. XXV–XXIX
	Frag. of Sb	Schøyen, MS 1909	Brooke, DJD XXVI (1998), pl. XXIV
1Q29	Lit. of 3 Tongues of Fire (apocrMoses[b]?)	663	Milik, DJD I (1955), pl. XXX
1Q30	Liturgical Text A?	BNP	Milik, DJD I (1955), pl. XXX
1Q31	Liturgical Text B?	BNP	Milik, DJD I (1955), pl. XXX
1Q32	NJ ar	BNP	Milik, DJD I (1955), pl. XXXI
1Q33	M (unopened scroll)	SHR	Sukenik, *DSSHU* pls. XVI–XXXIV, 47; figs. 11–13, 26–28
	col. I		Sukenik, *DSSHU* (1955), pl. XVI
	col. II		Sukenik, *DSSHU* (1955), pl. XVII
	col. III		Sukenik, *DSSHU* (1955), pl. XVIII
	col. IV		Sukenik, *DSSHU* (1955), pl. XIX
	col. V		Sukenik, *DSSHU* (1955), pl. XX
	col. VI		Sukenik, *DSSHU* (1955), pl. XXI
	col. VII		Sukenik, *DSSHU* (1955), pl. XXII
	col. VIII		Sukenik, *DSSHU* (1955), pl. XXIII
	col. IX		Sukenik, *DSSHU* (1955), pl. XXIV
	col. X		Sukenik, *DSSHU* (1955), pl. XXV
	col. XI		Sukenik, *DSSHU* (1955), pl. XXVI
	col. XII		Sukenik, *DSSHU* (1955), pl. XXVII
	col. XIII		Sukenik, *DSSHU* (1955), pl. XXVIII
	col. XIV		Sukenik, *DSSHU* (1955), pl. XXIX
	col. XV		Sukenik, *DSSHU* (1955), pl. XXX
	col. XV inc. frags. 1 + 9		Sukenik, *DSSHU* (1955), fig. 27
	col. XVI		Sukenik, *DSSHU* (1955), pl. XXXI
	col. XVII		Sukenik, *DSSHU* (1955), pl. XXXII
	col. XVIII		Sukenik, *DSSHU* (1955), pl. XXXIII
	col. XIX		Sukenik, *DSSHU* (1955), pl. XXXIV
	frags. 1–10		Sukenik, *DSSHU* (1955), pl. XLVII
		DAJ	Milik, DJD I (1955), pl. XXXI
1Q34	LitPr[a]	DAJ	Milik, DJD I (1955), pl. XXXI
1Q34bis	LitPr[b]	A. Samuel	Milik, DJD I (1955)
1QH[a]	H[a] (unopened scroll)	SHR	Sukenik, *DSSHU* (1955), pls. XXXV–LVIII; figs. 14–17, 29–30
	col. I		Sukenik, *DSSHU* (1955), pl. XXXV
	col. II		Sukenik, *DSSHU* (1955), pl. XXXVI
	col. III		Sukenik, *DSSHU* (1955), pl. XXXVII
	col. IV		Sukenik, *DSSHU* (1955), pl. XXXVIII
	col. V		Sukenik, *DSSHU* (1955), pl. XXXIX
	col. VI		Sukenik, *DSSHU* (1955), pl. XLVII
	col. VII		Sukenik, *DSSHU* (1955), pl. XLI
	col. VIII		Sukenik, *DSSHU* (1955), pl. XLII
	col. IX		Sukenik, *DSSHU* (1955), pl. XLIII
	col. X		Sukenik, *DSSHU* (1955), pl. XLIV
	col. XI		Sukenik, *DSSHU* (1955), pl. XLV
	col. XII		Sukenik, *DSSHU* (1955), pl. XLVI
	col. XIII		Sukenik, *DSSHU* (1955), pl. XLVII
	col. XIV		Sukenik, *DSSHU* (1955), pl. XLVIII
	col. XV		Sukenik, *DSSHU* (1955), pl. XLIX
	col. XVI		Sukenik, *DSSHU* (1955), pl. L
	col. XVII		Sukenik, *DSSHU* (1955), pl. LI
	col. XVIII		Sukenik, *DSSHU* (1955), pl. LII

	frag. 1		Sukenik, *DSSHU* (1955), pl. LIII
	frag. 2		Sukenik, *DSSHU* (1955), pl. LIII
	frag. 3		Sukenik, *DSSHU* (1955), pl. LIV
	frag. 4		Sukenik, *DSSHU* (1955), pl. LIV
	frag. 5		Sukenik, *DSSHU* (1955), pl. LV
	frag. 6		Sukenik, *DSSHU* (1955), pl. LV
	frag. 7		Sukenik, *DSSHU* (1955), pl. LV
	frag. 8		Sukenik, *DSSHU* (1955), pl. LV
	frag. 9		Sukenik, *DSSHU* (1955), pl. LV
	frag. 10		Sukenik, *DSSHU* (1955), pl. LVI
	frag. 11		Sukenik, *DSSHU* (1955), pl. LVI
	frag. 12		Sukenik, *DSSHU* (1955), pl. LVI
	frag. 13		Sukenik, *DSSHU* (1955), pl. LVI
	frag. 14		Sukenik, *DSSHU* (1955), pl. LVI
	frag. 15		Sukenik, *DSSHU* (1955), pl. LVI
	frag. 15 bis		Sukenik, *DSSHU* (1955), pl. LVI
	frags. 16–44		Sukenik, *DSSHU* (1955), pl. LVII
	frags. 45–66		Sukenik, *DSSHU* (1955), pl. LVIII
1Q35	H[b]	DAJ	Milik, DJD I (1955), pl. XXXI
1Q36	Hymns	DAJ	Milik, DJD I (1955), pl. XXXII
1Q37	Hymnic Compositions?	DAJ	Milik, DJD I (1955), pls. XXXII–XXXIII
1Q38	Hymnic Compositions?	BNP	Milik, DJD I (1955), pls. XXXII–XXXIII
1Q39	Hymnic Compositions?	BNP	Milik, DJD I (1955), pls. XXXII–XXXIII
1Q40	Hymnic Compositions?	BNP	Milik, DJD I (1955), pls. XXXII–XXXIII
1Q41	Unclassified frags.	653	Milik, DJD I (1955), pls. XXXIII–XXXV
1Q42	Unclassified frags.	653	Milik, DJD I (1955), pls. XXXIII–XXXV
1Q43	Unclassified frags.	653	Milik, DJD I (1955), pls. XXXIII–XXXV
1Q44	Unclassified frags.	653	Milik, DJD I (1955), pls. XXXIII–XXXV
1Q45	Unclassified frags.	653	Milik, DJD I (1955), pls. XXXIII–XXXV
1Q46	Unclassified frags.	653	Milik, DJD I (1955), pls. XXXIII–XXXV
1Q47	Unclassified frags.	653	Milik, DJD I (1955), pls. XXXIII–XXXV
1Q48	Unclassified frags.	653	Milik, DJD I (1955), pls. XXXIII–XXXV
1Q49	Unclassified frags.	653	Milik, DJD I (1955), pls. XXXIII–XXXV
1Q50	Unclassified frags.	BNP	Milik, DJD I (1955), pls. XXXIII–XXXV
1Q51	Unclassified frags.	BNP	Milik, DJD I (1955), pls. XXXIII–XXXV
1Q52	Unclassified frags.	BNP	Milik, DJD I (1955), pls. XXXIII–XXXV
1Q53	Unclassified frags.	BNP	Milik, DJD I (1955), pls. XXXIII–XXXV
1Q54	Unclassified frags.	BNP	Milik, DJD I (1955), pls. XXXIII–XXXV
1Q55	Unclassified frags.	BNP	Milik, DJD I (1955), pls. XXXIII–XXXV
1Q56	Unclassified frags.	BNP	Milik, DJD I (1955), pls. XXXIII–XXXV
1Q57	Unclassified frags.	BNP	Milik, DJD I (1955), pls. XXXIII–XXXV
1Q58	Unclassified frags.	BNP	Milik, DJD I (1955), pls. XXXIII–XXXV
1Q59	Unclassified frags.	BNP	Milik, DJD I (1955), pls. XXXIII–XXXV
1Q60	Unclassified frags.	BNP	Milik, DJD I (1955), pls. XXXIII–XXXV
1Q61	Unclassified frags.	BNP	Milik, DJD I (1955), pls. XXXIII–XXXV
1Q62	Unclassified frags.	BNP	Milik, DJD I (1955), pls. XXXIII–XXXV
1Q63	Unclassified frags. ar	BNP	Milik, DJD I (1955), pl. XXXV
1Q64	Unclassified frags. ar	BNP	Milik, DJD I (1955), pl. XXXV
1Q65	Unclassified frags. ar	BNP	Milik, DJD I (1955), pl. XXXV
1Q66	Unclassified frags. ar	BNP	Milik, DJD I (1955), pl. XXXV
1Q67	Unclassified frags. ar	BNP	Milik, DJD I (1955), pl. XXXV
1Q68	Unclassified frags. ar	BNP	Milik, DJD I (1955), pl. XXXV
1Q69	papUnclassified frags.	652	Milik, DJD I (1955), pl. XXXVI
1Q70	papUnclassified frags. (r + v)	DAJ	Milik, DJD I (1955), pl. XXXVII
1Q70bis	papUnclassified frags.	A. Samuel	
1Q71	Dan[a]	A. Samuel	*RevQ* 5; Barthélemy, DJD I (1955), 150 (no pl.); Ulrich, DJD XVI (2000)
1Q72	Dan[b]	MS 1926/4, Schøyen	*RevQ* 5; Barthélemy, DJD I (1955), 151 (no pl.)

187

2Q1	Gen	643	Baillet, DJD III (1962), pl. X
2Q2	Exod[a]	643	Baillet, DJD III (1962), pl. X
2Q3	Exod[b]	739	Baillet, DJD III (1962), pl. XI
2Q4	Exod[c]	742	Baillet, DJD III (1962), pl. XII
2Q5	paleoLev	742	Baillet, DJD III (1962), pl. XII
2Q6	Num[a]	742	Baillet, DJD III (1962), pl. XII
2Q7	Num[b]	742	Baillet, DJD III (1962), pl. XII
2Q8	Num[c]	742	Baillet, DJD III (1962), pl. XII
2Q9	Num[d?]	742	Baillet, DJD III (1962), pl. XII
2Q10	Deut[a]	742	Baillet, DJD III (1962), pl. XII
2Q11	Deut[b]	742	Baillet, DJD III (1962), pl. XII
2Q12	Deut[c]	742	Baillet, DJD III (1962), pl. XII
2Q13	Jer	741	Baillet, DJD III (1962), pl. XIII
2Q14	Ps	741	Baillet, DJD III (1962), pl. XIII
2Q15	Job	741	Baillet, DJD III (1962), pl. XIII
2Q16	Ruth[a]	62	Baillet, DJD III (1962), pl. XIV
2Q17	Ruth[b]	644	Baillet, DJD III (1962), pl. XV
2Q18	Sir	644	Baillet, DJD III (1962), pl. XV
2Q19	Jub[a]	644	Baillet, DJD III (1962), pl. XV
2Q20	Jub[b]	644	Baillet, DJD III (1962), pl. XV
2Q21	apocrMoses?	644	Baillet, DJD III (1962), pl. XV
2Q22	apocrDavid?	644	Baillet, DJD III (1962), pl. XV
2Q23	apocrProph	644	Baillet, DJD III (1962), pl. XV
2Q24	NJ ar	645	Baillet, DJD III (1962), pl. XVI
2Q25	Juridical Text	740	Baillet, DJD III (1962), pl. XVII
2Q26	EnGiants ar (*olim* Fragment of Ritual?)	740	Baillet, DJD III (1962), pl. XVII; re-edition: Stuckenbruck, DJD XXXVI (2000)
2Q27	Unclassified frags.	740	Baillet, DJD III (1962), pl. XVII
2Q28	Unclassified frags.	740	Baillet, DJD III (1962), pl. XVII
2Q29	Unclassified frags.	740	Baillet, DJD III (1962), pl. XVII
2Q30	Unclassified frags.	740	Baillet, DJD III (1962), pl. XVII
2Q31	Unclassified frags.	740	Baillet, DJD III (1962), pl. XVII
2Q32	Unclassified frags.	740	Baillet, DJD III (1962), pl. XVII
2Q33	Unclassified frags.	740	Baillet, DJD III (1962), pl. XVII
2QX1	Debris in box	749	
3Q1	Ezek	648	Baillet, DJD III (1962), pl. XVIII
3Q2	Ps	648	Baillet, DJD III (1962), pl. XVIII
3Q3	Lam	648	Baillet, DJD III (1962), pl. XVIII
3Q4	pIsa	648	Baillet, DJD III (1962), pl. XVIII
3Q5	Jub (*olim* apProph)	648	Baillet, DJD III (1962), pl. XVIII
3Q6	Hymn	648	Baillet, DJD III (1962), pl. XVIII
3Q7	TJud?	648	Baillet, DJD III (1962), pl. XVIII
3Q8	Text Mentioning Angel of Peace	745	Baillet, DJD III (1962), pl. XIX
3Q9	Sectarian Text	745	Baillet, DJD III (1962), pl. XIX
3Q10	Unclassified frags.	745	Baillet, DJD III (1962), pl. XIX
3Q11	Unclassified frags.	745	Baillet, DJD III (1962), pl. XIX
3Q12	Unclassified frags. ar	745	Baillet, DJD III (1962), pl. XIX
3Q13	Unclassified frags. ar	745	Baillet, DJD III (1962), pl. XIX
3Q14	Unclassified frags.	745	Baillet, DJD III (1962), pl. XIX
3Q15	Copper Scroll (unopened scroll)	DAJ	Milik, DJD III (1962), pl. XLIII
	col. I		Milik, DJD III (1962), pls. XLVIII–XLIX
	col. II		Milik, DJD III (1962), pls. L–LI
	col. III		Milik, DJD III (1962), pls. LII–LIII
	col. IV		Milik, DJD III (1962), pls. LIV–LV
	col. V		Milik, DJD III (1962), pls. LVI–LVII
	col. VI		Milik, DJD III (1962), pls. LVIII–LIX
	col. VII		Milik, DJD III (1962), pls. LX–LXI
	col. VIII		Milik, DJD III (1962), pls. LXII–LXIII
	col. IX		Milik, DJD III (1962), pls. LXIV–LXV

	col. X			Milik, DJD III (1962), pls. LXVI–LXVII
	col. XI			Milik, DJD III (1962), pls. LXVIII–LXIX
	col. XII			Milik, DJD III (1962), pls. LXX–LXXI
3QX1	Largely uninscribed frags.	743		
3QX2	Uninscribed frags.	744		
3QX3	Uninscribed frags.	746		
3QX4	Leather knot in box	747		
3QX5	Debris in box	748		
3QX6	Squeeze of 3Q15 clay	1009		
4Q1	Gen–Exod[a]	169	C1	Davila, DJD XII (1994), pls. I–V
		397	C7a	
		391	C7b	
4Q2	Gen[b]	215	C2	Davila, DJD XII (1994), pls. VI–VIII
4Q3	Gen[c]	393	C3	Davila, DJD XII (1994), pl. IX
4Q4	Gen[d]	1071	C4	Davila, DJD XII (1994), pl. IX
4Q5	Gen[e]	420	C5	Davila, DJD XII (1994), pl. X
4Q6	Gen[f]	273	C2b	Davila, DJD XII (1994), pl. XI
4Q7	Gen[g]	275	C2a	Davila, DJD XII (1994), pl. XII
4Q8	Gen[h1]	275	C2a	Davila, DJD XII (1994), pl. XII
	Gen[h2]	275, 725	C2a	Davila, DJD XII (1994), pl. XII
	Gen[h–para]	275, 725	C2a	Davila, DJD XII (1994), pl. XII
	Gen[h–title]	1073	C4b	Davila, DJD XII (1994), pl. XII
4Q9	Gen[j]	1072	C4a	Davila, DJD XII (1994), pl. XIII
4Q10	Gen[k]	393	C5a	Davila, DJD XII (1994), pl. XII
4Q11	paleoGen–Exod[l]	402	Sn1b	Skehan et al., DJD IX (1992), pls. I–VI
		204	Sn1b	
		422	Sn2	
		398	Sn3	
		395	Sn3b	
4Q12	paleoGen[m]	1125	Sn1a	Skehan et al., DJD IX (1992), pl. VI
	for Gen[n] see 4Q576			
4Q13	Exod[b]	659	C6	Cross, DJD XII (1994), pls. XIV–XV
4Q14	Exod[c]	1075	C8a	Sanderson, DJD XII (1994), pl. XVI–XX
		1074	C8b	
		1076	C8c	
4Q15	Exod[d]	242	C9	Sanderson, DJD XII (1994), pl. XXI
4Q16	Exod[e]	396	C10a	Sanderson, DJD XII (1994), pl. XXI
4Q17	Exod–Lev[f]	1002	C11	Cross, DJD XII (1994), pl. XXII
4Q18	Exod[g]	1075	C10b	Sanderson, DJD XII (1994), pl. XXI
4Q19	Exod[h]	201	C15c	Sanderson, DJD XII (1994), pl. XXI
4Q20	Exod[j]	201	C15e	Sanderson, DJD XII (1994), pl. XXI
4Q21	Exod[k]	201	C15d	Sanderson, DJD XII (1994), pl. XXI
4Q22	paleoExod[m]	1005	Sn4	Skehan et al., DJD IX (1992), pls. VII–XXXIII
		1126	Sn5	
		661	Sn6	
		1127	Sn7	
		1128	Sn8	
		1129	Sn9	
		1130	Sn10	
		1131	Sn11	
		1132	Sn12	
		1133	Sn13	
		1134	Sn14	
		1135	Sn15	
		DAJ	Sn15a	
		1136	Sn16	
		1137	Sn16a	
		1155	Sn51	

		1156	Sn51a	
		1157	Sn51b	
		1154	Sn52	
		1158	Sn52	
		1158	Sn53	
		1160	Sn54	
		1159	Sn55	
		1161	Sn56	
		1162	Sn57	
		1163	Sn58	
4Q23	Lev–Num[a]	272	C12a	Ulrich, DJD XII (1994), pls. XXIII–XXX
		271	C12b	
		419	C16a	
		399	C16b	
		401	C17a	
		418	C17b	
4Q24	Lev[b]	1077	C13b	Ulrich, DJD XII (1994), pls. XXXI–XXXIV
		1078	C13c	
		1079	C13a	
4Q25	Lev[c]	316	C14	Tov, DJD XII (1994), pl. XXXV
4Q26	Lev[d]	198	C15b	Tov, DJD XII (1994), pl. XXXVI
4Q26a	Lev[e]	197	C15a	Tov, DJD XII (1994), pl. XXXVII
4Q26b	Lev[g]	197	C15a	Tov, DJD XII (1994), pl. XXXVII
	for Lev[h] see 4Q249j			
4Q27	Num[b]	1080	C19a	Jastram, DJD XII (1994), pls. XXXVIII–XLIX
		1081A	C19b	
		1081B	C19b	
		1082	C20a	
		1083	C20b	
		1084A	C21a	
		1084B	C21a	
		1085A	C21b	
		1085B	C21b	
		1086A	C22a	
		1086B	C22a	
		1087	C22b	
		1088	C22c	
4Q28	Deut[a]	256	C23	Crawford, DJD XIV (1995), pl. I
4Q29	Deut[b]	1089	C24	Duncan, DJD XIV (1995), pl. II
4Q30	Deut[c]	243	C25a	Crawford, DJD XIV (1995), pls. III–IX
		237	C25b	
		238	C25c	
4Q31	Deut[d]	323	C26	Crawford, DJD XIV (1995), pl. X
4Q32	Deut[e]	233	C27	Duncan, DJD XIV (1995), pl. XI
4Q33	Deut[f]	322	C28a	Crawford, DJD XIV (1995), pls. XII–XV
		317	C28b	
4Q34	Deut[g]	400	C31b	Crawford, DJD XIV (1995), pl. XVI
4Q35	Deut[h]	389	C29	Duncan, DJD XIV (1995), pls. XVII–XVIII
4Q36	Deut[i]	323		Crawford, DJD XIV (1995), pl. XIX
4Q37	Deut[j]	170	C30a	Duncan, DJD XIV (1995), pls. XX–XXIII
		172	C30b	
		171	C30c	
4Q38	Deut[k1]	1090	C31a	Duncan, DJD XIV (1995), pls. XXIV
4Q38a	Deut[k2]	1090	C31c	Duncan, DJD XIV (1995), pl. XXV
4Q38b	Deut[k3]	172		Duncan, DJD XIV (1995), pl. XXV
4Q39	Deut[l]	390	C32a	Duncan, DJD XIV (1995), pl. XXVI
4Q40	Deut[m]	255	C32b	Duncan, DJD XIV (1995), pls. XXVII
4Q41	Deut[n]	981	C32c	Crawford, DJD XIV (1995), pls. XXVIII–XXIX
4Q42	Deut[o]	1091	C32d	Crawford, DJD XIV (1995), pl. XXX

		178	C32d	
4Q43	Deut[p]	1091	C32d	Crawford, DJD XIV (1995), pl. XXXI
4Q44	Deut[q]	676	Sn19	Skehan and Ulrich, DJD XIV (1995) pl. XXXI
4Q45	paleoDeut[r]	1138	Sn17	Skehan et al., DJD IX (1992), pls. XXXIV–XXXVI
		1139	Sn18	
4Q46	paleoDeut[s]	1139	Sn58	Skehan et al., DJD IX (1992), pl. XXXVII
4Q47	Josh[a]	1092	C33a	Ulrich, DJD XIV (1995), pls. XXXII–XXXIV
		1093	C33b	
4Q48	Josh[b]	392	C34	Tov, DJD XIV (1995), pl. XXXV
4Q49	Judg[a]	305	C35a	Trebolle, DJD XIV (1995), pl. XXXVI
4Q50	Judg[b]	1123	C35b	Trebolle, DJD XIV (1995), pl. XXXVI
4Q51	Sam[a]	998	C36	Cross, Parry, DJD XVII (in press),
		1094	C37a	
		1095	C37b	
		1096	C38	
		1097	C39a	
		1098	C39b	
		1099	C40a	
		1100	C40b	
		1101	C41a	
		1102	C41b	
		1103	C42	
		1104	C43a	
		1105	C43b	
		1106	C44a	
		1107	C44b	
4Q52	Sam[b]	206	C45a	Cross, Parry, DJD XVII (in press)
		195	C45b	
4Q53	Sam[c]	405	C46a	Ulrich, DJD XVII (in press),
		406	C46b	
4Q54	Kgs	1108	C47	Trebolle, DJD XIV (1995), pl. XXXVII
4Q55	Isa[a]	266	Sn20	Skehan, Ulrich, DJD XV (1997), pls. I–II
		660	Sn20a	
4Q56	Isa[b]	1140	Sn21	Skehan, Ulrich, DJD XV (1997), pls. III–VI
		1141	Sn21	
4Q57	Isa[c]	363	Sn22	Skehan, Ulrich, DJD XV (1997), pls. VII–XII
		382	Sn22	
		387	Sn22	
4Q58	Isa[d]	250	Sn23	Skehan, Ulrich, DJD XV (1997), pls. XIII–XV
		236	Sn24a	
4Q59	Isa[e]	262	Sn27	Skehan, Ulrich, DJD XV (1997), pls. XVI–XVII
4Q60	Isa[f]	324	Sn28	Skehan, Ulrich, DJD XV (1997), pls. XVIII–XX
4Q61	Isa[g]	175	Sn29a	Skehan, Ulrich, DJD XV (1997), pl. XXI
4Q62	Isa[h]	262	Sn27	Skehan, Ulrich, DJD XV (1997), pl. XXI
		261	Sn29c	
4Q63	Isa[j]	1142	Sn29b	Skehan, Ulrich, DJD XV (1997), pl. XXII
4Q64	Isa[k]	250	Sn25	Skehan, Ulrich, DJD XV (1997), pl. XXII
4Q65	Isa[l]	262	Sn27	Skehan, Ulrich, DJD XV (1997), pl. XXII
		262	Sn27	
4Q66	Isa[m]	261	Sn29c	Skehan, Ulrich, DJD XV (1997), pl. XXII
4Q67	Isa[n]	261	Sn29c	Skehan, Ulrich, DJD XV (1997), pl. XXIII
4Q68	Isa[o]	261	Sn29c	Skehan, Ulrich, DJD XV (1997), pl. XXIII
4Q69	papIsa[p]	261	Sn29c	Skehan, Ulrich, DJD XV (1997), pl. XXIII
4Q69a	Isa[q]			Skehan, Ulrich, DJD XV (1997), pl. XXIII
4Q69b	Isa[r]			Skehan, Ulrich, DJD XV (1997), pl. XXIII
4Q70	Jer[a]	1109	C48a	Tov, DJD XV (1997), pls. XXIV–XXIX
		1110	C48b	

		1111	C48c	
4Q71	Jer[b]	152	C49	Tov, DJD XV (1997), pl. XXX
4Q72	Jer[c]	671	C50a	Tov, DJD XV (1997), pls. XXXI–XXXVII
		246	C50b	
		244	C52	
		232	C51a	
		245	C51b	
4Q72a	Jer[d]	152	C49	Tov, DJD XV (1997), pl. XXXVIII
4Q72b	Jer[e]	152	C49	Tov, DJD XV (1997), pl. XXXVIII
4Q73	Ezek[a]	1112	C53	Sanderson, DJD XV (1997), pl. XXXIX
4Q74	Ezek[b]	207	C54	Sanderson, DJD XV (1997), pl. XL
4Q75	Ezek[c]	207	C54bis	Sanderson, DJD XV (1997), pl. XL
4Q76	XII[a]	296	C55a	Fuller, DJD XV (1997), pls. XLI–XLIII
		1114	C55b	
		314	C56	
4Q77	XII[b]	1113	C57	Fuller, DJD XV (1997), pl. XLIV
4Q78	XII[c]	162	C58a	Fuller, DJD XV (1997), pls. XLV–XLVII
		161	C58b	
4Q79	XII[d]	410	C59	Fuller, DJD XV (1997), pl. XLVII
4Q80	XII[e]	258	C60	Fuller, DJD XV (1997), pl. XLVIII
4Q81	XII[f]	1115	C60bis	Fuller, DJD XV (1997), pl. XLVIII
4Q82	XII[g] (unopened scroll)	1143	Sn30	Fuller, DJD XV (1997), pls. XLIX–LVI
		1144	Sn31	
		1145	Sn32	
		1146	Sn33	
		1147	Sn34	
		1164	Sn59	
		1165	Sn60	
		1166	Sn61	
		1167	Sn62	
		1168	Sn63	
		1169	Sn64	
		1170	Sn65	
		1171	Sn65a	
4Q83	Ps[a]	1148	Sn35	Skehan, Ulrich, Flint, DJD XVI (2000), pls. I–II
4Q84	Ps[b]	383	Sn36	Skehan, Ulrich, Flint, DJD XVI (2000), pls. III–VI
		360	Sn37a	
		999	Sn37	
4Q85	Ps[c]	312	Sn38	Skehan, Ulrich, Flint, DJD XVI (2000), pls. VII–IX
		312	Sn39	
4Q86	Ps[d]	225	Sn40	Skehan, Ulrich, Flint, DJD XVI (2000), pl. X
4Q87	Ps[e]	263	Sn41	Skehan, Ulrich, Flint, DJD XVI (2000), pls. XI–XII
4Q88	Ps[f]	1149	Sn42a	Skehan, Ulrich, Flint, DJD XVI (2000), pls. XIII–XIV
		436	Sn40	
4Q89	Ps[g]	1150	Sn43	Skehan, Ulrich, Flint, DJD XVI (2000), pl. XV
4Q90	Ps[h]	1150	Sn43	Skehan, Ulrich, Flint, DJD XVI (2000), pl. XV
4Q91	Ps[i]	1151	Sn43	Skehan, Ulrich, Flint, DJD XVI (2000), pl. XVI
4Q92	Ps[k]	1151	Sn43	Skehan, Ulrich, Flint, DJD XVI (2000), pl. XVII
4Q93	Ps[l]	1151	Sn43	Skehan, Ulrich, Flint, DJD XVI (2000), pl. XVII
4Q94	Ps[m]	1151	Sn43	Skehan, Ulrich, Flint, DJD XVI (2000), pl. XVII

4Q95	Ps[n]	1151	Sn43	Skehan, Ulrich, Flint, DJD XVI (2000), pl. XVIII
4Q96	Ps[o]	1151	Sn43	Skehan, Ulrich, Flint, DJD XVI (2000), pl. XVIII
4Q97	Ps[p] (*olim* 4Q237)	1151	Sn43	Skehan, Ulrich, Flint, DJD XVI (2000), pl. XVIII
4Q98	Ps[q]	Inst. Cath. Paris		Skehan, Ulrich, Flint, DJD XVI (2000), pl. XIX
4Q98a	Ps[r]	1151	Sn43	Skehan, Ulrich, Flint, DJD XVI (2000), pl. XIX
4Q98b	Ps[s]			Skehan, Ulrich, Flint, DJD XVI (2000), pl. XIX
4Q98c	Ps[t] (*olim* 4QPs[s] frag. 1)	1151?		Skehan, Ulrich, Flint, DJD XVI (2000), pl. XIX
4Q98d	Ps[u] (*olim* 4QPs[s] frag. 2)	1151?		Skehan, Ulrich, Flint, DJD XVI (2000), pl. XIX
4Q98e	Ps[v]			
4Q98f	Ps[w]			Fitzmyer, DJD XVI (2000)
4Q98g	Ps[x] (*olim* 4Q236)	304	M127	Skehan, Ulrich, Flint, DJD XVI (2000), pl. XVIII
4Q99	Job[a]	1116	C61	Ulrich, DJD XVI (2000), pl. XXI
4Q100	Job[b]	1117	C61bis	Ulrich, DJD XVI (2000), pl. XXII
4Q101	paleoJob[c]	1152	Sn44	Skehan et al., DJD IX (1992), pl. XXXVII
4Q102	Prov[a]	1153	Sn45	Skehan, Ulrich, DJD XVI (2000), pl. XXII
4Q103	Prov[b]	1153	Sn45	Skehan, Ulrich, DJD XVI (2000), pl. XXIII
4Q104	Ruth[a]	410	C62a	Ulrich, DJD XVI (2000), pl. XXIV
4Q105	Ruth[b]	1117	C62b	Ulrich, DJD XVI (2000), pl. XXIV
4Q106	Cant[a]	1118	C64a	Tov, DJD XVI (2000), pl. XXIV
4Q107	Cant[b]	1119	C64	Tov, DJD XVI (2000), pl. XXV
4Q108	Cant[c]	1118	C64b	Tov, DJD XVI (2000), pl. XXV
4Q109	Qoh[a]	DAJ	C65a	Ulrich, DJD XVI (2000), pl. XXVI
4Q110	Qoh[b]	1117	C65b	Ulrich, DJD XVI (2000), pl. XXVI
4Q111	Lam	667	C66	Cross, DJD XVI (2000), pls. XXVII–XXVIII
4Q112	Dan[a]	388	C67	Ulrich, DJD XVI (2000), pl. XXX–XXXIII
		394	C68	
4Q113	Dan[b]	1120	C69	Ulrich, DJD XVI 2000), pls. XXXIV–XXXV
		1121	C70	
4Q114	Dan[c]	224	C71	Ulrich, DJD XVI (2000), pl. XXXVI
4Q115	Dan[d]	1122	C72	Ulrich, DJD XVI (2000), pl. XXXVII
4Q116	Dan[e]	153	C76	Ulrich, DJD XVI (2000), pl. XXXVIII
4Q117	Ezra	1124	C73	Ulrich, DJD XVI (2000), pl. XXXIX
4Q118	Chr	1124	C74	Trebolle, DJD XVI (2000), pl. XL
4Q119	LXXLev[a]	1004	Sn46	Skehan et al., DJD IX (1992), pl. XXXVIII
4Q120	papLXXLev[b]	376	Sn47	Skehan et al., DJD IX (1992), pls. XXXIX–XLI
		378	Sn48	
		379	Sn48a	
4Q121	LXXNum	265	Sn49	Skehan et al., DJD IX (1992), pls. XLII–XLIII
4Q122	LXXDeut	265	Sn49	Skehan et al., DJD IX (1992), pl. XLIII
4Q123	paleo paraJosh	1152	Sn44	Skehan et al., DJD IX (1992), pl. XLVI
4Q124	paleoUnident. Text 1	1152	Sn44	Skehan et al., DJD IX (1992), pls. XLIV–XLV
4Q125	paleoUnident. Text 2	1152	Sn44	Skehan et al., DJD IX (1992), pl. XLVI
4Q126	Unidentified Text gr	265	Sn49	Skehan et al., DJD IX (1992), pl. XLVI
4Q127	pap paraExodus gr	374	Sn50	Skehan et al., DJD IX (1992), pl. XLVII
		375	Sn50a	Skehan et al., DJD IX (1992), pl. XLVII
4Q128	Phyl A		M1–4	Milik, DJD VI (1977), pls. VII, VIII, XXV
4Q129	Phyl B	211	M1–4	Milik, DJD VI (1977), pl. IX
4Q130	Phyl C	211	M1–4	Milik, DJD VI (1977), pls. X, XI
4Q131	Phyl D	173	M1–4	Milik, DJD VI (1977), pl. XII
4Q132	Phyl E	173	M1–4	Milik, DJD VI (1977), pls. XII, XIII
4Q133	Phyl F	173	M1–4	Milik, DJD VI (1977), pl. XIV
4Q134	Phyl G	809	M1–4	Milik, DJD VI (1977), pl. XV

4Q135	Phyl H		212	M1–4	Milik, DJD VI (1977), pl. XVI
4Q136	Phyl I		809	M1–4	Milik, DJD VI (1977), pl. XVII
4Q137	Phyl J			M1–4	Milik, DJD VI (1977), pl. XIX
4Q138	Phyl K		809	M1–4	Milik, DJD VI (1977), pl. XX
4Q139	Phyl L		211	M1–4	Milik, DJD VI (1977), pl. XXII
4Q140	Phyl M			M1–4	Milik, DJD VI (1977), pl. XXI
4Q141	Phyl N		212	M1–4	Milik, DJD VI (1977), pl. XXII
4Q142	Phyl O		211	M1–4	Milik, DJD VI (1977), pl. XXII
4Q143	Phyl P		809	M1–4	Milik, DJD VI (1977), pl. XXII
4Q144	Phyl Q		212	M1–4	Milik, DJD VI (1977), pl. XXIII
4Q145	Phyl R		212	M1–4	Milik, DJD VI (1977), pl. XXIII
4Q146	Phyl S		212	M1–4	Milik, DJD VI (1977), pl. XXIII
4Q147	Phyl T			M1–4	Milik, DJD VI (1977), pl. XXIV
4Q148	Phyl U		813	M1–4	Milik, DJD VI (1977), pl. XXV
4Q149	Mez A		813	M1–4	Milik, DJD VI (1977), pl. XXVI
4Q150	Mez B		210	M1–4	Milik, DJD VI (1977), pl. XXVI
4Q151	Mez C		174	M1–4	Milik, DJD VI (1977), pl. XXVII
4Q152	Mez D		174	M1–4	Milik, DJD VI (1977), pl. XXVI
4Q153	Mez E		174	M1–4	Milik, DJD VI (1977), pl. XXVI
4Q154	Mez F		813	M1–4	Milik, DJD VI (1977), pl. XXVI
4Q155	Mez G		173	M1–4	Milik, DJD VI (1977), pl. XXV
4Q156	tgLev	TgLev	299	M4a	Milik, DJD VI (1977), pl. XXVIII
4Q157	tgJob	TgJob	130	M4b	Milik, DJD VI (1977), pl. XXVIII
4Q158	BibPar (= 4QRP[a])	H–L	138		Allegro, DJD V (1968), pl. I
4Q159	Ordinances[a]	Ordin	474	A17	Allegro, DJD V (1968), pl. II
4Q160	VisSam	parSam	137	A14	Allegro, DJD V (1968), pl. III
4Q161	pIsa[a]	pIsa[a]	583, 585	A5–5′	Allegro, DJD V (1968), pls. IV–V
4Q162	pIsa[b]	pIsa[c]	DAJ	A6?	Allegro, DJD V (1968), pl. VI
4Q163	pap pIsa[c]	pIsa[b]	599, 584	A8a, b	Allegro, DJD V (1968), pls. VII–VIII
4Q164	pIsa[d]	pIsa[d]	291	A7?	Allegro, DJD V (1968), pl. IX
4Q165	pIsa[e]	pIsa[e]	587	A5′	Allegro, DJD V (1968), pl. IX
4Q166	pHos[a]	pHos	675	A9, 9′	Allegro, DJD V (1968), pl. X
4Q167	pHos[b]	pHos	354	A30	Allegro, DJD V (1968), pls. X–XI
4Q168	pMic?		326		Allegro, DJD V (1968), pl. XII
4Q169	pNah	pN	980	A10, 10′	Allegro, DJD V (1968), pls. XII–XIV
4Q170	pZeph		600	A11	Allegro, DJD V (1968), pl. XIV
4Q171	pPs[a]	pPs37, 45	600, 672	A11	Allegro, DJD V (1968), pls. XIV–XVII
4Q172	pUnid		600	A12	Allegro, DJD V (1968), pl. XVIII
4Q173	pPs[b]	pPs118, 127, 129	234, 290	A13	Allegro, DJD V (1968), pl. XVIII
4Q174	Flor (= 4QMidrEschat[a]?)		281, 286	A2–3	Allegro, DJD V (1968), pls. XIX–XX
4Q175	Test		DAJ	A1	Allegro, DJD V (1968), pl. XXI
4Q176	Tanḥ	Tanḥ	285, 293	A27, 27′	Allegro, DJD V (1968), pls. XXII–XXIII
4Q176 frags. 19–21	Jub? (instead of earlier 4Q176a)				Kister, *RevQ* 12 (1985–87): 529–36
4Q177	Catena A (= 4QMidrEschat[b]?)	Catena[a]	277, 289	A25	Allegro, DJD V (1968), pls. XXIV–XXV
4Q178	Unclassified frags. (= 4QMidrEschat[d]?)		160		Allegro, DJD V (1968), pl. XXV
4Q179	apocrLam A	Lament	235	A26	Allegro, DJD V (1968), pl. XXVI
4Q180	AgesCreat A	Wisd[c]	468	A23	Allegro, DJD V (1968), pl. XXVII
4Q181	AgesCreat B		473	A29?	Allegro, DJD V (1968), pl. XVIII
4Q182	Catena B (= 4QMidrEschat[c]?)	Catena[b]	160	A25′	Allegro, DJD V (1968), pl. XXVII
4Q183	MidrEschat[e]?		139	A16?	Allegro, DJD V (1968), pl. XXVI
4Q184	Wiles of the Wicked Woman	Wisd[a]	287	A20–22	Allegro, DJD V (1968), pl. XXVIII
4Q185	Sapiential Work		801	A31, 32?	Allegro, DJD V (1968), pls. XXIX–XXX
4Q186	Horoscope	Cryp[a]	109	A18	Allegro, DJD V (1968), pl. XXXI
4Q196	papTob[a] ar	Tb[a]	666	M5	Fitzmyer, DJD XIX (1995), pls. I–V
			851	M6	
			852	M7	
			822	M8	
			808	M9	

4Q197	Tob[b] ar	Tb[b]	132	M10	Fitzmyer, DJD XIX (1995), pls. VI–VII
			133	M11	
4Q198	Tob[c] ar	Tb[c]	231	M12	Fitzmyer, DJD XIX (1995), pl. VIII
4Q199	Tob[d] ar		231	M12	Fitzmyer, DJD XIX (1995), pl. VIII
4Q200	Tob[e]	Tb[h]	848	M13	Fitzmyer, DJD XIX (1995), pls. IX–X
			850	M14	
4Q201	En[a] ar (recto of 4Q338)	Hen[a]	821	M25	Milik, BE (1976), 139–63, 340–43, pls. I–V; re-edition: Stuckenbruck, DJD XXXVI (2000)
			904	M26	
4Q202	En[b] ar	Hen[c]	380	M29	Milik, BE (1976), 164–78, 344–46, pls. VI–IX
4Q203	EnGiants[a] ar		188	M28	Milik, BE (1976), 310–17, pls. XXX–XXXII; re-edition: Stuckenbruck, DJD XXXVI (2000), pls. II–III
		Hen[b]	189	M28	
			906	M28a	
4Q204	En[c] ar	Hen[b]	199	M27	Milik, BE (1976), 178–217, 346ff., pls. IX–XV
			200	M27a	
			191	M28	
			188	M28	
			189	M28′	
4Q205	En[d] ar	Hen[e]	142	M31	Milik, BE (1976), 217–25, 353–55, pls. XVI–XVII
4Q206	En[e] ar	Hen[d]	359	M30	Milik, BE (1976), 225–44, 355ff., pls. XVIII–XXI
			386	M30a	
			358	M30b	
4Q206 frags. 2–3	EnGiants[f?] ar		359		Milik, BE (1976), 235–36; Stuckenbruck, DJD XXXVI (2000), pl. III
4Q207	En[f] ar		143	M31a	Milik, BE (1976), 244–45, 359, pl. XXI
4Q208	Enastr[a] ar	Ha[b]	823	M35	Tigchelaar, García Martínez, DJD XXXVI (2000), pls. III–IV
			814	M35a	
4Q209	Enastr[b] ar	Ha[a]	846	M32	Milik, BE (1976), 278–96, pls. XXV–XXVII, XXX; re-edition: Tigchelaar, García Martínez, DJD XXXVI (2000), pls. VI–VIII
			847	M33	
			856	M34	
			857	M34	
4Q210	Enastr[c] ar	Ha[c]	229	M36	Milik, BE (1976), 284–88, pls. XXVIII, XXX
4Q211	Enastr[d] ar	Ha[d]	369	M36a	Milik, BE (1976), 296–97, pl. XXIX
4Q212	En[g] ar (also = Letter of Enoch)	HenV	227	M37	Milik, BE (1976), 245–72, 360–62, pls. XXI–XXIV
			228	M37a	
4Q213	Levi[a] ar	TL[a]	817	M41a	Stone, Greenfield, DJD XXII (1996), pl. I
4Q213a	Levi[b] ar (olim part of Levi[a])		249	M41	Stone, Greenfield, DJD XXII (1996), pl. II
4Q213b	Levi[c] ar (olim part of Levi[a])		816	M41b	Stone, Greenfield, DJD XXII (1996), pl. III
4Q214	Levi[d] ar (olim part of Levi[b])	TL[b]	370	M42b	Stone, Greenfield, DJD XXII (1996), pl. III
4Q214a	Levi[e] ar (olim part of Levi[b])		370	M42b	Stone, Greenfield, DJD XXII (1996), pl. IV
4Q214b	Levi[f] ar (olim part of Levi[b])		370	M42b	Stone, Greenfield, DJD XXII (1996), pl. IV
4Q215	TNaph	TN	368	M43	Stone, DJD XXII (1996), pl. V
4Q215a	Time of Righteousness (olim part of TNaph)		371	M43a	Stone, Chazon, DJD XXXVI (2000), pl. IX
4Q216	Jub[a]	Jb[a]	385	M 15	VanderKam, Milik, DJD XIII (1994), pls. I–II
			385	M16	
			384	M17	
4Q217	papJub[b?]		586	M126	VanderKam, Milik, DJD XIII (1994), pl. III
4Q218	Jub[c]	Jb[c]	849	M19	VanderKam, Milik, DJD XIII (1994), pl. IV
4Q219	Jub[d]	Jb[b]	300	M18	VanderKam, Milik, DJD XIII (1994), pl. IV
4Q220	Jub[e]		849	M19	VanderKam, Milik, DJD XIII (1994), pl. V
4Q221	Jub[f]	Jb[d]	361	M20	VanderKam, Milik, DJD XIII (1994), pl. VI

4Q222	Jub^g	Jb^e	230	M21	VanderKam, Milik, DJD XIII (1994), pl. V
4Q223	papJub^h	Jb^f	134	M22	VanderKam, Milik, DJD XIII (1994), pls. VII–IX
			135	M23	
4Q224	papJub^h		136	M24	VanderKam, Milik, DJD XIII (1994), pls. VII–IX
4Q225	psJub^a	psJb^c	311	M39a	VanderKam, Milik, DJD XIII (1994), pl. X
4Q226	psJub^b	psJb^a	811	M40	VanderKam, Milik, DJD XIII (1994), pl. XI
4Q227	psJub^c?	psJb^b	812	M39a	VanderKam, Milik, DJD XIII (1994), pl. XII
4Q228	Text with a Citation of Jub	citJub	309	M124	VanderKam, Milik, DJD XIII (1994), pl. XII
4Q229	Pseudep. work in mishnaic heb				(sic Milik's list; could not be located)
4Q230	Catalogue of Spirits^a				(sic Milik's list; could not be located)
4Q231	Catalogue of Spirits^b				(sic Milik's list; could not be located)
4Q232	NJ?				(sic Milik's list; could not be located; old name for 4Q365a)
4Q233	Frags. with place names				(sic Milik's list; could not be located)
4Q234	Exercitium Calami A		603		Yardeni, DJD XXXVI (2000), pl. X
4Q235	Unid. Text nab. (olim Book of Kings)		601	M129a	Yardeni, DJD XXVII (1997), pl. LV
4Q236	cancelled (= 4Q98g)		304	M127	Skehan, Ulrich, Flint, DJD XVI (2000), pl. XVIII
4Q237	cancelled (= 4Q97 Ps^p)				Skehan, Ulrich, Flint, DJD XVI (2000), pl. XVIII
4Q238	Hab 3				Ulrich, Flint, DJD XXXVI (2000)
4Q239	Pesher on the true Israel				(sic Milik's list; could not be located)
4Q240	Commentary on Canticles?				(sic Milik's list; could not be located)
4Q241	cancelled (now:4Q282 frags. h, i)				
4Q242	PrNab ar	sNab	248	M44	Collins, DJD XXII (1996), pl. VI
			665		
4Q243	psDan^a ar	psDan^a	854	M45	Collins, Flint, DJD XXII (1996), pls. VII–VIII
			908	M45a	
			855	M45b	
4Q244	psDan^b ar	psDan^b	853	M46	Collins, Flint, DJD XXII (1996), pl. IX
4Q245	psDan^c ar	psDan^c	247	M46a	Collins, Flint, DJD XXII (1996), pl. X
4Q246	apocrDan ar	psDan^d	209	M132	Puech, DJD XXII (1996), pl. XI
4Q247	Pesher on the Apocalypse of Weeks	PsHistC	377	M47a	Broshi, DJD XXXVI (2000), pl. X
4Q248	Historical Text A	PsHistE?	815	M47b	Eshel, Broshi, DJD XXXVI (2000), pl. X
4Q249	pap cryptA Midrash SeferMoshe (= recto of 4Q250) (title on verso of frag. 1 in square script)		589r	M108	Pfann, DJD XXXV (1999), pls. I–III
			589v		
			590	M109	
			598	M110	
			597	M111	
			596	M112	
			593	M113a	
4Q249a	pap cryptA Serekh ha-ʿEdah^a		598		Pfann, DJD XXXVI (2000)
4Q249b	pap cryptA Serekh ha-ʿEdah^b		596, 598		Pfann, DJD XXXVI (2000)
4Q249c	pap cryptA Serekh ha-ʿEdah^c		598		Pfann, DJD XXXVI (2000)
4Q249d	pap cryptA Serekh ha-ʿEdah^d		590		Pfann, DJD XXXVI (2000)
4Q249e	pap cryptA Serekh ha-ʿEdah^e		598		Pfann, DJD XXXVI (2000)
4Q249f	pap cryptA Serekh ha-ʿEdah^f				Pfann, DJD XXXVI (2000)
4Q249g	pap cryptA Serekh ha-ʿEdah^g				Pfann, DJD XXXVI (2000)
4Q249h	pap cryptA Serekh ha-ʿEdah^h				Pfann, DJD XXXVI (2000)
4Q249i	pap cryptA Serekh ha-ʿEdah^i				Pfann, DJD XXXVI (2000)
4Q249j	pap cryptA Lev^h?		590		Pfann, DJD XXXVI (2000)
4Q249k	pap cryptA Text Quoting Leviticus A		590		Pfann, DJD XXXVI (2000)
4Q249l	pap cryptA Text Quoting Leviticus B		590, 598		Pfann, DJD XXXVI (2000)
4Q249m	pap cryptA Hodayot-like Text D				Pfann, DJD XXXVI (2000)

4Q249n	pap cryptA Liturgical Work E?		590		Pfann, DJD XXXVI (2000)
4Q249o	pap cryptA Liturgical Work F?				Pfann, DJD XXXVI (2000)
4Q249p	pap cryptA Prophecy?				Pfann, DJD XXXVI (2000)
4Q249q	pap cryptA Frag. Mentioning Planting		589, 590		Pfann, DJD XXXVI (2000)
4Q249r	pap cryptA Unid. Text A		598		Pfann, DJD XXXVI (2000)
4Q249s	pap cryptA Unid. Text B		598		Pfann, DJD XXXVI (2000)
4Q249t	pap cryptA Unid. Text C				Pfann, DJD XXXVI (2000)
4Q249u	pap cryptA Unid. Text D				Pfann, DJD XXXVI (2000)
4Q249v	pap cryptA Unid. Text E				Pfann, DJD XXXVI (2000)
4Q249w	pap cryptA Unid. Text F				Pfann, DJD XXXVI (2000)
4Q249x	pap cryptA Unid. Text G				Pfann, DJD XXXVI (2000)
4Q249y	pap cryptA Unid. Text H				Pfann, DJD XXXVI (2000)
4Q249z	pap cryptA Miscellaneous Frags.				Pfann, DJD XXXVI (2000)
4Q250	pap cryptA Text Concerning Cultic Service A		593	M113a	Pfann, DJD XXXVI (2000)
4Q250a	pap cryptA Text Concerning Cultic Service B (r + v)		593	M113a	Pfann, DJD XXXVI (2000)
4Q250b	pap cryptA Text Related to Isa 11 (r + v)		593		Pfann, DJD XXXVI (2000)
4Q250c	pap cryptA Unid. Text J (recto of 4Q250d)				Pfann, DJD XXXVI (2000)
4Q250d	pap cryptA Unid. Text K (verso of 4Q250c)				Pfann, DJD XXXVI (2000)
4Q250e	pap cryptA Unid. Text L (recto of 4Q250f)				Pfann, DJD XXXVI (2000)
4Q250f	pap cryptA Unid. Text M (verso of 4Q250e)				Pfann, DJD XXXVI (2000)
4Q250g	pap cryptA Unid. Text N (r+v)				Pfann, DJD XXXVI (2000)
4Q250h	pap cryptA Unid. Text O (r+v)				Pfann, DJD XXXVI (2000)
4Q250i	pap cryptA Unid. Text P (r+v)				Pfann, DJD XXXVI (2000)
4Q250j	pap cryptA Misc. Texts (r+v)				Pfann, DJD XXXVI (2000)
4Q251	Halakha A	Hlk^a	702	M80	Larson, Lehmann, Schiffman, DJD XXXV (1999), pls. III–IV
			711	M81	
4Q252	CommGen A (*olim* PBless; pGen)	pGen B	668	M38	Brooke, DJD XXII (1996), pls. XII–XIII
			670	M131	
4Q253	CommGen B	pGenVI^b	819	M38a	Brooke, DJD XXII (1996), pl. XIV
4Q253a	CommMal (*olim* part of CommGen B)	pGenVI^b	819	M38a	Brooke, DJD XXII (1996), pl. XIV
4Q254	CommGen C	pGen A	113	M125	Brooke, DJD XXII (1996), pl. XV
4Q254a	CommGen D	pGenVI^a	820	M38	Brooke, DJD XXII (1996), pl. XVI
4Q255	papS^a (= verso [?] of 4Q433a)	S^a	177	M49	Alexander, Vermes, DJD XXVI (1998), pl. I
4Q256	S^b (*olim* S^d)	S^b	907	M50	Alexander, Vermes, DJD XXVI (1998), pls. II–V
			905	M50a	
4Q257	papS^c	S^c	858	M51	Alexander, Vermes, DJD XXVI (1998), pls. VI–IX
			859	M51a	
				M51′	
4Q258	S^d (*olim* S^b)	S^d	140	M52	Alexander, Vermes, DJD XXVI (1998), pls. X–XIII
			141	M53	
4Q259	S^e	S^e	810, 818	M54	Alexander, Vermes, DJD XXVI (1998), pls. XIV–XVI
4Q260	S^f	S^f	366	M55	Alexander, Vermes, DJD XXVI (1998), pl. XVII
4Q261	S^g	S^g	705	M56	Alexander, Vermes, DJD XXVI (1998), pls. XVIII–XIX
4Q262	S^h	S^h	105	M57	Alexander, Vermes, DJD XXVI (1998), pl. XX
4Q263	S^i	S^i	251	M57a	Alexander, Vermes, DJD XXVI (1998), pl. XXI

4Q264	S^j	S^j	297	M57b	Alexander, Vermes, DJD XXVI (1998), pl. XXI
4Q264a	Halakha B (*olim* S^z)	S^z	110		Baumgarten, DJD XXXV (1999), pl. V
4Q265	Miscellaneous Rules (*olim* Serekh Damascus)	SD	306		Baumgarten, DJD XXXV (1999), pls. V–VIII
			307	M78′	
			308		
4Q266	D^a (*olim* D^b)	D^b	701	M59a	Baumgarten, DJD XVIII (1996), pls. I–XVII
			680	M60	
			699	M60	
			704+	M61	
			700	M62	
			686	M63	
			687	M63	
			707	M64	
			688	M59, 65	
			706	M65	
			689	M66	
4Q267	D^b (*olim* D^d)	D^d	106	M69	Baumgarten, DJD XVIII (1996), pls. XVIII–XXI
			107	M70	
4Q268	D^c (*olim* D^a)	D^a	373	M58	Baumgarten, DJD XVIII (1996), pl. XXII
4Q269	D^d (*olim* D^f)	D^f	220	M75	Baumgarten, DJD XVIII (1996), pls. XXIII–XXV
			221	M75	
4Q270	D^e	D^e	698	M71	Baumgarten, DJD XVIII (1996), pls. XXVI–XXXVI
			685	M72	
			690	M73	
			697	M74	
			703	M74	
4Q271	D^f (*olim* D^c)	D^c	357	M67	Baumgarten, DJD XVIII (1996), pls. XXXVII–XXXIX
			362	M68	
4Q272	D^g	D^g	219	M76a	Baumgarten, DJD XVIII (1996), pl. XL
4Q273	papD^h	D^h	108	M77	Baumgarten, DJD XVIII (1996), pls. XLI–XLII
4Q274	Tohorot A	ThrA	182	M82a	Baumgarten, DJD XXXV (1999), pl. VIII
4Q275	Communal Ceremony (*olim* Tohorot B^a)	ThrB^a/S^x	679	M79b	Alexander, Vermes, DJD XXVI (1998), pl. XXII
4Q276	Tohorot B^a (*olim* B^b)	ThrB^b	111	M82a	Baumgarten, DJD XXXV (1999), pl. IX
4Q277	Tohorot B^b (*olim* B^c)	ThrB	111	M82a	Baumgarten, DJD XXXV (1999), pl. IX
4Q278	Tohorot C	ThrC	111	M82a	Baumgarten, DJD XXXV (1999), pl. IX
4Q279	Four Lots (*olim* Tohorot D?)	Sy	111	M82b	Alexander, Vermes, DJD XXVI (1998), pl. XXIII
4Q280	Curses (*olim* Ber^f)	Brk^z	223	M76c	Nitzan, DJD XXIX (1999), pl. I
4Q281a–f	Unidentified Fragments A, a–f		304		Fitzmyer, DJD XXXVI (2000), pl. XI
4Q282a–t	Unidentified Fragments B, a–t (frags. h, i: *olim* 4Q241)		303		Fitzmyer, DJD XXXVI (2000), pls. XI–XII
4Q283	cancelled				
4Q284	Purification Liturgy	Sndt	239	M83	Baumgarten, DJD XXXV (1999), pl. X
4Q284a	Harvesting (*olim* Tohorot G + Leqet)	Lqt	679	M79b	Baumgarten, DJD XXXV (1999), pl. XI
4Q285	Sefer ha-Milḥamah (*olim* Serekh ha-Milḥamah)	BM	301	M48	Vermes, Alexander, DJD XXXVI (2000), pls. XIII–XIV
4Q286	Ber^a	B^a	709	M84	Nitzan, DJD XI (1998), pls. I–IV
			691	M85	
			692	M85a	
4Q287	Ber^b	B^b	381	M86	Nitzan, DJD XI (1998), pls. V–VI
4Q288	Ber^c	B^c	222	M85b	Nitzan, DJD XI (1998), pl. VII
4Q289	Ber^d	B^d	222	M87a	Nitzan, DJD XI (1998), pl. VII
4Q290	Ber^e				Nitzan, DJD XI (1998), pl. VII
4Q291	Work Containing Prayers A	B^w	222	M87d	Nitzan, DJD XXIX (1999), pl. I

4Q292	Work Containing Prayers B	B^x	223	M87c	Nitzan, DJD XXIX (1999), pl. I
4Q293	Work Containing Prayers C	B^y	222	M87b	Nitzan, DJD XXIX (1999), pl. I
4Q294	Sapiential-Didactic Work C		618		Tigchelaar, DJD XXXVI (2000), pl. XV
4Q295	cancelled				
4Q296	cancelled				
4Q297	cancelled				
4Q298	cryptA Words of the Maskil to All Sons of Dawn	DS	898	M113	Pfann, Kister, DJD XX (1997), pls. I–II
4Q299	Myst^a	Myst^a	605	M117	Schiffman, DJD XX (1997), pls. III–VII
			604	M117a	
			594	M118	
			595	M119	
			592	M120	
4Q300	Myst^b	Myst^b	591	M116	Schiffman, DJD XX (1997), pl. VIII
4Q301	Myst^c?	Myst^c	582	M121	Schiffman, DJD XX (1997), pl. IX
4Q302	papAdmonitory Parable (*olim* Praise of God)	SapA	356	M122	Nitzan, DJD XX (1997), pls. X–XII
4Q302a	cancelled (now part of 4Q302) (*olim* Parable of the Tree)		333	M123	
4Q303	Meditation on Creation A (*olim* MedCreat A^a)	SapC	350	M124b	Lim, DJD XX (1997), pl. XIII
4Q304	Meditation on Creation B (*olim* MedCreat A^b)		295	M124b	Lim, DJD XX (1997), pl. XIII
4Q305	Meditation on Creation C (*olim* MedCreat B)		295	M124	Lim, DJD XX (1997), pl. XIII
4Q306	Men of People who Err (*olim* SapB)	SapB	350		Lim, DJD XXXVI (2000), pl. XV
4Q307	Text Mentioning Temple (*olim* SapWork E)		295?	Msap frag.	Lim, DJD XXXVI (2000), pl. XV
4Q308	Sapiential frags.?				(*sic* Milik's list; could not be located)
4Q309	Cursive work ar				(*sic* Milik's list; could not be located)
4Q310	papText ar				(*sic* Milik's list; could not be located)
4Q311	papUnclassified text				(*sic* Milik's list; could not be located)
4Q312	Heb text in Phoenician cursive?				(*sic* Milik's list; could not be located)
4Q313	cryptA Miqṣat Maʿaśê ha-Torah^g?				Pfann, DJD XXXVI (2000)
4Q313a	cryptA Cal. Doc. E				Pfann, DJD XXXVI (2000)
4Q313b	cryptA Unid. Text Q				Pfann, DJD XXXVI (2000)
4Q313c	cryptA Unid. Text R				Pfann, DJD XXXVI (2000)
4Q314	cancelled				
4Q315	cancelled				
4Q316	cancelled				
4Q317	cryptA Phases of the Moon (*olim* AstrCrypt)		896	M101	Milik, *BE* (1976), 68–69; Pfann, DJD XXI (2000)
			899	M101a	
			903	M102	
			902	M103	
			897	M104	
			900	M105	
4Q318	Zodiology and Brontology ar	Br	805	M100	Sokoloff, Greenfield, DJD XXXVI (2000), pls. XVI–XVII
4Q319	Otot (*olim* 4QS^b + 4QS^e; 4Q260b)		683	M97	Milik, *BE* (1976), 62; DJD XXI (2000)
			695	M97a	
			696	M98	
			708	M99	
4Q320	Cal. Doc. Mishmarot A (*olim* Mishmarot A)	Mish A	681	M90	Talmon with Ben Dov, DJD XXI (2000)
			682	M91	
4Q321	Cal. Doc. Mishmarot B (*olim* Mishmarot B^a)	Mish B^a	372	M88	Talmon with Ben Dov, DJD XXI (2000)
			365	M89	
4Q321a	Cal. Doc. Mishmarot C (*olim* Mishmarot B^b)	Mish B^b	190	M92a	Talmon with Ben Dov, DJD XXI (2000)

4Q322	Mishmarot A (*olim* Mishmarot Cᵃ)	Mish Cᵃ	694	M94a	Talmon with Ben Dov, DJD XXI (2000)
4Q323	Mishmarot B (*olim* Mishmarot Cᵇ)	Mish Cᵇ	694	M95a	Talmon with Ben Dov, DJD XXI (2000)
4Q324	Mishmarot C (*olim* Mishmarot Cᶜ; recto of 4Q355)	Mish Cᶜ	694	M95b	Talmon with Ben Dov. DJD XXI (2000)
4Q324a	Mishmarot D (*olim* Mishmarot Cᵈ)	Mish Cᵈ	684	M95c	Talmon with Ben Dov, DJD XXI (2000)
4Q324b	papCal. Doc.? A (*olim* Mishmarot Cᵉ)	Mish Cᵉ	302	M95′a	Talmon with Ben Dov, DJD XXI (2000)
4Q324c	cryptA Cal. Doc. B		240	M107	Pfann, DJD XXI (2000)
			241	M106	
4Q324d	Mishmarot E				Talmon with Ben Dov, DJD XXI (2000)
4Q325	Cal. Doc. Mishmarot D (*olim* Mishmarot D)	Mish D	226	M93a	Talmon with Ben Dov, DJD XXI (2000)
4Q326	Cal. Doc. C (*olim* Mishmarot Eᵃ)	Mish Eᵃ	693	M96b	Talmon with Ben Dov, DJD XXI (2000)
4Q327	cancelled (see 4Q394 frags. 1–2)				
4Q328	Mishmarot F (*olim* Mishmarot Fᵃ)	Mish Fᵃ	693	M92b	Talmon with Ben Dov, DJD XXI (2000)
4Q329	Mishmarot G (*olim* Mishmarot Fᵇ)	Mish Fᵇ	710	M93b	Talmon with Ben Dov. DJD XXI (2000)
4Q329a	Mishmarot H (*olim* Mishmarot G)	Mish G	710	M94b	Talmon with Ben Dov, DJD XXI (2000)
4Q330	Mishmarot I (*olim* Mishmarot H)	Mish H	710	M94c	Talmon with Ben Dov, DJD XXI (2000)
4Q331	papHistorical Text C		302	M95a	Fitzmyer, DJD XXXVI (2000), pl. XVIII
4Q332	Historical Text D		694	M95a	Fitzmyer, DJD XXXVI (2000), pl. XVIII
4Q333	Historical Text E		694	M95b	Fitzmyer, DJD XXXVI (2000), pl. XIX
4Q334	Ordo	Ordo	710	M94d	Glessmer, DJD XXI (2000)
4Q335–336	Astronomical frags.?				(*sic* Milik's list; could not be located)
4Q337	Cal. Doc. F		710	M96c	Glessmer, DJD XXI (2000)
4Q338	Genealogical List? (= verso of 4Q201)		821		Tov, DJD XXXVI (2000), pl. XX
4Q339	List of False Prophets ar		377	M47a	Broshi, Yardeni, DJD XIX (1995), pl. XI
4Q340	List of Netinim		346	M130	Broshi, Yardeni, DJD XIX (1995), pl. XI
4Q341	Exercitium Calami C (*olim* 4QTher; List of Proper Names)		346	M130a	Naveh, DJD XXXVI (2000), pl. XIX
4Q342	Letter? ar (r + v)		602	M129e	Yardeni, DJD XXVII (1997), fig. 28, pl. LIV
4Q343	Letter nab (r + v)		601	M129a	Yardeni, DJD XXVII (1997), fig. 28, pl. LV
4Q344	Debt Acknowledgement ar		602	M129b	Yardeni, DJD XXVII (1997), fig. 29, pl. LVI
4Q345	Deed A ar or heb (r + v)		602	M129c	Yardeni, DJD XXVII (1997), fig. 29, pl. LVI
4Q346	Deed of Sale ar		603		Yardeni, DJD XXVII (1997), fig. 30, pl. LVII
4Q346a	Unidentified Fragment (A)		603		Yardeni, DJD XXVII (1997), fig. 30, pl. LVII
4Q347	papDeed F ar (= part of XHev/Se 32)		184		Yardeni, DJD XXVII (1997), fig. 19, pl. XXI
4Q348	Deed B heb? (r + v)		602	M129d	Yardeni, DJD XXVII (1997), fig. 29, pl. LVIII
4Q349	cancelled				
4Q350	Account gr (= v of 4Q460 frag. 9)		254		Cotton, DJD XXXVI (2000), pl. XXI
4Q351	Account of Cereal A ar		603		Yardeni, DJD XXVII (1997), fig. 30, pl. LIX
4Q352	papAccount of Cereal B ar or heb		184		Yardeni, DJD XXVII (1997), fig. 31, pl. LIX
4Q352a	papAccount A ar or heb		184		Yardeni, DJD XXVII (1997), fig. 31, pl. LIX
4Q353	papAccount of Cereal or Liquid ar or heb		184		Yardeni, DJD XXVII (1997), fig. 30, pl. LX
4Q354	Account B ar or heb		603		Yardeni, DJD XXVII (1997), fig. 30, pl. LX
4Q355	Account C ar or heb (= verso of 4Q324)		694		Yardeni, DJD XXXVI (2000), pl. XXI
4Q356	Account D ar or heb		603		Yardeni, DJD XXVII (1997), fig. 30, pl. LX
4Q357	Account E ar or heb		603		Yardeni, DJD XXVII (1997), fig. 30, pl. LX
4Q358	papAccount F? ar or heb		184		Yardeni, DJD XXVII (1997), fig. 30, pl. LX
4Q359	papDeed C? ar or heb		184		Yardeni, DJD XXVII (1997), fig. 30, pl. LX
4Q360	Exercitium Calami B		603	M130c	Yardeni, DJD XXXVI (2000), pl. XXI
4Q360a	papUnidentified Fragments ar (B)		184		Yardeni, DJD XXVII (1997), fig. 31, pl. LXI
4Q360b	Unidentified Fragment C		603		Yardeni, DJD XXVII (1997), fig. 30, pl. LXI
4Q361	papUnidentified Fragment gr		184		Cotton, DJD XXVII (1997), pl. LXI
4Q362	cryptB undeciphered frags. A		901	M114	Pfann, DJD XXXVI (2000)
4Q363	cryptB undeciphered frags. B		367	M115	Pfann, DJD XXXVI (2000)
			364	M115a	
4Q363a	cryptC Text		112	M115b	Pfann, DJD XXXVI (2000)

4Q364	RP^b		483	SL	Tov, White, DJD XIII (1994), pls. XIII–XXI
		SL1	484	SL1	
			477	SL2	
			482	SL2′	
			459	SL3	
			458	SL	
4Q365	RP^c	SL2	800	SL4	Tov, White, DJD XIII (1994), pls. XXII–XXXII
			807	SL7	
			480	SL21	
			475	SL11?	
			460	SL6	
4Q365a	T^a?	JNh	475		Tov, White, DJD XIII (1994), pls. XXXIII–XXXIV
			480		
4Q366	RP^d		257	SL7	Tov, White, DJD XIII (1994), pl. XXXV
4Q367	RP^e		467	SL7	Tov, White, DJD XIII (1994), pl. XXXV
4Q368	apocrPent. A	SL5	268	SL5	Vanderkam, DJD XXXVI (2000)
4Q369	Prayer of Enosh (Prayer Concerning God and Israel?)	SL6	264	SL78+9a	Attridge, Strugnell, DJD XIII (1994), pl. XXXVII
4Q370	AdmonFlood (olim apocrFlood)	SL8	341	SL28	Newsom, DJD XIX (1995), pl. XII
4Q371	apocrJoseph^a	SL9	176	SL97, Sy49a	Schuller, Bernstein, DJD XXX (in press)
4Q372	apocrJoseph^b	SL10	337	SL10	Schuller, Bernstein, DJD XXX (in press)
4Q373	apocrJoseph^c	SL16	469	SL16	Schuller, Bernstein, DJD XXXVI (2000)
4Q374	Exod/Conq. Trad. (olim apocrMoses A)	SL11	476	SL11?	Newsom, DJD XIX (1995), pl. XIII
4Q375	apocrMoses^a (olim apocrMoses B)	SL13	122a	SL12	Strugnell, DJD XIX (1995), pl. XIV
4Q376	apocrMoses^b? (olim 3 Tongues of Fire)	SL45	355	SL46	Strugnell, DJD XIX (1995), pl. XV
4Q377	apocrPent. B (olim apocrMoses C)	SL12	122b	SL12′	Vanderkam, DJD XXXVI (2000)
			122b	SL12′	
4Q378	apocrJosh^a (olim Psalms of Joshua^a)	SL14	167	SL15′	Newsom, DJD XXII (1996), pls. XVII–XX
			168	SL15	
4Q379	apocrJosh^b (olim Psalms of Joshua^b)	SL15 Flag. (frag. 1)	479	SL13	Newsom, DJD XXII (1996), pls. XXI–XXV
			481	SL14	
4Q380	Non-Canonical Psalms A	SL17	283	S17	Schuller, DJD XI (1998), pl. VIII
4Q381	Non-Canonical Psalms B	SL18	472	SL18	Schuller, DJD XI (1998), pls. IX–XV
			471	SL18b	
			478	SL19	
			470	SL19a	
4Q382	pap paraKings et al. (olim papTehilot Ha-ʾAvot)	SL19	351	SL20	Olyan, DJD XIII (1994), pls. XXXVIII–XLI
			339	SL20a	
			338	SL21b	
			340	SL7	
4Q383	apocrJer A	SL20	519	SL24b, c	Dimant, DJD XXX (in press)
			519	SL30b	
4Q384	papApocrJer B?	SL21	120	SL29	Smith, DJD XIX (1995), pl. XVI
4Q385	psEzek^a	SL22	270	SL22	Dimant, DJD XXX (in press)
			274	SL22	
4Q385a	apocrJer C^a (olim psMos^a)	SL22	274	SL22a	Dimant, DJD XXX (in press)
4Q385b	psEzek^c (olim 4Q385 frag. 24, apocrJer C)	SL22	267	SL23	Dimant, DJD XXX (in press)
4Q386	psEzek^b	SL23	269	SL48	Dimant, DJD XXX (in press)
4Q387	Jer C^b (olim psMos^b)	SL24	525	SL24a	Dimant, DJD XXX (in press)
4Q387a	apocrJer D	SL24	525	SL24a	Dimant, DJD XXX (in press)
4Q388	psEzek^d	SL25	125	SL25	Dimant, DJD XXX (in press)
4Q388a	Jer C^c (olim psMos^c)	SL25	125	SL25	Dimant, DJD XXX (in press)

4Q389	Jer C^d (*olim* psMos^d) ??	SL27	349	SL27	Dimant, DJD XXX (in press)
4Q389a	Jer E (*olim* apocrMos^e) ??	SL27	349	SL27	Dimant, DJD XXX (in press)
4Q390	apocrJer E (psMos^e)	SL26	524	SL30	Dimant, DJD XXX (in press)
4Q391	pap psEzek^e		454	SL94.1	Smith, DJD XIX (1995), pls. XVII–XXV
			523	SL94	
			453	SL95.1	
			455	SL95	
4Q392	Works of God (*olim* liturgical work)	SL30	126	SL25a	Falk, DJD XXIX (1999), pls. II–III
4Q393	Communal Confession (*olim* liturgical work)	SL29	124	SL26	Falk, DJD XXIX (1999), pls. II–III
4Q394	MMT^a	SL31	336	SL32	Qimron, Strugnell, DJD X (1994), pls. I–III
			335	SL32	
4Q394 1–2	Cal. Doc. D (*olim* 4Q327; Mishmarot E^b)	Mish E^b	693	M96a	Talmon with Ben Dov, DJD XXI (2000)
4Q395	MMT^b	SL32	187	SL35a	Qimron, Strugnell, DJD X (1994), pl. III
4Q396	MMT^c	SL33	520	SL33	Qimron, Strugnell, DJD X (1994), pl. IV
			526	SL33	
4Q397	MMT^d	SL34	121b	SL34	Qimron, Strugnell, DJD X (1994), pls. V–VI
			157a	SL35b	
			121a	SL34	
4Q398	papMMT^e	SL35	157b	SL72	Qimron, Strugnell, DJD X (1994), pls. VII–VIII
			157c	SL72	
4Q399	MMT^f	SL36	292	SL82a	Qimron, Strugnell, DJD X (1994), pl. VIII
4Q400	ShirShabb^a	SL37	674	SL40	Newsom, DJD XI (1998), pl. XVI
4Q401	ShirShabb^b	SL37	491	SL40′	Newsom, DJD XI (1998), pls. XVII–XVIII
			43		
4Q402	ShirShabb^c	SL41	282	SL41	Newsom, DJD XI (1998 pl. XVIII)
4Q403	ShirShabb^d	SL39	155	SL42	Newsom, DJD XI (1998), pl. XX
4Q404	ShirShabb^e	SL38	517	SL43b	Newsom, DJD XI (1998), pl. XXI
4Q405	ShirShabb^f	SL40	669	SL37b	Newsom, DJD XI (1998), pls. XXII–XXX
			506	SL36	
			518	SL37	
			507	SL38	
			497	SL37a	
			504	SL39	
			503	SL39a	
4Q406	ShirShabb^g		155	SL42	Newsom, DJD XI (1998), pl. XXXI
4Q407	ShirShabb^h	SL41	127	SL49d	Newsom, DJD XI (1998), pl. XXXI
4Q408	apocrMoses^c?	SL84	253	SL84	Steudel, DJD XXXVI (2000), pl. XXII
4Q409	Liturgical Work A	SL47	292	SL43a	Qimron, DJD XXIX (1999), pl. IV
4Q410	Vision and Interpretation (*olim* sap. work)	SL46	510	SL46	Steudel, DJD XXXVI (2000), pl. XXII
4Q411	Sapiential Hymn(*olim* sap. work)		292	SL82c	Steudel, DJD XX (1997), pl. XIV
4Q412	Sapiential-Didactic Work A (*olim* sap. work)	SL82	292	SL82b	Steudel, DJD XX (1997), pl. XIV
4Q413	Comp. conc. Div. Provid. (*olim* sap. work)	SL50	127	SL42d	Qimron, DJD XX (1997), pl. XIV
4Q414	RitPur A (*olim* Baptismal Liturgy) (= verso of 4Q415)	SL51	488	SL47	Eshel, DJD XXXV (1999), pls. XI–XII
			487	SL47a	
4Q415	Instruction^a (*olim* Sap.Work A^d) (= recto of 4Q414)	SL52	488	SL47	Strugnell, Harrington, DJD XXXIV, (1999), pls. I–II
			487	SL47a	
4Q416	Instruction^b (*olim* Sap. Work A^b)	SL53	181	SL53	Strugnell, Harrington, DJD XXXIV, (1999), pls. III–VII
			180	SL48a	
4Q417	Instruction^c (*olim* Sap. Work A^c)	SL54	329	SL50	Strugnell, Harrington, DJD XXXIV, (1999), pls. VIII–XI
			331	SL50′	
			321	SL51	

4Q418	Instruction[d] (olim Sap. Work A[a])	SL55	505	SL53	Strugnell, Harrington, DJD XXXIV (1999), pls. XII–XXVII
			486	SL53a	
			493	SL54	
			489	SL55	
			494	SL56	
			495	SL56a	
			500	SL57	
			499	SL57a	
			496	SL58	
			498	SL58a	
			502	SL59a	
4Q418a	Instruction[e]	SL59b	511		Strugnell, Harrington, DJD XXXIV (1999), pls. XXVIII–XXIX
4Q418b	Text with Quotation from Psalm 107?				Strugnell, Harrington, DJD XXXIV (1999), pl. XXIX
4Q418c	Instruction[f?]				Strugnell, Harrington, DJD XXXIV (1999), pl. XXIX
4Q419	Sap. Work B	SL56	509	SL52	Tanzer, DJD XXXVI (2000), pl. XXIII
4Q420	Ways of Righteousness[a] (olim Sap. Work D[a])	SL58	509	SL52, 61b	Elgvin, DJD XX (1997), pl. XV
4Q421	Ways of Righteousness[b] (olim Sap. Work D[b])	SL57	512	SL61a	Elgvin, DJD XX (1997), pl. XVI
4Q422	Paraphrase of Gen and Exod	SL59	165, 166	SL62′ 62	Elgvin, Tov, DJD XIII (1994), pls. XLII–XLIII
4Q423	Instruction[g] (olim Sap. Work A[e] and E; olim Tree of Knowledge)	SL60	183	SL60′	Elgvin, DJD XXXIV (1999), pls. XXX–XXXI
			185	SL60	
4Q424	Instruction-like Work	SL61	123	SL61	Tanzer, DJD XXXVI (2000), pls. XXIII–XXIV
4Q425	Sapiential-Didactic Work B (olim Sap. Work C)	SL62	501	SL14b	Steudel, DJD XX (1997), pl. XVII
4Q426	Sapiential-Hymnic Work A (olim sap. work)	SL63	276	SL63	Steudel, DJD XX (1997), pl. XVIII
4Q427	H[a]	H[a]	115	SL65	Schuller, DJD XXIX (1999), pls. IV–VI
			116	SL65	
4Q428	H[b]	H[b]	515	SL68	Schuller, DJD XXIX (1999), pls. VII–XI
			514	SL69	
			514	SL69	
			521	SL68′	
			514	SL69	
4Q429	H[c]	H[c]	522	SL64	Schuller, DJD XXIX (1999), pls. XI–XII
			522	SL64	
4Q430	H[d]	H[d]	352	SL66	Schuller, DJD XXIX (1999), pl. XII
4Q431	H[e]	H[f]	513	SL69′ 11b, 67	Schuller, DJD XXIX (1999), pls. XII, XXVIII
4Q432	papH[f]	H[e]	117	SL70	Schuller, DJD XXIX (1999), pls. XIII–XIV
			118	SL71, 72	
4Q433	Hodayot-like Text A	SL70	513	SL69′ 11b, 67	Schuller, DJD XXIX (1999), pl. XV
4Q433a	papHodayot-like Text B (= recto[?] of 4Q255)	4	177		Schuller, DJD XXIX (1999), pl. XV
4Q434	Barkhi Nafshi[a]	SL71	156	SL93	Weinfeld, Seely, DJD XXIX (1999), pls. XVII–XIX
				SL93a	
4Q435	Barkhi Nafshi[b]	SL73	327	SL73b	Weinfeld, Seely, DJD XXIX (1999), pl. XX
4Q436	Barkhi Nafshi[c]	SL72	325	SL73a	Weinfeld, Seely, DJD XXIX (1999), pl. XXI
4Q437	Barkhi Nafshi[d]	SL74	325	SL73a	Weinfeld, Seely, DJD XXIX (1999), pls. XXII–XXIII
			516	SL74	
4Q438	Barkhi Nafshi[e]	SL87	259	SL87	Weinfeld, Seely, DJD XXIX (1999), pls. XXIII–XXIV

4Q439	Lament by a Leader (*olim* Work Similar to Barkhi Nafshi)	SL76	334	SL76	Weinfeld, Seely, DJD XXIX (1999), pl. XXIV
4Q440	Hodayot-like Text C	SL77	508	SL77	Schuller, DJD XXIX (1999), pl. XVI
4Q440a	Hodayot-like Text D (*olim* 4QHᵃ frag. 14)				Lange, DJD XXXVI (2000), pl. XXV
4Q440b	Fragment Mentioning a Court		196		Lange, DJD XXXVI (2000), pl. XXV
4Q441	Individual Thanksgiving A	SL78	492	SL78	Chazon, DJD XXIX (1999), pl. XXV
4Q442	Individual Thanksgiving B	SL79	492	SL79, 71′	Chazon, DJD XXIX (1999), pl. XXV
4Q443	Personal Prayer	SL80	345	SL80a	Chazon, DJD XXIX (1999), pl. XXV
4Q444	Incantation	SL81	194	SL81a	Chazon, DJD XXIX (1999), pl. XXVI
4Q445	Lament A	SL82	490	SL83a	Tigchelaar, DJD XXIX (1999), pl. XXVI
4Q446	Poetic Text A	SL83	490	SL83b	Tigchelaar, DJD XXIX (1999), pl. XXVI
4Q447	Poetic Text B		490	SL83c	Tigchelaar, DJD XXIX (1999), pl. XXVI
4Q448	Apocr. Psalm and Prayer	SL85	490	SL85	Eshel et al., DJD XI (1998), pl. XXXII
4Q449	Prayer A	SL112	186	SL81	Chazon, DJD XXIX (1999), pl. XXVII
4Q450	Prayer B?		186	SL81	Chazon, DJD XXIX (1999), pl. XXVII
4Q451	Prayer C	SL108	186	SL81	Chazon, DJD XXIX (1999), pl. XXVII
4Q452	Prayer D?		186	SL81	Chazon, DJD XXIX (1999), pl. XXVII
4Q453	Lament B	SL105	186	SL81	Chazon, DJD XXIX (1999), pl. XXVII
4Q454	Prayer E?		186	SL81	Chazon, DJD XXIX (1999), pl. XXVII
4Q455	Didactic Work C (*olim* Prayer F)		186	SL81	Chazon, DJD XXXVI (2000), pl. XXVII
4Q456	Halleluyah		186	SL81	Chazon, DJD XXIX (1999), pl. XXVII
4Q457a	Creation?	SL44	355	SL42b	Chazon, DJD XXIX (1999), pl. XXVII
4Q457b	Eschatological Hymn (*olim* prayer)	SL44	355	SL42b	Chazon, DJD XXIX (1999), pl. XXVII
4Q458	Narrative A	SL90	442	SL90	Larson, DJD XXXVI (2000), pl. XXV
4Q459	Narr. Work Ment. Lebanon (*olim* pseud. work)	SL103	254	SL103	Larson, DJD XXXVI (2000), pl. XXV
4Q460	Narr. Work and Prayer (*olim* pseud. work) (frag. 9 = recto of 4Q350)	SL75	254	SL75	Larson, DJD XXXVI (2000), pl. XXVI
4Q461	Narrative B	SL113	441	SL89b	Larson, DJD XXXVI (2000), pl. XXVII
4Q462	Narrative C	SL89	163	SL89a	Smith, DJD XIX (1995), pl. XXVI
4Q463	Narrative D	SL111–112	441	SL89c	Smith, DJD XIX (1995), pl. XXVII
4Q464	Exposition on the Patriarchs	SL7	264	SL78+9a	Stone, Eshel, DJD XIX (1995), pl. XXVIII
4Q464a	Narrative E		264		Stone, Eshel, DJD XIX (1995), pl. XXIX
4Q464b	Unclassified Frags.		264		Stone, Eshel, DJD XIX (1995), pl. XXIX
4Q465	papText Mentioning Samson?		268	SL81	Larson, DJD XXXVI (2000), pl. XXVII
4Q466	Text Ment. the Congregation of the Lord		203		Pike, DJD XXXVI (2000), pl. XXVII
4Q467	Text Mentioning "Light to Jacob"		203		Pike, DJD XXXVI (2000), pl. XXVII
4Q468a–d	Unidentified Fragments C, a–f		304		Broshi, DJD XXXVI (2000), pl. XXVIII
4Q468e	Historical Text F		303		Broshi, DJD XXXVI (2000), pl. XXVIII
4Q468f	Historical Text G		131		Lange, DJD XXXVI (2000), pl. XXVIII
4Q468g	Eschatological Work A		131		Lange, DJD XXXVI (2000), pl. XXVIII
4Q468h	Hymnic Text A		492		Lange, DJD XXXVI (2000), pl. XXIX
4Q468i	Sectarian Text		239		Lange, DJD XXXVI (2000), pl. XXIX
4Q468j	papUnclass. frags.				Lange, DJD XXXVI (2000), pl. XXIX
4Q468k	Hymnic Text B?				Lange, DJD XXXVI (2000), pl. XXIX
4Q468l	Frag. Mentioning Qoh 1:8–9				Lange, DJD XXXVI (2000), pl. XXIX
4Q468m–bb	Unidentified Fragments D				Ernst, Lange, DJD XXXVI (2000), pls. XXIX–XXX
4Q469	Narrative I	SL	519	SL30b	Larson, DJD XXXVI (in press)
4Q470	Text Mentioning Zedekiah	SL470	519	SL24c	Larson, Schiffman, Strugnell, DJD XIX (1995), pl. XXIX
4Q471	War Scroll-like Text B (*olim* Mh)	SL86	129	SL86	E. and H. Eshel, DJD XXXVI (2000), pl. XXX
4Q471a	Polemical Text	SL86	129	SL86	Eshel, Kister, DJD XXXVI (2000)
4Q471b	Self-Glorification Hymn (= 4QHe?) (*olim* Prayer of Michael)	SL86	129	SL86	Eshel, DJD XXIX (1999), pl. XXVIII
4Q471c	Prayer Concerning God and Israel				Eshel, DJD XXIX (1999), pl. XXVIII
4Q472	Eschatological Work B		129	SL86′	Elgvin, DJD XXXVI (2000)
4Q472a	Halakha C		129	SL86′	Elgvin, DJD XXXV (1999), pl. XII

4Q473	The Two Ways	SL109	444	SL92A	Elgvin, DJD XXII (1996), pl. XXVI
4Q474	Text Concerning Rachel and Joseph (*olim* apocrJosephA; sap. work)	SL106	444	SL92B	Elgvin, DJD XXXVI (2000), pl. XXXI
4Q475	Renewed Earth (*olim* sap. work)		Flag.	SL106	Elgvin, DJD XXXVI (2000), pl. XXXI
4Q476	Liturgical Work B	SL91	128	SL91	Elgvin, DJD XXIX (1999), pl. XXVIII
4Q476a	Liturgical Work C	SL91	128	SL91	Elgvin, DJD XXIX (1999), pl. XXVIII
4Q477	Rebukes Reported by the Overseer (*olim* decrees)	SL88	443	SL88	Eshel, DJD XXXVI (2000), pl. XXXII
4Q478	papFrag. Mentioning Festivals (*olim* Tobit?)		194	SL81	Larson, Schiffman, DJD XXII (1996), pl. XXVI
4Q479	Text Mentioning Descendants of David		186	SL	Larson, Schiffman, DJD XXII (1996), pl. XXVII
4Q480	Narrative F		186	SL	Larson, Schiffman, DJD XXII (1996), pl. XXVII
4Q481	Text Mentioning Mixed Kinds		186	SL	Larson, Schiffman, DJD XXII (1996), pl. XXVII
4Q481a	apocrElisha (*olim* Frag. Ment. Elisha)		194	SL	Trebolle, DJD XXII (1996), pl. XXVIII
4Q481b	Narrative G	SL101	194	SL	Larson, Schiffman, DJD XXII (1996), pl. XXVIII
4Q481c	Prayer for Mercy	SL10b	194	SL	Larson, Schiffman, DJD XXII (1996), pl. XXVIII
4Q481d	Frags. with Red Ink		194	SL	Larson, Schiffman, DJD XXII (1996), pl. XXIX
4Q481e	Narrative H		194	SL	Larson, Schiffman, DJD XXII (1996), pl. XXIX
4Q481f	Unclassified Frags.				Pike, DJD XXXVI (2000)
4Q482	papJub^j?		13		Baillet, DJD VII (1982), pl. I
4Q483	papGen or papJub^j?		13		Baillet, DJD VII (1982), pl. I
4Q484	papTJud?		15		Baillet, DJD VII (1982), pl. I
4Q485	papProph		13		Baillet, DJD VII (1982), pl. II
4Q486	papSap A?		13		Baillet, DJD VII (1982), pl. I
4Q487	papSap B?		9, 10		Baillet, DJD VII (1982), pls. III–IV
4Q488	papApocryphon ar		15		Baillet, DJD VII (1982), pl. II
4Q489	papApocalypse ar		15		Baillet, DJD VII (1982), pl. II
4Q490	papFrags. ar		15		Baillet, DJD VII (1982), pl. II
4Q491	M^a		457, 1001	H1–2	Baillet, DJD VII (1982), pls. V–VI
4Q492	M^b		284	H3a	Baillet, DJD VII (1982), pl. VII
4Q493	M^c		344	H3c	Baillet, DJD VII (1982), pl. VIII
4Q494	M^d		344	H3b	Baillet, DJD VII (1982), pl. VIII
4Q495	M^e		344	H3b	Baillet, DJD VII (1982), pl. VIII
4Q496	papM^f (= verso of 4Q505 and 4Q509)		20–25		Baillet, DJD VII (1982), pls. X, XII, XIV, XVI–XVIII, XXII, XXIV
4Q497	papWar Scroll-like Text A (*olim* papM^g?; = verso of 4Q499)		28		Baillet, DJD VII (1982), pl. XXVI
4Q498	papSap/Hymn		12		Baillet, DJD VII (1982), pl. XXVII
4Q499	papHymns/Prayers (= recto of 4Q497)		28		Baillet, DJD VII (1982), pls. XV, XIX, XXV
4Q500	papBened		11		Baillet, DJD VII (1982), pl. XXVII
4Q501	apocrLam B	Bt 8	279	Bt8	Baillet, DJD VII (1982), pl. XXVIII
4Q502	papRitMar		1–6		Baillet, DJD VII (1982), pls. XXI, XXIV, XXIX–XXXIV
4Q503	papPrQuot (= recto of 4Q512)		461–466, 463a		Baillet, DJD VII (1982), pls. XXXV, XXXVII, XXXIX, XLI, XLIII, XLV–XLVIII
4Q504	DibHam^a	Bt 3	30, 421, 982	Bt3	Baillet, DJD VII (1982), pls. XLIX–LIII
4Q505	papDibHam^b (= r of 4Q496, 4Q506)		20		Baillet, DJD VII (1982), pl. XXIII
4Q506	papDibHam^c (= v of 4Q505, 4Q509)		20, 25–26		Baillet, DJD VII (1982), pls. XVIII, XX, XXIV
4Q507	PrFêtes^a	Bt 7	179	Bt7	Baillet, DJD VII (1982), pl. XXVIII
4Q508	PrFêtes^b	Bt 6	298	Bt6	Baillet, DJD VII (1982), pls. LIV, LXXII

205

4Q509	papPrFêtes[c] (= recto of 4Q496 and 4Q506)		16, 17, 20–26,		Baillet, DJD VII (1982), pls. IX, XI, XIII, XV, XVII, XIX, XXI, XXII
4Q510	Shir[a]	Bt 5	280	Bt5	Baillet, DJD VII (1982), pl. LV
4Q511	Shir[b]	Bt 4	403–404, 407–409, 411–417	Bt4	Baillet, DJD VII (1982), pls. LVI–LXIII, LXV, LXVII–LXXI
4Q512	papRitPur B (= verso of 4Q503)		461–466 463a		Baillet, DJD VII (1982), pls. XXXVI, XXXVIII, XL, XLII, XLIV–XLVIII
4Q513	Ordinances[b]	Bt 1	310, 315	Bt1	Baillet, DJD VII (1982), pls. LXXII–LXXIII
4Q514	Ordinances[c]	Bt 2	154	Bt2	Baillet, DJD VII (1982), pl. LXXIV
4Q515	papUnclassified frags.		14		Baillet, DJD VII (1982), pl. LXXV
4Q516	papUnclassified frags.				Baillet, DJD VII (1982), pls. LXXV, LXXVII
4Q517	papUnclassified frags.		31, 33		Baillet, DJD VII (1982), pls. LXXVI, LXXVII
4Q518	papUnclassified frags. (= recto of 4Q519)		31, 34		Baillet, DJD VII (1982), pl. LXXVIII
4Q519	papUnclassified frags. (= verso of 4Q518)		31, 34		Baillet, DJD VII (1982), pl. LXXIX
4Q520	papUnclassified frags. (verso)		35		Baillet, DJD VII (1982), pl. LXXX
4Q521	Messianic Apocalypse		330	Sy37	Puech, DJD XXV (1998), pls. I–III
4Q522	Prophecy of Joshua (apocrJosh[c]?) (olim Work with Place Names)		425	Sy16	Puech, DJD XXV (1998), pls. IV, V; Skehan, Ulrich, Flint, DJD XVI (2000), pl. XX
4Q523	Jonathan (olim Heb. frag. B)		288	Sy49b	Puech, DJD XXV (1998), pl. VI
4Q524	T[b] (olim halakhic text)		320	Sy48	Puech, DJD XXV (1998), pls. VI–VIII
4Q525	Beatitudes (olim Wisdom Text with Beatitudes)	Beat	423 424 432	Sy38 Sy39 Sy39b	Puech, DJD XXV (1998), pls. IX–XIII
4Q526	Testament? (olim Heb. frag. C)		252	Sy49c	Puech, DJD XXV (1998), pl. XIV
4Q527	Liturgical Work D? (olim Heb. frag. D)		252	Sy49c	Puech, DJD XXV (1998), pl. XIV
4Q528	Hymnic or Sapiential Work B (olim Heb. frag. E)		252	Sy49c	Puech, DJD XXV (1998), pl. XIV
4Q529	Words of Michael ar	kM	164	Sy1	Puech, DJD XXXI (2000)
4Q530	EnGiants[b] ar	psHenA	437	Sy2	Milik, BE (1976), 304–6; Puech, DJD XXXI (2000)
4Q531	EnGiants[c] ar	psHenB	328 342	Sy3 Sy4	Milik, BE (1976), 307–8; Puech, DJD XXXI (2000)
4Q532	EnGiants[d] ar	psHenC	148	Sy5	Puech, DJD XXXI (2000)
4Q533	EnGiants[e] ar (Eschat. Vision?)	arT/arU	428	Sy53b	Puech, DJD XXXI (2000)
4Q534	Noah[a] ar (olim Elect of God ar)	Mess ar	1006	Sy50 Sy51	Puech, DJD XXXI (2000)
4Q535	Noah[b] (olim Aramaic N)	mN	348	Sy4b	Puech, DJD XXXI (2000)
4Q536	Noah[c] (olim Aramaic C)	arC	451	Sy54a	Puech, DJD XXXI (2000)
4Q537	TJacob? ar	arN	260	Sy25	Puech, DJD XXXI (2000)
4Q538	TJud ar	TB	450	Sy8	Puech, DJD XXXI (2000)
4Q539	TJoseph ar (olim aJo ar)	arM	433	Sy55b	Puech, DJD XXXI (2000)
4Q540	apocrLevi[a]? ar (olim AhA [bis] = TLevi[g]? ar)	arA	150	Sy13b	Puech, DJD XXXI (2000)
4Q541	apocrLevi[b]? ar (olim AhA = TLevi[h]? ar)	AhA	149 147	Sy12 Sy13	Puech, DJD XXXI (2000)
4Q542	TQahat ar	TQ	193	Sy7b	Puech, DJD XXXI (2000)
4Q543	Visions of Amram[a] ar	h'A[a] h'A[b]	347 343	Sy10a Sy10b	Puech, DJD XXXI (2000)
4Q544	Visions of Amram[b] ar	h'A[c]	431	Sy11	Puech, DJD XXXI (2000)
4Q545	Visions of Amram[c] ar	h'A[d]	192	Sy9	Puech, DJD XXXI (2000)
4Q546	Visions of Amram[d] ar	h'A[e]	434	Sy14	Puech, DJD XXXI (2000)
4Q547	Visions of Amram[e] ar		144	Sy7	Puech, DJD XXXI (2000)

4Q548	Visions of Amramf ar	arB	427	Sy53	Puech, DJD XXXI (2000)
4Q549	Visions of Amramg? ar (*olim* Work Ment. Hur and Miriam ar)	AhC	447	Sy15	Puech, DJD XXXI (2000)
4Q550	PrEsthera ar	DCP	430	Sy17b	Puech, DJD XXXVII (in press)
4Q550a	PrEstherb ar	DCP	430	Sy17b	Puech, DJD XXXVII (in press)
4Q550b	PrEstherc ar	DCP	430	Sy17b	Puech, DJD XXXVII (in press)
4Q550c	PrEstherd ar	DCP	426/430	Sy17	Puech, DJD XXXVII (in press)
4Q550d	PrEsthere ar	DCP	426	Sy17	Puech, DJD XXXVII (in press)
4Q550e	PrEstherf ar	DCP	260		Puech, DJD XXXVII (in press)
4Q551	DanSuz? ar	arO	?	Sy18	Puech, DJD XXXVII (in press)
4Q552	Four Kingdomsa ar	QRa	278	Sy19	Puech, DJD XXXVII (in press)
4Q553	Four Kingdomsb ar	QRb	353	Sy20	Puech, DJD XXXVII (in press)
4Q554	NJa ar	Jna	319	Sy22	Puech, DJD XXXVII (in press)
			318	Sy23–24	
4Q555	NJb ar		205	Sy57	Puech, DJD XXXVII (in press)
4Q556	Visiona ar		446	Sy2b	Puech, DJD XXXVII (in press)
4Q557	Visionc ar	arQ	313	Sy29a	Puech, DJD XXXVII (in press)
4Q558	papVisionb ar		448	Sy26	Puech, DJD XXXVII (in press)
			452	Sy27	
			449	Sy28a	
			440	Sy28b	
4Q559	papBibChronology ar	ChrB	438	Sy30	Puech, DJD XXXVII (in press)
4Q560	Exorcism ar	OC	445	Sy36	Puech, DJD XXXVII (in press)
4Q561	Physiognomy/Horoscope ar	Hor ar	439	Sy52	Puech, DJD XXXVII (in press)
4Q562	Aramaic D	arD	332	Sy54b	Puech, DJD XXXVII (in press)
4Q563	Aramaic E	arE	159	Sy55a	Puech, DJD XXXVII (in press)
4Q564	Aramaic F	arF	433	Sy55b	Puech, DJD XXXVII (in press)
4Q565	Aramaic G	arG	433	Sy55b	Puech, DJD XXXVII (in press)
4Q566	Aramaic H	arH	433	Sy55b	Puech, DJD XXXVII (in press)
4Q567	Aramaic I	arI	433	Sy55b	Puech, DJD XXXVII (in press)
4Q568	Aramaic K	arK	433	Sy55b	Puech, DJD XXXVII (in press)
4Q569	Aramaic L	arL	433	Sy55b	Puech, DJD XXXVII (in press)
4Q570	Aramaic R	arR	429	Sy55c	Puech, DJD XXXVII (in press)
4Q571	Aramaic V	arV	435	Sy56	Puech, DJD XXXVII (in press)
4Q572	Aramaic W	arW	435	Sy56	Puech, DJD XXXVII (in press)
4Q573	Aramaic X	arX	435	Sy56	Puech, DJD XXXVII (in press)
4Q574	Aramaic Y	arY	435	Sy56	Puech, DJD XXXVII (in press)
4Q575	Aramaic Z	arZ1/arZ2	435	Sy56	Puech, DJD XXXVII (in press)
4Q576	Genn (*olim* part of 4Q524)		320	Sy48	Puech, DJD XXV (1998), pl. XV
4Q577	Text Mentioning the Flood		320	Sy48	Puech, DJD XXV (1998), pl. XV
4Q578	Historical Text B		320	Sy48	Puech, DJD XXV (1998), pl. XV
4Q579	Hymnic Work?		330		Puech, DJD XXV (1998), pl. XV
5Q1	Deut		97		Milik, DJD III (1962), pl. XXXVI
5Q2	Kgs		98		Milik, DJD III (1962), pl. XXXVI
5Q3	Isa		99		Milik, DJD III (1962), pl. XXXVI
5Q4	Amos		100		Milik, DJD III (1962), pl. XXXVI
5Q5	Ps		98, 100, 104		Milik, DJD III (1962), pl. XXXVII
5Q6	Lama		100		Milik, DJD III (1962), pls. XXXVII–XXXVIII
5Q7	Lamb		100		Milik, DJD III (1962), pl. XXXVIII
5Q8	Phyl.		100		Milik, DJD III (1962), pl. XXXVIII
5Q9	Work with Place Names (apocrJosh?)				Milik, DJD III (1962), pl. XXXVIII
5Q10	apocrMal				Milik, DJD III (1962), pl. XXXVIII
5Q11	S		101		Milik, DJD III (1962), pl. XXXVIII
5Q12	D		101		Milik, DJD III (1962), pl. XXXVIII
5Q13	Rule				Milik, DJD III (1962), pls. XXXIX–XL
5Q14	Curses		101		Milik, DJD III (1962), pl. XL
5Q15	NJ ar				Milik, DJD III (1962), pls. XL–XLI

5Q16	Unclassified frags.			Milik, DJD III (1962), pls. XLI–XLII
5Q17	Unclassified frags.			Milik, DJD III (1962), pls. XLI–XLII
5Q18	Unclassified frags.	102		Milik, DJD III (1962), pls. XLI–XLII
5Q19	Unclassified frags.	102		Milik, DJD III (1962), pls. XLI–XLII
5Q20	Unclassified frags.	102		Milik, DJD III (1962), pls. XLI–XLII
5Q21	Unclassified frag.	102		Milik, DJD III (1962), pls. XLI–XLII
5Q22	Unclassified frag.	102		Milik, DJD III (1962), pls. XLI–XLII
5Q23	Unclassified frag.			Milik, DJD III (1962), pls. XLI–XLII
5Q24	Unclassified frag. ar			Milik, DJD III (1962), pls. XLI–XLII
5Q25	Unclassified frags.	102		Milik, DJD III (1962), pl. XLII
5QX1	Uninscribed leather frag.	50		
6Q1	paleoGen	894		Baillet, DJD III (1962), pl. XX
6Q2	paleoLev	894		Baillet, DJD III (1962), pl. XX
6Q3	papDeut?	894		Baillet, DJD III (1962), pl. XX
6Q4	papKgs	894		Baillet, DJD III (1962), pls. XX–XXII
		895		
		738		
6Q5	papPs?	646		Baillet, DJD III (1962), pl. XXIII
6Q6	Cant	646		Baillet, DJD III (1962), pl. XXIII
6Q7	papDan	646		Baillet, DJD III (1962), pl. XXIII
6Q8	papEnGiants ar (*olim* apocrGen)	785		Baillet, DJD III (1962), pls. XXIV, XXIX; re-edition: Stuckenbruck, DJD XXXVI (2000)
6Q9	pap apocrSam–Kgs	785, 892		Baillet, DJD III (1962), pls. XXIV–XXV
6Q10	papProph	649		Baillet, DJD III (1962), pl. XXVI
6Q11	Allegory of the Vine	649		Baillet, DJD III (1962), pl. XXVI
6Q12	apocrProphecy	649		Baillet, DJD III (1962), pl. XXVI
6Q13	Priestly Prophecy	649		Baillet, DJD III (1962), pl. XXVI
6Q14	Apoc ar	649		Baillet, DJD III (1962), pl. XXVI
6Q15	D	649		Baillet, DJD III (1962), pl. XXVI
6Q16	papBened	737		Baillet, DJD III (1962), pl. XXVII
6Q17	papCalendrical Doc.	737		Baillet, DJD III (1962), pl. XXVII
6Q18	papHymn	737		Baillet, DJD III (1962), pl. XXVII
		29		unpublished
6Q19	Text Related to Genesis ar	893		Baillet, DJD III (1962), pl. XXVIII
6Q20	Deut?	893		Baillet, DJD III (1962), pl. XXVIII
6Q21	Prophetic Text?	893		Baillet, DJD III (1962), pl. XXVIII
6Q22	papUnclassified frags.	893		Baillet, DJD III (1962), pl. XXVIII
6Q23	papUnclassified frags. ar (Words of Michael?)	893		Baillet, DJD III (1962), pl. XXVIII
6Q24	papUnclassified frags.	893		Baillet, DJD III (1962), pl. XXVIII
6Q25	papUnclassified frags.	893		Baillet, DJD III (1962), pl. XXVIII
6Q26	papAccount or contract	784		Baillet, DJD III (1962), pl. XXIX
6Q27	papCursive unclassified frags.	784		Baillet, DJD III (1962), pl. XXIX
6Q28	papCursive unclassified frags.	784		Baillet, DJD III (1962), pl. XXIX
6Q29	papCursive unclassified frag.	784		Baillet, DJD III (1962), pl. XXIX
6Q30	papCursive unclassified frags.	784		Baillet, DJD III (1962), pl. XXIX
6Q31	papUnclassified frags.	784		Baillet, DJD III (1962), pl. XXIX
6QX1	papUnclassified frags.	786		
6QX2	Unclassified frags.	787		
7Q1	papLXXExod	789		Baillet, DJD III (1962), pl. XXX
7Q2	papEpJer gr	789		Baillet, DJD III (1962), pl. XXX
7Q3	papBiblical Text? gr	789		Baillet, DJD III (1962), pl. XXX
7Q4	papBiblical Text? gr (papEn gr?)	789		Baillet, DJD III (1962), pl. XXX; Muro, *RevQ* 70 (1997)
7Q5	papBiblical Text? gr	789		Baillet, DJD III (1962), pl. XXX
7Q6	papUnclassified frags. gr	789		Baillet, DJD III (1962), pl. XXX
7Q7	papUnclassified frags. gr	789		Baillet, DJD III (1962), pl. XXX

7Q8	papUnclassified frags. gr (papEn gr?)	789	Baillet, DJD III (1962), pl. XXX; Muro, RevQ 70 (1997)
7Q9	papUnclassified frags. gr	789	Baillet, DJD III (1962), pl. XXX
7Q10	papUnclassified frags. gr	789	Baillet, DJD III (1962), pl. XXX
7Q11	papUnclassified frags. gr (papEn gr?)	789	Baillet, DJD III (1962), pl. XXX; Puech, RevQ 70 (1997)
7Q12	papUnclassified frags. gr (papEn gr?)	789	Baillet, DJD III (1962), pl. XXX; Muro, RevQ 70 (1997)
7Q13	papUnclassified frags. gr (papEn gr?)	789	Baillet, DJD III (1962), pl. XXX; Puech, RevQ 70 (1997)
7Q14	papUnclassified frags. gr (papEn gr?)	789	Baillet, DJD III (1962), pl. XXX; Puech, RevQ 70 (1997)
7Q15	papUnclassified frags. gr	789	Baillet, DJD III (1962), pl. XXX
7Q16	papUnclassified frags. gr	789	Baillet, DJD III (1962), pl. XXX
7Q17	papUnclassified frags. gr	789	Baillet, DJD III (1962), pl. XXX
7Q18	papUnclassified frags. gr	789	Baillet, DJD III (1962), pl. XXX
7Q19	papImprint gr	789A	Baillet, DJD III (1962), pl. XXX
8Q1	Gen	788	Baillet, DJD III (1962), pl. XXXI
8Q2	Ps	788	Baillet, DJD III (1962), pl. XXXI
8Q3	Phyl	914	Baillet, DJD III (1962), pls. XXXII–XXXIII
8Q4	Mez	916	Baillet, DJD III (1962), pl. XXXIV
8Q5	Hymn	917	Baillet, DJD III (1962), pl. XXXV
8QX1	Reinforcing tabs	56	
8QX2–3	Thongs	57, 58	
9Q	papUnclassified frag.	917	Baillet, DJD III (1962), pl. XXXV
10Q	ostr?	918	Baillet, DJD III (1962), pl. XXXV
11Q1	paleoLev^a		Freedman, Mathews, PHLS (1985)
	frag. A (Lev 4:24–26)	1039	Freedman, Mathews, PHLS (1985), pl. 1; Puech, RB 96 (1989): 176 bis
	frag. B (Lev 10:4–7)	1039	Freedman, Mathews, PHLS (1985), pl. 1
	frag. C (Lev 11:27–32)	1039	Freedman, Mathews, PHLS (1985), pls. 1, 12
	frag. D (Lev 13:3–9)	1039	Freedman, Mathews, PHLS (1985), pl. 1; Puech, RB 96 (1989): 176 bis
	frag. E (Lev 13:39–43)	1039	Freedman, Mathews, PHLS (1985), pls. 2, 12
	frag. F (Lev 14:16–21)	1039	Freedman, Mathews, PHLS (1985), pls. 2, 12; Puech, RB 96 (1989): 176 bis
	frag. G (Lev 14:52–15:5/16:2–4)	1039	Freedman, Mathews, PHLS (1985), pl. 2
	frag. H (Lev 16:34–17:5)	1039	Freedman, Mathews, PHLS (1985), pls. 3, 12; Puech, RB 96 (1989): 176 ter
	frag. I (Lev 18:27–19:4)	1039	Freedman, Mathews, PHLS (1985), pls. 3, 13
	frag. J (Lev 20:1–6)	1039	Freedman, Mathews, PHLS (1985), pls. 4, 13; Puech, RB 96 (1989): 176 ter
	frag. K (Lev 21:6–11)	1039	Freedman, Mathews, PHLS (1985), pls. 4, 14
	frag. L (Lev 21a–27a, Lev. 21:7a–12a)	Paris	Freedman, Mathews, PHLS (1985), pl. 5; Puech, RB 96 (1989): 176 quat
	frag. M (Lev 16:1–6)	1039	Freedman, Mathews, PHLS (1985), pl. 6; Puech, RB 96 (1989): 176 bis
	col. 1 (Lev 22:21–27)	1039	Freedman, Mathews, PHLS (1985), pls. 6, 14, 20
	col. 2 (Lev 23:22–29)	1039	Freedman, Mathews, PHLS (1985), pls. 7, 15, 20
	col. 3 (Lev 24:9–14)	1039	Freedman, Mathews, PHLS (1985), pls. 8, 16, 20
	col. 4 (Lev 25:28–36)	1039	Freedman, Mathews, PHLS (1985), pls. 9, 17, 20
	col. 5 (Lev 26:17–26)	1039	Freedman, Mathews, PHLS (1985), pls. 10, 18, 20
	col. 6 (Lev 27:11–19)	1039	Freedman, Mathews, PHLS (1985), pls. 11, 19, 20

	frags. a–f	1022	Puech, *RB* 96 (1989): 176 bis
	frags.	614	Puech, *RB* 96 (1989): 176 ter
	frags.	567	Puech, *RB* 96 (1989)
	frags. aa–ai	988	Tigchelaar, *RevQ* 70 (1998)
11Q2	Lev[b]		García Martínez, Tigchelaar, van der Woude, DJD XXIII (1998), pl. I
	frag. 1 (Lev 7:34–35)	577	
	frags. 2, 8 (Lev 9:23–10:2)	566	
	frag. 3 (Lev 13:58–59)	615	
	frag. 4 (Lev 14:16–17)	1032	
	frags. 5 + 6 (Lev 15:18–19)	567, 577	
	frag. 7 (Lev 25:31–33)	567, 1016	
	frag. 9 (?)	567	
11Q3	Deut		García Martínez, Tigchelaar, van der Woude, DJD XXIII (1998), pl. II
	frag. 1 (Deut 1:4–5)	576	
	frag. 2 (Deut 2:28–30)	1016	
	frag. 3 (?)	1016	
11Q4	Ezek (unopened scroll)		Herbert, DJD XXIII (1998), pl. II
	scroll frags. after unsuccessful opening	1010	
	frag. 1 (Ezek 1:8–10)	1013–1013A	
	frag. 2 (Ezek 4:3–5)	1013–1013A	
	frag. 3a (Ezek 4:6)	1013–1013A	
	frags. 4–5 (Ezek 4:9–10)	1013–1013A	
	frags. 3b + 6 (Ezek 5:11–17)	1013–1013A	
	frag. 7 (Ezek 7:9–12)	1013–1013A	
	frag. 8	1013–1013A	
	frag. 9	1013–1013A	
11Q5	Ps[a] (unopened scroll)	977	Sanders, DJD IV (1965), pls. I–II
	frag. A (Ps 101:1–8; 102:1–2)	977	Sanders, DJD IV (1965), pl. III
	frag. B (Ps 101:1–8; 102:1–2)	977	Sanders, DJD IV (1965), pl. III
	frag. C I (Ps 101:1–8; 102:1–2)	977	Sanders, DJD IV (1965), pl. III
	frag. C II (Ps 102:18–29; 103?; 104)	977	Sanders, DJD IV (1965), pl. III
	frag. D (Ps 109:21–31)	976	Sanders, DJD IV (1965), pl. III
	frag. E (Ps 118:25–29; 104:1–6, 21–35; 147:1–2, 18–20; 105:1–11)	976?	García Martínez, Tigchelaar, van der Woude, DJD XXIII (1998), pls. IV–V
	frag. F (Ps 147:3?)	614B	García Martínez, Tigchelaar, van der Woude, DJD XXIII (1998), pl. V
	col. I (Ps 105:25–45)	979	Sanders, DJD IV (1965), pl. IV
	col. II (Ps 146:9?–10; 148:1–12)	979	Sanders, DJD IV (1965), pl. IV
	col. III (Ps 121:1–8; 122:1–9; 123:1–2)	979	Sanders, DJD IV (1965), pl. IV
	col. IV (Ps 124:7–8; 125:1–5; 126:1–6; 127:1)	979	Sanders, DJD IV (1965), pl. V
	col. V (Ps 128:3–6; 129:1–8; 130:1–8)	979	Sanders, DJD IV (1965), pl. V
	col. VI (Ps 132:8–18; 119:1–6)	979	Sanders, DJD IV (1965), pl. VI
	col. VII (Ps 119:15–28)	979	Sanders, DJD IV (1965), pl. VI
	col. VIII (Ps 119:37–49)	979	Sanders, DJD IV (1965), pl. VII
	col. IX (Ps 119:59–73)	979	Sanders, DJD IV (1965), pl. VII
	col. X (Ps 119:82–96)	979	Sanders, DJD IV (1965), pl. VIII
	col. XI (Ps 119:105–20)	979	Sanders, DJD IV (1965), pl. VIII
	col. XII (Ps 119:128–42)	979	Sanders, DJD IV (1965), pl. IX
	col. XIII (Ps 119:150–64)	975	Sanders, DJD IV (1965), pl. IX

	col. XIV (Ps 119:171–6; 135:1–9)	975	Sanders, DJD IV (1965), pl. X
	col. XV (Ps 135:17–21; 136:1–16)	975	Sanders, DJD IV (1965), pl. X
	col. XVI (Ps 136:26b; 118:1?, 15, 16, 18, 19, ?, 29; 145:1–7)	975	Sanders, DJD IV (1965), pl. XI
	col. XVII (Ps 145:13–21+?)	975	Sanders, DJD IV (1965), pl. XI
	col. XVIII (Syriac Ps II)	975	Sanders, DJD IV (1965), pl. XII
	col. XIX (Plea for Deliverance)	978	Sanders, DJD IV (1965), pl. XII
	col. XX (Ps 139:8–24; 137:1)	978	Sanders, DJD IV (1965), pl. XIII
	col. XXI (Ps 137:9; 138:1–8; Sirach 51:13ff.)	978	Sanders, DJD IV (1965), pl. XIII
	col. XXII (Sirach 51:30; Apostr. to Zion; Ps 93:1–3)	978	Sanders, DJD IV (1965), pl. XIV
	col. XXIII (Ps 141:5–10; 133:1–3; 144:1–7)	978	Sanders, DJD IV (1965), pl. XIV
	col. XXIV (Ps 144:15; Syriac Ps III)	978	Sanders, DJD IV (1965), pl. XV
	col. XXV (Ps 142:4–8; 143:1–8)	974	Sanders, DJD IV (1965), pl. XV
	col. XXVI (Ps 149:7–9; 150:1–6; Hymn to the Creator)	974	Sanders, DJD IV (1965), pl. XVI
	col. XXVII (2 Sam 23:7; David's Comps; Ps 140:1–5)	974	Sanders, DJD IV (1965), pl. XVI
	col. XXVIII (Ps 134:1–3; 151A; 151B)	576	Sanders, DJD IV (1965), pl. XVII
11Q6	Ps^b		García Martínez, Tigchelaar, van der Woude, DJD XXIII (1998), pl. III
	frag. 1 (Ps 77:18–78:1)	606	
	frag. 2 (Ps 119:163–165)	614	
	frag. 3 (Ps 118:1, 15–16)	613	
	frags. 4 + 5 (Plea for Deliverance)	576	
	frag. 6 (Apostrophe to Zion)	621B	
	frag. 7 (Ps 141:10; 133; 144:1–2)	576, 621B	
	frag. 8 (Ps 109:3–4?)	1032	
	frag. 9 (?)	1032	
11Q7	Ps^c		García Martínez, Tigchelaar, van der Woude, DJD XXIII (1998), pl. VI
	frags. 1 + 2 (Ps 2:1–8)	606	
	frag. 3 (Ps 9:3–7)	606	
	frags. 4 + 6 + 7 (Ps 12:5–14:6)	606	
	frag. 5 (Ps 12:6–9)	614	
	frag. 8 (Ps 17:9–18:12)	606	
	frag. 9 (Ps 18:15–17?)	614	
	frag. 10 (Ps 19:4–8)	621B	
	frag. 11 (Ps 25:2–7)	1027	
11Q8	Ps^d		
	frag. 1 (Ps 6:2–4)	?	García Martínez, Tigchelaar, van der Woude, DJD XXIII (1998), pl. VII
	frag. 2 (Ps 9:3–6)	1025	García Martínez, Tigchelaar, van der Woude, DJD XXIII (1998), pl. VII
	frag. 3 (Ps 18:26–29; olim Mas1g?; XQPs)	78–79*	Flint, DJD XVI (2000); García Martínez, Tigchelaar, van der Woude, DJD XXIII (1998), pl. VII
	frag. 4 (Ps 18:39–42)	619	García Martínez, Tigchelaar, van der Woude, DJD XXIII (1998), pl. VII
	frag. 5 (Ps 36:13–37:4)	621B	García Martínez, Tigchelaar, van der Woude, DJD XXIII (1998), pl. VII
	frag. 6 (Ps 39:13–40:2)	569	García Martínez, Tigchelaar, van der Woude, DJD XXIII (1998), pl. VII
	frag. 7 (Ps 43:1–3)	569	García Martínez, Tigchelaar, van der Woude, DJD XXIII (1998), pl. VII
	frag. 8 (Ps 45:6–8)	621B	García Martínez, Tigchelaar, van der Woude, DJD XXIII (1998), pl. VII
	frag. 9 (Ps 59:5–8)	569	García Martínez, Tigchelaar, van der Woude, DJD XXIII (1998), pl. VII
	frag. 10 (Ps 68:1–5)	569	García Martínez, Tigchelaar, van der Woude, DJD XXIII (1998), pl. VII

	frag. 11 (Ps 68:14–18)	569	García Martínez, Tigchelaar, van der Woude, DJD XXIII (1998), pl. VII
	frag. 12 (Ps 78:5–12)	569, 621B	García Martínez, Tigchelaar, van der Woude, DJD XXIII (1998), pl. VII
	frag. 13 (Ps 81:4–9)	569	García Martínez, Tigchelaar, van der Woude, DJD XXIII (1998), pl. VII
	frag. 14 (Ps 86:11–14)	621B	García Martínez, Tigchelaar, van der Woude, DJD XXIII (1998), pl. VIII
	frag. 15 (Ps 115:16–116:1)	581A	García Martínez, Tigchelaar, van der Woude, DJD XXIII (1998), pl. VIII
	frag. 16 (Ps 78:36–37?)	580	García Martínez, Tigchelaar, van der Woude, DJD XXIII (1998), pl. VIII
	frag. 17 (Ps 60:9?)	1032	García Martínez, Tigchelaar, van der Woude, DJD XXIII (1998), pl. VIII
11Q9	Ps^e? (Ps 50:3–7)	1016	García Martínez, Tigchelaar, van der Woude, DJD XXIII (1998), pl. VIII
11Q10	tgJob (unopened scroll)		
	col. I (Job 17:14–18:4)	635	García Martínez, Tigchelaar, van der Woude, DJD XXIII (1998), pl. IX
	col. II (Job 19:11–19)	627	García Martínez, Tigchelaar, van der Woude, DJD XXIII (1998), pl. IX
	col. III (Job 19:29–20:6)	627	García Martínez, Tigchelaar, van der Woude, DJD XXIII (1998), pl. IX
	col. IV (Job 21:2–10)	628	García Martínez, Tigchelaar, van der Woude, DJD XXIII (1998), pl. IX
	col. V (Job 21:20–27)	628	García Martínez, Tigchelaar, van der Woude, DJD XXIII (1998), pl. IX
	col. VI (Job 22:3–9)	636	García Martínez, Tigchelaar, van der Woude, DJD XXIII (1998), pl. X
	col. VIi (Job 22:16–22)	636	García Martínez, Tigchelaar, van der Woude, DJD XXIII (1998), pl. X
	col. VIIA (Job 23:1–8)		García Martínez, Tigchelaar, van der Woude, DJD XXIII (1998), pl. X
	col. VIII (Job 24:12–17)	636	García Martínez, Tigchelaar, van der Woude, DJD XXIII (1998), pl. X
	col. IX (Job 24:24–26:2)	633	García Martínez, Tigchelaar, van der Woude, DJD XXIII (1998), pl. X
	col. X (Job 26:10–27:4)	633	García Martínez, Tigchelaar, van der Woude, DJD XXIII (1998), pl. XI
	col. XI (Job 27:11–20)	637	García Martínez, Tigchelaar, van der Woude, DJD XXIII (1998), pl. XI
	col. XII (Job 28:4–13)	637	García Martínez, Tigchelaar, van der Woude, DJD XXIII (1998), pl. XI
	col. XIII (Job 28:20–28)	637	García Martínez, Tigchelaar, van der Woude, DJD XXIII (1998), pl. XI
	col. XIV (Job 29:7–16)	632	García Martínez, Tigchelaar, van der Woude, DJD XXIII (1998), pl. XII
	col. XV (Job 29:24–30:4)	632	García Martínez, Tigchelaar, van der Woude, DJD XXIII (1998), pl. XII
	col. XVI (Job 30:13–20)	631	García Martínez, Tigchelaar, van der Woude, DJD XXIII (1998), pl. XII
	col. XVII (Job 30:25–31:1)	567, 631	García Martínez, Tigchelaar, van der Woude, DJD XXIII (1998), pl. XII
	col. XVIII (Job 31:8–16)	624, 631	García Martínez, Tigchelaar, van der Woude, DJD XXIII (1998), pl. XII
	col. XIX (Job 31:26–32)	624	García Martínez, Tigchelaar, van der Woude, DJD XXIII (1998), pls. XII–XIII
	col. XX (Job 31:40–32:3)	624	García Martínez, Tigchelaar, van der Woude, DJD XXIII (1998), pl. XIII
	col. XXI (Job 32:10–17)	634	García Martínez, Tigchelaar, van der Woude, DJD XXIII (1998), pl. XIII
	col. XXII (Job 33:6–16)	634	García Martínez, Tigchelaar, van der Woude, DJD XXIII (1998), pl. XIII
	col. XXIII (Job 33:24–32)	629, 635	García Martínez, Tigchelaar, van der Woude, DJD XXIII (1998), pl. XIV
	col. XXIV (Job 34:6–17)	621, 629	García Martínez, Tigchelaar, van der Woude, DJD XXIII (1998), pl. XIV

	col. XXV (Job 34:24–34)	621	García Martínez, Tigchelaar, van der Woude, DJD XXIII (1998), pl. XIV
	col. XXVI (Job 35:6–15)	626	García Martínez, Tigchelaar, van der Woude, DJD XXIII (1998), pl. XV
	col. XXVII (Job 36:7–16)	626, 630	García Martínez, Tigchelaar, van der Woude, DJD XXIII (1998), pl. XV
	col. XXVIII (Job 36:23–33)	623, 630	García Martínez, Tigchelaar, van der Woude, DJD XXIII (1998), pl. XV
	col. XXIX (Job 37:10–19)	635, 638	García Martínez, Tigchelaar, van der Woude, DJD XXIII (1998), pl. XVI
	col. XXX (Job 38:3–13)	638	García Martínez, Tigchelaar, van der Woude, DJD XXIII (1998), pl. XVI
	col. XXXI (Job 38:23–34)	638	García Martínez, Tigchelaar, van der Woude, DJD XXIII (1998), pl. XVII
	col. XXXII (Job 39:1–11)	638	García Martínez, Tigchelaar, van der Woude, DJD XXIII (1998), pl. XVII
	col. XXXIII (Job 39:20–29)	638	García Martínez, Tigchelaar, van der Woude, DJD XXIII (1998), pl. XVIII
	col. XXXIV (Job 40:5–14[15?])	638	García Martínez, Tigchelaar, van der Woude, DJD XXIII (1998), pl. XVIII
	col. XXXV (Job 40:23–31)	638	García Martínez, Tigchelaar, van der Woude, DJD XXIII (1998), pl. XIX
	col. XXXVI (Job 41:7–17)	638	García Martínez, Tigchelaar, van der Woude, DJD XXIII (1998), pl. XIX
	col. XXXVII (Job 41:25–42:2; 40:5; 42:4–6)	638	García Martínez, Tigchelaar, van der Woude, DJD XXIII (1998), pl. XX
	col. XXXVIII (Job 42:9–12)	638	García Martínez, Tigchelaar, van der Woude, DJD XXIII (1998), pl. XX
	frags. A1, A3, A5	635	García Martínez, Tigchelaar, van der Woude, DJD XXIII (1998), pl. XXI
	frags. A7, A9, A10	567	García Martínez, Tigchelaar, van der Woude, DJD XXIII (1998), pl. XXI
	frag. A8	581	García Martínez, Tigchelaar, van der Woude, DJD XXIII (1998), pl. XXI
	frags. A11–19	625	García Martínez, Tigchelaar, van der Woude, DJD XXIII (1998), pl. XXI
	frag. G	—	García Martínez, Tigchelaar, van der Woude, DJD XXIII (1998), pl. XXI
	frags. N, O	—	García Martínez, Tigchelaar, van der Woude, DJD XXIII (1998), pl. XXI
	frag. P	—	García Martínez, Tigchelaar, van der Woude, DJD XXIII (1998), pl. XXI
11Q11	apocrPs (unopened scroll: *olim* apocrPsª)		García Martínez, Tigchelaar, van der Woude, DJD XXIII (1998), pl. LIII
	frags. 1 + 2	619	García Martínez, Tigchelaar, van der Woude, DJD XXIII (1998), pl. XXII
	frags. 3 + 4	1032	García Martínez, Tigchelaar, van der Woude, DJD XXIII (1998), pl. XXII
	col. I	612	García Martínez, Tigchelaar, van der Woude, DJD XXIII (1998), pl. XXII
	col. II	61	García Martínez, Tigchelaar, van der Woude, DJD XXIII (1998), pl. XXIII
	col. III	61	García Martínez, Tigchelaar, van der Woude, DJD XXIII (1998), pl. XXIII
	col. IV	61	García Martínez, Tigchelaar, van der Woude, DJD XXIII (1998), pl. XXIV
	col. V (Ps 91)	61	García Martínez, Tigchelaar, van der Woude, DJD XXIII (1998), pl. XXIV
	col. VI	61, 612	García Martínez, Tigchelaar, van der Woude, DJD XXIII (1998), pl. XXV
	handle sheet and wooden handle	612	García Martínez, Tigchelaar, van der Woude, DJD XXIII (1998), pl. XXII
11Q12	Jub		García Martínez, Tigchelaar, van der Woude, DJD XXIII (1998), pl. XXVI
	frag. 1 (Jub 4:6–11)	619, 621B	
	frag. 2 (Jub 4:13–14)	606	
	frag. 3 (Jub 4:16–17 [4:11–12?])	?	

213

	frag. 4 (Jub 4:17–18?)	621B	
	frag. 5 (Jub 4:29–30)	619	
	frag. 6 (Jub 4:31)	621B	
	frag. 7 (Jub 5:1–2)	619	
	frag. 8 (Jub 12:15–17)	619	
	frag. 9 (Jub 12:28–29)	619	
	frag. 10?	621B	
	frag. 11?	614	
	frag. 12?	614B	
	frag. 13?	619	
11Q13	Melch		García Martínez, Tigchelaar, van der Woude, DJD XXIII (1998), pl. XXVII
	frags. 1a, 1b, 2–9	579	
	frag. 1c	1031	
	frag. 10	621B	
	frag. 11	1032	
11Q14	Sefer ha-Milḥamah (olim Ber)		García Martínez, Tigchelaar, van der Woude, DJD XXIII (1998), pl. XXVIII
	frags. 1a, 1b, 1e, 3	607	
	frag. 1c	?	
	frag. 1d	567	
	frag. 1f	607	
	frag. 2	614	
	frag. 4	615	
11Q15	Hymns[a]		García Martínez, Tigchelaar, van der Woude, DJD XXIII (1998), pl. XXIX
	frag. 1	576	
	frag. 2	1025	
	frags. 3, 4	621B	
11Q16	Hymns[b]	614	García Martínez, Tigchelaar, van der Woude, DJD XXIII (1998), pl. XXIX
11Q17	ShirShabb (unopened scroll)		García Martínez, Tigchelaar, van der Woude, DJD XXIII (1998), pl. LIII
	frag. 1	567	García Martínez, Tigchelaar, van der Woude, DJD XXIII (1998), pl. XXX
	frags. 2–4, 6, 8, 10–12, 14–15, 28–29, 34	565	García Martínez, Tigchelaar, van der Woude, DJD XXIII (1998), pls. XXX, XXXI, XXXIV
	frags. 5, 26b, 27, 30, 31	—	García Martínez, Tigchelaar, van der Woude, DJD XXIII (1998), pls. XXX, XXXIV
	frag. 26a	1032	García Martínez, Tigchelaar, van der Woude, DJD XXIII (1998), pl. XXXIV
	frags. 7, 9, 13, 23, 24	618	García Martínez, Tigchelaar, van der Woude, DJD XXIII (1998), pls. XXX–XXXI, XXXIII
	frags. 21a, 22	618	García Martínez, Tigchelaar, van der Woude, DJD XXIII (1998), pl. XXXII
	frag. 25	618	García Martínez, Tigchelaar, van der Woude, DJD XXIII (1998), pl. XXXIII
	frag. 16	609	García Martínez, Tigchelaar, van der Woude, DJD XXIII (1998), pl. XXXI
	frags. 17–19, 33	609	García Martínez, Tigchelaar, van der Woude, DJD XXIII (1998), pls. XXXI–XXXII
	frag. 20	609	García Martínez, Tigchelaar, van der Woude, DJD XXIII (1998), pl. XXXII
	frag. 32	621B	García Martínez, Tigchelaar, van der Woude, DJD XXIII (1998), pl. XXXIV
	frag. 35	614	García Martínez, Tigchelaar, van der Woude, DJD XXIII (1998), pl. XXXIV
	frags. 36, 42	1032	García Martínez, Tigchelaar, van der Woude, DJD XXIII (1998), pl. XXXIV
	frag. 37	1034	García Martínez, Tigchelaar, van der Woude, DJD XXIII (1998), pl. XXX

	frags. 38–41	1030	García Martínez, Tigchelaar, van der Woude, DJD XXIII (1998), pl. XXXIII
11Q18	NJ ar (unopened scroll)		García Martínez, Tigchelaar, van der Woude, DJD XXIII (1998), pl. LIII
	frags. 1–4, additional frags.	578A	García Martínez, Tigchelaar, van der Woude, DJD XXIII (1998), pls. XXXV, XL
	frags. 5–9	578	García Martínez, Tigchelaar, van der Woude, DJD XXIII (1998), pls. XXXV–XXXVI
	frags. 10–11	574, 572, 615	García Martínez, Tigchelaar, van der Woude, DJD XXIII (1998), pl. XXXVI
	frags. 12–13	564, 572	García Martínez, Tigchelaar, van der Woude, DJD XXIII (1998), pls. XXXVI, XXXVII
	frags. 14–15	564, 568	García Martínez, Tigchelaar, van der Woude, DJD XXIII (1998), pl. XXXVII
	frags. 16, 21	572, 617	García Martínez, Tigchelaar, van der Woude, DJD XXIII (1998), pls. XXXVII, XXXVIII
	frags. 17–18	611	García Martínez, Tigchelaar, van der Woude, DJD XXIII (1998), pls. XXXVII, XXXVIII
	frags. 19–20	575	García Martínez, Tigchelaar, van der Woude, DJD XXIII (1998), pl. XXXVIII
	frags. 22–24	573, 572, 615	García Martínez, Tigchelaar, van der Woude, DJD XXIII (1998), pl. XXXVIII
	frags. 25–27	570, 572, 615	García Martínez, Tigchelaar, van der Woude, DJD XXIII (1998), pl. XXXXIX
	frags. 28–31	571, 572, 614B	García Martínez, Tigchelaar, van der Woude, DJD XXIII (1998), pl. XXXXIX
	frags. 32–37 petrified remnants of scroll	572, 1030	García Martínez, Tigchelaar, van der Woude, DJD XXIII (1998), pl. XXXXIX
11Q19	Tᵃ (unopened scroll)	SHR	Yadin, Temple Scroll (1983)
	col. I	SHR	Yadin, Temple Scroll (1983), pl. 16
	col. II	SHR	Yadin, Temple Scroll (1983), pl. 17
	col. III	SHR	Yadin, Temple Scroll (1983), pl. 18
	col. IV	SHR	Yadin, Temple Scroll (1983), pl. 19
	col. V	SHR	Yadin, Temple Scroll (1983), pl. 20
	col. VI	SHR	Yadin, Temple Scroll (1983), pl. 21
	col. VII	SHR	Yadin, Temple Scroll (1983), pl. 22
	col. VIII	SHR	Yadin, Temple Scroll (1983), pl. 23
	col. IX	SHR	Yadin, Temple Scroll (1983), pl. 24
	col. X	SHR	Yadin, Temple Scroll (1983), pl. 25
	col. XI	SHR	Yadin, Temple Scroll (1983), pl. 26
	col. XII	SHR	Yadin, Temple Scroll (1983), pl. 27
	col. XIII	SHR	Yadin, Temple Scroll (1983), pl. 28
	col. XIV	SHR	Yadin, Temple Scroll (1983), pl. 29
	col. XV	SHR	Yadin, Temple Scroll (1983), pl. 30
	col. XVI	SHR	Yadin, Temple Scroll (1983), pl. 31
	col. XVII	SHR	Yadin, Temple Scroll (1983), pl. 32
	col. XVIII	SHR	Yadin, Temple Scroll (1983), pl. 33
	col. XIX	SHR	Yadin, Temple Scroll (1983), pl. 34
	col. XX	SHR	Yadin, Temple Scroll (1983), pl. 35
	col. XXI	SHR	Yadin, Temple Scroll (1983), pl. 36
	col. XXII	SHR	Yadin, Temple Scroll (1983), pl. 37
	col. XXIII	SHR	Yadin, Temple Scroll (1983), pl. 38
	col. XXIV	SHR	Yadin, Temple Scroll (1983), pl. 39
	col. XXV	SHR	Yadin, Temple Scroll (1983), pl. 40
	col. XXVI	SHR	Yadin, Temple Scroll (1983), pl. 41
	col. XXVII	SHR	Yadin, Temple Scroll (1983), pl. 42
	col. XXVIII	SHR	Yadin, Temple Scroll (1983), pl. 43
	col. XXIX	SHR	Yadin, Temple Scroll (1983), pl. 44
	col. XXX	SHR	Yadin, Temple Scroll (1983), pl. 45

	col. XXXI	SHR	Yadin, *Temple Scroll (1983)*, pl. 46
	col. XXXII	SHR	Yadin, *Temple Scroll (1983)*, pl. 47
	col. XXXIII	SHR	Yadin, *Temple Scroll (1983)*, pl. 48
	col. XXXIV	SHR	Yadin, *Temple Scroll (1983)*, pl. 49
	col. XXXV	SHR	Yadin, *Temple Scroll (1983)*, pl. 50
	col. XXXVI	SHR	Yadin, *Temple Scroll (1983)*, pl. 51
	col. XXXVII	SHR	Yadin, *Temple Scroll (1983)*, pl. 52
	col. XXXVIII	SHR	Yadin, *Temple Scroll (1983)*, pl. 53
	col. XXXIX	SHR	Yadin, *Temple Scroll (1983)*, pl. 54
	col. XL	SHR	Yadin, *Temple Scroll (1983)*, pl. 55
	col. XLI	SHR	Yadin, *Temple Scroll (1983)*, pl. 56
	col. XLII	SHR	Yadin, *Temple Scroll (1983)*, pl. 57
	col. XLIII	SHR	Yadin, *Temple Scroll (1983)*, pl. 58
	col. XLIV	SHR	Yadin, *Temple Scroll (1983)*, pl. 59
	col. XLV	SHR	Yadin, *Temple Scroll (1983)*, pl. 60
	col. XLVI	SHR	Yadin, *Temple Scroll (1983)*, pl. 61
	col. XLVII	SHR	Yadin, *Temple Scroll (1983)*, pl. 62
	col. XLVIII	SHR	Yadin, *Temple Scroll (1983)*, pl. 63
	col. XLIX	SHR	Yadin, *Temple Scroll (1983)*, pl. 64
	col. L	SHR	Yadin, *Temple Scroll (1983)*, pl. 65
	col. LI	SHR	Yadin, *Temple Scroll (1983)*, pl. 66
	col. LII	SHR	Yadin, *Temple Scroll (1983)*, pl. 67
	col. LIII	SHR	Yadin, *Temple Scroll (1983)*, pl. 68
	col. LIV	SHR	Yadin, *Temple Scroll (1983)*, pl. 69
	col. LV	SHR	Yadin, *Temple Scroll (1983)*, pl. 70
	col. LVI	SHR	Yadin, *Temple Scroll (1983)*, pl. 71
	col. LVII	SHR	Yadin, *Temple Scroll (1983)*, pl. 72
	col. LVIII	SHR	Yadin, *Temple Scroll (1983)*, pl. 73
	col. LIX	SHR	Yadin, *Temple Scroll (1983)*, pl. 74
	col. LX	SHR	Yadin, *Temple Scroll (1983)*, pl. 75
	col. LXI	SHR	Yadin, *Temple Scroll (1983)*, pl. 76
	col. LXII	SHR	Yadin, *Temple Scroll (1983)*, pl. 77
	col. LXIII	SHR	Yadin, *Temple Scroll (1983)*, pl. 78
	col. LXIV	SHR	Yadin, *Temple Scroll (1983)*, pl. 79
	col. LXV	SHR	Yadin, *Temple Scroll (1983)*, pl. 80
	col. LXVI	SHR	Yadin, *Temple Scroll (1983)*, pl. 81
	col. LXVII	SHR	Yadin, *Temple Scroll (1983)*, pl. 82
11Q20	T^b frags. 1a, 1c, 1e, 2, 9, 10b, 11b, 15a–b, 20, 26, 28b	577	García Martínez, Tigchelaar, van der Woude, DJD XXIII (1998), pls. XLI–XLIV, XLVI
	frag. 7	577	García Martínez, Tigchelaar, van der Woude, DJD XXIII (1998), pl. XLII
	frags. 1b, 4a, 11a, 21, 22, 23a–c, 25, 30a	580	García Martínez, Tigchelaar, van der Woude, DJD XXIII (1998), pls. XLI–XLIII, XLV, XLVII
	frag. 30b	580	
	frags. 8a–b, 10a, 10c, 10e–f	608, 1031	García Martínez, Tigchelaar, van der Woude, DJD XXIII (1998), pls. XLII, XLIII
	frag. 10g	608	
	frags. 10d, 41	607	García Martínez, Tigchelaar, van der Woude, DJD XXIII (1998), pls. XLIII, XLVII
	frag. 13	610	García Martínez, Tigchelaar, van der Woude, DJD XXIII (1998), pl. XLIV
	frag. 17	566	García Martínez, Tigchelaar, van der Woude, DJD XXIII (1998), pl. XLIV
	frags. 1d, 6b, 28a, 36, 37	614	García Martínez, Tigchelaar, van der Woude, DJD XXIII (1998), pls. XLI, XLII, XLVI, XLVII
	frags. 3, 18, 29	567	García Martínez, Tigchelaar, van der Woude, DJD XXIII (1998), pls. XLII, XLIV, XLVI
	frags. 4b, 42	1032	García Martínez, Tigchelaar, van der Woude, DJD XXIII (1998), pls. XLII, XLVII

	frags. 5, 27, 33, 40	621B	García Martínez, Tigchelaar, van der Woude, DJD XXIII (1998), pls. XLII, XLVII
	frags. 6a, 6c, 12, 15c, 16, 24, 38, 39	614B	García Martínez, Tigchelaar, van der Woude, DJD XXIII (1998), pls. XLII–XLV, XLVII
	frag. 14	1020	
	frags. 19, 23d, 34, 35	613	García Martínez, Tigchelaar, van der Woude, DJD XXIII (1998), pls. XLIV, XLV, XLVII
	frag. 31	606, 615	García Martínez, Tigchelaar, van der Woude, DJD XXIII (1998), pl. XLVII
	frag. 32	1016	García Martínez, Tigchelaar, van der Woude, DJD XXIII (1998), pl. XLVII
11Q21	T^c?		García Martínez, Tigchelaar, van der Woude, DJD XXIII (1998), pl. XLVIII
	frag. 1	619	
	frag. 2	614	
	frag. 3	567	
11Q22	paleoUnidentified Text		García Martínez, Tigchelaar, van der Woude, DJD XXIII (1998), pl. XLVIII
	frag. 1	?	
	frag. 2	?	
	frags. 3, 4	614	
	frag. 5	?	
	frag. 6	1020	
	frag. 7	1032	
11Q23	CryptA Unidentified Text	613	García Martínez, Tigchelaar, van der Woude, DJD XXIII (1998), pl. XLVIII
11Q24	Unidentified Text ar	567	García Martínez, Tigchelaar, van der Woude, DJD XXIII (1998), pl. XLIX
11Q25	Unidentified Text A		García Martínez, Tigchelaar, van der Woude, DJD XXIII (1998), pl. XLIX
	frags. 1, 2	567	
	frag. 3	621B	
	frag. 4	614	
	frag. 5	1032	
	frags. 6–8	581A	
11Q26	Unidentifed Text B		García Martínez, Tigchelaar, van der Woude, DJD XXIII (1998), pl. XLIX
	frag. 1	621B	
	frags. 2, 3	567	
11Q27	Unidentified Text C	614B	García Martínez, Tigchelaar, van der Woude, DJD XXIII (1998), pl. XLIX
11Q28	papUnidentified Text D	988	García Martínez, Tigchelaar, van der Woude, DJD XXIII (1998)
11Q29	Frag. Related to Serekh ha-Yaḥad	615	García Martínez, Tigchelaar, van der Woude, DJD XXIII (1998), pl. L
11Q30	Unclassified Fragments	567	García Martínez, Tigchelaar, van der Woude, DJD XXIII (1998), pls. L–LI
		581A	
		615	
		621B	
		988	
		1016	
		1031	
		1032	
		1034	
11Q31	Unidentified wads	563	García Martínez, Tigchelaar, van der Woude, DJD XXIII (1998), pl. LII
XQ1–4	Phyl. 1–4	SHR	Yadin, *Tefillin from Qumran* (1969)
XQ6	Offering ar	Private	Lemaire, DJD XXXVI (2000), pl. XXXII
XQ7		SHR	Lange, DJD XXXVIII (2000)

| Kh.Q | Ostracon 1 | | | | Cross, Eshel, DJD XXXVI (2000), pl. XXXIII |
| Kh.Q | Ostracon 2 | | | | Cross, Eshel, DJD XXXVI (2000), pl. XXXIV |

2. Wadi Daliyeh

ITEM NO.	COMPOSITION	OLD PLATE	INVEN- TORY	FORMER SIGLA	PUBLICATION
WDSP 1	papDeed of Slave Sale A ar		554r		Gropp, DJD XXVIII (in press)
WDSP 2	papDeed of Slave Sale B ar		555		Gropp, DJD XXVIII (in press)
WDSP 3	papDeed of Slave Sale C ar		558		Gropp, DJD XXVIII (in press)
WDSP 4	papDeed of Slave Sale D ar		553		Gropp, DJD XXVIII (in press)
WDSP 5	papDeed of Slave Sale E ar		559		Gropp, DJD XXVIII (in press)
WDSP 6	papDeed of Slave Sale F ar		548		Gropp, DJD XXVIII (in press)
WDSP 7	papDeed of Slave Sale G ar		549r		Gropp, DJD XXVIII (in press)
			549v		
WDSP 8	papDeed of Slave Sale H ar		755r		Gropp, DJD XXVIII (in press)
			755v		
WDSP 9	papDeed of Slave Sale I ar (r + v)		552r		Gropp, DJD XXVIII (in press)
			552v		
WDSP 10	papLoan with Pledge of Slave A? ar		551r		Gropp, DJD XXVIII (in press)
			551v		
WDSP 11	papDeed of Slave Sale J? ar (recto)		754r		Gropp, DJD XXVIII (in press)
WDSP 11a	papSettlement of Dispute? ar (verso)		754v		
WDSP 12	papLoan with Pledge of Slave B? ar		920		Gropp, DJD XXVIII (in press)
WDSP 13	papPledge of Slave C? ar (recto)		757r		Gropp, DJD XXVIII (in press)
WDSP 13a	papRelease of Pledged Slave? ar (verso)		757v		
WDSP 14	papDeed of Conveyance of Public Rooms ar		562		Gropp, DJD XXVIII (in press)
WDSP 15	papDeed of House Sale ar		560		Gropp, DJD XXVIII (in press)
WDSP 16	papDeed of Pledge of Vineyard? ar		561		Gropp, DJD XXVIII (in press)
WDSP 17	papReceipt of Payment in Relation to a Pledge ar		751		Gropp, DJD XXVIII (in press)
WDSP 18	papDeed of Slave Sale K ar		750		Gropp, DJD XXVIII (in press)
WDSP 19	papDeed of Slave Sale L ar		557		Gropp, DJD XXVIII (in press)
WDSP 20	papDeed of Slave Sale M ar		919C		Gropp, DJD XXVIII (in press)
WDSP 21	papDeed of Sale A ar		919B		Gropp, DJD XXVIII (in press)
WDSP 22	papDeed of Slave Sale N? ar		556		Gropp, DJD XXVIII (in press)
WDSP 23	papDeed of Settlement? ar (r + v)		752r		Gropp, DJD XXVIII (in press)
			752v		
WDSP 24	papDeed of Sale B? ar		756		Gropp, DJD XXVIII (in press)
WDSP 25	papDeed of SaleC ? ar		756		Gropp, DJD XXVIII (in press)
WDSP 26	papDeed of Slave Sale O? ar		756		Gropp, DJD XXVIII (in press)
WDSP 27	papPledge of Slave D? ar		758		Gropp, DJD XXVIII (in press)
WDSP 28	papMiscellaneous Fragments A ar		759B		
WDSP 29	papMiscellaneous Fragments B ar (r + v)		544r		
			544v		
WDSP 30	papMiscellaneous Fragments C ar		545		
WDSP 31	papMiscellaneous Fragments D ar		546		
WDSP I.3	papFrag. Nos 26–29 ar		547		Cross, DIWD (1974), pl. 60; Gropp, DJD XXVIII (in press)
WDSP 32	papMiscellaneous Fragments E ar		550		
WD pap 33	papMiscellaneous Fragments F ar		557 (757?)		
WDSP 34	papMiscellaneous Fragments G ar		753		
WDSP 35	papMiscellaneous Fragments H ar (recto)		759r		Gropp, DJD XXVIII (in press)
WDSP 35a	papMiscellaneous Fragments I ar (verso)		759v		
WDSP 36	papMiscellaneous Fragments ar		919A		

3. Ketef Jericho

Jer 1	papList of Loans ar		E. and H. Eshel, DJD XXXVIII (2000)
Jer 2	papDeed of Sale A ar		E. and H. Eshel, DJD XXXVIII (2000)
Jer 3	Deed of Sale B ar		E. and H. Eshel, DJD XXXVIII (2000)
Jer 4–5d	papUnidentified Text(s) gr		Cohen, DJD XXXVIII (2000)
Jer 4	papDeed of Sale or Lease? gr	K28556	Cohen, DJD XXXVIII (2000)
Jer 5a–d	pap gr		Cohen, DJD XXXVIII (2000)
Jer 5e	papTransaction Concerning Seeds gr		Cohen, DJD XXXVIII (2000)
Jer 6	papUnidentified Text		E. Eshel, DJD XXXVIII (2000)
Jer 7	papSale of Date Crop		E. Eshel and Misgav, DJD XXXVIII (2000)
Jer 8–30	papUnidentified Texts		DJD XXXVIII (2000)
Jer 31	papDeed of Sale? gr		Cotton, DJD XXXVIII (2000)
Jer 32	papDeed of Sale? gr		Cotton, DJD XXXVIII (2000)
Jer 33	papTreasury Receipt gr		Cotton, DJD XXXVIII (2000)
Jer 34–34g	pap gr		Cohen, DJD XXXVIII (2000)
Jer 34	papWritten Order? gr		Cohen, DJD XXXVIII (2000)
Jer 34a	papUnidentified Text gr		Cohen, DJD XXXVIII (2000)
Jer 34b	papList of Witnesses? gr		Cohen, DJD XXXVIII (2000)
Jer c–g	papUnidentified Texts gr		Cohen, DJD XXXVIII (2000)

4. Khirbet Mird

APHM 1	papByzantine Protocols arab	A33a1	1201	Grohmann, *APHM* (1963)
APHM 2	papByzantine Protocols arab	A1a1	1183	Grohmann, *APHM* (1963)
APHM 3	papByzantine Protocols arab	A23a1	1179	Grohmann, *APHM* (1963)
APHM 4	papByzantine Protocols arab	A23a2	1179	Grohmann, *APHM* (1963)
APHM 5	papProtocols arab	A30b2	1218	Grohmann, *APHM* (1963)
APHM 6	papProtocols arab	38r	1177r	Grohmann, *APHM* (1963)
APHM 7	papProtocols arab	A30b1	1218	Grohmann, *APHM* (1963)
APHM 8	papSignatures of Witnesses arab	A27.3	1258	Grohmann, *APHM* (1963)
APHM 9	papConclusion of Contract of Sale arab	28.5r	1212	Grohmann, *APHM* (1963)
APHM 10	papGalil-script Letter Frags. arab	36	1203	Grohmann, *APHM* (1963)
APHM 11	papGalil-script Letter Frags. arab	37	1261	Grohmann, *APHM* (1963)
APHM 12	papGalil-script Letter Frags. arab	4A	1174	Grohmann, *APHM* (1963)
APHM 13	papGalil-script Letter Frags. arab	4B	1192	Grohmann, *APHM* (1963)
APHM 14	papGalil-script Letter Frags. arab	4C	1192	Grohmann, *APHM* (1963)
APHM 15	papGalil-script Letter Frags. arab	4D	1192	Grohmann, *APHM* (1963)
APHM 16	papGalil-script Letter Frags. arab	A32a1	1260	Grohmann, *APHM* (1963)
APHM 17	papGalil-script Letter Frags. arab	A11a1	1187	Grohmann, *APHM* (1963)
APHM 18	papReply Re: An Act of Violence arab	35		Grohmann, *APHM* (1963)
APHM 19	papOrder for Investigation of Robbery arab	12.1v	1249	Grohmann, *APHM* (1963)
APHM 20	papFrag. of Official Letter arab	26.1r	1209	Grohmann, *APHM* (1963)
APHM 21	papFrag. of Official Letter arab	2.2	1222	Grohmann, *APHM* (1963)
APHM 22	papConclusion of Official Letter? arab	A4	1196	Grohmann, *APHM* (1963)
APHM 23	papLetter to the Governor arab	11	1257	Grohmann, *APHM* (1963)
APHM 24	papFrag. of Report of an Official arab	17.4	1259	Grohmann, *APHM* (1963)
APHM 25	papFrag. of Official Letter arab	29	1245	Grohmann, *APHM* (1963)
APHM 26	papFrag. of Official Letter arab	28.4r	1212	Grohmann, *APHM* (1963)
APHM 27	papFrag. of Official Letter arab	28.4v	1212	Grohmann, *APHM* (1963)
APHM 28	papFrag. of Official Letter arab	A31a1	1246	Grohmann, *APHM* (1963)
APHM 29	papFrag. of Official Letter arab	28.3v	1212	Grohmann, *APHM* (1963)
APHM 30	papFrag. of Official Letter arab	28.3r	1209	Grohmann, *APHM* (1963)
APHM 31	papFrag. of Official Letter arab	10.1	1252	Grohmann, *APHM* (1963)
APHM 32	papFrag. of Official Letter arab	4.1r	1213	Grohmann, *APHM* (1963)
APHM 33	papAdministrative List arab	A34a2	1240	Grohmann, *APHM* (1963)
	papAdministrative List arab	A35.1,4	1240	Grohmann, *APHM* (1963)

APHM 34	papAdministrative List arab	18.6	1216		Grohmann, *APHM* (1963)
APHM 35	papEconomic Text arab	26a3v	1209		Grohmann, *APHM* (1963)
APHM 36	papEconomic Text arab	A14a1	1188r		Grohmann, *APHM* (1963)
APHM 37	papEconomic Text arab	A14b1	1188v		Grohmann, *APHM* (1963)
APHM 38	papEconomic Text arab	28.1	1212		Grohmann, *APHM* (1963)
APHM 39	papEconomic Text arab	A22a	1185r		Grohmann, *APHM* (1963)
APHM 40	papEconomic Text arab	A22b3	1185v		Grohmann, *APHM* (1963)
APHM 41	papEconomic Text arab	A27a1	1258		Grohmann, *APHM* (1963)
APHM 42	Private Letter arab	32	1176		Grohmann, *APHM* (1963)
APHM 43r	Private Letter arab	A34a1	1251		Grohmann, *APHM* (1963)
APHM 43v	Private Letter arab	A34b1	1251		Grohmann, *APHM* (1963)
APHM 44	Private Letter arab	38v	1177v		Grohmann, *APHM* (1963)
APHM 45	Private Letter arab	13a1	1244		Grohmann, *APHM* (1963)
APHM 46	Private Letter arab	13.1	1244		Grohmann, *APHM* (1963)
APHM 47	Private Letter arab	5.2	1194		Grohmann, *APHM* (1963)
APHM 48r	Private Letter arab	A34a4r	1251		Grohmann, *APHM* (1963)
APHM 48v	Private Letter arab	A34a4v	1251		Grohmann, *APHM* (1963)
APHM 49	Private Letter arab	40	1254		Grohmann, *APHM* (1963)
APHM 50	Private Letter arab	6	1250		Grohmann, *APHM* (1963)
APHM 51	Private Letter arab	33	1248		Grohmann, *APHM* (1963)
APHM 52	Private Letter arab	34	1248		Grohmann, *APHM* (1963)
APHM 53	Private Letter arab	18.3	1216		Grohmann, *APHM* (1963)
APHM 54	Private Letter arab	3	1172		Grohmann, *APHM* (1963)
APHM 55	Private Letter arab	22Bgr	Louvain		Grohmann, *APHM* (1963)
APHM 56	Private Letter arab	15.1r	1206		Grohmann, *APHM* (1963)
APHM 57	Private Letter arab	15.2			Grohmann, *APHM* (1963)
APHM 58	Private Letter arab	15.3r	1206		Grohmann, *APHM* (1963)
APHM 59	Private Letter arab	15.1v	1206		Grohmann, *APHM* (1963)
APHM 60	Private Letter arab	14.2r	1217		Grohmann, *APHM* (1963)
APHM 61	Private Letter arab	14.2v	1217		Grohmann, *APHM* (1963)
APHM 62	Private Letter arab	14a3v	1217		Grohmann, *APHM* (1963)
APHM 63	Private Letter arab	A3a2v	1181		Grohmann, *APHM* (1963)
APHM 64	Private Letter arab	14.5			Grohmann, *APHM* (1963)
APHM 65	Private Letter arab	14a5			Grohmann, *APHM* (1963)
APHM 66r	Private Letter arab	18.4	1216		Grohmann, *APHM* (1963)
APHM 66v	Private Letter arab	18a4	1216		Grohmann, *APHM* (1963)
APHM 67	Private Letter arab	18.1r	1216		Grohmann, *APHM* (1963)
APHM 68	Private Letter arab	26.24	1209		Grohmann, *APHM* (1963)
APHM 69	Private Letter arab	5.1r	1194		Grohmann, *APHM* (1963)
APHM 70	Private Letter arab	7.2	1213		Grohmann, *APHM* (1963)
APHM 71	Literary Text arab	28.11r	1212		Grohmann, *APHM* (1963)
APHM 72	Literary Text arab	37	1261		Grohmann, *APHM* (1963)
APHM 73	Literary Text arab	A19.1	1230		Grohmann, *APHM* (1963)
APHM 74	Frags. of Protocol Texts	A17a1	1219		Grohmann, *APHM* (1963)
APHM 75	Frags. of Protocol Texts	A23a3	1179		Grohmann, *APHM* (1963)
APHM 76	Frags. of Protocol Texts	A17a4	1219		Grohmann, *APHM* (1963)
APHM 77	Frags. of Protocol Texts	A17a3	1219		Grohmann, *APHM* (1963)
APHM 78	Frags. of Protocol Texts	A30.3	1218		Grohmann, *APHM* (1963)
APHM 79	Frag. of Official Letter	A33.2	1201		Grohmann, *APHM* (1963)
APHM 80	Frag. of List	A10a1	1226		Grohmann, *APHM* (1963)
APHM 81r	Frag. of List	A34.3	1251		Grohmann, *APHM* (1963)
APHM 81v	Frag. of List		1251		Grohmann, *APHM* (1963)
APHM 82	Frag. of Economic Text	30.3	1207		Grohmann, *APHM* (1963)
APHM 83	Frag. of Economic Text	17.2	1259		Grohmann, *APHM* (1963)
APHM 84	Frag. of Private Letter	41	1247		Grohmann, *APHM* (1963)
APHM 85	Frag. of Private Letter	A13a	1180r		Grohmann, *APHM* (1963)
APHM 86	Frag. of Private Letter	A13b	1180v		Grohmann, *APHM* (1963)
APHM 87	Frag. of Private Letter	A15a1	1229		Grohmann, *APHM* (1963)
APHM 88	Frag. of Private Letter	A35.34	1253		Grohmann, *APHM* (1963)

APHM 89	Frag. of Private Letter	A19a5	1230	Grohmann, *APHM* (1963)
APHM 90	Frag. of Private Letter	12.2	1249	Grohmann, *APHM* (1963)
APHM 91	Frag. of Private Letter	2.5	1222	Grohmann, *APHM* (1963)
APHM 92	Frag. of Private Letter	30.1r	1207	Grohmann, *APHM* (1963)
APHM 93	Frag. of Private Letter	18.2v	1216	Grohmann, *APHM* (1963)
APHM 94	Frag. of Private Letter	13B1gr	Louvain	Grohmann, *APHM* (1963)
APHM 95	Frag. of Private Letter	12.5	1249	Grohmann, *APHM* (1963)
APHM 96	Frag. of Private Letter	A27.2	1258	Grohmann, *APHM* (1963)
APHM 97	Frag. of Private Letter	3.1r	1181	Grohmann, *APHM* (1963)
APHM 98	Frag. of Private Letter	28.7	1212	Grohmann, *APHM* (1963)
APHM 99	Frag. of Private Letter	13B2gr	Louvain	Grohmann, *APHM* (1963)
APHM 100	Frag. of Drawing	A23a4	1179	Grohmann, *APHM* (1963)
	Aland p83 (Mt 20:23–25)	16gr	Louvain	
	Aland p83 (Mt 20:30–31?)	16Bgr	Louvain	
	Aland p83	29gr	Louvain	
	Aland p83	29Bgr	Louvain	
	Aland p84 (Mk 2:3–5; Jn 17:3)	26gr	Louvain	
	Aland p84 (Mk 2:8–9; Jn 17:7–8)	26Bgr	Louvain	
	Aland p84 (Mk 6:30–31, 33–34)	27gr	Louvain	
	Aland p84 (Mk 6:36–37, 39–41)	27Bgr	Louvain	
	Aland p84	4gr	Louvain	
	Aland p84	4Bgr	Louvain	
	Aland p84	11gr	Louvain	
	Aland p84	11Bgr	Louvain	
	Uncial 0244 (Acts 11:29–12:1)	8gr	Louvain	
	Uncial 0244 (Acts 12:2–5)	8Bgr	Louvain	
	Josh 22:6–7, 9–10 cpa		1238	
	Mt 21:30–34 cpa		1238	
	Lk 3:1, 3–4		1238	
Mird Acts cpa	Acts cpa		657	Perrot, *RB* 70 (1963): pl. XIX
			657	Perrot, *RB* 70 (1963): pl. XIX
			657	Perrot, *RB* 70 (1963): pl. XVIII
	Col 1:16–18, 20b–21 cpa		1238	Perrot, *RB* 70 (1963): pl. XIX
papMird A	papLetter from Monk Gabriel to Abbot		656	Milik, *RB* 60 (1953): pl. XIX
MirdAmul cpa			Louvain	Baillet, *Le Muséon* 76 (1963): 375–401
	Plaster with Syriac Inscription	S2	1234	
	papFrag.	S3	1227	
	Alphabet gr	G1a	Louvain	van Haelst, *Ancient Society* 22 (1991): 306–15, pl. III
	Tropologion gr	G1b	Louvain	van Haelst, *Ancient Society* 22 (1991): 306–15, pl. III
	Tropologion gr	G2a	Louvain	van Haelst, *Ancient Society* 22 (1991): 306–15, pl. IV
	Tropologion gr	G2b	Louvain	van Haelst, *Ancient Society* 22 (1991): 306–15, pl. V
	Alphabet (joined with G4b) gr	G3a	Louvain	van Haelst, *Ancient Society* 22 (1991): 316, pl. VII
	Greek papyri	G3b	Louvain	
	Greek papyri	G4a	Louvain	
	Alphabet (joined with G3a) gr	G4b	Louvain	van Haelst, *Ancient Society* 22 (1991): 316, pl. VII
	Greek papyri	G5a	Louvain	
	Greek papyri	G5b	Louvain	
	Greek papyri	G6a	Louvain	
	Greek papyri	G6b	Louvain	
	Greek papyri	G7a	Louvain	
	Greek papyri	G7b	Louvain	
	Greek papyri	G8a	Louvain	
	Ecclesiastical Letter gr	G8b	Louvain	van Haelst, *Ancient Society* 22 (1991): 305–6, pl. II

221

Greek papyri	G9a	Louvain		
Greek papyri	G9b	Louvain		
Greek papyri	G10a	Louvain		
Greek papyri	G10b	Louvain		
Greek papyri	G11a	Louvain		
Greek papyri	G11b	Louvain		
Greek papyri	G12	Louvain		
Greek papyri	G13	Louvain		
Greek papyri	G14a	Louvain		
Greek papyri	G14b	Louvain		
Greek papyri	G15a	Louvain		
Greek papyri	G15b	Louvain		
Greek papyri	G16a	Louvain		
Greek papyri	G16b	Louvain		
Greek papyri	G17a	Louvain		
Greek papyri	G17b	Louvain		
Greek papyri	G18	Louvain		
Greek papyri	G19	Louvain		
Greek papyri	G20a	Louvain		
Greek papyri	G20b	Louvain		
Greek papyri	G21a	Louvain		
Greek papyri	G21b	Louvain		
Monastic Letter gr	G22a	Louvain		van Haelst, *Ancient Society* 22 (1991): 302–5, pl. I
Doxastica gr	G22b	Louvain		van Haelst, *Ancient Society* 22 (1991): 315–16, pl. VI
Greek papyri	G23a	Louvain		
Greek papyri	G23b	Louvain		
Greek papyri	G24a	Louvain		
Greek papyri	G24b	Louvain		
Greek papyri	G25a	Louvain		
Greek papyri	G25b	Louvain		
Greek papyri	G26a	Louvain		
Greek papyri	G26b	Louvain		
Greek papyri	G27a	Louvain		
Greek papyri	G27b	Louvain		
Greek papyri	G28a	Louvain		
Greek papyri	G28b	Louvain		
Greek papyri	G31a	Louvain		
Greek papyri	G31b	Louvain		

5. Wadi Nar

Nar 1	papFrag. gr		1015	DJD XXXVIII (2000)
Nar 2	papFrags. sem		1018	
Nar 3	Frag. gr		1023	DJD XXXVIII (2000)
Nar 4	papUnclass. frags.		1054	
Nar 5	Leather and linen frags.		1055	

6. Wadi Ghweir

Ghweir? 1	papCursive frag. gr		1019	Cotton?, DJD XXXVIII (2000)
Ghweir? 2	paperFrag. sem		1019	

7. Wadi Murabbaᶜat

Mur 1 frags. 1–3	Gen		806	Milik, DJD II (1961), pl. XIX
Mur 1 frags. 4–5	Exod		824	Milik, DJD II (1961), pl. XX
Mur 1 frags. 6–7	Num		832	Milik, DJD II (1961), pl. XXI
Mur 2	Deut		832	Milik, DJD II (1961), pl. XXI

Mur 3	Isa	833	Milik, DJD II (1961), pl. XXII
Mur 4	Phyl	650	Milik, DJD II (1961), pls. XXII–XXIV
Mur 5	Mez	792	Milik, DJD II (1961), pl. XXIV
Mur 6	Unidentified Literary Text	792	Milik, DJD II (1961), pl. XXV
Mur 7	Contract?	793	Milik, DJD II (1961), pl. XXV
Mur 8	Account of Cereals and Vegetables ar	793	Milik, DJD II (1961), pl. XXV
Mur 9	Account	830	Milik, DJD II (1961), pl. XXVI
Mur 10A	Account (palimpsest)	830	Milik, DJD II (1961), pl. XXVI
Mur 10B	Abecedary (palimpsest)	830	Milik, DJD II (1961), pl. XXVI
Mur 11	Abecedary	830	Milik, DJD II (1961), pl. XXVII
Mur 12	Unclassified frag.	874	Milik, DJD II (1961), pl. XXVII
Mur 13	Unclassified frag.	874	Milik, DJD II (1961), pl. XXVII
Mur 14	Unclassified frag.	874	Milik, DJD II (1961), pl. XXVII
Mur 15	Unclassified frag.	874	Milik, DJD II (1961), pl. XXVII
Mur 16	Unclassified frag.	874 r + v	Milik, DJD II (1961), pl. XXVII
Mur 17A	papLetter (palimpsest)	835	Milik, DJD II (1961), pl. XXVIII
Mur 17B	papList of Personal Names (palimpsest)	835	Milik, DJD II (1961), pl. XXVIII
Mur 18	papAcknowledgement of Debt ar	834 r + v	Milik, DJD II (1961), pl. XXIX
Mur 19	papWrit of Divorce ar	879 r + v	Milik, DJD II (1961), pls. XXX–XXXI
Mur 20	papMarriage Contract ar	879 r + v	Milik, DJD II (1961), pls. XXX–XXXI
Mur 21	papMarriage Contract ar	875 r + v	Milik, DJD II (1961), pls. XXXII–XXXIII
Mur 22	papDeed of Sale of Land	882 r + v	Milik, DJD II (1961), pls. XXXIII–XXXIV
Mur 23	papDeed of Sale? ar	840 r + v	Milik, DJD II (1961), pl. XXXIV
Mur 24	papFarming Contracts	825, 828	Milik, DJD II (1961), pls. XXXV–XXXVII
Mur 25	papDeed of Sale of Land ar	r + v	Milik, DJD II (1961), pl. XXXVIII
Mur 26	papDeed of Sale ar	725	Milik, DJD II (1961), pls. XXXIX–XL bis
Mur 27	papDeed of Sale ar	797	Milik, DJD II (1961), pls. XXXIX–XL bis
Mur 28	papDeed of Sale ar	884 r + v	Milik, DJD II (1961), pls. XXXIX–XL bis
Mur 29	papDeed of Sale	836 r + v	Milik, DJD II (1961), pl. XLI–XLI bis
Mur 30	papDeed of Sale of Plot	791 r + v	Milik, DJD II (1961), pls. XLI bis–XLII bis
Mur 31	papFrags. of Deeds of Sale	790 r + v	Milik, DJD II (1961), pl. XLII bis
Mur 32	papDeed Concerning Money ar	883	Milik, DJD II (1961), pl. XLIII
Mur 33	papDeed Concerning Money ar	878	Milik, DJD II (1961), pl. XLIII
Mur 34	papContract ar	798	Milik, DJD II (1961), pl. XLIII
Mur 35	papContract ar	798	Milik, DJD II (1961), pl. XLIII
Mur 36	papContract	837	Milik, DJD II (1961), pl. XLIII
Mur 37	papContracts and Signatures	878	Milik, DJD II (1961), pls. XLIII–XLIV
Mur 38	papContracts and Signatures	837	Milik, DJD II (1961), pls. XLIII–XLIV
Mur 39	papContracts and Signatures	837	Milik, DJD II (1961), pls. XLIII–XLIV
Mur 40	papContracts and Signatures	794	Milik, DJD II (1961), pls. XLIII–XLIV
Mur 41	papList of Personal Names	837	Milik, DJD II (1961), pl. XLIV
Mur 42	papLetter from Beit-Mashiko to Yeshua b. Galgula	639	Milik, DJD II (1961), pl. XLV
Mur 43	papLetter from Shimʿon b. Kosba to Yeshua b. Galgula	640	Milik, DJD II (1961), pl. XLVI
Mur 44	papLetter from Shimʿon b. Kosba to Yeshua b. Galgula	720	Milik, DJD II (1961), pl. XLVI
Mur 45	papLetter	829	Milik, DJD II (1961), pl. XLVII
Mur 46	papLetter Sent from Ein Gedi	829	Milik, DJD II (1961), pl. XLVII
Mur 47	papLetter	873	Milik, DJD II (1961), pl. XLVIII
Mur 48	papLetter	837	Milik, DJD II (1961), pl. XLVIII
Mur 49	papLetter	873	Milik, DJD II (1961), pl. XLVIII
Mur 50	papLetter?	837	Milik, DJD II (1961), pl. XLVIII
Mur 51	papLetter?	873	Milik, DJD II (1961), pl. XLVIII
Mur 52	papLetter?	831	Milik, DJD II (1961), pl. XLVIII
Mur 53	papUndeciphered Text	826	Milik, DJD II (1961), pls. XLIX–LI
Mur 54	papUndeciphered Text	880	Milik, DJD II (1961), pls. XLIX–LI
Mur 55	papUnclassified frags.	826	Milik, DJD II (1961), pls. XLIX–LI
Mur 56	papUnclassified frags.	794	Milik, DJD II (1961), pls. XLIX–LI

Mur 57	papUnclassified frags.	826	Milik, DJD II (1961), pls. XLIX–LI
Mur 58	papUnclassified frags.	826	Milik, DJD II (1961), pls. XLIX–LI
Mur 59	papUnclassified frags.	826	Milik, DJD II (1961), pls. XLIX–LI
Mur 60	papUnclassified frags.	826	Milik, DJD II (1961), pls. XLIX–LI
Mur 61	papUnclassified frags.	826	Milik, DJD II (1961), pls. XLIX–LI
Mur 62	papUnclassified frag.	798	Milik, DJD II (1961), pls. XLIX–LI
Mur 63	papUnclassified frag.	798	Milik, DJD II (1961), pls. XLIX–LI
Mur 64	papUnclassified frag.	798	Milik, DJD II (1961), pls. XLIX–LI
Mur 65	papUnclassified frag.	798	Milik, DJD II (1961), pls. XLIX–LI
Mur 66	papUnclassified frag.	798	Milik, DJD II (1961), pls. XLIX–LI
Mur 67	papUnclassified frag.	798	Milik, DJD II (1961), pls. XLIX–LI
Mur 68	papUnclassified frag.	798	Milik, DJD II (1961), pls. XLIX–LI
Mur 69	papUnclassified frag.	798	Milik, DJD II (1961), pls. XLIX–LI
Mur 70	papUnclassified frag.	794	Milik, DJD II (1961), pls. XLIX–LI
Mur 71	papFrag. nab	881	Milik, DJD II (1961), pl. LI
Mur 72	ostr ar	1066	Milik, DJD II (1961), pl. LII
Mur 73	ostrAbecedary and List of Personal Names	1033	Milik, DJD II (1961), pl. LII
Mur 74	ostrList of Personal Names	1049	Milik, DJD II (1961), pl. LIII
Mur 75	ostrPersonal Name	1037	Milik, DJD II (1961), pls. LIII–LIV
Mur 76	ostrPersonal Name	1052	Milik, DJD II (1961), pls. LIII–LIV
Mur 77	ostrPersonal Name	1052	Milik, DJD II (1961), pls. LIII–LIV
Mur 78	ostrAbecedary	1014	Milik, DJD II (1961), pls. LIV–LV
Mur 79	ostrAbecedary	1049	Milik, DJD II (1961), pls. LIV–LV
Mur 80	ostrAbecedary	1036	Milik, DJD II (1961), pls. LIV–LV
Mur 81	ostrUnclassified	1050	Milik, DJD II (1961), pl. LV
Mur 82	ostrUnclassified	1037	Milik, DJD II (1961), pl. LV
Mur 83	ostrUnclassified	1037	Milik, DJD II (1961), pl. LV
Mur 84	ostrUnclassified	1037	Milik, DJD II (1961), pl. LV
Mur 85	ostrUnclassified	1028, 1037	Milik, DJD II (1961), pl. LV
Mur 86	ostrUnclassified	1028	Milik, DJD II (1961), pl. LV
Mur 87	ostrPersonal Name	1035	Milik, DJD II (1961), pl. LV
Mur 88	XII (unopened scroll)		
	col. I (Joel 2:20)	?	Milik, DJD II (1961), pl. LVI
	col. II (Joel 2:26–4:16)	?	Milik, DJD II (1961), pl. LVI
	col. III (Amos 1:5–2:1)	?	Milik, DJD II (1961), pl. LVI
	col. VI (Amos)	64	Milik, DJD II (1961), pl. LVII
	col. VII (Amos 7:3–8:7)	64	Milik, DJD II (1961), pl. LVII
	col. VIII (Amos 8:11–9:15)	64	Milik, DJD II (1961), pl. LVIII
	col. IX (Obad 1–21)	64	Milik, DJD II (1961), pl. LIX
	col. X (Jonah 1:1–3:2)	64, 213	Milik, DJD II (1961), pl. LX
	col. XI (Jonah 3:2–Mic 1:5)	65, 213	Milik, DJD II (1961), pl. LXI
	col. XII (Mic 1:5–3:4)	65	Milik, DJD II (1961), pl. LXII
	col. XIII (Mic 3:4–4:12)	65	Milik, DJD II (1961), pl. LXIII
	col. XIV (Mic 4:12–6:7)	65	Milik, DJD II (1961), pl. LXIV
	col. XV (Mic 6:11–7:17)	65	Milik, DJD II (1961), pl. LXV
	col. XVI (Mic 7:17–Nah 2:12)	65, 66	Milik, DJD II (1961), pl. LXVI
	col. XVII (Nah 2:13–3:19)	66	Milik, DJD II (1961), pl. LXVII
	col. XVIII (Hab 1:3–2:11)	66	Milik, DJD II (1961), pl. LXVIII
	col. XIX (Hab 2:18–Zeph 1:1)	66	Milik, DJD II (1961), pl. LXIX
	col. XX (Zeph 1:11–3:6)	66, 67	Milik, DJD II (1961), pl. LXX
	col. XXI (Zeph 3:8–Hag 1:11)	67	Milik, DJD II (1961), pl. LXXI
	col. XXII (Hag 1:12–2:10)	67	Milik, DJD II (1961), pl. LXXII
	col. XXIII (Hag 2:12–Zech 1:4)	67	Milik, DJD II (1961), pl. LXXII
	Unidentified frags.	540	Milik, DJD II (1961), pl. LXXIII
Mur 89	Account of Money gr	728	Benoit, DJD II (1961), pl. LXXIV
Mur 90	Account of Cereals and Vegetables gr	728	Benoit, DJD II (1961), pl. LXXV
Mur 91	Account of Cereals and Vegetables gr	841	Benoit, DJD II (1961), pl. LXXVI
Mur 92	Account of Cereal gr	841	Benoit, DJD II (1961), pl. LXXVI
Mur 93	Account? gr	841	Benoit, DJD II (1961), pl. LXXVI

Mur 94	Resume of Accounts gr	843	Benoit, DJD II (1961), pl. LXXVII
Mur 95	List of Personal Names gr	723	Benoit, DJD II (1961), pl. LXXVIII
Mur 96	Account of Cereals gr	723	Benoit, DJD II (1961), pl. LXXVIII
Mur 97	Account of Cereals gr	723	Benoit, DJD II (1961), pl. LXXVIII
Mur 98	Accounts? gr	911	Benoit, DJD II (1961), pl. LXXIX
Mur 99	Accounts? gr	911	Benoit, DJD II (1961), pl. LXXIX
Mur 100	Accounts? gr	911	Benoit, DJD II (1961), pl. LXXIX
Mur 101	Accounts? gr	911	Benoit, DJD II (1961), pl. LXXIX
Mur 102	Accounts? gr	911	Benoit, DJD II (1961), pl. LXXIX
Mur 103	List of Personal Names gr	727	Benoit, DJD II (1961), pl. LXXX
Mur 104	Corners and Edges of Leather gr	727	Benoit, DJD II (1961), pl. LXXX
Mur 105	Corners and Edges of Leather gr	727	Benoit, DJD II (1961), pl. LXXX
Mur 106	Corners and Edges of Leather gr	727	Benoit, DJD II (1961), pl. LXXX
Mur 107	Corners and Edges of Leather gr	727	Benoit, DJD II (1961), pl. LXXX
Mur 108	papPhilosophical Text gr	713	Benoit, DJD II (1961), pl. LXXXI
Mur 109	papLiterary Text gr	712 r	Benoit, DJD II (1961), pls. LXXXII–LXXXIII
Mur 110	papLiterary Text gr	712 v	Benoit, DJD II (1961), pls. LXXXII–LXXXIII
Mur 111	papLiterary Text gr	712 r + v	Benoit, DJD II (1961), pls. LXXXII–LXXXIII
Mur 112	papLiterary Text gr	910 r	Benoit, DJD II (1961), pls. LXXXII–LXXXIII
Mur 113	papProceedings of Lawsuit gr	910 v	Benoit, DJD II (1961), pl. LXXXIV
Mur 114	papRecognition of Debt gr	641 r + v	Benoit, DJD II (1961), pl. LXXXV
Mur 115	papRemarriage Contract gr	716 r + v	Benoit, DJD II (1961), pls. LXXXVI–LXXXVIII
Mur 116	papMarriage Contract gr	715 r	Benoit, DJD II (1961), pl. LXXXIX
Mur 117	papExtracts from Official Ordinances gr	839 r + v	Benoit, DJD II (1961), pl. XC
Mur 118	papAccount gr	712 r + v	Benoit, DJD II (1961), pls. XCI–XCIV
Mur 119	papAccount gr	712 r + v	Benoit, DJD II (1961), pls. XCI–XCIV
Mur 120	papAccount gr	845	Benoit, DJD II (1961), pls. XCI–XCIV
Mur 121	papAccount gr	722	Benoit, DJD II (1961), pls. XCI–XCIV
Mur 122	papAccount gr	722	Benoit, DJD II (1961), pls. XCI–XCIV
Mur 123	papAccount gr	722	Benoit, DJD II (1961), pls. XCI–XCIV
Mur 124	papAccount gr	724	Benoit, DJD II (1961), pls. XCI–XCIV
Mur 125	papAccount gr	719	Benoit, DJD II (1961), pls. XCI–XCIV
Mur 126	papLiterary or Notarial Writing gr	717	Benoit, DJD II (1961), pl. XCV
Mur 127	papLiterary or Notarial Writing gr	722	Benoit, DJD II (1961), pl. XCV
Mur 128	papLiterary or Notarial Writing gr	724	Benoit, DJD II (1961), pl. XCV
Mur 129	papLiterary or Notarial Writing gr	722	Benoit, DJD II (1961), pl. XCV
Mur 130	papLiterary or Notarial Writing gr	712 r + v	Benoit, DJD II (1961), pl. XCV
Mur 131	papLiterary or Notarial Writing gr	712 r + v	Benoit, DJD II (1961), pl. XCV
Mur 132	papLiterary or Notarial Writing gr	717	Benoit, DJD II (1961), pl. XCV
Mur 133	papCursive Text gr	909	Benoit, DJD II (1961), pls. XCVI–XCVIII
Mur 134	papCursive Text gr	909	Benoit, DJD II (1961), pls. XCVI–XCVIII
Mur 135	papCursive Text gr	909	Benoit, DJD II (1961), pls. XCVI–XCVIII
Mur 136	papCursive Text gr	909	Benoit, DJD II (1961), pls. XCVI–XCVIII
Mur 137	papCursive Text gr	909	Benoit, DJD II (1961), pls. XCVI–XCVIII
Mur 138	papCursive Text gr	909	Benoit, DJD II (1961), pls. XCVI–XCVIII
Mur 139	papCursive Text gr	909	Benoit, DJD II (1961), pls. XCVI–XCVIII
Mur 140	papCursive Text gr	909	Benoit, DJD II (1961), pls. XCVI–XCVIII
Mur 141	papCursive Text gr	909	Benoit, DJD II (1961), pls. XCVI–XCVIII
Mur 142	papCursive Text gr	909	Benoit, DJD II (1961), pls. XCVI–XCVIII
Mur 143	papCursive Text gr	909 r + v	Benoit, DJD II (1961), pls. XCVI–XCVIII
Mur 144	papCursive Text gr	909	Benoit, DJD II (1961), pls. XCVI–XCVIII
Mur 145	papCursive Text gr	717	Benoit, DJD II (1961), pls. XCVI–XCVIII
Mur 146	papCursive Text gr	712 r + v	Benoit, DJD II (1961), pls. XCVI–XCVIII
Mur 147	papCursive Text gr	719	Benoit, DJD II (1961), pls. XCVI–XCVIII
Mur 148	papCursive Text gr	717	Benoit, DJD II (1961), pls. XCVI–XCVIII
Mur 149	papCursive Text gr	717	Benoit, DJD II (1961), pls. XCVI–XCVIII
Mur 150	papCursive Text gr	724	Benoit, DJD II (1961), pls. XCVI–XCVIII
Mur 151	papCursive Text gr	722	Benoit, DJD II (1961), pls. XCVI–XCVIII

Mur 152	papCursive Text gr	724	Benoit, DJD II (1961), pls. XCVI–XCVIII
Mur 153	papCursive Text gr	724	Benoit, DJD II (1961), pls. XCVI–XCVIII
Mur 154	papCursive Text gr	722	Benoit, DJD II (1961), pls. XCVI–XCVIII
Mur 155	papDocument gr	913	Benoit, DJD II (1961), pl. XCIX
Mur 156	Christian Liturgical Text gr	718 r + v	Benoit, DJD II (1961), pl. C
Mur 157	Magical Text gr	721	Benoit, DJD II (1961), pl. C
Mur 158	Unclassified frags. lat	844	Benoit, DJD II (1961), pl. CI
Mur 159	Cursive Text lat	838	Benoit, DJD II (1961), pl. CI
Mur 160	Unclassified frags. lat	838	Benoit, DJD II (1961), pl. CII
Mur 161	Unclassified frags. lat	838	Benoit, DJD II (1961), pl. CII
Mur 162	Unclassified frags. lat	838	Benoit, DJD II (1961), pl. CII
Mur 163	Unclassified frags. lat	838	Benoit, DJD II (1961), pl. CII
Mur 164	Document in Shorthand gr	802	Benoit, DJD II (1961), pls. CIII–CV
Mur 164a	Document in Shorthand gr	802	
Mur 164b	Document in Shorthand gr	802	
Mur 165	ostr gr	1051	Benoit, DJD II (1961), pl. CV
Mur 166	ostr gr	1051	Benoit, DJD II (1961), pl. CV
Mur 167	ostr gr	1051	Benoit, DJD II (1961), pl. CV
Mur 168	ostr lat	1051	Benoit, DJD II (1961), pl. CV
Mur 169	Receipt arab	721	Grohmann, DJD II (1961), pl. CVI
Mur 170	Sales Contract arab	730	Grohmann, DJD II (1961), pl. CVI
Mur 171	Magical Text arab	721 r + v	Grohmann, DJD II (1961), pl. CVI
Mur 172	Religious or Magical Text arab	721	Grohmann, DJD II (1961), pl. CVI
Mur 173	Amulet arab	642 r + v	Grohmann, DJD II (1961), pl. CVII
Mur?	Gen (Gen 33:18–34:3)		Puech, *RevQ* 10 (1979–81): 163–66

8. Wadi Sdeir

Sdeir 1	Gen	984	Murphy, DJD XXXVIII (2000)
Sdeir 2	papPromissory Note? ar	985 r + v	Yardeni, DJD XXXVIII (2000)
Sdeir 3	Unidentified Text A gr	986 r + v	DJD XXXVIII (2000)
Sdeir 4	Unidentified Text B gr	983 r + v	DJD XXXVIII (2000)

9. Naḥal Ḥever

5/6Ḥev 1a	Num^a (*olim* 5/6Ḥev 41)	534	Flint, DJD XXXVIII (2000)
5/6Ḥev 1b	Ps (*olim* 5/6 Ḥev 40) (+ XḤev/Se 4)	888	Flint, DJD XXXVIII (2000)
		890	
		891	
5/6Ḥev 1	papDowry Settlement? nab [P.Yadin 1] (BA bdl. 15)	r	Yadin, Yardeni, Levine, JDS (in press)
		v	
5/6Ḥev 2	papSale of Property nab [P.Yadin 2] (BA bdl. 16)	216* r	Yadin, Yardeni, Levine, JDS (in press)
		v	
5/6Ḥev 3	papSale of Property nab [P.Yadin 3] (BA bdl. 14a)	r	Yadin, Yardeni, Levine, JDS (in press)
		v	
5/6Ḥev 4	papFragmentary Deed nab [P.Yadin 4] (BA bdl. 14b)	r	Yadin, Yardeni, Levine, JDS (in press)
		v	
5/6Ḥev 5	papDeposit gr [P.Yadin 5] (BA bdl. 11c1, 11c2)	104*	Lewis, JDS 2 (1989), pl. 1
			Lewis, JDS 2 (1989), pl. 2
5/6Ḥev 6	papLease of Land? nab [P.Yadin 6] (BA bdl. 11b)	142*	
5/6Ḥev 7	papDeed of Gift ar [P.Yadin 7] (BA bdl. 6)	207* r	Yadin, Greenfield, Yardeni, *ErIsr* 25 (1996): 383–403
		v	
5/6Ḥev 8	papSale of Donkeys ar [P.Yadin 8] (BA bdl. 11a1)	144*	Yadin, Yardeni, Levine, JDS (in press)

5/6Ḥev 9	papQuittance nab [P.Yadin 9] (BA bdl. 11a2)	145*	Yadin, Yardeni, Levine, JDS (in press)
5/6Ḥev 10	papMarriage Contract ar [P.Yadin 10] (BA bdl. 7c)	205* r	Yadin, Greenfield, Yardeni, *IEJ* 44 (1994): 75–101
		v	
5/6Ḥev 11	papLoan on Hypothec gr [P.Yadin 11] (BA bdl. 13)	134* r	Lewis, JDS 2 (1989), pl. 3
		v	Lewis, JDS 2 (1989), pl. 4
5/6Ḥev 12	papExtract from Council Minutes gr [P.Yadin 12] (BA bdl. 5f)	137* r	Lewis, JDS 2 (1989), pl. 5
		v	Lewis, JDS 2 (1989), pl. 6
5/6Ḥev 13	papPetition to Governor gr [P.Yadin13] (BA bdl. 11d)	139*	Lewis, JDS 2 (1989), pl. 7
5/6Ḥev 14	papSummons gr [P.Yadin 14] (BA bdl. 10c)	141* r	Lewis, JDS 2 (1989), pl. 8
		v	Lewis, JDS 2 (1989), pl. 9
5/6Ḥev 15	papDeposition gr [P.Yadin 15] (BA bdl. 2)	215* r	Lewis, JDS 2 (1989), pls. 10, 11
		v	Yadin, Greenfield, JDS 2 (1989), pl. 12
5/6Ḥev 16	papRegistration of Land gr [P.Yadin 16] (BA bdl. 7b)	123* r	Lewis, JDS 2 (1989), pl. 13
		v	Yadin, Greenfield, JDS 2 (1989), pl. 14
5/6Ḥev 17	papDeposit gr [P.Yadin 17] (BA bdl. 7a)	140* r	Lewis, JDS 2 (1989), pl. 15
		v	Yadin, Greenfield, JDS 2 (1989), pl. 16
5/6Ḥev 18	papMarriage Contract gr [P.Yadin 18] (BA bdl. 1)	r	Lewis, JDS 2 (1989), pls. 17, 18
		v	Yadin, Greenfield, JDS 2 (1989), pl. 19
5/6Ḥev 19	papDeed of Gift gr [P.Yadin 19] (BA bdl. 8b)	108* r	Lewis, JDS 2 (1989), pl. 20
		v	Yadin, Greenfield, JDS 2 (1989), pl. 21
5/6Ḥev 20	papConcession of Rights gr [P.Yadin 20] (BA bdl. 8a)	r	Lewis, JDS 2 (1989), pls. 22, 23
		v	Yadin, Greenfield, JDS 2 (1989), pl. 24
5/6Ḥev 21	papPurchase of a Date Crop gr [P.Yadin 21] (BA bdl. 3)	105* r	Lewis, JDS 2 (1989), pl. 25
		v	Lewis, JDS 2 (1989), pl. 26
5/6Ḥev 22	papSale of a Date Crop gr [P.Yadin 22] (BA bdl. 10d)	r	Lewis, JDS 2 (1989), pl. 27
		v	Lewis, JDS 2 (1989), pl. 28
5/6Ḥev 23	papSummons gr [P.Yadin 23] (BA bdl. 10a)	110* r	Lewis, JDS 2 (1989), pls. 29, 30
		v	Lewis, JDS 2 (1989), pl. 31
5/6Ḥev 24	papDeposition gr [P.Yadin 24] (BA bdl. 10e)	116*	
5/6Ḥev 25	papSummons, Countersum. gr [P.Yad. 25] (BA bdl. 10b)	206*	Lewis, JDS 2 (1989), pls. 32, 33
5/6Ḥev 26	papSummons and Reply gr [P.Yadin 26] (BA bdl. 9)	124* r	Lewis, JDS 2 (1989), pl. 34
		v	Lewis, JDS 2 (1989), pl. 35
5/6Ḥev 27	papReceipt gr [P.Yadin 27] (BA bdl. 4)		Lewis, JDS 2 (1989), pl. 36
5/6Ḥev 28	papJudiciary Rule gr [P.Yadin 28] (BA bdl. 5a)	121*	Lewis, JDS 2 (1989), pl. 37
5/6Ḥev 29	papJudiciary Rule gr [P.Yadin 29] (BA bdl. 5a bis)	122*	Lewis, JDS 2 (1989), pl. 38
5/6Ḥev 30	papJudiciary Rule gr [P.Yadin 30]	120*	
5/6Ḥev 31	papContract? gr [P.Yadin 31] (BA bdl. 14c)	136*	
5/6Ḥev 32	papContract? gr [P.Yadin 32] (BA bdl. 18)		
5/6Ḥev 32a	papContract? gr [P.Yadin 32a] (BA bdl. 17)		
5/6Ḥev 33	Petition gr [P.Yadin 33] (BA bdl. 5b)	118* r	Lewis, JDS 2 (1989), pl. 39
		v	

227

5/6Hev 34	papPetition gr [P.Yadin 34] (BA bdl. 12)	208*	
5/6Hev 35	papSummons? gr [P.Yadin 35] (BA bdl. 11e)	109*	
5/6Hev 36	papFragment nab [P.Yadin 36] (= XHev/Se Nab. 1)	99*	Yadin, Greenfield, Yardeni, Levine, JDS (in press)
		654	
		655	
		867	
5/6Hev 37	papMarriage Contract gr (= XHev/Se gr 65)	138*	Lewis, JDS 2 (1989), pl. 40
	[P.Yadin 37] (BA bdl. 9/10)		
5/6Hev 38	papUnclassified Text nab [P.Yadin 38] (BA bdl. 4[a])	r	Yadin, Greenfield, Yardeni, Levine, JDS (in press)
		v	
5/6Hev 39	papUnclassified Frag. nab [P.Yadin 39] (BA bdl. 4[b])	115*	Yadin, Greenfield, Yardeni, Levine, JDS (in press)
5/6Hev 40	Ps [P.Yadin 40] (= 5/6Hev 1b)		
5/6Hev 41	Num [P.Yadin 41] (= 5/6Hev 1a)	27*, 103*	
5/6Hev 42	papLease Contract ar [P.Yadin 42] (EG bdl. 2)	102*	Yadin, Greenfield, Yardeni, Levine, JDS (in press)
5/6Hev 43	papReceipt ar [P.Yadin 43] (EG bdl. 1)	129* r	Yadin, Greenfield, Yardeni, Levine, JDS (in press)
		v	
5/6Hev 44	papLease of Land [P.Yadin 44] (EG bdl. 5)		Yadin, IEJ 12 (1962): pl. 48C; Yadin, Greenfield, Yardeni, Levine, JDS (in press)
5/6Hev 45	papLease of Land [P.Yadin 45] (EG bdl. 6)	126*	Yadin, Greenfield, Yardeni, Levine, JDS (in press)
5/6Hev 46	papLease of Land [P.Yadin 46] (EG bdl. 7)		Yadin, Greenfield, Yardeni, Levine, JDS (in press)
5/6Hev 47a, b	papDeed of Sale of Half of a Garden ar I [P.Yadin 47 I, II]	117* r	Yadin, Greenfield, Yardeni, Levine, JDS (in press)
		v	
5/6Hev 48	Uninscribed Leather [P.Yadin 48]		
5/6Hev 49	papLetter [P.Yadin 49] (BK bdl. 11)		Yadin, Greenfield, Yardeni, Levine, JDS (in press)
5/6Hev 50	papLetter [P.Yadin 50] (BK bdl. 7)		Yadin, Greenfield, Yardeni, Levine, JDS (in press)
5/6Hev 51	papLetter [P.Yadin 51] (BK bdl. 4)	128*	Yadin, Greenfield, Yardeni, Levine, JDS (in press)
5/6Hev 52	papLetter gr [P.Yadin 52] (BK bdl. 2)		Lifschitz, Aegyptus 42 (1962): 240ff.; Cotton, JDS 3 (in press)
5/6Hev 53	papLetter ar [P.Yadin 53] (BK bdl. 3)	100*	Yadin, Greenfield, Yardeni, Levine, JDS (in press)
5/6Hev 54	woodLetter ar [P.Yadin 54]	119*	Yadin, Greenfield, Yardeni, Levine, JDS (in press)
5/6Hev 55	papLetter ar [P.Yadin 55] (BK bdl. 13)		Yadin, Greenfield, Yardeni, Levine, JDS (in press)
5/6Hev 56	papLetter ar [P.Yadin 56] (BK bdl. 10)	114*	Yadin, Greenfield, Yardeni, Levine, JDS (in press)
5/6Hev 57	papLetter ar [P.Yadin 57] (BK bdl. 14)		Yadin, Greenfield, Yardeni, Levine, JDS (in press)
5/6Hev 58	papLetter ar [P.Yadin 58] (BK bdl. 9)	107*	Yadin, Greenfield, Yardeni, Levine, JDS (in press)
5/6Hev 59	papLetter gr [P.Yadin 59] (BK bdl. 5)	213*	Lifschitz, Aegyptus 42 (1962): 258ff.; Cotton, JDS 3 (in press)
5/6Hev 60	papLetter ar? [P.Yadin 60] (BK bdl. 8)		Yadin, Greenfield, Yardeni, Levine, JDS (in press)
5/6Hev 61	papLetter [P.Yadin 61] (BK bdl. 6)	127*, 131*	Yadin, Greenfield, Yardeni, Levine, JDS (in press)
5/6Hev 62	papLetter ar? [P.Yadin 62] (BK bdl. 12)	133*	Yadin, Greenfield, Yardeni, Levine, JDS (in press)
5/6Hev 63	papPalimpsest Letter ar [P.Yadin 63]	125*	Yadin, Greenfield, Yardeni, Levine, JDS (in press)
5/6Hev 64	papFrag. gr [P.Yadin 64]	106*	Cotton, JDS 3 (in press)

8Ḥev 1	8ḤevXII gr		Tov, DJD VIII (1990)
	col. 2 (Jon 1:14–2:7)	539	Tov, DJD VIII (1990), pls. I, II
	col. 3 (Jon 3:2–5, 7–10; 4:1–2, 5)	539, 539A	Tov, DJD VIII (1990), pls. I, III
	col. 4 (Mic 1:1–7a)	539	Tov, DJD VIII (1990), pls. I, IV
	col. 5 (Mic 1:7b–8)	532	Tov, DJD VIII (1990), pl. IV
	col. 6 (Mic 2:7–8; 3:5–6)	529, 532	Tov, DJD VIII (1990), pl. V
	col. 7 (Mic 4:3–5)	529, 531	Tov, DJD VIII (1990), pl. V
	col. 8 (Mic 4:6–10; 5:1–4[5])	530, 531	Tov, DJD VIII (1990), pl. VI
	col. 9 (Mic 5:4[5]–6[7])	530	Tov, DJD VIII (1990), pl. VI
	col. 13 (Nah 1:13–14)	539A	Tov, DJD VIII (1990), pl. VII
	col. 14 (Nah 2:5–10, 14)	535, 539A	Tov, DJD VIII (1990), pl. VIII
	col. 15 (Nah 3:6–17)	535, 539A	Tov, DJD VIII (1990), pl. IX
	col. 16 (Hab 1:5–11)	528	Tov, DJD VIII (1990), pl. X
	col. 17 (Hab 1:14–17; 2:1–8a)	63, 530	Tov, DJD VIII (1990), pls. XI, XVIII
	col. 18 (Hab 2:13–20)	63	Tov, DJD VIII (1990), pls. XII, XVIII
	col. 19 (Hab 3:9–15)	63	Tov, DJD VIII (1990), pls. XIII, XVIII
	col. 20 (Zeph 1:1–6a)	63	Tov, DJD VIII (1990), pls. XIV, XVIII
	col. 21 (Zeph 1:13–18)	63	Tov, DJD VIII (1990), pls. XV, XVIII
	col. 22 (Zeph 2:9–10)	63	Tov, DJD VIII (1990), pls. XV, XVIII
	col. 23 (Zeph 3:6–7)	63	Tov, DJD VIII (1990), pls. XV, XVIII
	col. 28 (Zech 1:1–4)	530	Tov, DJD VIII (1990), pl. XVI
	col. 29 (Zech 1:12–15)	530	Tov, DJD VIII (1990), pl. XVI
	col. 30 (Zech 1:19–2:4, 7–12)	530, 539A	Tov, DJD VIII (1990), pl. XVII
	col. 31 (Zech 2:16–3:7)	530, 539A	Tov, DJD VIII (1990), pl. XVII
	col. B1 (Zech 8:19–23a)	538	Tov, DJD VIII (1990), pl. XIX
	col. B2 (Zech 8:23b–9:5)	538	Tov, DJD VIII (1990), pl. XIX
	Unclassified Frags. 1–6	537–539	Tov, DJD VIII (1990), pl. XX
8Ḥev 2	Prayer	223*, 225*	Aharoni, IEJ 12 (1962): pl. 30F; Morgenstern, DJD XXXVIII (2000)
8Ḥev 3	papFrags.	222*	Aharoni, IEJ 12 (1962): pl. 30E
8Ḥev 4	papUnidentified Text gr	221*	Cotton, DJD XXXVIII (2000)
8Ḥev 5	ostr	IAA	Aharoni, IEJ 12 (1962): pl. 29A
8Ḥev 6	ostr	IAA	Aharoni, IEJ 12 (1962): pl. 29B
8Ḥev	ostrFrags.	IAA	Aharoni, IEJ 12 (1962): pl. 31A–D

10. Naḥal Ḥever/Seiyal

XḤev/Se 1	Numᵃ (= part of 5/6Ḥev 1a)		Flint, DJD XXXVIII (2000)
XḤev/Se 2	Numᵇ	534	Flint, DJD XXXVIII (2000)
XḤev/Se 3	Deut	534	Flint, DJD XXXVIII (2000)
XḤev/Se 4	Ps (= part of 5/6Ḥev 1b)		
XḤev/Se 5	Phylactery	886	Morgenstern, Segal, DJD XXXVIII (2000)
XḤev/Se 6	Eschatological Hymn	889	Morgenstern, DJD XXXVIII (2000)
XḤev/Se 7	Deed of Sale A ar (r + v)	889	Yardeni, DJD XXVII (1997), fig. 1, pl. I
XḤev/Se 8	papDeed of Sale B ar and heb	533	Yardeni, DJD XXVII (1997), figs. 2–3, pl. II
XḤev/Se 8a	papDeed of Sale C ar	651	Yardeni, DJD XXVII (1997), figs. 4–5, pl. III
XḤev/Se 9	papDeed of Sale D ar	543	Yardeni, DJD XXVII (1997), figs. 6–8, pls. IV–V
XḤev/Se 9a	papUnclassified Fragment A ar	543	Yardeni, DJD XXVII (1997), fig. 9, pl. VI
XḤev/Se 10	papReceipt for Payment of a Fine? ar	736	Yardeni, DJD XXVII (1997), fig. 9, pl. VII
XḤev/Se 11	papMarriage Contract? ar	736	Yardeni, DJD XXVII (1997), fig. 9, pl. VII
XḤev/Se 12	papReceipt for Dates ar	736	Yardeni, DJD XXVII (1997), fig. 10, pls. VIII–IX
XḤev/Se 13	papWaiver of Claims? Ar	736	Yardeni, DJD XXVII (1997), fig. 11, pls. VIII–IX
XḤev/Se 14	papFragment of a Deed ar?	542	Yardeni, DJD XXVII (1997), fig. 12, pl. X
XḤev/Se 15	papUnclassified Fragment B	542	Yardeni, DJD XXVII (1997), fig. 12, pl. X
XḤev/Se 16–17	papUnclassified Fragments C–D	542	Yardeni, DJD XXVII (1997), fig. 12, pl. X
XḤev/Se 18	papUnclassified Fragment E	542	Yardeni, DJD XXVII (1997), fig. 12, pl. X
XḤev/Se 19	papUnclassified Fragment F	542	Yardeni, DJD XXVII (1997), fig. 12, pl. X

XHev/Se 20	(cancelled)		
XHev/Se 21	papDeed of Sale E ar	527	Yardeni, DJD XXVII (1997), figs. 12–13, pls. XI–XII
XHev/Se 22	papDeed of Sale F? ar	735	Yardeni, DJD XXVII (1997), fig. 14, pl. XIII
XHev/Se 23	papDeed of Sale G ar	536	Yardeni, DJD XXVII (1997), fig. 15, pl. XIV
XHev/Se 24	papDeed A ar	536	Yardeni, DJD XXVII (1997), fig. 15, pl. XV
XHev/Se 24a	papDeed B ar	536	Yardeni, DJD XXVII (1997), fig. 15, pl. XVI
XHev/Se 25	papDeed C ar	542	Yardeni, DJD XXVII (1997), fig. 16, pl. XVII
XHev/Se 26	papText Dealing with Deposits and Barley ar	542	Yardeni, DJD XXVII (1997), fig. 16, pl. XVII
XHev/Se 27	papDeed D ar	542	Yardeni, DJD XXVII (1997), fig. 16, pl. XVIII
XHev/Se 28	papUnclassified Fragment G ar	536	Yardeni, DJD XXVII (1997), fig. 17, pl. XIX
XHev/Se 29	papUnclassified Fragments H	732, 733	Yardeni, DJD XXVII (1997), fig. 17, pl. XIX
XHev/Se 30	papLetter to Shimʿon ben Kosibah	542	Yardeni, DJD XXVII (1997), fig. 18, pl. XX
XHev/Se 31	papDeed E ar	734	Yardeni, DJD XXVII (1997), fig. 19, pl. XXI
XHev/Se 32	papDeed F ar (+ 4Q347)	184, 734	Yardeni, DJD XXVII (1997), fig. 19, pl. XXI
XHev/Se 33	papUnclassified Fragment I ar	734	Yardeni, DJD XXVII (1997), fig. 19, pl. XXII
XHev/Se 34	papDeed G ar	734	Yardeni, DJD XXVII (1997), fig. 19, pl. XXII
XHev/Se 35	papUnclassified Fragment J ar	734	Yardeni, DJD XXVII (1997), fig. 19, pl. XXII
XHev/Se 36	papUnclassified Fragment K	734	Yardeni, DJD XXVII (1997), fig. 19, pl. XXII
XHev/Se 37	papDeed H ar?	734	Yardeni, DJD XXVII (1997), fig. 20, pls. XXIII–XXIV
XHev/Se 38	papUnclassified Fragments L	865	Yardeni, DJD XXVII (1997), fig. 20, pl. XXV
XHev/Se 39	papUnclassified Fragment M	865	Yardeni, DJD XXVII (1997), fig. 20, pl. XXV
XHev/Se 40	papUnclassified Fragment N	865	Yardeni, DJD XXVII (1997), fig. 20, pl. XXV
XHev/Se 41	papUnclassified Fragment O	865	Yardeni, DJD XXVII (1997), fig. 20, pl. XXV
XHev/Se 42	papUnclassified Fragment P	865	Yardeni, DJD XXVII (1997), fig. 21, pl. XXV
XHev/Se 43	papUnclassified Fragment Q	865	Yardeni, DJD XXVII (1997), fig. 21, pl. XXV
XHev/Se 44	papUnclassified Fragment R	865	Yardeni, DJD XXVII (1997), fig. 21, pl. XXV
XHev/Se 45	papUnclassified Fragment S	865	Yardeni, DJD XXVII (1997), fig. 21, pl. XXV
XHev/Se 46	papUnclassified Fragment T	865	Yardeni, DJD XXVII (1997), fig. 21, pl. XXV
XHev/Se 47a	papUnclassified Fragment U	865	Yardeni, DJD XXVII (1997), fig. 21, pl. XXVI
XHev/Se 47b	papUnclassified Fragment V	865	Yardeni, DJD XXVII (1997), fig. 21, pl. XXVI
XHev/Se 47c	papUnclassified Fragment W	865	Yardeni, DJD XXVII (1997), fig. 21, pl. XXVI
XHev/Se 47d	papUnclassified Fragment X	865	Yardeni, DJD XXVII (1997), fig. 21, pl. XXVI
XHev/Se 47e	papUnclassified Fragment Y	865	Yardeni, DJD XXVII (1997), fig. 21, pl. XXVI
XHev/Se 47f	papUnclassified Fragment Z	865	Yardeni, DJD XXVII (1997), fig. 21, pl. XXVI
XHev/Se 47g	papUnclassified Fragment AA	865	Yardeni, DJD XXVII (1997), fig. 21, pl. XXVI
XHev/Se 47h	papUnclassified Fragment BB	865	Yardeni, DJD XXVII (1997), fig. 21, pl. XXVI
XHev/Se 48	(cancelled)		
XHev/Se 49	Promissory Note	Priv. Coll.	Yardeni, DJD XXVII (1997), figs. 22–23, pl. XXVII

XHev/Se 50	papDeed of Sale H ar (= part of Mur 26)	725, BTS 7163		Yardeni, DJD XXVII (1997), figs. 24–26, pls. XXVII–XXX
XHev/Se 60	papTax (or Rent) Receipt from Mahoza gr	866		Cotton, DJD XXVII (1997), fig. 27, pls. XXXI–XXXII
XHev/Se 61	papConclusion to a Land Declaration gr	866		Cotton, DJD XXVII (1997), pls. XXXI, XXXIII
XHev/Se 62	papLand Declaration gr			Cotton, DJD XXVII (1997), pls. XXXIV–XXXVII
XHev/Se 63	papDeed of Renunciation of Claims gr	866		Cotton, DJD XXVII (1997), pls. XXXI, XXXVIII
XHev/Se 64	papDeed of Gift gr	869		Cotton, DJD XXVII (1997), fig. 27, pls. XXXIX–XL
XHev/Se 65	papMarriage Contract gr	99		Cotton, DJD XXVII (1997), pl. XLI
XHev/Se 66	papLoan with Hypothec gr	732		Cotton, DJD XXVII (1997), pl. XLII
XHev/Se 67	papText Mentioning Timber gr	866		Cotton, DJD XXVII (1997), pls. XXXI, XLIII
XHev/Se 68	papText Mentioning a Guardian gr	866		Cotton, DJD XXVII (1997), pls. XXXI, XLIV
XHev/Se 69	papCancelled Marriage Contract gr	870		Cotton, DJD XXVII (1997), pls. XLV–XLVI
XHev/Se 70	papUnidentified Fragment A gr	866		Cotton, DJD XXVII (1997), pls. XXXI, XLVII
XHev/Se 71	papUnidentified Fragment B gr	866		Cotton, DJD XXVII (1997), pls. XXXI, XLVII
XHev/Se 72	papUnidentified Fragment C gr	866		Cotton, DJD XXVII (1997), pls. XXXI, XLVII
XHev/Se 73	papEnd of a Document gr	731		Cotton, DJD XXVII (1997), pl. XLVII
XHev/Se 74–139	papUnidentified Fragments gr	732		Cotton, DJD XXVII (1997), pl. XLVIII
XHev/Se 140–169	papUnidentified Fragments gr	731		Cotton, DJD XXVII (1997), pl. XLIX
XHev/Se Nab. 1	papContract nab (= 5/6Hev 36)	654, 655, 867		Starcky, RB61 (1954), 161–181, pls. I–III; Yardeni, Levine, JDS (in press)
XHev/Se Nab. 2	papContract nab	862 r, v		Yardeni, Levine, JDS (in press)
XHev/Se Nab. 3	papContract nab	863 r, v		Yardeni, Levine, JDS (in press)
XHev/Se Nab. 4	papContract nab	868		Yardeni, Levine, JDS (in press)
XHev/Se Nab. 5	papContract nab	864 r, v		Yardeni, Levine, JDS (in press)
XHev/Se Nab. 6	papFrag. nab (olim "Wadi Habara")	860, 860A		Yardeni, Levine, JDS (in press)
Hev/Se? 1–12	papUnidentified Fragments gr	3001		Cotton, DJD XXVII (1997), pl. L
Hev/Se? 13–14	papUnidentified Fragments gr	3004		Cotton, DJD XXVII (1997), pl. LI
Hev/Se? 15–23	papUnidentified Fragments gr	3005		Cotton, DJD XXVII (1997), pl. LI
Hev/Se? 24–35	papUnidentified Fragments gr	3006		Cotton, DJD XXVII (1997), pl. LII
Hev/Se? 36–57	papUnidentified Fragments gr	3007		Cotton, DJD XXVII (1997), pl. LIII

11. Naḥal Mishmar

1Mish 1	papOfficial Document			Bar Adon, IEJ 11 (1961): pl. 13E
1Mish 2	papList of Names and Account gr (recto) (verso)			Lifshitz, IEJ 11 (1961): pl. 23H (cf. 13D) Cotton, DJD XXXVIII (2000) Lifshitz, IEJ 11 (1961): pl. 23I
1Mish 3	papPromissory Note?			Bar Adon, EAEHL (1977), 3:690
1Mish 4	ostrUnclassified			Bar Adon, EAEHL (1977), 3:690
1Mish 5	ostrUnclassified			Bar Adon, EAEHL (1977), 3:690
1Mish 6	ostrUnclassified			Bar Adon, EAEHL (1977), 3:690
1Mish 7	ostrUnclassified			Bar Adon, EAEHL (1977), 3:690
1Mish 8	ostrUnclassified gr			Bar Adon, EAEHL (1977), 3:690

12. Naḥal Ṣeʾelim

34Ṣe 1	Phylactery	220*		Aharoni, IEJ 11 (1961): pl. 11

34Şe 2	Num			Aharoni, *IEJ* 11 (1961): pl. 11; Morgenstern, DJD XXXVIII (2000)
34Şe 3a	papDeed A			Morgenstern, DJD XXXVIII (2000)
34Şe 3b	Deed B			Morgenstern, DJD XXXVIII (2000)
34Şe 4	papCensus List from Judaea or Arabia gr	226, 229		Cotton, DJD XXXVIII (2000)
34Şe 5	papAccount gr	226		Cotton, DJD XXXVIII (2000)

13. Masada

Mas1	Gen (*olim* Mas1i Jub)	91*	1039–1317	Talmon, *Masada VI* (1999), illustr. 2
Mas1a	Lev^a	195*	1039–1270	Talmon, *Masada VI* (1999), illustr. 3
Mas1b	Lev^b	198*	92–480	Talmon, *Masada VI* (1999), illustr. 4
Mas1c	Deut	196*	1043/1–4	Talmon, *Masada VI* (1999), illustr. 6
Mas1d	Ezek	197*	1043–2220	Talmon, *Masada VI* (1999), illustr. 8
Mas1e	Ps^a	237*	1039–1160	Talmon, *Masada VI* (1999), illustr. 9
Mas1f	Ps^b	81*	1103–1742	Talmon, *Masada VI* (1999), illustr. 10
Mas1g	(cancelled; see 11QPs^d)			
Mas1h	Sir	238*	1109–1537	Yadin, *Ben Sira Scroll* (1965), pls. 1–9
Mas1j	Jub or psJub	236*	1276–1786	Talmon, *Masada VI* (1999), illustr. 14
Mas1k	ShirShabb	232*	1039–1200	Newsom, DJD XI (1998), pl. XIX; Talmon, *Masada VI* (1999), illustr. 15
Mas1l	apocrJosh (*olim* paraJosh)	90*	1039–1211	Talmon, *Masada VI* (1999), illustr. 13
Mas1m	apocrGen (*olim* apEsther?)	82–83*	1045–1350, 1375	Talmon, *Masada VI* (1999), illustr. 12
Mas1n	Qumran-type Frag. (*olim* sectarian? frag.)	92*	1063–1747	Talmon, *Masada VI* (1999), illustr. 16
Mas1o r	pap paleoText of Sam. Origin (recto)	235*	1039–320	Talmon, *Masada VI* (1999), illustr. 18
Mas1o v	pap paleoUnidentified Text (verso)	235*	1039–1320	Talmon, *Masada VI*(1999), illustr. 18
Mas1p	Unclassified frag. ar?	93*	1039–1274	Talmon, *Masada VI* (1999), illustr. 17
Mas1–553	ostrLetters			Yadin, Naveh, *Masada I* (1989)
Mas554	ostrLetter		16–89/1	Yadin, Naveh, *Masada I* (1989), pl. 45
Mas555	ostrLetter		92A–587	Yadin, Naveh, *Masada I* (1989), pl. 45
Mas556	ostrLetter		146–479, 786	Yadin, Naveh, *Masada I* (1989), pl. 45
Mas557–720	ostrMisc.			Yadin, Naveh, *Masada I* (1989)
Mas721 r	papVirgil lat (recto)	70*	1039–1210	Cotton, Geiger, *Masada II* (1989), pl. 1
Mas721 v	papVirgil lat (verso)	70*	1039–1210	Cotton, Geiger, *Masada II* (1989), pl. 1
Mas722	papLegionary Pay Record lat	64*	1039–1122	Cotton, Geiger, *Masada II* (1989), pl. 2
Mas723	papMedical Care in the Roman Army lat	59*	1039–1195	Cotton, Geiger, *Masada II* (1989), pl. 4
Mas724 r	papLetter to Iulius Lupus lat (recto)	212*	1039–1161	Cotton, Geiger, *Masada II* (1989), pl. 4
Mas724 v	papLetter to Iulius Lupus lat (verso)	212*	1039–1161	Cotton, Geiger, *Masada II* (1989), pl. 4
Mas725	papThe Balsam Trade lat	233*	1039–1122/1	Cotton, Geiger, *Masada II* (1989), pl. 5
Mas726	papLetter Concerning a Centurion lat	67–68*	1039–1267	Cotton, Geiger, *Masada II* (1989), pl. 5
Mas727	papMilitary Document lat	67–68*	1039–1267	Cotton, Geiger, *Masada II* (1989), pl. 5
Mas728	papLetter lat	77*	1039–1272	Cotton, Geiger, *Masada II* (1989), pl. 5
Mas728a	papLetter lat	50–53*	1039–1272	Cotton, Geiger, *Masada II* (1989), pl. 6
Mas729	papMilitary Document lat	71*	1039–1159	Cotton, Geiger, *Masada II* (1989), pl. 6
Mas730	papMilitary Document? lat	61*	1039–1159	Cotton, Geiger, *Masada II* (1989), pl. 6
Mas731	papMilitary Document? lat (r + v)	46*	1039–1307/2	Cotton, Geiger, *Masada II* (1989), pl. 6
Mas732	papFrag. lat	56–58*	1039–1271	Cotton, Geiger, *Masada II* (1989), pl. 7
Mas733	papFrag. lat	57*	1039–1271	Cotton, Geiger, *Masada II* (1989), pl. 7
Mas734	papFrag. lat	50–53*	1039–1272	Cotton, Geiger, *Masada II* (1989), pl. 7
Mas735	papFrag. lat	47–49*	1039–1273	Cotton, Geiger, *Masada II* (1989), pl. 7
Mas736	papFrag. lat		1039–1273	Cotton, Geiger, *Masada II* (1989), pl. 7
Mas737	papFrag. lat	55*	1039–1299	Cotton, Geiger, *Masada II* (1989), pl. 7
Mas738	Frag. lat	63*	1264–2063	Cotton, Geiger, *Masada II* (1989), pl. 7
Mas739	papLiterary Text? gr	54*	1264–2007	Cotton, Geiger, *Masada II* (1989), pl. 8

Mas740	papDocuments? gr	60*	92–401	Cotton, Geiger, *Masada II* (1989), pl. 8
Mas741	papLetter of Abakantos to Judas gr	45*	1039–1307/1	Cotton, Geiger, *Masada II* (1989), pl. 8
Mas742	papByzantine Document gr	69*	1029–2234	Cotton, Geiger, *Masada II* (1989), pl. 9
Mas743	woodTablet gr	65*	1039–1302	Cotton, Geiger, *Masada II* (1989), pl. 9
Mas744	papList of Names? gr	50-53*	1039–1271, 272	Cotton, Geiger, *Masada II* (1989), pl. 9
Mas745	papLetter gr	50-53*	1039–1272	Cotton, Geiger, *Masada II* (1989), pl. 9
Mas746	papLetter(s) gr	47-49*	1039–1273	Cotton, Geiger, *Masada II* (1989), pl. 9
Mas747	papFrag. gr	66*	1045–1641	Cotton, Geiger, *Masada II* (1989), pl. 10
Mas748	papBilingual List of Names lat-gr	62*	1276–1890	Cotton, Geiger, *Masada II* (1989), pl. 10
Mas749	papFrags. lat or gr	43*, 233*		Cotton, Geiger, *Masada II* (1989), pl. 10
Mas750–927	ostrMisc. lat and gr			Cotton, Geiger, *Masada II* (1989)
Mas928–945	Graffiti			Cotton, Geiger, *Masada II* (1989)
Mas946–951	Amphora stamps lat			Cotton, Geiger, *Masada II* (1989)

233

Appendix G:
Concordance of Ugaritic Texts

Subject	CTU[1]	UT	CTA[2]	RS	Translations
Baal and Yamm	1.1	ʿnt	1	3.361	*UNP* 7; *COS*
	II:1–III:30	pl. ix	ii 1–iii 30		1.86; *ANET*,
	IV:1–V:28	pl. x	iv 1–v 28		129–42 (for
					Baal texts)
Baal and Yamm	1.2	137	2	3.367 + 3.346	*UNP* 8; *COS*
	I:1–17		i 1–17		1.86
	II:1–15	129	ii 1–15		
	III:1–24	68	iii 1–24		
	IV:1–40		iv 1–40		
Baal and ʿAnat	1.3	ʿnt	3	2.[014] + 3.363	*UNP* 9; *COS*
	I:1–II:41	I:1–II:41	i 1–ii 41		1.86
	III:1–3	II:42–44	iii 1–3		
	III:4–47	III:1–44	iii 4–47		
	IV:1–46	IV:45–90	iv 1–46		
	IV:48–55	pl. vi:IV:1–8	iv 48–55		
	V:1–43	V:9–51	v 1–43		
	VI:1–25	VI:1–25	vi 1–25		
Baal's Palace	1.4	51	4	2.[008] +	*UNP* 10; *COS*
	I:1–IV:62	I:1–IV:62	i 1–iv 62	3.341 + 3.347	1.86
	V:1–65	V:63–127	v 1–65		
	VI:1–VIII:49	VI:1–VIII:49	vi 1–viii 49		
Baal and Mot	1.5	67	5	2.[022] +	*UNP* 11; *COS*
	I:1–III:30	I:1–III:29	i 1–iii 30	3.[565]	1.86
	IV:1–VI:31	IV:1–VI:31	iv 1–vi 31		
Baal and Mot	1.6	62:1–28	6	2.[009] + 5.155	*UNP* 12; *COS*
	I:1–28	49:I:1–39	i 1–28		1.86
	I:29–67	49:II:1–III:24	i 29–67		
	II:1–III:24	49:IV:25–51	ii 1–iii 24		
	IV:1–27	49:V:1–VI:38	iv 1–27		
	V:1–VI:38	62:38–57	v 1–vi 38		
	VI:39–58		vi 39–58		
Variant Version of Baal	1.8		8	3.364	*UNP* 14
	(I) II:1–17		(I) II:1–17		
Baal and the Cow	1.10	76	10	3.362 + 5.181	*UNP* 15
	I:1–18	I:1–18	i 1–18		
	I:20–24	I:19–23	i 20–24		
	II:1–38	II:1–38	ii 1–38		
	III:1–37	III:2–38	iii 1–37		
A Birth	1.11		11	3.319	*UNP* 16
	1–19		1–19		

[1] For complete indexes of excavation numbers and publications, see CTU, 607–623 and 639–649.

[2] For a table of concordances of CTA with earlier editions, see *CTA*, xix–xxxiv.

The Poem of Baal Haddu	1.12 I:1–II:6 II:7–61	75 I:1–II:6 II:8–62	12 i 1–ii 6 ii 7–61	2.[012]	*UNP* 17
Hymn to ʿAnat	1.13 1–36	6 1–36	13 1–36	1.006	
Kirta Legend	1.14 I:1–43 II:1–51 III:1–59 IV:1–52 V:1–28 V:30–45 VI:1–41	Krt 1–43 54–104 105–163 164–215 216–243 246–261 266–306	14 i 1–43 ii 1–51 iii 1–59 iv 1–52 v 1–28 v 30–45 vi 1–41	2.[003] + 3.324 + 3.344 + 3.414	*UNP* 1; *COS* 1.102; *ANET*, 142–49 (for all of Keret)
Kirta Legend	1.15 I:1–VI:9	128 I:1–VI:9	15 i 1–vi 9	3.343 + 3.345	*UNP* 2; *COS* 1.102
Kirta Legend	1.16 I:1–62 II:1–58 III:1–17 IV:1–17 V:1–36 V:37–52 VI:1–59	125:1–62 125:63–120 126:III:1–17 126:IV:2–18 126:V:1–36 126:V:38–53 127:1–59	16 i 1–62 ii 1–58 iii 1–17 iv 1–17 v 1–36 v 37–52 vi 1–59	3.325 + 3.342 + 3.408	*UNP* 3; *COS* 1.102
Aqhat Legend	1.17 I:1–47 II:1–47 V:1–VI:55	*2 Aqht* I:2–48 II:1–47 V:1–VI:55	17 i 1–47 ii 1–47 v 1–vi 55	2.[004]	*UNP* 4; *COS* 1.103; *ANET*, 149–55 (for all of Aqhat)
Aqhat Legend	1.18 I:1–34 IV:1–42	*3 Aqht* rev.:1–34 obv.:1–42	18 I 1–34 iv 1–42	3.340	*UNP* 5; *COS* 1.103
Aqhat Legend	1.19 I:1–49 II:1–57 III:1–56 IV:1–61	*1 Aqht* 1–49 50–106 107–162 163–223	19 i 1–49 ii 1–57 iii 1–56 iv 1–61	3.322 + 3.349 + 3.366	*UNP* 6; *COS* 1.103
Rephaim Texts	1.20 I:1–II:12	121 I:1–II:12	20 i 1–ii 12	3.348	*UNP* 20
Rephaim Texts	1.21 II:1–13	122 1–13	21 ii 1–13	2.[019] + 5.155	*UNP* 21
Rephaim Texts	1.22 I:1–28 II:1–26	124:1–28 123:1–26	22 i 1–28 ii 1–26	2.[024]	*UNP* 22
The Birth of Gods Dawn and Dusk	1.23 1–76	52 1–76	23 1–76	2.002	*UNP* 23; *COS* 1.87
The Wedding of the Moon Gods	1.24 1–50	77 1–50	24 1–50	5.194	*UNP* 24
Sacrifices	1.39 1–22	1 1–22	34 1–22	1.001	
Ritual	1.40 1–43	2 1–43	32 1–43	1.002 + 1.002[A]	

Sacrifices/Ritual	1.41 1–55	3 1–55	35 1–55	1.003 + 2.[005]	COS 1.95
List of Deities	1.47 1–34	17 1–34	29 1–34	1.017	
Ritual/Song	1.96 1–13			22.225	UNP 26
Incantation against Snake Bite	1.100 1–79	607 1–79		24.244	UNP 25; COS 1.94
List of Kings	1.113 1–26			24.257	COS 1.104
El's Feast	1.114 1–31	601 1–31		24.258	UNP 19; COS 1.97
Variant Version of Baal and Mot	1.333 1–19			24.293	UNP 13

Appendix H:
Greek and Latin Works and Their Abbreviations

EXPLANATORY NOTES REGARDING THE TABLE (see also §8.3.14)

(1) For Greek works as for Latin works, a Latin title and abbreviation are normally used; but if the work is well known under its Greek name, this may be provided in parentheses following the Latin title. In a few cases where scholars almost always use a Greek title instead, we give a Greek abbreviation and a Greek title, both transliterated. We do not use Greek abbreviations in Greek characters.

(2) For many better-known works, English as well as Latin titles are given. For Greek and Latin classical and patristic works, however, we prefer to use Latin abbreviations in notes even if English titles are used in the text of the book. If English abbreviations are used, the author should provide a list of these.

(3) Anonymous works in this table are alphabetized by their abbreviations, which are given in bold italics to distinguish them from works of the preceding author. Naturally, when such an abbreviation is used it should be set italic but not bold.

(4) Abbreviations of spurious works are bracketed.

(5) For the sake of completeness, some titles are included that are short enough that they need no abbreviation.

(6) The table is very selective in its choice of authors; but for authors that are included we have tried to offer complete lists of their works.

ABBREVIATIONS	LATIN (OR GREEK) TITLE	ENGLISH TITLE
Achilles Tatius		
Leuc. Clit.	Leucippe et Clitophon	The Adventures of Leucippe and Cleitophon
Aelian		
Nat. an.	De natura animalium	Nature of Animals
Var. hist.	Varia historia	
Aeschines		
Ctes.	In Ctesiphonem	Against Ctesiphon
Fals. leg.	De falsa legatione	False Embassy
Tim.	In Timarchum	Against Timarchus
Aeschylus		
Ag.	Agamemnon	Agamemnon
Cho.	Choephori	Libation-Bearers
Eum.	Eumenides	Eumenides
Pers.	Persae	Persians
Prom.	Prometheus vinctus	Prometheus Bound
Sept.	Septem contra Thebas	Seven against Thebes
Suppl.	Supplices	Suppliant Women
Aesop		
Fab.	Fabulae	Fables

237

ABBREVIATIONS	LATIN (OR GREEK) TITLE	ENGLISH TITLE
Albinus		
Epit.	Epitome doctrinae platonicae (Didaskalikos)	Handbook of Platonism
Intr.	Introductio in Platonem (Prologus or Eisagōgē)	Introduction to Plato
Alexander of Aphrodisias		
De an.	De anima	
Comm. An. post.	In Analytica posteriora commentariorum fragmenta	
Comm. An. pr.	In Aristotelis Analyticorum priorum librum i commentarium	
Comm. Metaph.	In Aristotelis Metaphysica commentaria	
Comm. Mete.	In Aristotelis Meteorologicorum libros commentaria	
Comm. Sens.	In librum De sensu commentarium	
Comm. Top.	In Aristotelis Topicorum libros octo commentaria	
Fat.	De fato	
Mixt.	De mixtione	
Probl.	Problemata	
Ambrose		
Abr.	De Abraham	
Apol. Dav.	Apologia prophetae David	
Aux.	Sermo contra Auxentium de basilicis tradendis	
Bon. mort.	De bono mortis	Death as a Good
Cain	De Cain et Abel	
Enarrat. Ps.	Enarrationes in XII Psalmos davidicos	
Exc.	De excessu fratris sui Satyri	
Exh. virginit.	Exhortatio virginitatis	
Fid.	De fide	
Exp. Isa.	Expositio Isaiae prophetae	
Exp. Luc.	Expositio Evangelii secundum Lucam	
Exp. Ps. 118	Expositio Psalmi CXVIII	
Expl. symb.	Explanatio symboli ad initiandos	
Fid. Grat.	De fide ad Gratianum	
Fug.	De fuga saeculi	Flight from the World
Hel.	De Helia et Jejunio	
Hex.	Hexaemeron libri sex	Six Days of Creation
Hymn.	Hymni	
Incarn.	De incarnationis dominicae sacramento	The Sacrament of the Incarnation of the Lord
Instit.	De institutione virginis	
Isaac	De Isaac vel anima	Isaac, or The Soul
Jac.	De Jacob et vita beata	Jacob and the Happy Life
Job	De interpellatione Job et David	The Prayer of Job and David
Jos.	De Joseph patriarcha	
Myst.	De mysteriis	The Mysteries
Nab.	De Nabuthae historia	
Noe	De Noe et arca	
Ob. Theo.	De obitu Theodosii	
Ob. Val.	De obitu Valentiniani consolatio	
Off.	De officiis ministrorum	
Paen.	De paenitentia	
Parad.	De paradiso	Paradise
Patr.	De benedictionibus patriarcharum	The Patriarchs
Sacr.	De sacramentis	The Sacraments
Sacr. regen.	De sacramento regenerationis sive de philosophia	
Spir.	De Spiritu Sancto	The Holy Spirit
Symb.	Explanatio symboli	
Tob.	De Tobia	
Vid.	De viduis	
Virg.	De virginibus	
Virginit.	De virginitate	
Anaximenes of Lampsacus		
Rhet. Alex.	Rhetorica ad Alexandrum (Ars rhetorica)	
Andronicus		
[Pass.]	De passionibus	The Passions
Anth. pal.	Anthologia palatina	Palatine Anthology

ABBREVIATIONS	LATIN (OR GREEK) TITLE	ENGLISH TITLE
Anth. plan.	*Anthologia planudea*	*Planudean Anthology*

Antoninus Liberalis
| *Metam.* | *Metamorphōseōn synagōgē* | |

Apollonius of Rhodes
| *Argon.* | *Argonautica* | *Argonautica* |

Apollonius Sophista
| *Lex. hom.* | *Lexicon homericum* | *Homeric Lexicon* |

Appian
| *Bell. civ.* | *Bella civilia* | *Civil Wars* |
| *Hist. rom.* | *Historia romana* | *Roman History* |

Apuleius
Apol.	*Apologia (Pro se de magia)*	*Apology*
De deo Socr.	*De deo Socratico*	
Dogm. Plat.	*De dogma Platonis*	
Flor.	*Florida*	
Metam.	*Metamorphoses*	*The Golden Ass*

Aratus
| *Phaen.* | *Phaenomena* | |

Archimedes
Aequil.	*De planorum aequilibriis*	*The Equilibriums of Planes or Centers of Gravity of Planes*
Aren.	*Arenarius*	*The Sand-reckoner*
Assumpt.	*Liber assumptorum*	
Bov.	*Problema bovinum*	
Circ.	*Dimensio circuli*	*Measurement of the Circle*
Con. sph.	*De conoidibus et sphaeroidibus*	*On Conoids and Spheroids*
Eratosth.	*Ad Eratosthenem methodus*	*To Eratosthenes on the Method of Mechanical Theorems*
Fluit.	*De corporibus fluitantibus*	*On Floating Bodies*
Quadr.	*Quadratura parabolae*	*Quadrature of the Parabola*
Sph. cyl.	*De sphaera et cylindro*	*On the Sphere and the Cylinder*
Spir.	*De lineis spiralibus*	*On Spirals*
Stom.	*Stomachion*	

Aretaeus
Cur. acut.	*De curatione acutorum morborum*	
Cur. diut.	*De curatione diuturnorum morborum*	
Sign. acut.	*De causis et signis acutorum morborum*	
Sign. diut.	*De causis et signis diuturnorum morborum*	

Aristophanes
Ach.	*Acharnenses*	*Acharnians*
Av.	*Aves*	*Birds*
Eccl.	*Ecclesiazusae*	*Women of the Assembly*
Eq.	*Equites*	*Knights*
Lys.	*Lysistrata*	*Lysistrata*
Nub.	*Nubes*	*Clouds*
Pax	*Pax*	*Peace*
Plut.	*Plutus*	*The Rich Man*
Ran.	*Ranae*	*Frogs*
Thesm.	*Thesmophoriazusae*	
Vesp.	*Vespae*	*Wasps*

Aristotle
De an.	*De anima*	*Soul*
An. post.	*Analytica posteriora*	*Posterior Analytics*
An. pr.	*Analytica priora*	*Prior Analytics*
Ath. pol.	*Athēnaīn politeia*	*Constitution of Athens*
[Aud.]	*De audibilibus*	*Sounds*
Cael.	*De caelo*	*Heavens*
Cat.	*Categoriae*	*Categories*
l.]	*De coloribus*	*Colors*
Div. somn.	*De divinatio per somnum*	*Prophesying by Dreams*
Ep.	*Epistulae*	*Letters*
Eth. eud.	*Ethica eudemia*	*Eudemian Ethics*

ABBREVIATIONS	LATIN (OR GREEK) TITLE	ENGLISH TITLE
Eth. nic.	Ethica nichomachea	Nichomachean Ethics
Gen. an.	De generatione anamalium	Generation of Animals
Gen. corr.	De generatione et corruptione	Generation and Corruption
Hist. an.	Historia animalium	History of Animals
Inc. an.	De incessu animalium	Gait of Animals
Insomn.	De insomniis	
Int.	De interpretatione	Interpretation
Juv. sen.	De juventute et senectute	Youth and Old Age
[Lin. ins.]	De lineis insecabilibus	Indivisible Lines
Long. brev.	De longitudine et brevitate vitae	Longevity and Shortness of Life
[Mag. mor.]	Magna moralia	
[Mech.]	Mechanica	Mechanics
Mem. rem.	De memoria et reminiscentia	Memory and Reminiscence
Metaph.	Metaphysica	Metaphysics
Mete.	Meteorologica	Meteorology
[Mir. ausc.]	De mirabilibus auscultationibus	On Marvelous Things Heard
Mot. an.	De motu animalium	Movement of Animals
[Mund.]	De mundo	
[Oec.]	Oeconomica	Economics
Part. an.	De partibus animalium	Parts of Animals
[Physiogn.]	Physiognomonica	Physiognomonics
Phys.	Physica	Physics
[Plant.]	De plantis	Plants
Poet.	Poetica	Poetics
Pol.	Politica	Politics
[Probl.]	Problemata	Problems
Protr.	Protrepticus	
Resp.	De respiratione	Respiration
Rhet.	Rhetorica	Rhetoric
[Rhet. Alex.]	Rhetorica ad Alexandrum (see Anaximenes)	Rhetoric to Alexander
Sens.	De sensu et sensibilibus	Sense and Sensibilia
Somn.	De somniis	Dreams
Somn. vig.	De somno et vigilia	Sleep and Waking
Soph. elench.	Sophistici elenchi (Top. 9)	Sophistical Refutations
[Spir.]	De spiritu	
Top.	Topica	Topics
[Vent.]	De ventorum situ et nominibus	Situations and Names of Winds
[Virt. vit.]	De virtutibus et vitiis	Virtues and Vices
Vit. mort.	De vita et morte	Life and Death
[Gorg.]	De Gorgia	
[Xen.]	De Xenophane	
[Zen.]	De Zenone	

Arrian

Anab.	Anabasis	
Epict. diss.	Epicteti dissertationes	
Peripl. M. Eux.	Periplus Maris Euxini	
Tact.	Tactica	

Artemidorus Daldianus

Onir.	Onirocritica	

Athanasius

Apol. Const.	Apologia ad Constantium	Defense before Constantius
Apol. sec.	Apologia secunda (= Apologia contra Arianos)	Defense against the Arians
[Apoll.]	De incarnatione contra Apollinarium	On the Incarnation against Apollinaris
C. Ar.	Orationes contra Arianos	Orations against the Arians
Decr.	De decretis	Defense of the Nicene Definition
Dion.	De sententia Dionysii	On the Opinion of Dionysius
Ep. Adelph.	Epistula ad Adelphium	Letter to Adelphius
Ep. Aeg. Lib.	Epistula ad episcopos Aegypti et Libyae	Letter to the Bishops of Egypt and Libya
Ep. Afr.	Epistula ad Afros episcopos	Letter to the Bishops of Africa
Ep. Amun	Epistula ad Amun	Letter to Ammoun
Ep. cler. Alex.	Epistula ad clerum Alexandriae	Letter to the Clergy of Alexandria
Ep. cler. Mareot.	Epistula ad clerum Mareotae	Letter to the Clergy of the Mareotis
Ep. Drac.	Epistula ad Dracontium	Letter to Dracontius
Ep. encycl.	Epistula encyclica	Circular Letter
Ep. Epict.	Epistula ad Epictetum	Letter to Epictetus
Ep. fest.	Epistulae festales	Festal Letters
Ep. Jo. Ant.	Epistula ad Joannem et Antiochum presbyteros	Letter to John and Antiochus
Ep. Jov.	Epistula ad Jovianum	Letter to Jovian

ABBREVIATIONS	LATIN (OR GREEK) TITLE	ENGLISH TITLE
Ep. Marcell.	Epistula ad Marcellinum de interpretatione Psalmorum	Letter to Marcellinus on the Interpretation of the Psalms
Ep. Max.	Epistula ad Maximum	Letter to Maximus
Ep. mon. 1	Epistula ad monachos i	First Letter to Monks.
Ep. mon. 2	Epistula ad monachos ii	Second Letter to Monks
Ep. mort. Ar.	Epistula ad Serapionem de more Arii	Letter to Serapion concerning the Death of Arius
Ep. Ors. 1	Epistula ad Orsisium i	First Letter to Orsisius
Ep. Ors. 2	Epistula ad Orsisium ii	Second Letter to Orsisius
Ep. Pall.	Epistula ad Palladium	Letter to Palladius
Ep. Rufin.	Epistula ad Rufinianum	Letter to Rufinianus
Ep. Serap.	Epistulae ad Serapionem	Letters to Serapion concerning the Holy Spirit
Ep. virg. (Copt.)	Epistula ad virgines (Coptice)	First (Coptic) Letter to Virgins
Ep. virg. (Syr.)	Epistula ad virgines (Syriace)	Second (Syriac) Letter to Virgins
Ep. virg. (Syr./Arm.)	Epistula ad virgines (Syriace et Armeniace)	Letter to Virgins
Ep. virg. (Theod.)	Epistula exhortatora ad virgines apud Theodoretum	Letter to Virgins
Fug.	Apologia de fuga sua	Defense of His Flight
C. Gent.	Contra gentes	Against the Pagans
H. Ar.	Historia Arianorum	History of the Arians
Hen. sōm.	Henos sōmatos	Encyclical Letter of Alexander concerning the Deposition of Arius
Hom. Jo. 12:27	In illud Nunc anima mea turbata est	Homily on John 12:27
Hom. Matt. 11:27	In illud Omnia mihi tradita sunt	Homily on Matthew 11:27
Hom. Luc. 12:10	In illud Qui dixerit verbum in filium	Homily on Luke 12:10
Inc.	De incarnatione	On the Incarnation
Mor. et val.	De morbo et valitudine	On Sickness and Health
Narr. fug.	Narratio ad Ammonium episcopum de fuga sua	Report of Athanasius concerning Theodorus
Syn.	De synodis	On the Councils of Ariminum and Seleucia
Tom.	Tomus ad Antiochenos	Tome to the People of Antioch
Vit. Ant.	Vita Antonii	Life of Antony

Athenaeus

Deipn.	Deipnosophistae	

Athenagoras

Leg.	Legatio pro Christianis	
Res.	De resurrectione	

Augustine

Acad.	Contra Academicos	Against the Academics
Adim.	Contra Adimantum	Against Adimantus
Adnot. Job	Adnotationum in Job liber I	Annotations on Job
Agon.	De agone christiano	Christian Combat
An. orig.	De anima et eius origine	The Soul and Its Origin
Arian.	Contra sermonem Arianorum	
Bapt.	De baptismo contra Donatistas	Baptism
Beat.	De vita beata	
Bon. conj.	De bono conjugali	The Good of Marriage
Brev. coll.	Breviculus collationis cum Donatistis	
Catech.	De catechizandis rudibus	Catechizing the Uninstructed
Civ.	De civitate Dei	The City of God
Coll. Max.	Collatio cum Maximino Arianorum episcopo	
Conf.	Confessionum libri XIII	Confessions
Cons.	De consensu evangelistarum	Harmony of the Gospels
Contin.	De continentia	Continence
Corrept.	De correptione et gratia	Admonition and Grace
Cresc.	Contra Cresconium Donatistam	
Cur.	De cura pro mortuis gerenda	The Care to Be Taken for the Dead
Dial.	Principia dialecticae	
Disc.	De disciplina christiana	
Div.	De divinitate daemonum	The Divination of Demons
Div. quaest. LXXXIII	De diversis quaestionibus LXXXIII	Eighty-three Different Questions
Div. quaest. Simpl.	De diversis quaestionibus ad Simplicianum	
Doctr. chr.	De doctrina christiana	Christian Instruction
Don.	Post collationem adversus Donatistas	
C. du. ep. Pelag.	Contra duas epistulas Pelagianorum ad Bonifatium	Against the Two Letters of the Pelagians
Duab.	De duabus animabus	Two Souls
Dulc.	De octo Dulcitii quaestionibus	The Eight Questions of Dulcitius
Emer.	De gestis cum Emerino	
Enarrat. Ps.	Enarrationes in Psalmos	Enarrations on the Psalms
Enchir.	Enchiridion de fide, spe, et caritate	Enchiridion on Faith, Hope, and Love

241

ABBREVIATIONS	LATIN (OR GREEK) TITLE	ENGLISH TITLE
Exp. Gal.	Expositio in epistulam ad Galatas	
Exp. quaest. Rom.	Expositio quarumdam quaestionum in epistula ad Romanos	
Faust.	Contra Faustum Manichaeum	Against Faustus the Manichaean
Fel.	Contra Felicem	Against Felix
Fid.	De fide rerum quae non videntur	Faith in Things Unseen
Fid. op.	De fide et operibus	Faith and Works
Fid. symb.	De fide et symbolo	Faith and the Creed
Fort.	Contra Fortunatum	Against Fortunatus
Fund.	Contra epistulam Manichaei quam vocant Fundamenti	Against the Letter of the Manichaeans That They Call "The Basics"
Gaud.	Contra Gaudentium Donatistarum episcopum	Against Gaudentius the Donatist Bishop
Gen. imp.	De Genesi ad litteram imperfectus liber	On the Literal Interpretation of Genesis: An Unfinished Book
Gen. litt.	De Genesi ad litteram	On Genesis Litarally Interpreted
Gen. Man.	De Genesi contra Manichaeos	On Genesis against the Manicheans
Gest. Pelag.	De gestis Pelagii	Proceedings of Pelagius
Gramm.	De grammatica	
Grat.	De gratia et libero arbitrio	Grace and Free Will
Grat. Chr.	De gratia Christi, et de peccato originali	The Grace of Christ and Original Sin
Haer.	De haeresibus	Heresies
Immort. an.	De immortalitate animae	The Immortality of the Soul
Incomp. nupt.	De incompetentibus nuptiis	Adulterous Marriages
Adv. Jud.	Tractatus adversus Judaeos	In Answer to the Jews
C. Jul.	Contra Julianum	Against Julian
C. Jul. op. imp.	Contra secundam Juliani responsionem imperfectum opus	Against Julian: Opus Imperfectum
Leg.	Contra adversarium legis et prophetarum	
Lib.	De libero arbitrio	Free Will
C. litt. Petil.	Contra litteras Petiliani	
Locut. Hept.	Locutionum in Heptateuchum libri septem	
Mag.	De magistro	
Man.	De moribus Manichaeorum	The Morals of the Manichaeans
Maxim.	Contra Maximinum Arianum	Against Maximinus the Arian
De mend.	De mendacio	On Lying
C. mend.	Contra mendacium	Against Lying (to Consentius)
Mor. eccl.	De moribus ecclesiae catholicae	The Way of Life of the Catholic Church
Mor. Manich.	De moribus Manichaeorum	The Way of Life of the Manichaeans
Mus.	De musica	Music
Nat. bon.	De natura boni contra Manichaeos	The Nature of the Good
Nat. grat.	De natura et gratia	Nature and Grace
Nat. orig.	De natura et origine animae	The Nature and Origin of the Soul
Nupt.	De nuptiis et concupiscentia ad Valerium comitem	Marriage and Concupiscence
Oct. quaest. Vet. Test.	De octo quaestionibus ex Veteri Testamento	Eight Questions from the Old Testament
Op. mon.	De opere monachorum	The Work of Monks
Ord.	De ordine	
Parm.	Contra epistulam Parmeniani	
Pat.	De patientia	Patience
Pecc. orig.	De peccato originali	Original Sin
Pecc. merit.	De peccatorum meritis et remissione	Guilt and Remission of Sins
Perf.	De perfectione justitiae hominis	Perfection in Human Righteousness
Persev.	De dono perseverantiae	The Gift of Perseverance
Praed.	De praedestinatione sanctorum	The Predestination of the Saints
Priscill.	Ad Orosium contra Priscillianistas et Origenistas	To Orosius against the Priscillianists and the Origenists
Psal. Don.	Psalmus contra partem Donati	
Quaest. ev.	Quaestionum evangelicarum libri II	
Quaest. Hept.	Quaestiones in Heptateuchum	
Quaest. Matt.	Quaestiones in evangelium Matthaei	
Quant. an.	De quantitate animae	The Magnitude of the Soul
Reg.	Regula ad servos Dei	
Retract.	Retractationum libri II	Retractations
Rhet.	De rhetorica, Rhetores Latini	
Secund.	Contra Secundinum Manichaeum	
Serm.	Sermones	
Serm. Dom.	De sermone Domini in monte	Sermon on the Mount
Solil.	Soliloquiorum libri II	Soliloquies
Spec.	De scriptura sancta speculum	
Spir. et litt.	De spiritu et littera	The Spirit and the Letter
Symb.	De symbolo ad catechumenos	The Creed: For Catechumens
Tract. ep. Jo.	In epistulam Johannis ad Parthos tractatus	Tractates on the First Epistle of John
Tract. Ev. Jo.	In Evangelium Johannis tractatus	Tractates on the Gospel of John
Trin.	De Trinitate	The Trinity

242

ABBREVIATIONS	LATIN (OR GREEK) TITLE	ENGLISH TITLE
Unic. bapt.	De unico baptismo	
Unit. eccl.	De unitate ecclesiae	The Unity of the Church
Util. cred.	De utilitate credendi	The Usefulness of Believing
Util. jej.	De utilitate jejunii	The Usefulness of Fasting
Ver. rel.	De vera religione	True Religion
Vid.	De bono viduitatis	The Excellence of Widowhood
Virginit.	De sancta virginitate	Holy virginity
Vit. Christ.	De vita christiana	The Christian Life

Aulus Gellius

Noct. att.	Noctes atticae	Attic Nights
Bell. afr.	Bellum africum	African War
Bell. alex.	Bellum alexandrinum	Alexandrian War

Bion

Epitaph. Adon.	Epitaphius Adonis	Lament for Adonis
[Epith. Achil.]	Epithalamium Achillis et Deidameiae	Epithalamium to Achilles and Deidamea

Caesar

Bell. civ.	Bellum civile	Civil War
Bell. gall.	Bellum gallicum	Gallic War

Callimachus

Aet.	Aetia (in P.Oxy. 2079)	Causes
Epigr.	Epigrammata	Epigrams
Hec.	Hecala	Hecale
Hymn.	Hymni	Hymns
Hymn. Apoll.	Hymnus in Apollinem	Hymn to Apollo
Hymn. Cer.	Hymnus in Cererem	Hymn to Ceres or Demeter
Hymn. Del.	Hymnus in Delum	Hymn to Delos
Hymn. Dian.	Hymnus in Dianam	Hymn to Diana or Artemis
Hymn. Jov.	Hymnus in Jovem	Hymn to Jove or Zeus
Hymn. lav. Pall.	Hymnus in lavacrum Palladis	Hymn to the Baths of Pallas

Can. ap.	Canones apostolicae	Apostolic Canons

Cato

Agr.	De agricultura (De re rustica)	Agriculture
Orig.	Origines	Origins

Ceb. Tab.	Cebetis Tabula	

Chariton

Chaer.	De Chaerea et Callirhoe	Chaereas and Callirhoe

Chrysostom   *See John Chrysostom*

Cicero

Acad.	Academicae quaestiones	
Acad. post.	Academica posteriora (Lucullus)	
Acad. pr.	Academica priora	
Agr.	De Lege agraria	
Amic.	De amicitia	
Arch.	Pro Archia	
Att.	Epistulae ad Atticum	
Aug.	De auguriis	
Balb.	Pro Balbo	
Brut.	Brutus or De claris oratoribus	
Caecin.	Pro Caecina	
Cael.	Pro Caelio	
Cat.	In Catalinam	
Clu.	Pro Cluentio	
Corn.	Pro Cornelio de maiestate	
Deiot.	Pro rege Deiotaro	
Div.	De divinatione	
Div. Caec.	Divinatio in Caecilium	
Dom.	De domo suo	
Ep. Brut.	Epistulae ad Brutum	
Epigr.	Epigrammata	
Fam.	Epistulae ad familiares	
Fat.	De fato	
Fin.	De finibus	
Flac.	Pro Flacco	

243

ABBREVIATIONS	LATIN (OR GREEK) TITLE	ENGLISH TITLE
Font.	*Pro Fonteio*	
Har. resp.	*De haruspicum responso*	
Inv.	*De inventione rhetorica*	
Leg.	*De legibus*	
Leg. man.	*Pro Lege manilia (De imperio Cn. Pompeii)*	
Lig.	*Pro Ligario*	
Lim.	*Limon*	
Mar.	*Marius*	
Marcell.	*Pro Marcello*	
Mil.	*Pro Milone*	
Mur.	*Pro Murena*	
Nat. d.	*De natura deorum*	
Off.	*De officiis*	
Opt. gen.	*De optimo genere oratorum*	
De or.	*De oratore*	
Or. Brut.	*Orator ad M. Brutum*	
Parad.	*Paradoxa Stoicorum*	
Part. or.	*Partitiones oratoriae*	
Phil.	*Orationes philippicae*	
Pis.	*In Pisonem*	
Planc.	*Pro Plancio*	
Prov. cons.	*De provinciis consularibus*	
Quint. fratr.	*Epistulae ad Quintum fratrem*	
Quinct.	*Pro Quinctio*	
Rab. Perd.	*Pro Rabirio Perduellionis Reo*	
Rab. Post.	*Pro Rabirio Postumo*	
Red. pop.	*Post reditum ad populum*	
Red. sen.	*Post reditum in senatu*	
Resp.	*De republica*	
Rosc. com.	*Pro Roscio comoedo*	
Rosc. Amer.	*Pro Sexto Roscio Amerino*	
Scaur.	*Pro Scauro*	
Sen.	*De senectute*	
Sest.	*Pro Sestio*	
Sull.	*Pro Sulla*	
Tim.	*Timaeus*	
Tog. cand.	*Oratio in senatu in toga candida*	
Top.	*Topica*	
Tull.	*Pro Tullio*	
Tusc.	*Tusculanae disputationes*	
Vat.	*In Vatinium*	
Verr.	*In Verrem*	

Clement of Alexandria

Ecl.	*Eclogae propheticae*	*Extracts from the Prophets*
Exc.	*Excerpta ex Theodoto*	*Excerpts from Theodotus*
Paed.	*Paedagogus*	*Christ the Educator*
Protr.	*Protrepticus*	*Exhortation to the Greeks*
Quis div.	*Quis dives salvetur*	*Salvation of the Rich*
Strom.	*Stromata*	*Miscellanies*

Cod. justin. | *Codex justinianus* |

Cod. theod. | *Codex theodosianus* |

Columella

Arb.	*De arboribus*	
Rust.	*De re rustica*	

Const. ap. | *Constitutiones apostolicae* | *Apostolic Constitutions* |

Cornutus

Nat. d.	*De natura deorum (Epidromē tōn kata tēn Hellēniken theologian paradedomenōn)*	*Summary of the Traditions concerning Greek Mythology*

Corp. herm. | *Corpus hermeticum* |

Cosmas Indicopleustes

Top.	*Topographia christiana*	*Christian Topography*

Cyprian

Demetr.	*Ad Demetrianum*	*To Demetrian*

ABBREVIATIONS	LATIN (OR GREEK) TITLE	ENGLISH TITLE
Dom. or.	De dominica oratione	The Lord's Prayer
Don.	Ad Donatum	To Donatus
Eleem.	De opere et eleemosynis	Works and Almsgiving
Fort.	Ad Fortunatum	To Fortunatus: Exhortation to Martyrdom
Hab. virg.	De habitu virginum	The Dress of Virgins
[Idol.]	Quod idola dii non sint	That Idols Are Not Gods
Laps.	De lapsis	The Lapsed
Mort.	De mortalitate	Mortality
Pat.	De bono patientiae	The Advantage of Patience
Sent.	Sententiae episcoporum de haereticis baptizandis	
Test.	Ad Quirinum testimonia adversus Judaeos	To Quirinius: Testomonies against the Jews
Unit. eccl.	De catholicae ecclesiae unitate	The Unity of the Catholic Church
Zel. liv.	De zelo et livore	Jealousy and Envy

Demetrius

Eloc.	De elocutione (Peri hermēneias)	Style

Demosthenes

Andr.	Adversus Androtionem	Against Androtion
[Apat.]	Contra Apatourium	Against Apaturius
1–3 Aphob.	In Aphobum	1–3 Against Aphobus
Aristocr.	In Aristocratem	Against Aristocrates
1–2 Aristog.	In Aristogitonem	1–2 Against Aristogeiton
1 [2] Boeot.	Contra Boeotum i–ii	1–2 Against Boeotos
Call.	Contra Calliclem	Against Callicles
[Callip.]	Contra Callipum	Against Callipus
Chers.	De Chersoneso	On the Chersonese
Con.	In Cononem	Against Conon
Cor. trier.	De corona trierarchiae	On the Trierarchic Crown
Cor.	De corona	On the Crown
[Dionys.]	Contra Dionysodorum	Against Dionysodorus
Epitaph.	Epitaphius	Funeral Oration
[Erot.]	Eroticus	Eroticus
Eub.	Contra Eubulidem	Against Eubulides
[Euerg.]	In Evergum et Mnesibulum	Against Evergus and Mnesibulus
Exord.	Exordia (Prooemia)	
Fals. leg.	De falsa legatione	False Embassy
Halon.	De Halonneso	On the Halonnesus
[Lacr.]	Contra Lacritum	Against Lacritus
[Leoch.]	Contra Leocharem	Against Leochares
Lept.	Adversus Leptinem	Against Leptines
[Macart.]	Contra Macartatum	Against Macartatus
Meg.	Pro Megalopolitanis	For the Megalopolitans
Mid.	In Midiam	Against Meidias
Naus.	Contra Nausimachum et Xenopeithea	Against Nausimachus
[Neaer.]	In Neaeram	Against Neaera
Nicostr.	Contra Nicostratum	Against Nicostratus
[Olymp.]	In Olympiodorum	Against Olympiodorus
1–3 Olynth.	Olynthiaca i–iii	1–3 Olynthiac
1–2 Onet.	Contra Onetorem	1–2 Against Onetor
De pace	De pace	On the Peace
C. Phorm.	Contra Phormionem	Against Phormio
Pro Phorm.	Pro Phormione	For Phormio
Pant.	Contra Pantaenetum	Against Pantaenetus
1–3 [4] Philip.	Philippica i–iv	1–4 Philippic
[Poly.]	Contra Polyclem	Against Polycles
Rhod. lib.	De Rhodiorum libertate	On the Liberty of the Rhodians
Spud.	Contra Spudiam	Against Spudia
1 [2] Steph.	In Stephanum i–ii	1–2 Against Stephanus
Symm.	De symmoriis	On the Symmories
[Syntax.]	Peri syntaxeōs	On Organization
[Theocr.]	In Theocrinem	Against Theocrines
[Tim.]	Contra Timotheum	Against Timotheus
Timocr.	In Timocratem	Against Timocrates
Zenoth.	Contra Zenothemin	Against Zenothemis

Didymus

Comm. Eccl.	Commentarii in Ecclesiasten	
Comm. Job	Commentarii in Job	
Comm. Oct. Reg.	Commentarii in Octateuchum et Reges	
Comm. Ps.	Commentarii in Psalmos	
Comm. Zach.	Commentarii in Zachariam	
Dial. haer.	Dialogus Didymi Caeci cum haeretico	

ABBREVIATIONS	LATIN (OR GREEK) TITLE	ENGLISH TITLE
Enarrat. Ep. Cath.	*In Epistulas Catholicas brevis enarratio*	
Fr. Cant.	*Fragmentum in Canticum canticorum*	
Fr. 1 Cor.	*Fragmenta in Epistulam i ad Corinthios*	
Fr. 2 Cor.	*Fragmenta in Epistulam ii ad Corinthios*	
Fr. Heb.	*Fragmentum in Epistulam ad Hebraeos*	
Fr. Jer.	*Fragmenta in Jeremiam*	
Fr. Jo.	*Fragmenta in Joannem*	
Fr. Prov.	*Fragmenta in Proverbia*	
Fr. Ps.	*Fragmenta in Psalmos*	
Fr. Rom.	*Fragmenta in Epistulam ad Romanos*	
In Gen.	*In Genesim*	
Incorp.	*De incorporeo*	
Man.	*Contra Manichaeos*	
Philos.	*Ad philosophum*	
Trin.	*De Trinitate*	

Dig.	*Digesta*	

Dinarchus

Aristog.	*In Aristogitonem*	*Against Aristogiton*
Demosth.	*In Demosthenem*	*Against Demosthenes*
Phil.	*In Philoclem*	*Against Philocles*

Dio Chrysostom

Achill.	*Achilles (Or. 58)*	*Achilles and Cheiron*
Admin.	*De administratione (Or. 50)*	*His Past Record*
Aegr.	*De aegritudine (Or. 16)*	*Pain and Distress of Spirit*
Alex.	*Ad Alexandrinos (Or. 32)*	*To the People of Alexandria*
Apam.	*Ad Apamenses (Or. 41)*	*To the Apameians*
Aud. aff.	*De audiendi affectione (Or. 19)*	*Fondness for Listening*
Avar.	*De avaritia (Or. 17)*	*Covetousness*
Borysth.	*Borysthenitica (Or. 36)*	*Borysthenic Discourse*
Cel. Phryg.	*Celaenis Phrygiae (Or. 35)*	*At Celaenae in Phrygia*
Charid.	*Charidemus (Or. 30)*	
Chrys.	*Chryseis (Or. 61)*	
Compot.	*De compotatione (Or. 27)*	*Symposia*
Conc. Apam.	*De concordia cum Apamensibus (Or. 40)*	*On Concord with Apamea*
Consuet.	*De consuetudine (Or. 76)*	*Custom*
Consult.	*De consultatione (Or. 26)*	*Deliberation*
Cont.	*Contio (Or. 47)*	*In the Public Assembly at Prusa*
In cont.	*In contione (Or. 48)*	*Political Address in the Assembly*
[Cor.]	*Corinthiaca (Or. 37)*	*Corinthian Discourse*
Def.	*Defensio (Or. 45)*	*Defense*
Dei cogn.	*De dei cognitione (Or. 12)*	*Man's First Conception of God (Olympic Discourse)*
Dial.	*Dialexis (Or. 42)*	*In His Native City*
Dic. exercit.	*De dicendi exercitatione (Or. 18)*	*Training for Public Speaking*
Diffid.	*De diffidentia (Or. 74)*	*Distrust*
Diod.	*Ad Diodorum (Or. 51)*	*To Diodorus*
Divit.	*De divitiis (Or. 79)*	*Wealth*
Exil.	*De exilio (Or. 13)*	*Banishment*
Fel.	*De felicitate (Or. 24)*	*Happiness*
Fel. sap.	*De quod felix sit sapiens (Or. 23)*	*The Wise Man is Happy*
Fid.	*De fide (Or. 73)*	*Trust*
1 Fort.	*De fortuna i (Or. 63)*	*Fortune 1*
2 Fort.	*De fortuna ii (Or. 64)*	*Fortune 2*
3 Fort.	*De fortuna iii (Or. 65)*	*Fortune 3*
Gen.	*De genio (Or. 25)*	*The Guiding Spirit*
1 Glor.	*De gloria i (Or. 66)*	*Reputation*
2 Glor.	*De gloria ii (Or. 67)*	*Popular Opinion*
3 Glor.	*De gloria iii (Or. 68)*	*Opinion*
Grat.	*Gratitudo (Or. 44)*	*Friendship for His Native Land*
Hab.	*De habitu (Or. 72)*	*Personal Appearance*
Hom.	*De Homero (Or. 53)*	*Homer*
Hom. Socr.	*De Homero et Socrate (Or. 55)*	*Homer and Socrates*
Invid.	*De invidia (Or. 77/78)*	*Envy*
Isthm.	*Isthmiaca (Or. 9)*	*Isthmian Discourse*
De lege	*De lege (Or. 75)*	*Law*
Lib.	*De libertate (Or. 80)*	*Freedom*
Lib. myth.	*Libycus mythos (Or. 5)*	*A Libyan Myth*
1 Melanc.	*Melancomas i (Or. 29)*	*Melancomas 1*
2 Melanc.	*Melancomas ii (Or. 28)*	*Melancomas 2*
Ness.	*Nessus (Or. 60)*	*Nessus, or Deianeira*
Nest.	*Nestor (Or. 57)*	*Homer's Portrayal of Nestor*
Nicaeen.	*Ad Nicaeenses (Or. 39)*	*To the Nicaeans*

ABBREVIATIONS	LATIN (OR GREEK) TITLE	ENGLISH TITLE
Nicom.	Ad Nicomedienses (Or. 38)	To the Nicomedians
De pace	De pace et bello (Or. 22)	Peace and War
Philoct. arc.	De Philoctetae arcu (Or. 52)	Appraisal of the Tragic Triad
Philoct.	Philoctetes (Or. 59)	
De philosophia	De philosophia (Or. 70)	Philosophy
De philosopho	De philosopho (Or. 71)	The Philosopher
Pol.	Politica (Or. 43)	Political Address
Pulchr.	De pulchritudine (Or. 21)	Beauty
Rec. mag.	Recusatio magistratus (Or. 49)	Refusal of the Office of Archon
Regn.	De regno (Or. 56)	Kingship
1 Regn.	De regno i (Or. 1)	Kingship 1
2 Regn.	De regno ii (Or. 2)	Kingship 2
3 Regn.	De regno iii (Or. 3)	Kingship 3
4 Regn.	De regno iv (Or. 4)	Kingship 4
Regn. tyr.	De regno et tyrannide (Or. 62)	Kingship and Tyranny
Rhod.	Rhodiaca (Or. 31)	To the People of Rhodes
Sec.	De secessu (Or. 20)	Retirement
Serv.	De servis (Or. 10)	Servants
1 Serv. lib.	De servitute et libertate i (Or. 14)	Slavery and Freedom 1
2 Serv. lib.	De servitute et libertate ii (Or. 15)	Slavery and Freedom 2
Socr.	De Socrate (Or. 54)	Socrates
1 Tars.	Tarsica prior (Or. 33)	First Tarsic Discourse
2 Tars.	Tarsica altera (Or. 34)	Second Tarsic Discourse
Troj.	Trojana (Or. 11)	Trojan Discourse
Tumult.	De tumultu (Or. 46)	Protest against Mistreatment
Tyr.	De tyrannide (Or. 6)	Diogenes, or On Tyranny
Ven.	Venator (Or. 7)	The Hunter (Eubeoan Discourse)
Virt. (Or. 8)	De virtute (Or. 8)	Virtue
Virt. (Or. 69)	De virtute (Or. 69)	Virtue

Dionysius of Halicarnassus

1–2 Amm.	Epistula ad Ammaeum i–ii	
Ant. or.	De antiquis oratoribus	
Ant. rom.	Antiquitates romanae	
Comp.	De compositione verborum	
Dem.	De Demosthene	
Din.	De Dinarcho	
Is.	De Isaeo	
Isocr.	De Isocrate	
Lys.	De Lysia	
Pomp.	Epistula ad Pompeium Geminum	
[Rhet.]	Ars rhetorica	
Thuc.	De Thucydide	
Thuc. id.	De Thucydidis idiomatibus	

Dioscorides Pedanius

[Alex.]	Alexipharmaca	
Mat. med.	De materia medica	

Epictetus

Diatr.	Diatribai (Dissertationes)	
Gnom.	Gnomologium	
Ench.	Enchiridion	

Epiphanius

Pan.	Panarion (Adversus haereses)	Refutation of All Heresies

Euripides

Alc.	Alcestis	
Andr.	Andromache	
Bacch.	Bacchae	Bacchanals
Cycl.	Cyclops	
Dict.	Dictys	
El.	Electra	
Hec.	Hecuba	
Hel.	Helena	Helen
Heracl.	Heraclidae	Children of Hercules
Herc. fur.	Hercules furens	Madness of Hercules
Hipp.	Hippolytus	
Hyps.	Hypsipyle	
Iph. aul.	Iphigenia aulidensis	Iphigeneia at Aulis
Iph. taur.	Iphigenia taurica	Iphigeneia at Tauris
Med.	Medea	

ABBREVIATIONS	LATIN (OR GREEK) TITLE	ENGLISH TITLE
Orest.	*Orestes*	
Phoen.	*Phoenissae*	*Phoenician Maidens*
Rhes.	*Rhesus*	
Suppl.	*Supplices*	*Suppliants*
Tro.	*Troades*	*Daughters of Troy*

Eusebius

Chron.	*Chronicon*	*Chronicle*
Coet. sanct.	*Ad coetum sanctorum*	*Oration of the Emperor Constantine Which He Addressed to the Assembly of the Saints*
Comm. Isa.	*Commentarius in Isaiam*	*Commentary on Isaiah*
Comm. Ps.	*Commentarius in Psalmos*	*Commentary on the Psalms*
Dem. ev.	*Demonstratio evangelica*	*Demonstration of the Gospel*
Eccl. theol.	*De ecclesiastica theologia*	*Ecclesiastical Theology*
Ecl. proph.	*Eclogae propheticae*	*Extracts from the Prophets*
Hier.	*Contra Hieroclem*	*Against Hierocles*
Hist. eccl.	*Historia ecclesiastica*	*Ecclesiastical History*
Laud. Const.	*De laudibus Constantini*	*Praise of Constantine*
Marc.	*Contra Marcellum*	*Against Marcellus*
Mart. Pal.	*De martyribus Palaestinae*	*The Martyrs of Palestine*
Onom.	*Onomasticon*	
Praep. ev.	*Praeparatio evangelica*	*Preparation for the Gospel*
Theoph.	*Theophania*	*Divine Manifestation*
Vit. Const.	*Vita Constantini*	*Life of Constantine*

Firmicus Maternus

Err. prof. rel.	*De errore profanarum religionum*	
Math.	*Mathesis*	

Gaius

Inst.	*Institutiones*	

Gorgias

Hel.	*Helena*	
Pal.	*Palamedes*	

Gregory of Nazianzus

Ep.	*Epistulae*	
Or. Bas.	*Oratio in laudem Basilii*	

Gregory of Nyssa

Deit.	*De deitate Filii et Spiritus Sancti*	

Gregory the Great

Moral.	*Expositio in Librum Job, sive Moralium libri xxv*	*Moralia*

Heliodorus

Aeth.	*Aethiopica*	

Heraclitus

All.	*Allegoriae (Quaestiones homericae)*	

Herodotus

Hist.	*Historiae*	*Histories*

Hesiod

Op.	*Opera et dies*	*Works and Days*
[Scut.]	*Scutum*	*Shield*
Theog.	*Theogonia*	*Theogony*

Hieronymus **See Jerome**

Hippocrates

Acut.	*De ratione victus in morbis acutis* (Περὶ διαίτης ὀξέων)	*Regimen in Acute Diseases*
Aff.	*De affectionibus* (Περὶ παθῶν)	*Affections*
Alim.	*De alimento* (Περὶ τροφῆς)	*Nutriment*
Aph.	*Aphorismata* (Ἀφορισμοί)	*Aphorisms*
De arte	*De arte* (Περὶ τέχνης)	*The Art*

248

ABBREVIATIONS	LATIN (OR GREEK) TITLE	ENGLISH TITLE
Artic.	De articulis reponendis (Περὶ ἄρθρων ἐμβολῆς)	Joints
Carn.	De carne (Περὶ σαρκῶν)	Fleshes
Coac.	Praenotiones coacae (Κωακαὶ προγνώσεις)	
Decent.	De habitu decenti (Περὶ εὐσχημοσύνης)	Decorum
Dent.	De dentitione (Περὶ ὀδοντοφυίης)	Dentition
Epid.	Epidemiae (Ἐπιδημίαι)	Epidemics
Fist.	Fistulae (Περὶ συρίγγων)	Fistulas
Fract.	De fracturis (Περὶ ἀγμῶν)	Fractures
Genit.	Genitalia (Περὶ γονῆς)	Genitals
Int.	De affectionibus internis (Περὶ τῶν ἐντὸς παθῶν)	Internal Affections
Jusj.	Jus jurandum (Ὅρκος)	The Oath
Lex	Lex (Νόμος)	Law
Liq.	De liquidorum usu (Περὶ ὑγρῶν χρήσιος)	Use of Liquids
Loc. hom.	De locis in homine (Περὶ τόπων τῶν κατὰ ἀνθρώπων)	Places in Man
Med.	De medico (Περὶ ἰητροῦ)	The Physician
Mochl.	Mochlichon	Instruments of Reduction
Morb.	De morbis (Περὶ νούσων)	Diseases
Morb. sacr.	De morbo sacro (Περὶ ἱερῆς νούσου)	The Sacred Disease
Mul.	De morbis mulierum (Γυναικεῖα)	Female Diseases
Nat. hom.	De natura hominis (Περὶ φύσιος ἀνθρώπου)	Nature of Man
Nat. mul.	De natura muliebri (Περὶ γυναικείης φύσιος)	Nature of Woman
Nat. puer.	De natura pueri (Περὶ φύσιος παιδίου)	Nature of the Chile
Oct.	De octimestri partu (Περὶ ὀκταμήνου)	
Off.	De officina medici (Κατ' ἰητρεῖον)	In the Surgery
Praec.	Praeceptiones (Παραγγελίαι)	Precepts
Progn.	Prognostica (Προγνωστικόν)	Prognostic
Prorrh.	Prorrhetica (Προρρητικόν)	Prorrhetic
Septim.	De septimestri partu (Περὶ ἑπταμήνου)	
Steril.	De sterilitate (Περὶ ἀφόρων)	Sterility
Vict.	De victu (Περὶ διαίτης)	Regimen
Vict. salubr.	De ratione victus salubris (Περὶ διαίτης ὑγιεινῆς)	Regimen in Health
Vet. med.	De vetere medicina (Περὶ ἀρχαίης ἰητρικῆς)	Ancient Medicine

Hippolytus

Antichr.	De antichristo	
Ben. Is. Jac.	De benedictionibus Isaaci et Jacobi	
Can. pasch.	Canon paschalis	
In Cant.	In Canticum canticorum	
Cant. Mos.	In canticum Mosis	
Chron.	Chronicon	
Comm. Dan.	Commentarium in Danielem	
Fr. Prov.	Fragmenta in Proverbia	
Fr. Ps.	Fragmenta in Psalmos	
Haer.	Refutatio omnium haeresium (Philosophoumena)	Refutation of All Heresies
Helc. Ann.	In Helcanam et Annam	
Noet.	Contra haeresin Noeti	
Trad. ap.	Traditio apostolica	The Apostolic Tradition
Univ.	De universo	

Homer

Il.	Ilias	Iliad
Od.	Odyssea	Odyssey

Horace

Ars	Ars poetica	
Carm.	Carmina	Odes
Ep.	Epistulae	Epistles
Epod.	Epodi	Epodes
Saec.	Carmen saeculare	
Sat.	Satirae	Satires

Irenaeus

Epid.	Epideixis tou apostolikou kērygmatos	Demonstration of the Apostolic Preaching
Haer.	Adversus haereses	Against Heresies

249

ABBREVIATIONS	LATIN (OR GREEK) TITLE	ENGLISH TITLE
Isocrates		
Aeginet.	Aegineticus (Or. 19)	
Antid.	Antidosis (Or. 15)	
Archid.	Archidamus (Or. 6)	
Areop.	Areopagiticus (Or. 7)	
Big.	De bigis (Or. 16)	On the Team of Horses
Bus.	Busiris (Or. 11)	
Callim.	In Callimachum (Or. 18)	Against Callimachus
De pace	De pace (Or. 8)	
Demon.	Ad Demonicum (Or. 1)	
Ep.	Epistulae	
Euth.	In Euthynum (Or. 21)	
Evag.	Evagoras (Or. 9)	
Hel. enc.	Helenae encomium (Or. 10)	
Loch.	In Lochitum (Or. 20)	
Nic.	Nicocles (Or. 3)	
Ad Nic.	Ad Nicoclem (Or. 2)	
Panath.	Panathenaicus (Or. 12)	
Paneg.	Panegyricus (Or. 4)	
Phil.	Philippus (Or. 5)	
Plat.	Plataicus (Or. 14)	
Soph.	In sophistas (Or. 13)	
Trapez.	Trapeziticus (Or. 17)	On the Banker

Jerome		
Chron.	Chronicon Eusebii a Graeco Latine redditum et continuatum	
Comm. Abd.	Commentariorum in Abdiam liber	
Comm. Agg.	Commentariorum in Aggaeum liber	
Comm. Am.	Commentariorum in Amos libri III	
Comm. Eccl.	Commentarii in Ecclesiasten	
Comm. Eph.	Commentariorum in Epistulam ad Ephesios libri III	
Comm. Ezech.	Commentariorum in Ezechielem libri XVI	
Comm. Gal.	Commentariorum in Epistulam ad Galatas libri III	
Comm. Habac.	Commentariorum in Habacuc libri II	
Comm. Isa.	Commentariorum in Isaiam libri XVIII	
Comm. Jer.	Commentariorum in Jeremiam libri VI	
Comm. Joel.	Commentariorum in Joelem liber	
Comm. Jon.	Commentariorum in Jonam liber	
Comm. Mal.	Commentariorum in Malachiam liber	
Comm. Matt.	Commentariorum in Matthaeum libri IV	
Comm. Mich.	Commentariorum in Michaeum libri II	
Comm. Nah.	Commentariorum in Nahum liber	
Comm. Os.	Commentariorum in Osee libri III	
Comm. Phlm.	Commentariorum in Epistulam ad Philemonem liber	
Comm. Ps.	Commentarioli in Psalmos	
Comm. Soph.	Commentariorum in Sophoniam libri III	
Comm. Tit.	Commentariorum in Epistulam ad Titum liber	
Comm. Zach.	Commentariorum in Zachariam libri III	
Did. Spir.	Liber Didymi de Spiritu Sancto	
Epist.	Epistulae	
Expl. Dan.	Explanatio in Danielem	
Helv.	Adversus Helvidium de Mariae virginitate perpetua	
Hom. Matth.	Homilia in Evangelium secundum Matthaeum	
Interp. Job	Libri Job versio, textus hexaplorum	
Jo. Hier.	Adversus Joannem Hierosolymitanum liber	
Jov.	Adversus Jovinianum libri II	
Lucif.	Altercatio Luciferiani et orthodoxi seu dialogus contra Luciferianos	
Mon. Pachom.	Monitorum Pachomii versio latina	
Monogr.	Tractatus de monogrammate	
Nom. hebr.	De nominibus hebraicis (Liber nominum)	
Orig. Hom. Cant.	Homiliae II Origenis in Canticum canticorum Latine redditae	
Orig. Jer. Ezech.	Homiliae XXVIII in Jeremiam et Ezechielem Graeco Origenis Latine redditae	
Orig. Hom. Luc.	In Lucam homiliae XXXIX ex Graeco Origenis Latine conversae	
Orig. Princ.	De principiis	

ABBREVIATIONS	LATIN (OR GREEK) TITLE	ENGLISH TITLE
Pelag.	Adversus Pelagianos dialogi III	
Psalt. Hebr.	Psalterium secundum Hebraeos	
Qu. hebr. Gen.	Quaestionum hebraicarum liber in Genesim	
Reg. Pachom.	Regula S. Pachomii, e Graeco	
Ruf.	Adversus Rufinum libri III	
Sit.	De situ et nominibus locorum Hebraicorum (Liber locorum)	
Tract. Isa.	Tractatus in Isaiam	
Tract. Marc.	Tractatus in Evangelium Marci	
Tract. Ps.	Tractatus in Psalmos	
Tract. var.	Tractatus varii	
Vigil.	Adversus Vigilantium	
Vir. ill.	De viris illustribus	
Vit. Hil.	Vita S. Hilarionis eremitae	
Vit. Malch.	Vita Malchi monachi	
Vit. Paul.	Vita S. Pauli, primi eremitae	

John Chrysostom

Adfu.	Adversus eos qui non adfuerant	
Aeg.	In martyres Aegyptios	
Anna	De Anna	
Anom.	Contra Anomoeos	
Ant. exsil.	Sermo antequam iret in exsilium	
Ascens.	In ascensionem domini nostri Jesu Christi	
Bab.	De sancto hieromartyre Babyla	Babylas the Martyr
Bab. Jul.	De Babyla contra Julianum et gentiles	
Bapt.	De baptismo Christi	
Barl.	In sanctum Barlaam martyrem	
Bern.	De sanctis Bernice et Prosdoce	
Catech. illum.	Catecheses ad illuminandos	
Catech. jur.	Catechesis de juramento	
Catech. ult.	Catechesis ultima ad baptizandos	
Cath.	Adversus Catharos	
Coemet.	De coemeterio et de cruce	
Comm. Isa.	Commentarius in Isaiam	
Comm. Job	Commentarius in Job	
Comp. reg. mon.	Comparatio regis et monachi	
Compunct. Dem.	Ad Demetrium de compunctione	
Compunct. Stel.	Ad Stelechium de compunctione	
Cruc.	De cruce et latrone homiliae II	
Cum exsil.	Sermo cum iret in exsilium	
Dav.	De Davide et Saule	
Delic.	De futurae vitae deliciis	
Diab.	De diabolo tentatore	
Diod.	Laus Diodori episcopi	
Dros.	De sancta Droside martyre	
Educ. lib.	De educandis liberis	
El. vid.	In Eliam et viduam	
Eleaz. puer.	De Eleazaro et septem pueris	
Eleem.	De eleemosyna	
Ep. carc.	Epistula ad episcopos, presbyteros et diaconos in carcere	
Ep. Cyr.	Epistula ad Cyriacum	
1 Ep. Innoc.	Ad Innocentium papam epistula I	
2 Ep. Innoc.	Ad Innocentium papam epistula II	
Ep. Olymp.	Epistulae ad Olympiadem	
Ep. Theod.	Letter to Theodore	
Eust.	In sanctum Eustathium Antiochenum	
Eutrop.	In Eutropium	
Exp. Ps.	Expositiones in Psalmos	
Fat. prov.	De fato et providentia	
Fem. reg.	Quod regulares feminae viris cohabitare non debeant	
Fr. Ep. Cath.	Fragmenta in Epistulas Catholicas	
Freq. conv.	Quod frequenter conveniendum sit	
Goth. concin.	Homilia habita postquam presbyter Gothus concionatus fuerat	
Grat.	Non esse ad gratiam concionandum	
Hom. Act.	Homiliae in Acta apostolorum	
Hom. Act. 9:1	De mutatione nominum	
Hom. Col.	Homiliae in epistulam ad Colossenses	
Hom. 1 Cor.	Homiliae in epistulam i ad Corinthios	
Hom. 1 Cor. 10:1	In dictum Pauli: Nolo vos ignorare	
Hom. 1 Cor. 11:19	In dictum Pauli: Oportet haereses esse	

ABBREVIATIONS	LATIN (OR GREEK) TITLE	ENGLISH TITLE
Hom. 1 Cor. 7:2	In illud: Propter fornicationes autem unusquisque suam uxorem habeat	
Hom. 2 Cor.	Homiliae in epistulam ii ad Corinthios	
Hom. 2 Cor. 11:1	In illud: Utinam sustineretis modicum	
Hom. 2 Cor. 4:13	In illud: Habentes eundem spiritum	
Hom. Eph.	Homiliae in epistulam ad Ephesios	
Hom. Gal.	Homiliae in epistulam ad Galatas commentarius	
Hom. Gal. 2:11	In illud: In faciem ei restiti	
Hom. Gen.	Homiliae in Genesim	
Hom. Heb.	Homiliae in epistulam ad Hebraeos	
Hom. Isa. 45:7	In illud Isaiae: Ego Dominus Deus feci lumen	
Hom. Isa. 6:1	In illud: Vidi Dominum	
Hom. Jer. 10:23	In illud: Domine, non est in homine	
Hom. Jo.	Homiliae in Joannem	
Hom. Jo. 5:17	In illud: Pater meus usque modo operatur	
Hom. Jo. 5:19	In illud: Filius ex se nihil facit	
Hom. Matt.	Homiliae in Matthaeum	
Hom. Matt. 18:23	De decem millium talentorum debitore	
Hom. Matt. 26:39	In illud: Pater, si possibile est, transeat	
Hom. Matt. 9:37	In illud: Messis quidem multa	
Hom. Phil.	Homiliae in epistulam ad Philippenses	
Hom. Phlm.	Homiliae in epistulam ad Philemonem	
Hom. princ. Act.	In principium Actorum	
Hom. Ps. 48:17	In illud: Ne timueris cum dives factus fuerit homo	
Hom. Rom.	Homiliae in epistulam ad Romanos	
Hom. Rom. 12:20	In illud: Si esurierit inimicus	
Hom. Rom. 16:3	In illud: Salutate Priscillam et Aquilam	
Hom. Rom. 5:3	De gloria in tribulationibus	
Hom. Rom. 8:28	In illud: Diligentibus deum omnia cooperantur in bonum	
Hom 1 Thess.	Homiliae in epistulam i ad Thessalonicenses	
Hom. 2 Thess.	Homiliae in epistulam ii ad Thessalonicenses	
Hom. 1 Tim.	Homiliae in epistulam i ad Timotheum	
Hom. 1 Tim. 5:9	In illud: Vidua eligatur	
Hom. 2 Tim.	Homiliae in epistulam ii ad Timotheum	
Hom. 2 Tim. 3:1	In illud: Hoc scitote quod in novissimis diebus	
Hom. Tit.	Homiliae in epistulam ad Titum	
Hom. Tit. 2:11	In illud: Apparuit gratia dei omnibus hominibus	
Ign.	In sanctum Ignatium martyrem	
Inan. glor.	De inani gloria	
Iter. conj.	De non iterando conjugio	
Adv. Jud.	Adversus Judaeos	Discourses against Judaizing Christians
Jud. gent.	Contra Judaeos et gentiles quod Christus sit deus	
Jul.	In sanctum Julianum martyrem	
Juv.	In Juventinum et Maximum martyres	
Kal.	In Kalendas	
Laed.	Quod nemo laeditur nisi a se ipso	No One Can Harm the Man Who Does Not Injure Himself
Laud. Max.	Quales ducendae sint uxores (=De laude Maximi)	
Laud. Paul.	De laudibus sancti Pauli apostoli	
Laz.	De Lazaro	
Lib. repud.	De libello repudii	
Liturg.	Liturgia	
Lucian.	In sanctum Lucianum martyrem	
Macc.	De Maccabeis	
Mart.	De sanctis martyribus; Homilia in martyres (must give vol./pg. ref.)	
Melet.	De sancto Meletio Antiocheno	
Natal.	In diem natalem Christi	
Non desp.	Non esse desperandum	
Oppugn.	Adversus oppugnatores vitae monasticae	
Ordin.	Sermo cum presbyter fuit ordinatus	
Paenit.	De paenitentia	
Paralyt.	In paralyticum demissum per tectum	
Pasch.	In sanctum pascha	
Pecc.	Peccata fratrum non evulganda	Against Publicly Exposing the Sins of the Brethren

ABBREVIATIONS	LATIN (OR GREEK) TITLE	ENGLISH TITLE
Pelag.	De sancta Pelagia virgine et martyre	
Pent.	De sancta pentecoste	
Phoc.	De sancto hieromartyre Phoca	
Praes. imp.	Homilia dicta praesente imperatore	
Prod. Jud.	De proditione Judae	
Prof. evang.	De profectu evangelii	Lowliness of Mind
Proph. obscurit.	De prophetarum obscuritate	
Quatr. Laz.	In quatriduanum Lazarum	
1 Redit.	Post reditum a priore exsilio sermo I	
2 Redit.	Post reditum a priore exsilio sermo II	
Regr.	De regressu	
Reliq. mart.	Homilia dicta postquam reliquiae martyrum	
Res. Chr.	Adversus ebriosos et de resurrectione domini nostri Jesu Christi	
Res. mort.	De resurrectione mortuorum	
Rom. mart.	In sanctum Romanum martyrem	
Sac.	De sacerdotio	Priesthood
Sanct. Anast.	Homilia dicta in templo sanctae Anastasiae	
Saturn.	Cum Saturninus et Aurelianus acti essent in exsilium	
Scand.	Ad eos qui scandalizati sunt	
Serm. Gen.	Sermones in Genesim	
Stag.	Ad Stagirium a daemone vexatum	
Stat.	Ad populum Antiochenum de statuis	
Stud. praes.	De studio praesentium	
Subintr.	Contra eos qui subintroductas habent virgines	
Terr. mot.	De terrae motu	
Theatr.	Contra ludos et theatra	
Theod. laps.	Ad Theodorum lapsum	Exhortation to Theodore after His Fall
Vid.	Ad viduam juniorem	To a Young Widow
Virginit.	De virginitate	

John Malalas
Chron.	Chronographia	

John Philoponus
Comm. De an.	In Aristotelis De anima libros commentaria	

Josephus   See §8.3.7

Justin
1 Apol.	Apologia i	First Apology
2 Apol.	Apologia ii	Second Apology
Dial.	Dialogus cum Tryphone	Dialogue with Trypho

Justinian
Edict.	Edicta	
Nov.	Novellae	

Juvenal
Sat.	Satirae	

Lactantius
Epit.	Epitome divinarum institutionum	Epitome of the Divine Institutes
Inst.	Divinarum institutionum libri VII	The Divine Institutes
Ir.	De ira Dei	The Wrath of God
Mort.	De morte persecutorum	The Deaths of the Persecutors
Opif.	De opificio Dei	The Workmanship of God

Longinus
[Subl.]	De sublimitate	On the Sublime

Longus
Daphn.	Daphnis and Chloe	

Lucian
Abdic.	Abdicatus	Disowned
Alex.	Alexander (Pseudomantis)	Alexander the False Prophet
[Am.]	Amores	Affairs of the Heart
Anach.	Anacharsis	
[Asin.]	Asinus (Lucius)	Lucius, or The Ass
Bis acc.	Bis accusatus	The Double Indictment

ABBREVIATIONS	LATIN (OR GREEK) TITLE	ENGLISH TITLE
Astr.	Astrologia	Astrology
Cal.	Calumniae non temere credendum	Slander
Cat.	Cataplus	The Downward Journey, or The Tyrant
Char.	Charon	
Demon.	Demonax	
Deor. conc.	Deorm concilium	Parliament of the Gods
Dial. d.	Dialogi deorum	Dialogues of the Gods
Dial. meretr.	Dialogi meretricii	Dialogues of the Courtesans
Dial. mort.	Diologi mortuorum	Dialogues of the Dead
Dom.	De domo	The Hall
Electr.	De electro	Amber, or The Swans
[Encom. Demosth.]	Demosthenous encomium	Praise of Demosthenes
Eunuch.	Eunuchus	The Eunuch
Fug.	Fugitivi	The Runaways
Gall.	Gallus	The Dream, or The Cock
Hermot.	Hermotimus (De sectis)	Hermotimus, or Sects
Icar.	Icaromenippus	
Imag.	Imagines	Essays in Portraiture
Pro imag.	Pro imaginibus	Essays in Portraiture Defended
Ind.	Adversus indoctum	The Ignorant Book-Collector
Jud. voc.	Judicium vocalium	The Consonants at Law
Jupp. conf.	Juppiter confutatus	Zeus Catechized
Jupp. trag.	Juppiter tragoedus	Zeus Rants
Laps.	Pro lapsu inter salutandum	A Slip of the Tongue in Greeting
Lex.	Lexiphanes	
Luct.	De luctu	Funerals
Men.	Menippus (Necyomantia)	Menippus, or Descent into Hades
Merc. cond.	De mercede conductis	Salaried Posts in Great Houses
Musc. laud.	Muscae laudatio	The Fly
Nav.	Navigium	The Ship, or The Wishes
Nigr.	Nigrinus	
Par.	De parasito	The Parasite
Peregr.	De morte Peregrini	The Passing of Peregrinus
Phal.	Phalaris	
[Philopatr.]	Philopatris	The Patriot
Philops.	Philopseudes	The Lover of Lies
Pisc.	Piscator	The Dead Come to Life, or The Fisherman
Pseudol.	Pseudologista	The Mistaken Critic
Rhet. praec.	Rhetorum praeceptor	A Professor of Public Speaking
Sacr.	De sacrificiis	Sacrifices
Salt.	De saltatione	The Dance
Sat.	Saturnalia	Conversation with Cronus
Scyth.	Scytha	The Scythian, or The Consul
Somn.	Somnium (Vita Luciani)	The Dream, or Lucian's Career
Symp.	Symposium	The Carousal, or The Lapiths
Syr. d.	De syria dea	The Goddess of Syria
Tim.	Timon	
Tox.	Toxaris	
Tyr.	Tyrannicida	The Tyrannicide
Ver. hist.	Vera historia	A True Story
Vit. auct.	Vitarum auctio	Philosophies for Sale

Menander

Dysk.	Dyskolos	
Epitr.	Epitrepontes	
Georg.	Georgos	
Mis.	Misoumenos	
Mon.	Monostichoi	
Phasm.	Phasma	
Perik.	Perikeiromenē	
Sam.	Samia	
Sik.	Sikyonios	
Thras.	Thrasonidis	

Methodius of Olympus

Lib. arb.	De libero arbitrio	
Res.	De resurrectione	
Symp.	Symposium (Convivium decem virginum)	

Minucius Felix

Oct.	Octavius	

Nepos

Ag.	Agesilaus	

ABBREVIATIONS	LATIN (OR GREEK) TITLE	ENGLISH TITLE
Alc.	*Alciabiades*	
Arist.	*Aristides*	
Att.	*Atticus*	
Cat.	*Cato*	
Chabr.	*Chabrias*	
Cim.	*Cimon*	
Con.	*Conon*	
Dat.	*Datames*	
Di.	*Dion*	
Epam.	*Epaminondas*	
Eum.	*Eumenes*	
Ham.	*Hamilcar*	
Han.	*Hannibal*	
Iph.	*Iphicrates*	
Lys.	*Lysander*	
Milt.	*Miltiades*	
Paus.	*Pausanias*	
Pel.	*Pelopidas*	
Phoc.	*Phocion*	
Reg.	*De regibus*	
Them.	*Themistocles*	
Thras.	*Thrasybulus*	
Timol.	*Timoleon*	
Timoth.	*Timotheus*	

Nicander

Alex.	*Alexipharmaca*	
Ther.	*Theriaca*	

Nicolaus of Damascus

Hist. univ.	*Historia universalis*	*Universal History (in Athenaeus)*
Vit. Caes.	*Vita Caesaris*	

Nonnus

Dion.	*Dionysiaca*	
Paraphr. Jo.	*Paraphrasis sancti evangelii Joannei*	

Orac. chald.	*De oraculis chaldaicis*	*Chaldaean Oracles*

Origen

Adnot. Deut.	*Adnotationes in Deuteronomium*	
Adnot. Exod.	*Adnotationes in Exodum*	
Adnot. Gen.	*Adnotationes in Genesim*	
Adnot. Jes. Nav.	*Adnotationes in Jesum filium Nave*	
Adnot. Judic.	*Adnotationes in Judices*	
Adnot. Lev.	*Adnotationes in Leviticum*	
Adnot. Num.	*Adnotationes in Numeros*	
Cant. (Adulesc.)	*In Canticum canticorum (libri duo quos scripsit in adulescentia)*	
Cels.	*Contra Celsum*	*Against Celsus*
Comm. Cant.	*Commentarius in Canticum*	
Comm. Gen.	*Commentarii in Genesim*	
Comm. Jo.	*Commentarii in evangelium Joannis*	
Comm. Matt.	*Commentarium in evangelium Matthaei*	
Comm. Rom.	*Commentarii in Romanos*	
Comm. ser. Matt.	*Commentarium series in evangelium Matthaei*	
Dial.	*Diologus cum Heraclide*	*Dialogue with Heraclides*
Enarrat. Job	*Enarrationes in Job*	
Engastr.	*De engastrimytho*	*Witch of Endor*
Ep. Afr.	*Epistula ad Africanum*	
Ep. Greg.	*Epistula ad Gregorium Thaumaturgum*	
Ep. ign.	*Epistula ad ignotum (Fabianum Romanum)*	
Exc. Ps.	*Excerpta in Psalmos*	
Exp. Prov.	*Expositio in Proverbia*	
Fr. Act.	*Fragmentum ex homiliis in Acta apostolorum*	
Fr. Cant.	*Libri x in Canticum canticorum*	
Fr. 1 Cor.	*Fragmenta ex commentariis in epistulam i ad Corinthios*	
Fr. Eph.	*Fragmenta ex commentariis in epistulam ad Ephesios*	
Fr. Exod.	*Fragmenta ex commentariis in Exodum*	

ABBREVIATIONS	LATIN (OR GREEK) TITLE	ENGLISH TITLE
Fr. Ezech.	Fragmenta ex commentariis in Ezechielem	
Fr. Heb.	Fragmenta ex homiliis in epistulam ad Hebraeos	
Fr. Jer.	Fragmenta in Jeremiam	
Fr. Jo.	Fragmenta in evangelium Joannis	
Fr. Lam.	Fragmenta in Lamentationes	
Fr. Luc.	Fragmenta in Lucam	
Fr. Matt.	Fragmenta ex commentariis in evangelium Matthaei	
Fr. Os.	Fragmentum ex commentariis in Osee	
Fr. Prin.	Fragmenta de principiis	
Fr. Prov.	Fragmenta ex commentariis in Proverbia	
Fr. Ps.	Fragmenta in Psalmos 1–150	
Fr. 1 Reg.	Fragmenta in librum primum Regnorum	
Fr. Ruth	Fragmentum in Ruth	
Hex.	Hexapla	
Hom. Cant.	Homiliae in Canticum	
Hom. Exod.	Homiliae in Exodum	
Hom. Ezech.	Homiliae in Ezechielem	
Hom. Gen.	Homiliae in Genesim	
Hom. Isa.	Homiliae in Isaiam	
Hom. Jer.	Homiliae in Jeremiam	
Hom. Jes. Nav.	In Jesu Nave homiliae xxvi	
Hom. Job	Homiliae in Job	
Hom. Judic.	Homiliae in Judices	
Hom. Lev.	Homiliae in Leviticum	
Hom. Luc.	Homiliae in Lucam	
Hom. Num.	Homiliae in Numeros	
Hom. Ps.	Homiliae in Psalmos	
Hom. 1 Reg.	Homiliae in I Reges	
Mart.	Exhortatio ad martyrium	Exhortation to Martyrdom
Or.	De oratione (Peri proseuchēs)	Prayer
Pasch.	De pascha	The Pascha
Philoc.	Philocalia	
Princ.	De principiis (Peri archōn)	First Principles
Res.	De resurrectione libri ii	
Schol. Apoc.	Scholia in Apocalypsem	
Schol. Cant.	Scholia in Canticum canticorum	
Schol. Luc.	Scholia in Lucam	
Schol. Matt.	Scholia in Matthaeum	
Sel. Deut.	Selecta in Deuteronomium	
Sel. Exod.	Selecta in Exodum	
Sel. Ezech.	Selecta in Ezechielem	
Sel. Gen.	Selecta in Genesim	
Sel. Jes. Nav.	Selecta in Jesum Nave	
Sel. Job	Selecta in Job	
Sel. Judic.	Selecta in Judices	
Sel. Lev.	Selecta in Leviticum	
Sel. Num.	Selecta in Numeros	
Sel. Ps.	Selecta in Psalmos	

Ovid

Am.	Amores	
Ars	Ars amatoria	
Fast.	Fasti	
Hal.	Halieutica	
Her.	Heroides	
Ib.	Ibis	
Med.	Medicamina faciei femineae	
Metam.	Metamorphoses	

Pausanias

Descr.	Graeciae description	Description of Greece

Peripl. M. Rubr.	Periplus Maris Rubri	The Periplus of the Erythraean Sea

Persius

Sat.	Satirae	

Philo	See §8.3.6

Philodemus of Gadara

Adv. Soph.	Adversus sophistas	

256

ABBREVIATIONS	LATIN (OR GREEK) TITLE	ENGLISH TITLE
D.	*De diis*	
Hom.	*De bono rege secundum Homerum*	
Ir.	*De ira*	
Lib.	*De libertate dicendi*	
Mort.	*De morte*	
Mus.	*De musica*	
Piet.	*De pietate*	
Rhet.	*Volumina rhetorica*	
Sign.	*De signis*	
Vit.	*De vitiis X*	

Philostratus

Ep.	*Epistulae*	
Gymn.	*De gymnastica*	
Imag.	*Imagines*	
Vit. Apoll.	*Vita Apollonii*	
Vit. soph.	*Vitae sophistarum*	

Photius

Lex.	*Lexicon*	

Pindar

Isthm.	*Isthmionikai*	*Isthmian Odes*
Nem.	*Nemeonikai*	*Nemean Odes*
Ol.	*Olympionikai*	*Olympian Odes*
Paean.	*Paeanes*	*Hymns*
Pyth.	*Pythionikai*	*Pythian Odes*
Thren.	*Threnoi*	*Dirges*

Plato

[Alc. maj.]	*Alcibiades major*	*Greater Alcibiades*
Apol.	*Apologia*	*Apology of Socrates*
[Ax.]	*Axiochus*	
Charm.	*Charmides*	
Crat.	*Cratylus*	
[Def.]	*Definitiones*	*Definitions*
Ep.	*Epistulae*	*Letters*
[Epin.]	*Epinomis*	
Euthyd.	*Euthydemus*	
Euthyphr.	*Euthyphro*	
Gorg.	*Gorgias*	
Hipparch.	*Hipparchus*	
Hipp. maj.	*Hippias major*	*Greater Hippias*
Hipp. min.	*Hippias minor*	*Lesser Hippias*
Lach.	*Laches*	
Leg.	*Leges*	*Laws*
Menex.	*Menexenus*	
[Min.]	*Minos*	
Phaed.	*Phaedo*	
Phaedr.	*Phaedrus*	
Phileb.	*Philebus*	
Pol.	*Politicus*	*Statesman*
Parm.	*Parmenides*	
Prot.	*Protagoras*	
Resp.	*Respublica*	*Republic*
Soph.	*Sophista*	*Sophist*
Symp.	*Symposium*	
Theaet.	*Theaetetus*	
Tim.	*Timaeus*	

Plautus

Amph.	*Amphitruo*	
Asin.	*Asinaria*	
Aul.	*Aulularia*	
Bacch.	*Bacchides*	
Capt.	*Captivi*	
Cas.	*Casina*	
Cist.	*Cistellaria*	
Curc.	*Curculio*	
Epid.	*Epidicus*	
Men.	*Menaechmi*	
Mil. glor.	*Miles gloriosus*	
Most.	*Mostellaria*	
Pers.	*Persae*	

ABBREVIATIONS	LATIN (OR GREEK) TITLE	ENGLISH TITLE
Poen.	*Poenulus*	
Pseud.	*Pseudolus*	
Rud.	*Rudens*	
Stic.	*Sticus*	
Trin.	*Trinummus*	
Truc.	*Truculentus*	
Vid.	*Vidularia*	

Pliny the Elder

Nat.	*Naturalis historia*	*Natural History*

Pliny the Younger

Ep.	*Epistulae*	
Ep. Tra.	*Epistulae ad Trajanum*	
Pan.	*Panegyricus*	

Plotinus

Enn.	*Enneades*	

Plutarch

Adol. poet. aud.	*Quomodo adolescens poetas audire debeat*	
Adul. am.	*De adulatore et amico*	
Adul. amic.	*Quomodo adulator ab amico internoscatur*	
Aem.	*Aemilius Paullus*	
Ag. Cleom.	*Agis et Cleomenes*	
Ages.	*Agesilaus*	
Alc.	*Alcibiades*	
Alex.	*Alexander*	
Alex. fort.	*De Alexandri magni fortuna aut virtute*	
Am. prol.	*De amore prolis*	
Amat.	*Amatorius*	
[Amat. narr.]	*Amatoriae narrationes*	
Amic. mult.	*De amicorum multitudine*	
[An ignis]	*Aquane an ignis utilior*	
An seni	*An seni respublica gerenda sit*	
An virt. doc.	*An virtus doceri possit*	
An vit.	*An vitiositas ad infelicitatem sufficiat*	
An. corp.	*Animine an corporis affectiones sint peiores*	
An. procr.	*De animae procreatione in Timaeo*	
An. procr. epit.	*Epitome libri de procreatione in Timaeo*	
Ant.	*Antonius*	
[Apoph. lac.]	*Apophthegmata laconica*	
Arat.	*Aratus*	
Arist.	*Aristides*	
Art.	*Artaxerxes*	
Brut.	*Brutus*	
Brut. an.	*Bruta animalia ratione uti*	
Caes.	*Caesar*	
Cam.	*Camillus*	
Cat. Maj.	*Cato Major*	*Cato the Elder*
Cat. Min.	*Cato Minor*	*Cato the Younger*
Cic.	*Cicero*	
Cim.	*Cimon*	
Cleom.	*Cleomenes*	
Cohib. ira	*De cohibenda ira*	
Adv. Col.	*Adversus Colotem*	
Comm. not.	*De communibus notitiis contra stoicos*	
Comp. Aem. Tim.	*Comparatio Aemilii Paulli et Timoleontis*	
Comp. Ag. Cleom. cum Ti. Gracch.	*Comparatio Agidis et Cleomenis cum Tiberio et Gaio Graccho*	
Comp. Ages. Pomp.	*Comparatio Agesilai et Pompeii*	
Comp. Alc. Cor.	*Comparatio Alcibiadis et Marcii Coriolani*	
Comp. Arist. Cat.	*Comparatio Aristidis et Catonis*	
Comp. Arist. Men. compend.	*Comparationis Aristophanis et Menandri compendium*	
Comp. Cim. Luc.	*Comparatio Cimonis et Luculli*	
Comp. Dem. Cic.	*Comparatio Demosthenis et Ciceronis*	
Comp. Demetr. Ant.	*Comparatio Demetrii et Antonii*	
Comp. Dion. Brut.	*Comparatio Dionis et Bruti*	
Comp. Eum. Sert.	*Comparatio Eumenis et Sertorii*	
Comp. Lyc. Num.	*Comparatio Lycurgi et Numae*	
Comp. Lys. Sull.	*Comparatio Lysandri et Sullae*	
Comp. Nic. Crass.	*Comparatio Niciae et Crassi*	
Comp. Pel. Marc.	*Comparatio Pelopidae et Marcelli*	

ABBREVIATIONS	LATIN (OR GREEK) TITLE	ENGLISH TITLE
Comp. Per. Fab.	Comparatio Periclis et Fabii Maximi	
Comp. Phil. Flam.	Comparatio Philopoemenis et Titi Flaminini	
Comp. Sol. Publ.	Comparatio Solonis et Publicolae	
Comp. Thes. Rom.	Comparatio Thesei et Romuli	
Conj. praec.	Conjugalia Praecepta	
[Cons. Apoll.]	Consolatio ad Apollonium	
Cons. ux.	Consolatio ad uxorem	
Cor.	Marcius Coriolanus	
Crass.	Crassus	
Cupid. divit.	De cupiditate divitiarum	
Curios.	De curiositate	
De esu	De esu carnium	
De laude	De laude ipsius	
Def. orac.	De defectu oraculorum	
Dem.	Demosthenes	
Demetr.	Demetrius	
Dion	Dion	
E Delph.	De E apud Delphos	
Eum.	Eumenes	
Exil.	De exilio	
Fab.	Fabius Maximus	
Fac.	De facie in orbe lunae	
Flam.	Titus Flamininus	
Fort.	De fortuna	
Fort. Rom.	De fortuna Romanorum	
Frat. amor.	De fraterno amore	
Galb.	Galba	
Garr.	De garrulitate	
Gen. Socr.	De genio Socratis	
Glor. Ath.	De gloria Atheniensium	
Her. mal.	De Herodoti malignitate	
Inim. util.	De capienda ex inimicis utilitate	
Inv. od.	De invidia et odio	
Is. Os.	De Iside et Osiride	
Lat. viv.	De latenter vivendo	
Lib. aegr.	De libidine et aegritudine	
[Lib. ed.]	De liberis educandis	
Luc.	Lucullus	
Lyc.	Lycurgus	
Lys.	Lysander	
Mar.	Marius	
Marc.	Marcellus	
Max. princ.	Maxime cum principibus philosophiam esse disserendum	
Mor.	Moralia	
Mulier. virt.	Mulierum virtutes	
[Mus.]	De musica	
Nic.	Nicias	
Num.	Numa	
Oth.	Otho	
Parsne an fac.	Parsne an facultas animi sit vita passiva	
Pel.	Pelopidas	
Per.	Pericles	
Phil.	Philopoemen	
Phoc.	Phocion	
[Plac. philos.]	De placita philosophorum	
Pomp.	Pompeius	
Praec. ger. rei publ.	Praecepta gerendae rei publicae	
Prim. frig.	De primo frigido	
Princ. iner.	Ad principem ineruditum	
Publ.	Publicola	
Pyrrh.	Pyrrhus	
Pyth. orac.	De Pythiae oraculis	
Quaest. conv.	Quaestionum convivialum libri IX	
Quaest. nat.	Quaestiones naturales (Aetia physica)	
Quaest. plat.	Quaestiones platonicae	
Quaest. rom.	Quaestiones romanae et graecae (Aetia romana et graeca)	
Rect. rat. aud.	De recta ratione audiendi	
[Reg. imp. apophth.]	Regum et imperatorum apophthegmata	
Rom.	Romulus	
Sept. sap. conv.	Septem sapientium convivium	
Sera	De sera numinis vindicta	
Sert.	Sertorius	
Sol.	Solon	

ABBREVIATIONS	LATIN (OR GREEK) TITLE	ENGLISH TITLE
Soll. an.	De sollertia animalium	
Stoic. abs.	Stoicos absurdiora poetis dicere	
Stoic. rep.	De Stoicorum repugnantiis	
Suav. viv.	Non posse suaviter vivi secundum Epicurum	
Sull.	Sulla	
Superst.	De superstitione	
Them.	Themistocles	
Thes.	Theseus	
Ti. C. Gracch.	Tiberius et Caius Gracchus	
Tim.	Timoleon	
Tranq. an.	De tranquillitate animi	
Trib. r. p. gen.	De tribus rei publicae generibus	
Tu. san.	De tuenda sanitate praecepta	
Un. rep. dom.	De unius in republica dominatione	
Virt. mor.	De virtute morali	
Virt. prof.	Quomodo quis suos in virtute sentiat profectus	
Virt. vit.	De virtute et vitio	
Vit. aere al.	De vitando aere alieno	
[Vit. poes. Hom.]	De vita et poesi Homeri	
Vit. pud.	De vitioso pudore	
[Vit. X orat.]	Vitae decem oratorum	

Pollux

Onom.	Onomasticon	

Porphyry

Abst.	De abstinentia	
Agalm.	Peri agalmatōn	
Aneb.	Epistula ad Anebonem	
Antr. nymph.	De antro nympharum	
Christ.	Contra Christianos	
Chron.	Chronica	
Comm. harm.	Eis ta harmonika Ptolemaiou hypomnēma	
Comm. Tim.	In Platonis Timaeum commentaria	
Exp. Cat.	In Aristotelis Categorias expositio per interrogationem et responsionem	
Isag.	Isagoge sive quinque voces	
Marc.	Ad Marcellam	
Philos. orac.	De philosophia ex oraculis	
Quaest. hom.	Quaestiones homericae	
Quaest. hom. Odd.	Quaestionum homericarum ad Odysseam pertinentium reliquiae	
Sent.	Sententiae ad intelligibilia ducentes	
Vit. Plot.	Vita Plotini	
Vit. Pyth.	Vita Pythagorae	

Ptolemy (the Gnostic)

Flor.	Epistula ad Floram	Letter to Flora

Quintilian

Decl.	Declamationes	
Inst.	Institutio oratoria	

Res gest. divi Aug.	Res gestae divi Augusti	

Rhet. Her.	Rhetorica ad Herennium	

Rufinus

Adam. Haer.	Adamantii libri Contra haereticos	
Anast.	Apologia ad Anastasium papam	
Apol. Hier.	Apologia adversus Hieronymum	
Apol. Orig.	Eusebii et Pamphyli Apologia Origenis	
Basil. hom.	Homiliae S. Basilii	
Ben. patr.	De benedictionibus patriarcharum	
Clem. Recogn.	Clementis quae feruntur Recognitiones	
Greg. Orat.	Gregorii Orationes	
Hist.	Eusebii Historia ecclesiastica a Rufino translata et continuata	
Hist. mon.	Historia monachorum in Aegypto	
Orig. Comm. Cant.	Origenis Commentarius in Canticum	
Orig. Hom. Exod.	Origenis in Exodum homiliae	

ABBREVIATIONS	LATIN (OR GREEK) TITLE	ENGLISH TITLE
Orig. Hom. Gen.	Origenis in Genesism homiliae	
Orig. Hom. Jos.	Origenis Homiliae in librum Josua	
Orig. Hom. Judic.	Origenis in librum Judicum homiliae	
Orig. Hom. Lev.	Origenis Homiliae in Leviticum	
Orig. Hom. Num.	Origenis in Numeros homiliae	
Orig. Princ.	Origenis Libri Peri archôn seu De principiis libri IV	
Orig. Hom. Ps.	Origenis Homiliae in Psalmos	
Orig. Comm. Rom.	Origenis Commentarius in epistulam ad Romanos	
Sent. Sext.	Sexti philosophi Sententiae a Rufino translatae	
Symb.	Commentarius in symbolum apostolorum	

Sallust

Bell. Cat.	Bellum catalinae	
Bell. Jug.	Bellum jugurthinum	
Hist.	Historiae	
Rep.	Epistulae ad Caesarem senem de re publica	

Seneca

Ag.	Agamemnon	
Apol.	Apolocyntosis	
Ben.	De beneficiis	
Clem.	De clementia	
Dial.	Dialogi	
Ep.	Epistulae morales	
Helv.	Ad Helviam	
Herc. fur.	Hercules furens	
Herc. Ot.	Hercules Otaeus	
Ira	De ira	
Lucil.	Ad Lucilium	
Marc.	Ad Marciam de consolatione	
Med.	Medea	
Nat.	Naturales quaestiones	
Phaed.	Phaedra	
Phoen.	Phoenissae	
Polyb.	Ad Polybium de consolatione	
Thy.	Thyestes	
Tranq.	De tranquillitate animi	
Tro.	Troades	
Vit. beat.	De vita beata	

Sextus Empiricus

Math.	Adversus mathematicos	Against the Mathematicians
Pyr.	Pyrrhoniae hypotyposes	Outlines of Pyrrhonism

Sophocles

Aj.	Ajax	
Ant.	Antigone	
El.	Elektra	
Ichn.	Ichneutae	
Oed. col.	Oedipus coloneus	
Oed. tyr.	Oedipus tyrannus	
Phil.	Philoctetes	
Trach.	Trachiniae	

Stobaeus

Ecl.	Eclogae	
Flor.	Florilegium	

Strabo

Geogr.	Geographica	Geography

Suetonius

Aug.	Divus Augustus	
Cal.	Gaius Caligula	
Claud.	Divus Claudius	
Dom.	Domitianus	
Galb.	Galba	
Gramm.	De grammaticis	
Jul.	Divus Julius	
Nero	Nero	
Otho	Otho	

ABBREVIATIONS	LATIN (OR GREEK) TITLE	ENGLISH TITLE
Poet.	De poetis	
Rhet.	De rhetoribus	
Tib.	Tiberius	
Tit.	Divus Titus	
Vesp.	Vespasianus	
Vit.	Vitellius	

Tacitus

Agr.	Agricola	
Ann.	Annales	
Dial.	Dialogus de oratoribus	
Germ.	Germania	
Hist.	Historiae	

Terence

Ad.	Adelphi	
Andr.	Andria	
Eun.	Eunuchus	
Haut.	Hauton timorumenos	
Hec.	Hecyra	
Phorm.	Phormio	

Tertullian

An.	De anima	The Soul
Apol.	Apologeticus	Apology
Bapt.	De baptismo	Baptism
Carn. Chr.	De carne Christi	The Flesh of Christ
Cor.	De corona militis	The Crown
Cult. fem.	De cultu feminarum	The Apparel of Women
Exh. cast.	De exhortatione castitatis	Exhortation to Chastity
Fug.	De fuga in persecutione	Flight in Persecution
Herm.	Adversus Hermogenem	Against Hermogenes
Idol.	De idololatria	Idolatry
Jejun.	De jejunio adversus psychicos	On Fasting, against the Psychics
Adv. Jud.	Adversus Judaeos	Against the Jews
Marc.	Adversus Marcionem	Against Marcion
Mart.	Ad martyras	To the Martyrs
Mon.	De monogamia	Monogamy
Nat.	Ad nationes	To the Heathen
Or.	De oratione	Prayer
Paen.	De paenitentia	Repentance
Pall.	De pallio	The Pallium
Pat.	De patientia	Patience
Praescr.	De praescriptione haereticorum	Prescription against Heretics
Prax.	Adversus Praxean	Against Praxeas
Pud.	De pudicitia	Modesty
Res.	De resurrectione carnis	The Resurrection of the Flesh
Scap.	Ad Scapulam	To Scapula
Scorp.	Scorpiace	Antidote for the Scorpion's Sting
Spect.	De spectaculis	The Shows
Test.	De testimonio animae	The Soul's Testimony
Ux.	Ad uxorem	To His Wife
Val.	Adversus Valentinianos	Against the Valentinians
Virg.	De virginibus velandis	The Veiling of Virgins

Theocritus

Id.		Idylls

Theodoret

Car.	De caritate	
Hist. eccl.	Historia ecclesiastica	Ecclesiastical History
Phil. hist..	Philotheos historia	History of the Monks of Syria

Theon of Alexandria

Comm. Alm.	Commentarium in Almagestum	Commentary on the Almagest

Theophilus

Autol.	Ad Autolycum	To Autolycus

Theophrastus

Caus. plant.	De causis plantarum	
Char.	Characteres	
Hist. plant.	Historia plantarum	
Sens.	De sensu	

ABBREVIATIONS	LATIN (OR GREEK) TITLE	ENGLISH TITLE
Tyconius		
Reg.	*Liber regularum*	
Varro		
Rust.	*De re rustica*	
Virgil		
Aen.	*Aeneid*	
Ecl.	*Eclogae*	
Georg.	*Georgica*	
Xenophon		
Ages.	*Agesilaus*	
Anab.	*Anabasis*	
Apol.	*Apologia Socratis*	
[Ath.]	*Respublica atheniensium*	
Cyn.	*Cynegeticus*	
Cyr.	*Cyropaedia*	
Eq.	*De equitande ratione*	
Eq. mag.	*De equitum magistro*	
Hell.	*Hellenica*	
Hier.	*Hiero*	
Lac.	*Respublica Lacedaemoniorum*	
Mem.	*Memorabilia*	
Oec.	*Oeconomicus*	
Symp.	*Symposium*	

Appendix I:
Hebrew and Greek Numbers

א	1		יט	19
ב	2		כ	20
ג	3		כא – כט	21–29
ד	4		ל	30
ה	5		מ	40
ו	6		נ	50
ז	7		ס	60
ח	8		ע	70
ט	9		פ	80
י	10		צ	90
יא	11		ק	100
יב	12		קי	110
יג	13		קכ	120
יד	14		קל	130
טו	15		קמ	140
טז	16		קנ	150
יז	17		קס	160
יח	18		קע	170

α′	1		μ′	40
β′	2		ν′	50
γ′	3		ξ′	60
δ′	4		ο′	70
ε′	5		π′	80
ϛ′	6		ϙ′	90
ζ′	7		ρ′	100
η′	8		σ′	200
θ′	9		τ′	300
ι′	10		υ′	400
ια′	11		φ′	500
ιβ′	12		χ′	600
ιγ′	13		ψ′	700
ιδ′	14		ω′	800
ιε′	15		ϡ′	900
ιϛ′	16		,α	1,000
ιζ′	17		,β	2,000
ιη′	18		,γ	3,000
ιθ′	19		,ι	10,000
κ′	20		,κ	20,000
κα′	21		,ρ	100,000
λ′	30			

Appendix J:
Editing and Proofreading Marks

For a thorough explanation of these marks, consult *CMS* 2.65–90, 3.19–36.

Instruction	In-Text Mark	Margin Mark
delete	These distinctions are not challenged by the covenant.	*e*
close up	chu rch doors	$\cap$
delete and close up	We must also remember that Cynics were not known for being well mannered to say the least.	*e*
insert	mesianic	s|
lowercase	the Bridegroom	*lc*
transpose words	Seminar Jesus	*tr*
spell out	7	*sp*
begin paragraph	. . . no happy solutions. Despite the differences . . .	¶
superscript	"humble"	*v*
insert space	Bar Kokhba	#
insert hair space	too close	*hr*
find and replace	A.D.	f/r → A.D.
overlapping or crashing text	"literal interpretation"	⸮
let original stand	God will add to that person the plagues	*stet*
CAPITAL	nibc	*cap*

SMALL CAPS	<u>LORD</u>	*sc*
italics	Biblia Hebraica Stuttgartensia	*ital*
boldface	apocalyptic community	*bf*
wrong font	His argument is truly unusual.	*wf*
increase/decrease point size	The number of scholars holding this view is infinitesimal.	*+ ps* / *- ps*
roman type	His distinctive thesis is that Moses was really a woman.	*rom*
insert comma	However, it may be that links with the parable of the Sower have been overemphasized.	⌃
insert period	Matthew's version of the beatitude may be a redactional improvement	⊙
insert semicolon	The succession of Psalms 65 and 66 may not be accidental, they may have formed part of the same preexilic liturgy.	
insert colon	See 2 Sam 2:31.	: |
insert parentheses	Paul asserts that the law's function has to do with transgression 3:19.	(|)
insert quote marks	The children of Wisdom are those who respond to Wisdom's message.	
insert hyphen	re-rejected	═ /
insert en dash	(cf. pp. 131-34 above)	$\frac{1}{N}$
insert em dash	This commentary—supplemented with maps, charts, and tables—provides a wealth of exegetical detail.	$\frac{1}{M}$

266

Index